BODIES OF WRITING, BODIES IN PERFORMANCE

GENDERS

GENDERS 23

BODIES OF WRITING, BODIES IN PERFORMANCE

Edited by Thomas Foster, Carol Siegel, and Ellen E. Berry

NEW YORK UNIVERSITY PRESS
NEW YORK AND LONDON

NEW YORK UNIVERSITY PRESS
New York and London

Copyright © 1996 by New York University
All rights reserved

ISBN 0-8147-2646-1 cloth
ISBN 0-8147-2647-X paperback

New York University Press books are printed on acid-free paper,
and their binding materials are chosen for strength and durability.

Manufactured in the United States of America

10 9 8 7 6 5 4 3 2 1

Contents

PART THREE

Performing Masculinities

PART ONE

Writing the Body: Violence, Representation, and Resistance in Women's Texts

Writing on the Body? Representation and Resistance in British Suffragette Accounts of Forcible Feeding

Caroline J. Howlett

I had decided to write the words "Votes for Women" on my body
—Constance Lytton, *Prisons and Prisoners*[1]

Does pain have a history? In her influential work *The Body in Pain*, Elaine Scarry suggests that it does not; drawing on the accounts of torture survivors, war casualties, and others, she evolves a theory of pain as transhistorical, transcultural phenomenon. Pain, Scarry maintains, has no relation to the external world, and therefore has an inherent "resistance to language" that makes it difficult to express. For Scarry, pain's resistance to language is essential to what it is: it does not depend on cultural or linguistic context. However, she goes on to speak of recent advances toward a diagnostic terminology of pain that have been made by doctors listening closely to the words patients use to describe their pain.[2] These developments seem to contradict Scarry's fundamental premise; they are predicated on the possibility of constituting pain in language.

Concepts such as pain, which are presumed to be "without history," are precisely those toward which Foucault urges us to turn our attention. In *The History of Sexuality* Foucault constructs a genealogy of sex, which posits that supposedly natural or innate desires and gender affiliations are

3

in fact produced by a regulatory discourse of sexuality that inscribes the subject. It ought also, he argues, be possible to construct genealogies of other "ahistorical" aspects of human experience, such as "sentiments, love, conscience, instincts," and also, I suggest, pain.[3]

Foucault's work on the professionalization of medicine over the last three centuries offers a way to begin to refute Scarry's argument that pain is inherently resistant to language.[4] It seems reasonable to posit that the increasing dominance of the medical establishment, with its claim to specialized knowledge about the "truth" of pain and illness, placed the voices of patients under erasure. That pain should be mystified and rendered difficult to translate into language clearly serves the interests of a professional medical body, who cannot then be challenged by claims from pain sufferers that they have a different, experiential knowledge of the truth of pain. Pain's apparent resistance to representation might then be seen as not inherent, but a product of a regulatory medical epistemology that resists all threats to its ascendancy.

I suggest, then, that it is not that pain is resistant to representation, but that representation is resistant to pain. Research into why this should be so, and into the different ways in and moments at which pain sufferers have attempted to break down this resistance, might allow us to construct a genealogy of pain: a genealogy of which this essay would form a part. The forcible feeding of militant suffragettes in British prisons between 1909 and 1914 provides a chilling object lesson in how well both the medical establishment and the state have been served historically by representation's resistance to pain.[5] There is no doubt that the problem of communicating the extent of their suffering to the general public severely hampered the suffragettes in their attempts to bring the force of public opinion to bear against this horrifying practice.

This article explores the strategies British suffragettes used in their accounts of forcible feeding to combat representation's resistance to pain. It is prefaced by a brief explanation of when and why forcible feeding was instituted in the prisons, which introduces my argument that the forcible feeding account was crucial to the construction of a shared suffragette subjectivity, which enabled suffragettes to resist the annihilation of their movement that the pain of forcible feeding was intended to produce. Representations of suffragettes in pain were deployed, not only by the suffragettes themselves, but also by the antisuffragist popular press. I show how the meaning of these images was reversed so that they would be read as images of suffragettes causing pain to others (as aggressive maenads) or to themselves (as hysterics); this reversal has many parallels with patriarchal representations of rape. The use made of these images exemplifies representation's resistance to pain; the pain of the suffragettes is not re-presented here so as to be readable as pain. As I suggest, images of women being forcibly fed were equally open to misinterpretation, even when women were in control of their production and presentation. I argue that, for a variety of reasons, suffragettes could have more hope of a sympathetic reception for written accounts of forcible feeding than for visual images.

I then attempt to trace a genealogy of the forcible feeding account. I begin with a discussion of the first wave of forcible feeding accounts, those produced between September 1909 and April 1910. Forcible feeding gradually became the focus of suffragette prison writing; I articulate the crucial role Constance Lytton's accounts played in this change of focus. The second wave of accounts, written after the reintroduction of forcible feeding in 1912, can, I argue, be seen as falling into two main groups: accounts that use the metaphor of rape (which center around the term "outrage"), and accounts that use the metaphor of an operation. These two representational practices tended to construct the subjectivities of their speakers in interestingly different ways.

From there I go on to consider the question of how far forcible feeding accounts, as representations of violence against the self, can be seen as re-inflicting that violence through the act of inscription. Constance Lytton's autobiography, which figures the experience of being forcibly fed as an act of mimicry, indicates the extent to which all forcible feeding accounts involve a more or less violent splitting of the subject.

THE INTRODUCTION OF FORCIBLE FEEDING

Forcible feeding, as it was carried out in British prisons between 1909 and 1914, was a brutal and life-threatening procedure. The hunger-striking prisoner was first held down on a chair or bed by several wardresses. Feeding was then carried out by doctors, either orally or nasally. If the feeding was oral, a gag made of wood or metal was inserted to prevent the mouth from closing; where the patient resisted, a metal gag was generally forced into the mouth, cutting the gums and lips and often breaking the teeth. Once the gag was inserted, it was screwed open to widen the mouth, and a thick rubber tube was inserted into the throat and pressed down into the stomach. Alternatively, a thinner rubber tube was inserted via the nostril, causing severe pain, particularly to the eyes. Food was then poured from a jug into the tube via a funnel; milk and Bovril were two of the commonest ingredients. Quantities given appear to have varied considerably; many suffragettes vomited continuously during the feeding, and few managed to hold the food down for any length of time. Damage to the tissues of the nose and throat was almost universal; on some occasions the tube was accidentally inserted into the windpipe so that food was poured into the lungs.

Forcible feeding for hunger-striking suffragette prisoners was introduced in September 1909. Suffragettes had been hunger striking, and thereby obtaining release, since June 1909. At this point in the suffrage campaign, the hunger strike was undertaken as a protest against the government's failure to afford suffragettes the status and privileges of political prisoners; instead, the women were being imprisoned in the "third division," with the ordinary criminals. On September 29 Herbert Gladstone (the home secretary) informed the House of Commons of his decision to introduce forcible feeding. It was, he declared, his duty to do so: forcible feeding was the only way the women's lives, which were "sacred," could be preserved (without releasing them and thus making a mockery of the law).[6] However, as the Liberal journalists Brailsford and Nevinson argued in a letter to the *Times*, Gladstone was thus discounting the alternative option of granting the WSPU's demand and officially recognizing the suffragettes as political prisoners.[7]

In the same Commons speech Gladstone describes forcible feeding as "hospital treatment." This enraged many doctors, hundreds of whom petitioned the prime minister to the effect that this epithet was no longer legitimate: most practitioners had ceased to forcibly feed self-starving patients, because the operation caused intense pain and sometimes even death. Had the government adopted forcible feeding in a genuine bid to keep the women alive, it would certainly have been administered above all to those women whose deaths were most likely to cause a national scandal: the famous, the titled, and the influential. However, the operation was generally avoided in such cases; the vast majority of those who were subjected to the ordeal repeatedly were relatively unknown middle- and working-class women. The actual motive behind forcible feeding is better expressed in a letter from Edward VII to Gladstone, dated 13

August 1909, in which the king urges his home secretary to institute forcible feeding in the prisons, since what he calls the "short term of martyrdom" of the hunger strike ending in release was, he judged, "more likely to attract than deter women from joining the ranks of the militant Suffragettes."[8] It was then as a deterrent that forcible feeding was adopted; its value to the government was not that it saved life but that it inflicted pain and had a perceived ability to decimate the movement.

HER ACCOUNT/MY EXPERIENCE: TERMS OF RESISTANCE

As Mary Jean Corbett has argued, forcible feeding was intended to cut suffragettes off from their cause and from each other, by subjecting them to so much pain that the experience of it and the fear of its return would fill up their whole consciousness, leaving no room for any abstract ideas or feelings of loyalty. Corbett argues that the many shared activities in which suffragettes participated, such as marching, demonstrating, and selling papers, were intended as ways of countering the experience of profound isolation suffered during forcible feeding.[9] She does not include writing and reading accounts of forcible feeding in her list of shared activities, but the number of these accounts and the frequency with which they appear in the suffrage papers testify to the importance attributed to these activities.

Reading accounts and writing one's own account of forcible feeding were crucial ways of setting one's own experience in the context of other suffragettes'. Forcible feeding accounts can be understood as offering a set of formulae within which a suffragette could write her experiences and highlight those aspects of the experience that were shared by many others. By writing these accounts, suffragettes could make their pain communicable and comprehensible, where it might otherwise have seemed debilitatingly private and inarticulate. In making their pain meaningful, they also prevented it from seeming pointless or irrelevant to others; the forcible feeding account constructed the pain as politically relevant because part of a shared project. The formulae that the forcible feeding account evolved became the terms of a language in which the suffragettes attempted to break the resistance of representation to pain.

These effects of the forcible feeding account were crucial to many suffragettes. In one of her accounts of forcible feeding, the militant suffragette and music hall comedian Kitty Marion describes how she once had food poured into her lungs during the feeding, an appallingly painful and terrifying experience. Another suffragette, Lilian Lenton, had the same experience at a later date, and Marion indicates that she found support in reading Lenton's story of her ordeal. "Reading her account in the 'Suff' [the *Suffragette*]," Marion writes, "it might have been my own description of my experience." [10] Marion here reveals the extent to which the forcible feeding account helped break down the isolation felt by pain sufferers, allowing suffragettes to enter into a shared subject position with others: to suffer forcible feeding is to enter into the subjectivity of any other suffragette who has been forcibly fed. Grace Roe, onetime editor of the *Suffragette*, made a similar point at her trial in Marylebone police court, where she declared, "Nobody who has not been forcibly fed knows what it is." [11] Only another suffragette who has been forcibly fed, Roe implies, can enter into the shared subject position Marion refers to: nobody else can understand what a forcibly fed suffragette has been through.

Perhaps Marion and Roe here provide one answer to Maud Ellmann's question: why was it that experiencing forcible feeding became such a sine qua non of suffragette identity? [12] The experience of forcible feeding had two effects: on the one hand it isolated suffragettes by alienating them from the rest of the (un-forcibly fed) world, while on the other it strengthened the bonds within the suffragette community to the extent that personal experience was no longer distinguishable from the experiences of the community as a whole. The accounts became increasingly intersubjective: one account begins to sound much like another as the words of other women become the means by which the suffragettes represent this (supposedly) private bodily ordeal. The increasing coalescence of the accounts around the metaphors of outrage and operation, discussed below, gives some flavor of this "repetitiveness." The accounts became points of unification, points at which the voices and experiences of many suffragettes merged. At her trial for conspiracy in June 1914, the WSPU organizer Nellie Hall told the court, "However vividly the horror of forcible feeding is described it cannot be realised except by those who have suffered its tortures. . . . I will use the description of Mary Richardson, which fits my case well: 'Warders and doctors go from cell to cell, and the cries and moans of our friends come to us, and it is almost worse than the feeding itself.' " [13]

Hall goes on to cite Richardson at length, and indeed it is not clear at what point she begins to speak in her "own" voice again. The citation is not an absolutely accurate rendition of any Richardson account with which I am familiar, although it is similar to some of them. Hall is rather speaking in a double voice: a voice that brings together her own experiences and "the moans and cries of [her] friends" into a single text.

Laura Ainsworth, a teacher and one of the first suffragettes to be forcibly fed in 1909, literally embodied this strategy of taking another's representation of forcible feeding as an "account" of one's own experience. Antonia Raeburn relates that, in October 1909, Ainsworth "armed herself" with a poster depicting forcible feeding that was currently being circulated—I guess this to be *Torturing Women in Prison*—and went to a Liberal meeting that the prime minister, Asquith, was attending. Ainsworth approached him, displayed her poster, and asked, "Why did you do this to me?"[14] An impersonal depiction of a "typical" suffragette being forcibly fed could, Ainsworth implies, articulate the individual experience of any forcibly fed suffragette; the ordeal is not an isolated and isolating bodily experience but a point of identification and union between many women.

"SCREAMING WITH IMPOTENT RAGE": REVERSING THE VIOLENCE

One crucial reason for producing pictorial representations of forcible feeding such as the one used by Ainsworth was to make the pain it caused socially visible. This was particularly important in the Edwardian period, when it was popularly believed (as it had been in the previous century) that pain, like any internal problem or pathology, should reveal itself in visible physical symptoms; as late as 1909, doctors were still claiming to be able to diagnose "moral diseases" such as masturbation by visual examination.[15] However, simply making their pain visible did not ensure that it would necessarily be read as the suffragists intended. The popular belief that physiognomic abnormalities were caused by psychological disturbances meant that images of women's faces contorted with pain were ripe for exploitation by their opponents.

In an article entitled "The Suffragette Face: New Type Evolved by Militancy" (fig. 1.), the antisuffragist *Daily Mirror* told its readers, "There is no longer any need for the militants to wear their colours, or their badges. Fanaticism has set its seal upon their faces and left a peculiar

FIG. 1. "The Suffragette Face: New Type Evolved by Militancy," *Daily Mirror*, (May 25, 1914): 5. Reproduced by permission of the author from Lisa Tickner, *The Spectacle of Women: Imagery of the Suffrage Campaign, 1907–1914* (London: Chatto, 1987), 171, and of the *Daily Mirror*.

expression which cannot be mistaken. Nowadays, indeed, any observant person can pick out a suffragette in a crowd of other women."[16] This argument is illustrated by a selection of photographs of women's faces taken at a WSPU demonstration. Most of the women look angry or exhausted; the pictures are accompanied by such captions as "Ecstasy on Arrest," "Dishevelled after Fighting," and "Rather Emotional." In most cases the faces alone are shown: there is no visible cause for their grimaces, which are thus implicitly attributed to the nursed grievances of the bitter minds referred to in the article. The only photograph featuring the police presents them as the victims of suffragette aggression: an apparently snarling woman is said to be "Attacking the Police." The majority of these photographs were taken at the demonstration outside Buckingham Palace on May 21, 1914. It is true that a small number of women retaliated against the rough treatment they received from the police on this occasion: Sylvia Pankhurst recalls that one woman brandished a horsewhip, but affirms that very few "used any force other than the persistent pressure of their bodies." She explains that the scale of police brutality was appalling and unprecedented. Women were punched, kicked, grabbed by the breasts, and struck with truncheons; May Billinghurst, a disabled suffragette, was tipped out of her wheelchair by policemen.[17]

In the center of the page is a picture of the WSPU coleader Emmeline Pankhurst, her face apparently contorted with emotion. This picture is cut from a larger photograph that is reproduced in her autobiography, where we can see the cause of her anguished expression: a policeman has lifted her from the ground by the waist, pinning her arms tightly to her sides.[18] Beneath the picture of the WSPU organizer Flora Drummond appears that of an unnamed suffragette, carrying the caption "Screaming with Impotent Rage." This picture has clearly been chosen because the two women look superficially similar, supporting the argument that the suffragette is a recognizable "type." However, the whole photograph, reproduced in Raeburn's *The Suffragette View*, tells a different story. Here we can see that the woman (named by Raeburn as Eleanor Higginson) is screaming, not in hysterical rage, but in agony: her arms are being twisted backwards by policemen.[19]

We see in the use made of these pictures that "elision of the scene of violence" that Lynn Higgins and Brenda Silver argue characterizes the male poetics of rape.[20] This elision is associated with a displacement of the violence, which is attributed to the raped woman rather than to the rapist. Patricia Joplin shows how this poetics of reversal works in the classical story of Philomela, who is raped by Tereus and plots revenge with her sister Procne. "Myth," she explains, "seeks to blame the women . . . the sisters must become *force-feeders;* they must turn out to be blood-thirsty" [my emphasis].[21] As Mieke Bal argues, the elision of the aggressive male act often means that rape is misread as self-inflicted violence. She cites as typical the conventional way of representing the story of Lucrezia in classical art. In Roman mythology, Lucrezia is raped by Tarquin and commits suicide afterwards in shame at the loss of her honor: Bal explains that the story is conventionally depicted using the scene of Lucrezia's suicide rather than that of her rape.[22] The story, whose semiotics already conveyed the message "rape is the woman's fault," now reads "rape is the woman's own act upon herself." In "The Suffragette Face," male acts of violence are similarly elided so that the appearance of anguish on the faces can be read as self-induced: a hysterical symptom.

Despite these dangers, many suffragists demanded visual representations of forcible feeding. In the WSPU leaflet *Doctors as Torturers,* which cites several doctors' views as to the brutality of forcible feeding, C. Barrow Burt comments, "I suppose it would be futile to ask for a fair photograph of the proceedings . . . but the scene might be reconstructed, so that we might see with our own eyes the sort of daily goings-on in the women's prisons."[23] In 1909 the Labour Party leader Keir Hardie protested to the *Daily News* in the following terms: "Women, worn and weak by hunger, are seized upon, held down by brute force, gagged, a tube inserted down the throat, and food poured or pumped into the stomach. Let British men think over the spectacle."[24] However, in the same letter he notes the fact that when the House of Commons, the elected representatives of British men, thought over the spectacle, they were moved not to horror but to "levity."

Images of women being punished or silenced were, after all, a staple of contemporary cartoon humor. Lisa Tickner's excellent study of the visual propaganda of the suffrage movement, *The Spectacle of Women,* includes two contemporary comic postcards depicting suffragettes being forcibly fed, which are reproduced below (fig. 2).[25] In "The Prevention of Hunger Strikes," the suffragette is skinny and unattractive, with huge feet (a characteristic all suffragettes were popularly believed to share); she

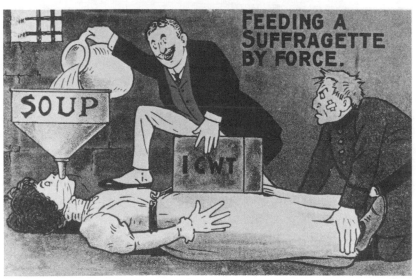

FIG. 2. "The Prevention of Hunger Strikes" and "Feeding a Suffragette by Force." Comic postcards of the suffrage era. Private collection of Patricia Leeming. Reproduced from Tickner, *The Spectacle of Women*, 107, by permission of the author. I have attempted to contact Patricia Leeming for her permission but unfortunately without success.

is held down by grinning wardresses while a maliciously gleeful doctor holds up a huge syringe.[26] In "Feeding a Suffragette by Force," the woman is well-dressed and much more attractive than most cartoon suffragettes; her feet are of average size and her rebellious nature is signaled only by the sticking plaster on the warder's cheek. The doctor who feeds her has his foot on her chest and looks debonair and humorous rather than malicious. While the supposed pleasure of "The Prevention of Hunger Strikes" comes from the fact that the tormented woman is ugly and unpopular, that of "Feeding a Suffragette by Force" comes from her very attractiveness: the viewer is invited to share in the doctor's enjoyment of this oral "rape."

Given this climate, suffragist visual representations of forcible feeding inevitably risked being viewed in a very different light from that which their producers intended. For this reason I dispute Tickner's argument that images produced by suffragists were ipso facto effective in countering the misogyny of this contemporary postcard "humor."[27] Certainly a suffragist representation of forcible feeding might try to disrupt this reaction: for instance, the WSPU poster *Modern Inquisition* (fig. 3), published in 1910, shows the tube entering the woman's body through the nose rather than through the mouth, in an attempt to avoid the connotations of silencing and of oral rape that "Feeding a Suffragette by Force" suggests.[28] However, the cover cartoon of the *Suffragette*, July 31, 1914, with its brutalized male warders leering over the agonized face of a suffragette, whose head is being pulled back, is in many ways distinguishable from these (unofficially) antisuffragist postcards only by context. Such an image of a woman being forcibly fed, regardless of its producer's intention, could equally be read as a horrific indictment of a misogynist culture in which women's bodies are violated or as a pleasing reassurance that, in spite of women's rebelliousness, men still have them under complete control.

Many suffragettes express similar reservations about using visual descriptions or images of forcible feeding in their written accounts. In her moving account of her imprisonment, Helen Gordon Liddle, the secretary of the Westminster branch of the WSPU, explicitly refuses to give too graphic a depiction of forcible feeding, on the grounds that she cannot control the spirit in which it will be read. She writes, "The prisoner is of the opinion that over the ordeal that follows a veil should be drawn. The

FIG. 3. *Modern Inquisition.* WSPU propaganda poster (1910). Suffragette Fellowship Collection at the Museum of London. Reproduced from Tickner, *The Spectacle of Women*, color plate 7, by permission of the author and of Diane Atkinson of the Museum of London.

principle underlying her act and its results is strong enough to justify it in her own eyes, but with the unseeing public it will not. Therefore why satisfy their mere animal curiosity?"[29]

Mary Richardson, famous as the suffragette who slashed the *Rokeby Venus*, explains in her autobiography that she was motivated to write her story when her memories were painfully brought back by going to see a film that included a forcible feeding scene: a scene that she was unable to stay and watch.[30] Richardson resists a cinematic portrayal of forcible feeding in her autobiography as she resisted it in the cinema; although she was forcibly fed on very many occasions, and at the time described the experience very vividly, she describes it in this text only once. The one self-consciously visual image she uses is also self-consciously alienated; having explained how the wardresses pinned her to the floor, she writes, "And now that the victim was trussed up and ready the doctors came in."[31] To any reader versed in suffragette literature, this image recalls the much-publicized gibe made by the doctor who forcibly fed Leslie Hall, that feeding her was "like stuffing a turkey for Christmas": an image that identifies eating with being eaten in a sinister gesture that underlines the deadly intentions behind forcible feeding (Pankhurst, *SM*, 329). This allusion, in the context of Richardson's "visual" image of her own ordeal, implies that a suffragette can construct such an image only by imaginatively stepping outside her body, thus alienating herself from the site of the very pain she is attempting to express. As we shall see later in my discussion of Constance Lytton's masquerade, visual images imply a spectator whose place (given that forcible feeding happened without independent witnesses, behind prison doors) could only be filled by the doctors and wardresses carrying out the feeding: not a position with which the suffragettes would wish to identify.

If the effect of forcible feeding was both literally and metaphorically to silence the suffragettes, then using visual images to combat it could be seen as self-defeating: after all, women in pictures cannot speak. By contrast, verbal accounts offered suffragettes a way to transform a torture that was intended to silence them into a place from which to speak. Such reversals were common in suffragette technique: one might compare their strategy of chaining themselves to trees or railings in order, first, to dramatize the shackled condition of womanhood, and second, to make that condition, which usually enforced silence and submission, into one from which to make speeches without the police being able to move them on.[32]

Written accounts, insofar as the strategies they employ in resistance to the pain were evolved by suffragettes themselves, offered suffragettes more hope of controlling the presentation of forcible feeding than the propaganda poster. Posters such as *Modern Inquisition* could be misread in the light of misogynist comic postcards such as those shown above: there was no directly equivalent comic version of the written forcible feeding account to encourage such misreading (although of course contemporary pornographic representations of rape might form an indirect equivalent).

The extremely articulate written forcible feeding accounts that suffragettes produced also had the effect of testifying to their authors' rationality. Underlining this was crucial; the only other group of people being forcibly fed in the same period in Britain were inmates in lunatic asylums, and forcible feeding thus constituted a slur on the suffragettes' sanity. Indeed, attempts were made by prison authorities to certify individual suffragettes as insane in order to legitimate the practice. Through their well-written descriptions of the ordeal they had undergone, suffragettes countered this slur. By extension, they also countered the slur against womanhood implicit in their disenfranchisement: the WSPU made much of the fact that by depriving women of votes the government was classing them with the insane, another disenfranchised group.[33]

Another benefit of written accounts was that they offered, at least in small part, some control over readership. A poster on the wall is viewed, and is intended to be viewed, by the general public. By contrast, written accounts for the most part appeared only in the suffrage press, and were thus read predominantly by other suffragists: most nonsuffragists simply did not see those papers. By virtue of the conditions of their publication, written accounts could be rather more confident of a sympathetic reception.

THE FIRST PHASE: 1909–10

To understand the genealogy of the representational strategies that came to predominate in forcible feeding accounts, it is essential to understand the pivotal role played by Lady Constance Lytton. Lytton was an aristocrat, the daughter of an earl and a lady-in-waiting, who became a militant suffragette and was imprisoned twice in 1909 under her own name. The second occasion fell in October, shortly after the introduction of forcible feeding. Along with her fellow suffragette prisoners she began the hunger strike, but unlike the others, Constance Lytton and Jane Brailsford (the wife of the Liberal journalist) were released without being forcibly fed: Lytton ostensibly because of her heart condition. Lytton believed that it was not her weak heart but her title that had saved her, and resolved to prove the point. To this end she disguised herself as a seamstress, took the pseudonym Jane Warton, and was once again arrested for militancy in Liverpool in January 1910. The heart of the working-class spinster Jane Warton evidently inspired less concern than that of the titled lady: she was not medically examined but was forcibly fed repeatedly, until at the end of January, her true identity having been discovered, she was released in critical condition. She suffered a heart attack and never recovered from the resulting paralysis. Lytton's experiences thus prove the falsity of the government's claim that forcible feeding was only resorted to in order to save life.

Lytton's masquerade fell at a crucial moment in the history of the movement. She was one of the last forcibly fed suffragettes to be released from prison before the WSPU leadership declared a truce from militancy in order to allow a bill for women's suffrage, known as the Conciliation Bill, to pass before the House of Commons. Her story was for this reason not quickly superseded by others, and so it remained in the public mind; she recounted something of her experiences in a speech at the Queen's Hall on January 31, 1910, which was published in *Votes for Women*, and also in several articles over the following months. Lytton became a reference point for discussions of forcible feeding after the close of its first phase; when in June 1910 *Votes for Women* published an article for "new readers" summing up the course of the movement so far, Lytton's case was the only example of forcible feeding discussed.[34]

Forcible feeding was suspended in February 1910. The new home secretary, Winston Churchill, devised a new prison "division" for suffragettes, known as rule 243a, which granted them most of the privileges of the first division and was thereby seen to obviate the need to hunger strike for political prisoner status. Men were not covered by this rule, however, and several male militant suffragist prisoners were forcibly fed in the interim. A WSPU pamphlet of 1911 that publicizes the forcible feeding of working-class suffragist William Ball cites Lytton's experiences, along with those of Mary Leigh, to remind the reader of the similar sufferings inflicted on women in 1909.[35] Also in 1911, the suffragette novelist Gertrude Colmore published a polemical novel entitled *Suffragette Sally*, featuring a fictionalized account of Constance Lytton's experiences in the character of Lady Geraldine Hill.[36] For Sally, the eponymous working-class co-heroine of the novel, Lady Hill is an inspirational role model. By the time forcible feeding was reintroduced in 1912, Lytton's version of the forcible feeding account was undoubtedly the most familiar one to the majority of suffragist readers.

The first phase of forcible feeding had caused much anger in the suffragist press, but forcible feeding itself had not always been stressed over the other kinds of ill-treatment to which imprisoned suffragettes were subjected. For instance, when the prison experiences of Selina Martin and Leslie Hall (two of the first militants to be forcibly fed) were first publicized in *Votes for Women*, the fact that they had been handcuffed and frog-marched was stressed over the fact that they had been forcibly fed, and the former tortures were described at much greater length than the latter. A leaflet about their ordeals was circulated in which the word "frog-march" was emboldened throughout.[37] Similarly, other first-wave accounts stress the horrors of handcuffing or of the hunger strike itself over those of forcible feeding.[38]

However, in 1912, shortly after the reintroduction of forcible feeding, Sylvia Pankhurst wrote a report about the experiences of Martin and Hall that places special emphasis on the horrors of the feeding itself, rather than on the accompanying violence.[39] From here on there is an increasing focus on forcible feeding itself in the accounts, to the erasure of most other kinds of violence the women underwent. This new emphasis, I argue, was in large part due to Lytton's early accounts, which overdetermined the prison experiences and accounts of hundreds of suffragettes who were to follow her.

Lytton's emphasis on the horrors of forcible feeding in her early accounts is partly explained by the fact that, apart from one occasion when she was slapped in the face by a doctor, she did not experience other forms of violence. However, Lytton also introduced a new tone to the forcible feeding account. Many of the early accounts tend to read as descriptions of a medical procedure rather than of the victim's emotions. Examples of these are the accounts of Mary Leigh, a committed militant who was involved in the first suffragette stone-throwing incident, and

Dorothy Pethick, also a window smasher and the sister of the WSPU treasurer Emmeline Pethick-Lawrence. Mary Leigh's account and Dorothy Pethick's letter to the press both concentrate on what was done to them, going into great detail about the methods and equipment used.[40] Both describe the pain of forcible feeding in quite objective, even medical terms. Leigh at one point remarks that during the feeding "great pain is experienced, both mental and physical," but it is only the physical aspect of the pain that she describes. "The sensation," she explains, "is most painful—the drums of the ears seem to be bursting and there is a horrible pain in the throat and the breast. . . . The after-effects are a feeling of faintness, a sense of great pain in the diaphragm or breast-bone, in the nose and the ears." Pethick's description of her pain has a similarly medical ring and is also presented in the passive voice. "It was not until within four days of my release," she writes, "and when the nasal passages were very much swollen and inflamed, that the tube was dipped in glycerine to facilitate its passage and relieve the agonizing pain."

For Lytton, however, to write or speak about forcible feeding was not just to describe someone else's act of violence against one; it was a self-representational act in itself, a mise-en-scène. In a speech she gave in January 1910, Lytton indicates that to be adequate, a description of forcible feeding must go beyond the merely medical: "It is like describing a hospital scene—and much worse."[41] Her description of her pain is far more subjective in tone than those of Leigh and Pethick, and is as concerned with the psychological aspect of the pain as with the physical, describing how it obliterated the contents of her consciousness: "I felt as though I were being killed. . . . I forgot what I was in there for, I forgot women, I forgot everything except my own sufferings, and I was completely overcome by them." Forcible feeding is not merely painful: it has the ability to annihilate the subject.

In another moving early account, Lytton speaks of the time when she was so ill after forcible feeding that she believed her death was imminent, and of the joy she felt at the prospect of release from her pain. However, she explains, she managed to shame herself out of submission to death, which she understood as an abdication from her duty. She closes this account with a passionate call to other women to come and share in her ordeal: "Women, as women, because you are women, come out in all your womanliness, and whether or not victory is for your day, at least each one of you make sure that the one course impossible to you is surrender of your share in the struggle."[42] Here Lytton makes forcible feeding the definitive experience, not only of suffragettes, but of womanhood. The culmination of the representational practice she here inaugurates can be seen in 1914, when the American feminist journalist Djuna Barnes felt moved to have herself forcibly fed and had herself photographed during the ordeal: she wrote an article about it for the *New York World Magazine* in which she stated that she had hereby "shared the greatest experience of the bravest of my sex."[43]

OUTRAGES AND OPERATIONS

In July 1912 two suffragette prisoners in Dublin were denied political prisoner status; they began a hunger strike and were forcibly fed over a period of nine weeks. In October of that year Emmeline Pankhurst inaugurated a new policy: hunger strike, not for political prisoner status, but for release. Hundreds of suffragettes followed her lead, and forcible feeding recommenced on an unprecedented scale. Forcible feeding accounts proliferated: they littered the pages of the suffrage newspapers *Votes for Women*, the *Suffragette*, and, later, the *Women's Dreadnought*; some were reprinted in pamphlet form.

My discussion of these second-wave accounts will focus on terms of resistance and submission. In general, those who represent themselves as resisting forcible feeding describe the ordeal through the metaphor of rape; by contrast, those who represent themselves as submitting passively use the metaphor of an operation. I shall examine the problems thrown up by these metaphors, and the way they work to produce different specific forms of male oppression and female pain as central to the common experience of women.

There is evidence to suggest that second-wave forcible feeding accounts were carefully constructed to produce maximum political effect. Emmeline Pankhurst offered the following counsel in a letter to fellow militant and forcible feeding survivor Myra Sadd Brown (whose husband had already written a letter of protest to the prison authorities):

It would really be so much more effective if you would write the account of what took place yourself that I should advise you to do so. I should try to confine your account to the points in regard to the way in which the tube returned, the fact that you had had an operation on your nose, [etc.] . . . describing what took place as graphically as possible, say what you do to me about the ordeal being terrible mentally and physically. . . . I should imagine it is a unique experience and therefore there is nothing exactly that one can liken it to.[44]

Pankhurst's view that the account should be "graphic" or pictorial, sticking as much as possible to medical facts, coupled with her caution as to whether metaphors would be appropriate, suggest that she may have been uneasy with the analogies some suffragettes were using in their accounts of forcible feeding. Most suffragettes felt that forcible feeding was a horrific assault on their persons, and many were implicitly equating the experience with rape. As Lisa Tickner notes, suffragettes never explicitly used the word "rape" to talk about forcible feeding.[45] However, it is important to point out that in this period the word "outrage" is very frequently used in places where we would today say "rape" or "sexual abuse," and this word occurs repeatedly in descriptions of forcible feeding. The resonances of the word are clear from an article in *Votes for Women*, which compares the "outrage" of forcible feeding, to which suffragettes were being subjected for minor or nominal crimes, to the comparative leniency of sentences recently imposed on men for "the outrage of young girls."[46] Writers who use the term "outrage" usually represent themselves as having resisted the feeding, as the only morally appropriate response: this too is evidence that they intended the term "outrage" to resonate as "rape." This resistance was also tactically important for other reasons. The home secretary frequently stated that the prisoners were not struggling against the feeding, and that this proved that the process was not really painful; some even implied that the women secretly enjoyed the experience (Pankhurst, *SM*, 447).[47]

Other suffragettes, however, chose to represent themselves as submitting passively to forcible feeding. This strategy too had its tactical importance: the government frequently asserted that forcible feeding was painful or dangerous only if the patient resisted, and that therefore any damage it caused to suffragettes was their own fault. Also violent resistance might be seen as contradicting the WSPU's dictum that they would never cause physical harm to any but themselves in the course of their fight for the vote, a pledge that was itself designed to counteract the popular antisuffragist practice of representing them as violent, rampaging maenads. Those suffragettes who did not resist forcible feeding usually describe it using the term "operation" (or a similar word) rather than "outrage." They tend to stress that, in spite of their submission, they still suffered terrible pain and injuries; that forcible feeding is inherently dangerous regardless of whether the patient struggles or not.

Mary Leigh's account was one of the first to be published; it appeared in *Votes for Women* on October 15, 1909, and was later reprinted as the pamphlet *Fed by Force*, cited above. This first-wave account is particularly interesting, in that it establishes the two terms that, I argue, demarcated the boundaries of representational choice for second-wave forcible feeding accounts. Leigh writes that she told the prison governor that while the practice of forcible feeding by the spoon could be described as an "operation," feeding by tube could only be described as an "outrage." Hence she represents herself as resisting the tube feeding; stressing that she "used no violence," Leigh states, "I resist and am overcome by weight of numbers." Leigh characterizes forcible feeding as a struggle whose sides are clearly gendered. All the acts of cruelty and threatening behaviors are attributed to the doctors and male warders, while the wardresses' only recorded role is to hold her down; during her first nasal feeding, she remembers, "the matron and two of the wardresses were in tears." As we shall see, this representational practice is also used by those who were to follow Leigh in using the imagery of rape. For Leigh, as for other resisters who used rape terminology, forcible feeding was, in the contemporary phrase, part of the "sex war" being waged against women. Dr. Frances Ede, speaking at the London Palladium in 1912 after a period of forcible feeding, comments, "There seems to be an innate cruelty in man which does not exist in woman . . . what the Government tell them to do they are apparently willing to carry out regardless of honour, chivalry and the protection that men say they afford to women."[48]

To resist or to submit? Few suffragettes are as frank, or as self-conscious, about the politics behind their representational choices as Kitty Marion, who was forcibly fed on many occasions throughout the suffrage years. On commencing her second hunger strike in June 1912, Marion (usually a "resister") decided to adopt a different strategy. She writes, "I decided not to struggle this time since I had been told how beneficial forcible feeding is and how invalids and babies submit to it. There's the rub, 'submit'. In spirit, we were not going to 'submit' to forcible feeding any more than to disenfranchisement. Heart and soul revolted and resisted, but this time I would let the body submit."[49] That Marion made this decision for strategic reasons, in an attempt to prove the falsity of the government's argument, rather than because she believed she would really save herself pain, is particularly evident in the manuscript version of this account, where she expresses her decision with greater irony. "Instead of struggling against it," she writes, "I thought I would submit quietly for a change, since the 'enemy' had always insisted on forcible feeding being 'life saving' and only our resistance injurious."[50] In fact this feeding went disastrously wrong and the food was poured into her lungs, causing her terrible pain. Marion evidently considered her case proved, as she does not mention having repeated the experiment.

Accounts deploying the metaphor of rape become increasingly common toward the end of the militant suffrage campaign. The Scottish suffragette Ethel Moorhead wrote of her ordeal in March 1914: "I was carried back to my cell feeling that I had been physically and spiritually outraged."[51] In July of that year Grace Roe declared, "It would be morally wrong if we did not struggle against such an outrage as that."[52] Sylvia Pankhurst too believed it was crucial that the suffragettes should both resist and be seen to resist forcible feeding. In a letter to her mother, Sylvia writes, "I am fighting, fighting, fighting . . . I am afraid they may be saying we don't resist. Yet my shoulders are bruised with struggling" (*SM*, 447). Pankhurst repeatedly uses the word "outrage" to describe the feeding, and, as Maud Ellmann notes, her description reads like an account of "oral rape" (*SM*, 444–46).[53]

Pankhurst's account, however, illustrates the problem with using the terminology of rape: the rhetoric of self-infliction that, as Bal argues, bedevils representations of rape. Describing her feelings of shame at not being able to throw up all the food they forced into her and thereby hasten her release, Pankhurst writes, "Every hour I remained seemed a shameful consent, an encouragement to the maintainers of outrage" (*SM*, 446). Corbett comments that "'consent' and submission were not appropriate categories to invoke in terms of this experience," but in a sense experiencing and representing forcible feeding as rape necessitated some sort of engagement with these terms.[54] Pankhurst is not making a perverse or inappropriate choice of words but rather demonstrating the extent to which the terminology of rape tends to elide male responsibility and attribute it instead to the raped woman. One of Mary Richardson's accounts displays a similar problem. "One struggles," Richardson explains, "also, because of another reason—a moral reason—for forcible feeding is an immoral assault as well as a painful physical one, and to remain passive under it would give one the feeling of sin—the sin of concurrence." [55]

This rhetorical reversal whereby rape becomes self-rape made some resisting suffragettes feel that to write about their experience of forcible feeding at all was to do themselves violence on top of that which had already been done to them. The suffragette who makes this point most clearly is Ada Cecile Wright, a resister who was imprisoned on six occasions between 1907 and 1913. Wright declares that she will not talk about the sufferings she endured during forcible feeding because "One feels sometimes as if it were a violation to one's self to write of them!" [sic]. [56]

The use of the metaphor of rape places issues of sexuality at the center of the suffragette identity. That accounts centering around this metaphor should have become more common in the later years of the movement is testimony to the increasing emphasis on these issues in suffragette literature of these years. Christabel Pankhurst's enormously influential work on venereal disease, *The Great Scourge and How to End It* (1913) identified exploitative and infecting male sexual practices as the root causes of female oppression. Pankhurst writes of the dominance of the "doctrine that women are sex and beyond that nothing," which she argues leads men to believe that "women are created primarily for the sex gratification of men." [57] As Jane Marcus notes, for Christabel votes for women and chastity for men were inextricably linked. [58] Using the metaphor of rape in forcible feeding accounts was another way of linking women's oppression and male sexuality: forcible feeding becomes a figure for a whole variety of sufferings undergone by women because of male sexual practices. As forcible feeding became the definitive experience of the suffragette movement and (by extension) of women in general, so its representation as rape made sexual abuse the definitive experience of womanhood.

Jane Marcus argues that suffragettes underwent forcible feeding in order to "point out to the public and to themselves that their common experience as women was unmistakably the experience of rape"; in this way they made themselves "political rape victims" and thus enabled an identification with poor and socially outcast women. [59] My qualification of this argument would be that in order to produce this reading of forcible feeding as rape, and thus to enable political identification with other women, suffragettes had to do some representational work; forcible feeding is not literally rape, and not all suffragettes read or experienced it as such.

For some suffragettes, forcible feeding was not rape precisely because the gendered positions that metaphor implies were not applicable. In accounts by resisters who use rape terminology, the male doctors are represented as the primary agents of violation; the wardresses are represented as less cruel and often as friendly. Kitty Marion, for instance, represents the wardresses as sympathetic to the point of actually sharing the suffragettes' pain: "The wardresses . . . had fearfully tearstained faces . . . and I wished that the 'brute things' who had ordered the f.f. [sic] could have suffered all these wardresses suffered, to say nothing of us."[60] In some accounts, however, resisting suffragettes reject rape terminology; these accounts are characterized by the equal emphasis they place on the cruelty of the wardresses. In one of Mary Richardson's accounts it is the wardresses who are "brutalised"; their cruelty is equal to that of the doctors.[61] Olive Walton, the secretary of the Tunbridge Wells branch of the WSPU, who was forcibly fed in Aylesbury prison in 1912, also rejects rape terminology and depicts the wardresses as hostile and brutal. In her statement for the WSPU she explains that on one occasion the wardresses came alone to feed her and she resisted, insisting that it was a job for the doctor. At this, she recalls, "the wardresses lost all control of themselves . . . one woman began to pummel me all over my breasts and stomach causing intense pain. I remember I called her a brute."[62]

In accounts by suffragettes who choose not to resist forcible feeding, terms like "outrage" and "brutal" are generally absent. The account of Myra Sadd Brown, the suffragette to whom Emmeline Pankhurst's letter cited above is written, is an example of this smaller but significant group. Brown's stated aim in writing her account is to counter the government's assertion that "forcible feeding is only dangerous when the patient resists" by showing that damage was caused to her nose and throat although "in my case there was no resistance and I did all in my power to assist the doctor during the operation."[63] The term "outrage" is absent from this account, which focuses almost exclusively on the medical failings of the doctors rather than on other forms of cruelty; forcible feeding is shown as a dangerous operation badly carried out. Brown stresses that though she told the doctor that her nose had been broken and operated on and therefore might be too narrow for the tube, "he did not examine my nose in any way," and neither did the deputy medical officer to whom she complained. As she explains, the doctor went on to bungle the job badly: "each time the tube was passed the throat could not retain it and it was choked up violently till the doctor himself was convinced that feeding could not take place by this method."

By using the passive voice, Brown is able to erase the imputation that she had any will in the matter of her body's "natural resistance," enacting a division between her body and herself that allows her to remain the innocent victim of malpractice. This representational technique is also deployed by other nonresisting suffragettes in their accounts, including Alice Farmer and Lilian Lenton.[64] Brown's official statement is an extended version of a letter she wrote to the *Woman's Platform* protesting their publication of an account of her case by Ellis Griffith on June 28, 1912. Griffith here argues that "the difficulty in feeding her arose entirely from the unusual power she possessed of contracting the throat muscles and bringing the tube out through her mouth."[65] In this way he replaces Brown's "innocent" version of her body with one more complicit with her will. Similarly, Griffith replaces Brown's objective bodily evidence of damage, the bleeding of her nose and throat, with the slippery evidence of Brown's word, asserting that "No trace of bleeding was observed nor did the prisoner at the time make any complaint of the kind, though she did afterwards." By way of conclusion, Griffith states that "if she suffered any pain, it was entirely due to the violent resistance she offered to what was necessary medical treatment."

The subject position constructed by these texts differs in important ways from that constructed by the accounts linking forcible feeding and rape. If the latter strategy can be read as a call to other women and an attempt to forge identification between women on the basis of a shared experience of rape, the latter may be read as a call to men. Accounts that center around the term "operation" were frequently written as protests to and/or about specific men in authority against specific blunders that took place. Even where such accounts argue that the operation is *always* carried out badly, the implication remains that there could be a way to do it that would be acceptable. It is not forcible feeding *per se*, but rather the doctors' cruel or cavalier attitude to women's bodies that is the problem.

The effectiveness of these accounts as protests against forcible feeding depends primarily on the extent to which the experiences referred to are understood as representative of the experiences of all suffragettes. The sufferings of their writers could be understood as exceptional, the result of an inept practitioner; the practice of forcible feeding in general thus remains unchallenged. However, these accounts could also be read as making forcible feeding a figure for women's maltreatment at the hands of the medical establishment, which is identified as a central aspect of women's oppression. They thereby suggest a critique of male abuse of power of a different kind from that found in the "rape" accounts, but one that is (arguably) of no less importance.

We may say, then, that forcible feeding accounts construct three different models of suffragette subjectivity. Accounts that represent resistance and use the metaphor of rape construct a large subject position that may encompass women other than suffragettes; this subject position makes the experience of rape definitive of female subjectivity, thus facilitating a political identification between many women. Accounts that represent submission and use the metaphor of an operation may also permit such identification through a definition of woman as victim of medical malpractice. They differ from the "rape" accounts in that they usually imply an alternative "good doctor" who could have performed the operation properly; the gender of this putative doctor is rarely specified and thus the broadly suffragist subject position these accounts invoke does not exclude men. The third group of accounts, which represent resistance but refuse the metaphor of rape, construct a subject position to which only forcibly fed suffragettes would have access; this strategy does not permit a universal female (or even feminist) subject and thus precludes identification with women other than suffragettes. However, the specifically suffragette subjectivity thus constructed is, within these bounds, extremely fluid and mutually reinforcing, enabling strong identification between many forcibly fed suffragettes.

REPRESENTING (AS) VIOLENCE

Ada Cecile Wright's assertion that writing an account of forcible feeding feels like "a violation to one's self" raises an interesting problem.[66] Is it possible to represent an act of violence against oneself without re-inflicting that violence? Is the representation of violence, in some sense, intrinsically violent? In *The Violence of Representation*, Armstrong and Tennenhouse suggest that all representations of people commit violence against those people, by suppressing their differences of, say, gender or ethnicity. "Whenever we speak for someone else," they argue, "we are inscribing her with our own . . . idea of order."[67] Violence would then be the result of any act of representation where there is a power differential between the person representing and the person being represented.

Elisabeth Bronfen suggests a different approach to the question. For her, representation as a tool is inherently violent, regardless of who is using it. Writing of the artist Ferdinand Hodler, who produced over seventy sketches and portraits of his dying lover Valentine Godé-Darel between 1914 and 1915, Bronfen poses the question: "[A]re Godé-Darel and her death made visible or invisible through these images?"[68] For Bronfen, the answer to this question lies not in the power relation between Hodler and Godé-Darel but in the viewer's relation to the images. She asks whether "every representation of dying is not violent precisely because it implies the safe position of a spectator." Bronfen suggests that the violence of representation is committed by the viewer, who in our culture must choose between the position of the "morally involved spectator," who treats the represented body as if it were real and thereby ignores the mechanisms of representation, and that of the "aesthetically involved spectator," who ignores the reality of the body being represented.[69] By implication, then, even if Godé-Darel had painted self-portraits on her deathbed, viewers of the paintings would in a sense be violating her simply by taking on these compromised positions as spectators. Still more disturbingly, insofar as she would become a spectator of her own painting, she would be violating herself. By analogy, the writer of a forcible feeding account would, through the act of representing her ordeal, inflict violence on herself further to that which she had already suffered.

I suggest that the question of whether or not the spectator (or reader) of a representation of violence reenacts the violence hinges crucially on precisely how safe from that violence the position of the spectator or reader is. For the fellow suffragette reader or viewer, representations of forcible feeding were very far from conferring "the safe position of a spectator"; rather, they reminded her of her own shattering experience of violence, and/or appealed to her sense of solidarity, urging her to go to prison and undergo the same torture as the depicted woman for the cause.

Constance Lytton's autobiography, *Prisons and Prisoners*, appeared in 1914, during the final months of the militant suffrage campaign. In this text Lytton gives details about her masquerade as Jane Warton that had not appeared in her earlier accounts and that raise fascinating questions

about the split subject of forcible feeding accounts and the role of mimicry in Lytton's strategy. Exploring these questions may help us determine the question of how far Lytton and other account writers violate
their identities through the self-representational act.

In *Prisons and Prisoners* Lytton explains that she first learned about
forcible feeding by going to a meeting in Birmingham where she heard
"the shadow of a girl" describe her recent experiences in prison. Lytton
says that this girl reminded her of the Fra Angelico paintings in St.
Mark's, Venice, and explains how she bought a book of these paintings:
"I looked through the book to choose one specially like the girl at Birmingham; there were several that reminded me of her. I had looked at
these pictures in my younger days, and . . . I had felt annoyed with the
man for painting beings so inhuman, women that were ethereal but so
little real, a look of purity that no living creature has. Now I had . . .
seen the thing portrayed in life" (*PP*, 201–2).

In the published version of *Prisons and Prisoners* this woman is not
named, but from the manuscript we learn that it was Laura Ainsworth.[70]
Ainsworth is presented as an image of a forcibly fed suffragette, a Fra
Angelico "portrayed in life"; the emphasis is on her appearance, and the
pity and horror it evokes in Lytton, rather than on what she says. Lytton
implicitly invokes our aesthetic rather than our moral indignation; we are
to be horrified at what was done to her, not because it is immoral, but
because she is beautiful.[71]

Through her masquerade as Jane Warton, Lytton similarly represents
herself as an image to be viewed rather than a "real person." Disguising
herself as "Jane Warton," Lytton sets out to turn herself into a portrayal
of a suffragette, and specifically an antisuffragist portrayal: "the *Punch*
version of a Suffragette." On two notable occasions in the text, perhaps
the moments at which Jane is subjected to the most degradation, Lytton
separates herself from her creation and makes "Jane" the object of her
externalized gaze. The first is at the police station when the arrested
suffragettes are asked to give their names:

It was the turn of Jane Warton. She walked across to the policeman, one shoulder
hitched slightly above the other, her hair sticking out straight behind. . . . The
large, grey woollen gloves were drawn up over the too short sleeves of her coat;
on the collar of it were worn portraits of Mrs. Pankhurst, Mrs. Lawrence and
Christabel, in small china brooches; her hat had a bit of tape with "Votes for

Women" written on it . . . and eye-glasses were fixed on her nose. Her standing out in the room was the signal for a convulsed titter from the other prisoners. "It's a shame to laugh at one of your fellow-prisoners," said the policeman behind the desk, and the tittering was hushed. It was all I could do not to laugh, and I thought to myself, "Is the *Punch* version of a Suffragette overdone?" As I got back to my companions they too were laughing, but I thought it wonderfully kind of the policeman to have spoken on my behalf. (*PP*, 249)

The status of Lytton's laughter, and thus of her subjectivity, is ambiguous in this passage. The laughter of the nonsuffragette prisoners is almost certainly (as the policeman believes) hostile or mocking; they knew nothing of Lytton's true identity and there is no reason to suppose that they could read her masquerade as masquerade; her appearance would have corresponded with portrayals of suffragettes they had seen in the papers and comic postcards. By contrast, the laughter of her suffragette companions is "knowing" laughter: they were aware of Lytton's true identity and their amusement is produced by the excessive quality of her mimicry. The status of Lytton's (suppressed) laughter, however, remains in doubt. Is she laughing with her companions at the success of her mimicry and the failure of the others to see the difference? Or is she laughing with the nonsuffragette prisoners at the sheer ridiculousness of Jane's appearance, thus approximating her own viewing position to that of the antisuffragist *Punch* reader?

In either case, what Lytton is clearly *not* doing is identifying herself, the subject of the laughter, with Jane, the object of the prisoners' contempt and the policeman's pity. Many studies of autobiographical discourse have pointed to the radical division in all such writing between the *I* who writes and the *I* who is written, where the writing *I* frequently stands in a privileged power position to the written, but the division is rarely so violent as in this case.[72] The writing and written selves in this part of *Prisons and Prisoners* are divided in many ways, with their different names, classes, and backgrounds. Constance Lytton is an educated, attractive, moneyed aristocrat, while Jane Warton is a working-class woman, poor, unknown, unattractive, and without influential friends. Even while masquerading as Jane Warton, Lytton cannot experience or represent the contempt of the other prisoners and the pity of the policeman as if she "really were" their object: that is, as if she were the ugly working-class woman she pretends to be.

The second occasion on which Lytton steps outside her assumed persona is when, after feeding her for the first time, a doctor slaps her face to show his contempt for her. Lytton writes,

At first it seemed such an utterly contemptible thing to have done that I could only laugh in my mind. Then suddenly I saw Jane Warton lying before me, and it seemed as if I were outside of her. She was the most despised, ignorant and helpless prisoner that I had seen. When she had served her time and was out of the prison, no one would believe anything she said, and the doctor, when he had fed her by force and tortured her body, struck her on the cheek to show her how he despised her! This was Jane Warton, and I had come to help her. (*PP*, 270)

Again, Lytton does not experience or represent this assault as if she "really were" Jane. She identifies herself as the observing Lytton, wanting to laugh at the doctor's petty cowardice in striking her after the feeding, but moved to pity by the sight of Jane's abject appearance. The point of the masquerade is not to enable her to *experience* the feeding as someone like Jane might have done, in all its misery and degradation. Lytton's revelation is visual, not experiential: she *sees* what happens to Jane, and this gives her the authority to write about it. Bronfen's notion that any representation of violence is itself violent, in that it implies the safe position of a spectator, has a particularly disquieting resonance here. The only possible position for a spectator of forcible feeding is, precisely, that of the doctors and wardresses performing the operation; no one else was allowed to watch. To view forcible feeding is therefore to come uncomfortably close to being the torturer oneself.[73]

Lytton's masquerade raises other uncomfortable questions as well, tapping into the fierce current debate in feminism around the politics of mimicry. Is "female female impersonation" of this kind to be celebrated for its disruptive effect on categories of gender, or condemned for the violence done to the identity of the woman mimicked? Naomi Schor, writing on George Sand's female female impersonations, argues that "ultimately *female travesty*, in the sense of women dressing up as or impersonating other women, constitutes by far the most disruptive form of *bisextuality*: for, whereas there is a long, venerable tradition of naturalized intersexual travesty in fiction, drama and opera, the exchange of *female* identities, the blurring of difference within difference, remains a largely marginal and unfamiliar form."[74] When women impersonate other women, differences between women are simultaneously highlighted and blurred, because the act of impersonation underlines the difference(s) of the other woman's identity even as it appropriates them. Female female impersonation might then subvert the tyranny of gender by proliferating the visible axes along which difference operates: sexual difference loses its primacy.

Carole-Anne Tyler, writing on Dolly Parton's claims to being a female female impersonator, holds a different view. She speaks of the belief many feminists share that by playing up or overacting femininity, women can disrupt it, calling attention to the artificiality of the conventions that encode a body as feminine. However, she argues, the excessive feminin- ity Parton displays is only readable as such from a specifically middle- class viewpoint. "From a middle class point of view," Tyler argues, "she overdoes it. She does not quite get femininity right. . . . Her taste for the excessive is in excessively bad taste." From some working-class points of view, Tyler suggests, Parton may well look like a perfectly ordinary woman. Mimicry, then, is performed "at the expense of the 'other' woman, unconscious and unconscionable."[75]

Of course, Lytton's masquerade is different from Parton's in that it is class, rather than femininity, that Lytton intends to problematize or play up. Her impersonation of a working-class woman is deliberately ugly, not in order to mock working-class women's failure to get femininity right, but because she has noticed that unattractive women prisoners usually receive worse treatment from the prison authorities. Lytton in- tends to maximize the number of oppressed groups with whom she identifies through her masquerade: not only working women, but also unfeminine women. There is no doubt that, in playing Jane, Lytton turns herself into a stereotype. It is nonetheless a moot question whether in doing so she commits violence against the working-class suffragettes of whom Jane is a stereotypical representation. Clearly, *Prisons and Prisoners,* which was widely read all over the world, publicized the sufferings of working-class suffragettes to an unprecedented extent. Perhaps more important, Lytton's accounts formed a model for other accounts that followed, a model that working-class suffragettes then used to articulate their own experiences. Through the forcible feeding account, personal narratives by ordinary women, whose voices would never otherwise have appeared in print, were published and read in large numbers. Lytton's masquerade had made working class suffragettes' prison experiences a matter of public interest, thus providing them with that point of insertion into the public sphere that, as many feminist scholars of autobiography have pointed out, has historically been so crucial for the production, and particularly the publication, of women's autobiographical writing.[76]

It must be pointed out that whatever reading we make of Lytton's masquerade, there was nothing playful about it. Submitting herself to the profound personal and physical pain of forcible feeding, which led first to partial paralysis and subsequently to her premature death, Lytton inscribed her mimicry of the "other suffragette(s)" painfully upon her own body. I suggest that the violent splitting of the subject of her autobiography can better be read as violence against herself than against the object(s) of her mimicry. Lytton de-centers her self to the extent that she identifies even the moment of her greatest suffering, directly after the feeding, as the suffering of another. Her subjectivity is constantly "haunted" by those other, unknown, working-class suffragettes like Selina Martin and Leslie Hall who have been and are going through the same ordeal (*PP*, 243).

Lytton knew that in the culture she was struggling to change, women's words were not heard and their writings were not read; Martin and Hall's accounts of their ordeals would never be read widely enough outside suffragette circles to make an impact. As "The Suffragette Face" article illustrates, if you were a woman in this period the only thing of yours that would be read was your body. The argument for undergoing forcible feeding might then run like this. The female body is a prime ground for signification; if as a woman you want to be read you must write what you have to say there. To show that women are violated and held in contempt in a male-dominated culture it is necessary to show that women's bodies are violated and held in contempt by men. A very effective way to do this is to put your own body into a situation in which women's bodies are routinely and institutionally violated by men and then to publicize that image of your body. And, to borrow a phrase from Judith Butler, Lytton knew that she had a "body that mattered"; an aristocratic body whose torture would not be tolerated by the public as those of "real" Jane Wartons had been.[77]

Lytton demonstrates her belief in this argument through her decision, while imprisoned under her own name in Holloway, "to write the words 'Votes for Women' on my body, scratching it in my skin with a needle, beginning over the heart and ending it on my face." Her plan was to write half the inscription and then show it to the doctors, explaining that if they did not stop giving her preferential treatment (keeping her in hospital when she was not ill) then she would write the rest. Testifying to her awareness of the press photograph as propaganda weapon, she explains that she intended to tell them "that as I knew how much appearances were respected by officials, I thought it well to warn them that the last letter and a full stop would come upon my cheek, and be still quite fresh and visible on the day of my release" (*PP*, 164). In fact, Lytton only completed the *V* in "Votes" before she was caught and had to show the doctors what she had done. Displaying the *V* with pride, Lytton comments, "I felt all a craftsman's satisfaction in my job. The V was very clearly and evenly printed in spite of the varying material of its background, a rib bone forming an awkward bump" (*PP*, 167). Horrifying though this strategy is, it indicates both Lytton's bravery and her astuteness in using her body as a canvas for the publicization of political messages. I suggest that Lytton's literal act of self-inscription, like her masquerade, can be read as a figure for what happens in all forcible feeding accounts. The ordeal of forcible feeding is made both personally bearable and politically valuable because it is interpreted as an inscription upon one's own body and identity of the physical and personal sufferings of many others; others with whom one therefore shares a subject position. The body and its pain are no longer private or incommunicable but replete with shared political meanings: they can be a source of unity and pride. Forcible feeding is no longer something done *to* one, but something one *does;* not only the accounts but even the ordeal itself becomes a self-representational act. The violence done by the representation of forcible feeding is not a new assault upon the victim but an integral part of the self-representational violent act that is forcible feeding.

LOSING THE PERSONAL

Christabel Pankhurst, the coleader of the WSPU, once declared, "To lose the personal in the great impersonal is to live!"[78] For suffragettes under the shadow of forcible feeding, I have suggested, such a loss or contextualization of the personal was essential; to remain in the lonely isolation of their pain was almost inevitably to fall into depression, illness, and silence. The forcible feeding account was one important way in which suffragettes constructed their identities as impersonal, part of a wider subjectivity including many women.

Kate Flint has acknowledged the good use the suffragettes made of the power of reading to form "a bridge between many women," but believes that they stressed communality in their reading practice at "the fatal cost of simultaneously suppressing the necessary recognition of heterogeneity."[79] The way the accounts I have been discussing share a set of common representational practices indicates that suffragettes stressed communality in their writing as well as in their reading practice. The question remains, however, whether this practice was "fatal" in its suppression of the differences between these women and their experiences. Forcible feeding accounts tend to follow one of a few patterns, centering around certain shared metaphors and stressing those aspects of the experience that are shared or highlighted by many women. Does this make them "violent representations," not only in that they re-present and thus risk re-inflicting violence, but also in that they do further violence by erasing the variety of ways suffragettes experienced forcible feeding? To argue this would be to assume that each suffragette had an entirely personal, original experience of forcible feeding that was unique to her. On the contrary, I argue that most suffragettes' experiences of forcible feeding were overdetermined by visual and textual representations of forcible feeding that they had already seen; it seems likely that in most cases there was no completely unmediated, pretextual experience that we could refer to or even posit.

Of course, suffragettes' experiences of forcible feeding were not *entirely* determined by representations they had previously seen, and it is very probable that the diversity of their experiences is not fully testified to in the existing accounts. However, I contest Flint's view that this suppression of experiential differences was "fatal" to the suffrage movement. For the suffragettes undergoing forcible feeding, I argue, emphasizing the heterogeneity among them would have been as fatal as Flint argues it was to suppress it. It should not be forgotten that the heterogeneity of the suffragettes, the differences and divisions between them, were a crucial part of the torturers' verbal weaponry; many suffragettes state that the prison officials tried to break their spirits by faking reports that other hunger strikers had broken down, that they were alone and their struggle was therefore meaningless, since "*all the others had given in.*"[80] Difference was deadly; to be different was to be isolated, both experientially and politically.

As Michèle Barrett has argued, "the inordinate value attached to experience in popular feminism is aligned to an excess of both relativism and pluralism."[81] Barrett contends that the emphasis on difference (understood as experiential diversity) in contemporary feminism tends toward humanism in that it takes for granted the transparency of experience and the stability and unity of the individual Cartesian subject who experiences. I suggest that our notion of representation and its relation to the subject needs to be broadened in recognition of the fact that in many cases oppressed groups, such as the suffragettes, need to construct for themselves a kind of communal "subject" for representation.[82] This communal subject, so far from committing violence against the identities of individual members of the group, may actually preserve and even constitute the possibility of such identities. "To lose the personal in the great impersonal is to live" may be the expression of a strategy for survival.

NOTES

All illustrations reproduced by kind permission of Lisa Tickner from *The Spectacle of Women: Imagery of the Suffrage Campaign 1907–1914* (London: Chatto, 1987). Specific thanks are due to Diane Atkinson for permission to reproduce *Modern Inquisition* from the Suffragette Fellowship Collection and to the *Daily Mirror* for permission to reproduce "The Suffragette Face." I should also like to thank Maud Ellmann and David Booth for their useful criticism of this article and for supporting and encouraging me in my work.

1. Constance Lytton, *Prisons and Prisoners: Some Personal Experiences* (London: Heinemann, 1914), 164. Further references to this work will be included parenthetically in the text (*PP*).

2. Elaine Scarry, *The Body in Pain: The Making and Unmaking of the World* (Oxford: Oxford University Press, 1985), 4–6.

3. Michel Foucault, "Nietzsche, Genealogy, History," in *The Foucault Reader*, ed. Paul Rabinow (Harmondsworth: Penguin, 1984), 76.

4. See, for instance, Michel Foucault, "The Politics of Health in the Eighteenth Century," in *The Foucault Reader*, 273–90.

5. A note on terminology: it has become conventional in discussions of the British suffrage movement to use the word "suffragette" to refer to militant suffragists and "suffragist" to refer to nonmilitants. However, this distinction is not observed by writers of the period, and I consider its observance likely to cause unnecessary confusion. In this article I use the term "suffragist" as I find it used in the period: that is, to refer to anyone—militant or nonmilitant, unionized or otherwise—who supports the campaign for women's suffrage. I use the term "suffragette" to refer to active and unionized militant women suffragists only. The three main militant suffrage societies were the Women's Social and Political Union (WSPU), the Women's Freedom League (WFL), and the East London

Federation of the Suffragettes (EFL). The nonmilitant societies were united under the banner of the National Union of Women's Suffrage Societies (NUWSS). The WSPU was closed to men but had a satellite, the Men's Political Union, which was also militant on occasion.

6. Midge Mackensie, *Shoulder to Shoulder: A Documentary* (London: Allen, 1975), 130.

7. Ibid., 131–32.

8. Ibid., 130.

9. Mary Jean Corbett, *Representing Femininity: Middle Class Subjectivity in Victorian and Edwardian Women's Autobiographies* (New York: Oxford University Press, 1992), 165.

10. Kitty Marion, Ms. Prison Account (in letter to Edith How-Martyn), The Suffragette Fellowship Collection at the Museum of London (hereafter SFC), accession no. 50.82/1124. Much of the material from this archive can be consulted on a set of microfilms entitled *Women's Social and Political Emancipation: The Suffragette Fellowship Collection at the Museum of London* (Brighton, Sussex: Harvester Microform, 1985). The same accession numbers are used for reference in either case.

11. *Suffragette* (June 5, 1914): 133; cited in Antonia Raeburn, *The Militant Suffragettes* (London: Joseph, 1973), 234. The *Suffragette* article gives extensive coverage of what was said by both Grace Roe and Nellie Hall at this trial. Both women reiterate Roe's point about the difficulty of describing forcible feeding to those who have not undergone it.

12. Maud Ellmann, *The Hunger Artists: Starving, Writing and Imprisonment* (London: Virago, 1993), 35.

13. "Miss Nellie Hall's Speech," *Suffragette* (July 13, 1914): 203.

14. Raeburn, *Militant Suffragettes*, 119. The poster *Torturing Women in Prison*, which is reprinted in *Votes for Women* (Oct. 29, 1909): 68, was published by the WSPU for their by-election campaign at Bermondsey. It is, as far as I know, the only suffragist poster representing forcible feeding that would have been available to Ainsworth as early as October 1909.

15. See, for instance, Howard A. Kelly, *Medical Gynaecology* (New York: Appleton, 1909), 292–95.

16. "The Suffragette Face: New Type Evolved by Militancy," *Daily Mirror* (May 25, 1914): 5.

17. E. Sylvia Pankhurst, *The Suffragette Movement: An Intimate Account of Persons and Ideals* (London: Virago, 1977), 552. Further references to this work will be included parenthetically in the text (*SM*).

18. Emmeline Pankhurst, *My Own Story* (London: Nash, 1914), 348.

19. Antonia Raeburn, *The Suffragette View* (London: Charles, 1976), 84.

20. Lynn A. Higgins and Brenda R. Silver, "Rereading Rape," in *Rape and Representation*, ed. Lynn A. Higgins and Brenda R. Silver (New York: Columbia University Press, 1991), 5.

21. Patricia Klindienset Joplin, "The Voice of the Shuttle Is Ours," in *Rape and Representation*, ed. Higgins and Silver, 49.

22. Mieke Bal, "Visual Poetics: Reading with the Other Art," in *Theory between the Disciplines: Authority/Vision/Poetics*, ed. Martin Kreiswirth and Mark A. Cheetham (Ann Arbor: Michigan University Press, 1990), 135–50.

23. *Doctors as Torturers* (London: WSPU, [c. 1912]).

24. Mackensie, *Shoulder to Shoulder*, 131.

25. Lisa Tickner, *The Spectacle of Women: Imagery of the Suffrage Campaign 1907–1914* (London: Chatto, 1987), 108.

26. On the myth of huge feet, see Frederick Pethick-Lawrence's autobiography, *Fate Has Been Kind* (London: Hutchinson, 1943), 85.

27. Tickner, *The Spectacle of Women*, 52.

28. Original copies of this poster are held in the Suffragette Fellowship Collection at the Museum of London and in the Fawcett Library.

29. Helen Gordon [Liddle], *The Prisoner: A Sketch* (Letchworth: Garden City Press, 1911), 39.

30. Mary R. Richardson, *Laugh a Defiance* (London: Weidenfeld, 1953), xii.

31. Ibid., 84.

32. See Christabel Pankhurst, *Unshackled: The Story of How We Won the Vote* (London: Hutchinson, 1959), 113.

33. See, for example, the Artists' Suffrage League poster *Convicts, Lunatics and Women!* (1908), rpt in Tickner, *The Spectacle of Women*, color plate 4.

34. *Votes for Women* (June 17, 1910): 610.

35. *Torture in an English Prison* (London: WSPU, [1911]).

36. G. Colmore, *Suffragette Sally* (London: Stanley Paul, 1911). Rpt as Gertrude Colmore, *Suffragettes: A Story of Three Women* (London: Pandora, 1984).

37. *Votes for Women* (Dec. 31, 1909 and Jan. 7, 1910); *Atrocities in an English Prison* (London: WSPU, [1909]).

38. See, for instance, the accounts of Nellie Taylor, *Votes for Women* (Dec. 31, 1909): 221, and Violet Bryant, *Votes for Women* (Feb. 4, 1910): 298.

39. Sylvia Pankhurst, Report on Forcible Feeding, SFC, acc. no. 57.70/12.

40. Mary Leigh, *Fed by Force* (London: WSPU, [1909]); Dorothy Pethick, Letter to the Press (Nov. 1, 1909), SFC, acc. no. 57.70/14.

41. "A Speech by Lady Constance Lytton," *Votes for Women* (Feb. 4, 1910): 292.

42. Constance Lytton, "A Message to Friends and Foes," *Votes for Women* (Apr. 22, 1910): 479.

43. Djuna Barnes, "How It Feels to Be Forcibly Fed," in *New York* (New York: Sun and Moon, 1989), 179.

44. Emmeline Pankhurst, Letter to Myra Sadd Brown (c. 1912), SFC, acc. no. 50.82/1136.

45. Tickner, *The Spectacle of Women*, 107.

46. "The Forcible Feeding Scandal," *Votes for Women* (Nov. 7, 1913): 85.

47. Kitty Marion describes how the wardresses taunted her with the gibe that she "seemed to prefer taking [her] food from the doctor, instead of giving in quietly." Unsigned Prison Account, SFC, acc. no. Z6083.

48. Frances Ede, Speech (delivered Apr. 5, 1912), SFC, acc. no. Z6084.

49. Kitty Marion, "Autobiography," SFC, acc. no. 50.82/1124.

50. Marion, Ms. Prison Account.

51. *Suffragette* (Mar. 6, 1914): 465.

52. *Suffragette* (July 17, 1914): 243. In the same issue Christabel Pankhurst describes forcible feeding as "an act of violence and indecency" (236).

53. Ellmann, *The Hunger Artists*, 33.

54. Corbett, *Representing Femininity*, 164.

55. *Suffragette* (Feb. 6, 1914): 269.

56. Ada Cecile Wright, "Personal Reminiscences," SFC, acc. no. 50.82/1135.

57. Christabel Pankhurst, *The Great Scourge and How to End It* (London: E. Pankhurst, 1913), 19–20.

58. Jane Marcus, *Suffrage and the Pankhursts* (London: Routledge, 1987), 14.

59. Jane Marcus, "The Asylums of Antaeus: Women, War and Madness: Is There a Feminist Fetishism?" in *The Difference Within: Feminism and Critical Theory*, ed. Elizabeth Meese and Alice Parker (Amsterdam: Benjamins, 1989), 73–74.

60. Marion, Ms. Prison Account. See also Janie Terrero, "Prison Experiences," SFC, acc. no. 60.15/13.

61. Mary Richardson, "Tortured Women: A Prisoner's Testimony," *Women's Dreadnought* (Aug. 8, 1914): 83.

62. Olive Walton, "Hunger Striking and Forcible Feeding in Aylesbury Prison," SFC, acc. no. 50.82/1131.

63. Myra Sadd Brown, Statement, SFC, acc. no. 50.82/1136.

64. Alice Farmer, Statement, SFC, acc. no. 58.87/61; Lilian Lenton, *Votes for Women* (Oct. 24, 1913): 44.

65. Ellis Griffith, Statement, SFC, acc. no. 50.82/1136.

66. Many other suffragettes also express a reluctance to describe their experiences, which could well stem from a similar disquiet. For instance, despite Emmeline Pankhurst's advice (cited above), Myra Sadd Brown refused to provide a graphic account of forcible feeding. She remarks, "I do not wish to speak of my mental or physical sufferings; they are indescribable" (Statement, SFC).

67. Nancy Armstrong and Leonard Tennenhouse, eds., *The Violence of Representation: Literature and the History of Violence* (London: Routledge, 1989), 25.

68. Elisabeth Bronfen, *Over Her Dead Body: Death, Femininity and the Aesthetic* (Manchester: Manchester University Press, 1992), 47.

69. Ibid., 44–45.

70. Constance Lytton, Ms. "Prisons and Prisoners," SFC, acc. no. 50.82/1125–1129.

71. Readers may be interested in a rare photograph of Ainsworth, apparently taken shortly after Lytton met her, which appears in B. M. Willmott Dobbie, *A Nest of Suffragettes in Somerset* (Bath: Batheaston Society, 1979), 33.

72. See, for instance, Paul de Man, "Autobiography as De-Facement," *Modern Language Notes* 94 (1979): 919–30; Leigh Gilmore, "A Signature of Lesbian Autobiography: 'Gertrice/Altrude,' " in *Autobiography and Questions of Gender*, ed. Shirley Neumann (London: Cass, 1991), 56–75.

73. Lytton herself expressed the idea that she had not really been forcibly fed, but only staged a representation of forcible feeding. Shortly after her ordeal, she wrote, "To think that I who have endured by far the least of all the 'forcibly fed' should be making people wake up more than all of them. . . . It is the other more heroic and first ones who have really done what I *seem* to have done." Letter to Alice Kerr, January 26, 1910, Fawcett Library Archives.

74. Naomi Schor, "Female Fetishism: The Case of George Sand," in *The Female Body in Western Culture*, ed. Susan Suleiman (Cambridge: Harvard University Press, 1986), 370. Cited in Marcus, "The Asylums of Antaeus," 75.

75. Carole-Anne Tyler, "The Feminine Look," in *Theory between the Disciplines*, ed. Kreiswirth and Cheetham, 208–10.

76. See especially Sidonie Smith, *A Poetics of Women's Autobiography: Marginality and the Fictions of Self-Representation* (Bloomington: Indiana University Press, 1987).

77. Judith Butler, *Bodies That Matter: On the Discursive Limits of "Sex"* (London: Routledge, 1993).

78. Pankhurst, *Unshackled*, 78.

79. Kate Flint, *The Woman Reader: 1837–1914* (Oxford: Clarendon, 1993), 248–49.

80. *Votes for Women* (Oct. 29, 1909): 67.

81. Michèle Barrett, "Some Different Meanings of the Concept of 'Difference': Feminist Theory and the Concept of Ideology," in *The Difference Within*, ed. Meese and Parker, 45.

82. Such an alternative model of subjecthood, which could be set against the Cartesian model, is suggested by Spinoza in his *Ethics*. Spinoza argues that "if, for example, two individuals of entirely the same nature are joined to one another, they compose an individual twice as powerful as each one." He advocates such a subjectivity as a political goal, declaring, "Man, I say, can wish for nothing more helpful to the preservation of his being than that all should so agree in all things that the Minds and Bodies of all would compose, as it were, one Mind and Body." E. M. Curley, *The Collected Works of Spinoza* (Princeton: Princeton University Press, 1985), vol. 1, 556.

Literary Representations of Battered Women: Spectacular Domestic Punishment

Frances L. Restuccia

The public execution . . . is a ceremonial by which a momentarily injured sovereignty is reconstituted. It restores that sovereignty by manifesting it at its most spectacular. . . . Its aim is to . . . bring into play . . . the dissymmetry between the subject who has dared to violate the law and the all-powerful sovereign who displays his strength. . . . [I]n this liturgy of punishment, there must be an emphatic affirmation of power and of its intrinsic superiority. And this superiority is not simply that of right, but that of the physical strength of the sovereign beating down upon the body of his adversary and mastering it.

— Michel Foucault, *Discipline and Punish*

Then he aimed the gun with drunken accuracy right into her face and fired. What Ruth remembered now with nausea and a feeling of cold dying, was Mem lying faceless among a scattering of gravel in a pool of blood, in which were scattered around her head like a halo, a dozen bright yellow oranges that glistened on one side from the light.

— Alice Walker, *The Third Life of Grange Copeland*

[O]f course he wanted the usual seating arrangement, . . . just so he could lie there like some kind of king, right? . . . I told him I just didn't feel like it. . . . [H]e kicked me. . . . The people at the Hilton looked at me and I could tell they were wondering how I'd ever get onstage that night looking the way I did, all beat-up and battered, with my one eye swollen almost shut.

— Tina Turner, *I, Tina*

POWER AND PAIN

If Nancy Armstrong and Leonard Tennenhouse are right about the intrinsic violence of representation, then Kathy Acker's martyr in *Blood and Guts in High School*, the woman who gets tied up with ropes, beaten a lot, "all gooky and bloody and screaming," full of "angry hurt pain inside"—like the typical victim fresh from battering who cannot communicate anything to anyone—can *never* express herself, or have her plight expressed by another, without that expression being implicated in the dominant power structure.[1] A logical extension of a deterministic strain of Foucauldianism as well as of feminist theories that insist upon the inescapable masculinity of the symbolic register, Armstrong and Tennenhouse's theory assumes that victims who manage somehow to find their way to expression become members of the ruling class, while authors who express their characters' victimization acquire power at their characters' expense. For, as they argue in their introduction to the collection *The Violence of Representation*, writing is "a form of violence in its own right"; reading and speaking too are implicated in power, in that they are exclusive, in that they necessarily reconstruct the world "around the polarities of Self and Other."[2] As a result "whenever we speak for someone else[,] we are inscribing her with our own (implicitly masculine) idea of order" (VR 25).[3] Women's as well as feminist discourse is by no means exempt from the colonizing that Armstrong and Tennenhouse indict. They have abstracted the logic of their theory deliberately from a female text— Brontë's *Jane Eyre*—in which Jane overcomes certain Others (Mrs. Reed, Mr. Brocklehurst, Blanche Ingram, Mr. Rochester, Others one might have thought worth overcoming; Bertha is conspicuously missing) in order to become a heroine, as well as to attain the status of narrator. Thus Jane suppresses difference and participates in the violence of representation. Even as Jane's power assumes benevolent forms, such as supervision and education, it is a kind of imperialism, rendering her claim to victim status illegitimate. Imperialism represents what is "culturally other as a negation of self," just as (this analogy presumes) Jane does in carving out her deep self, a subjectivity whose depth is what leads readers of the novel to become quite fond of her. Jane Eyre, in Armstrong and Tennenhouse's estimation, "is the progenitrix of a new gender, class, and race of selves in relation to whom all others are deficient. No less is at stake in granting such an individual power to author her own history" (VR 8).[4]

One can deduce from this reaction to Jane the hopelessness of academics—who are "directly involved in the violence of representation"—ever sidestepping power over those for whom they may wish to put power to beneficent use. To Armstrong and Tennenhouse, there is no refuge, no getting outside the hegemony: not in the "deepest recesses of the female psyche" or on "the loftiest pinnacles of art" (VR 25). All writing, speaking, reading beings—academics in particular—are "[c]ondemned to power" (VR 26). The only thing we can do (consequently) is to recognize the kinship between the violence of Jane Eyre's discourse and our own. We are, in Armstrong and Tennenhouse's essay, likewise compared to hospital staff who participate in the construction of the battered woman by refusing to inquire into the cause of her injured body. Armstrong and Tennenhouse end their introductory piece by turning to Teresa de Lauretis's commentary on the institutional complicity in battering of medical and other "'helping professions' (such as the police and the judiciary)"; de Lauretis looks at how women who are seeking help are boomeranged right back into the role of the battered victim.[5] Academics (to Armstrong and Tennenhouse) victimize similarly: "like the medical personnel in de Lauretis's study, we are, in naming, also constituting information as an event, transaction, or relationship. We are positioning it within our culture and in relation to ourselves. . . . We exercise the very form of power which . . . gained centrality as part of modern imperialism" (VR 26). Imperialists, Jane Eyre, emergency medical staff (deliberately oblivious to the battering that drives their patients to them), academics, writers, readers, speakers—all are complicit in the suppression of difference in the violence of representation.

Following Armstrong and Tennenhouse's logic, it would seem that if academics are as guilty of committing the violence of representation as de Lauretis's medical personnel, then de Lauretis (as an academic) is as guilty of committing the violence of representation as the medical personnel whose representational violence she brings to our attention. Even more extravagantly: a writer apparently writing on behalf of abused women would seem to enact semiotic violence, through representation, on par with the empirical violence "out there" in the world. Their "ultimate goal," Armstrong and Tennenhouse assert proudly, "is to demonstrate that the two cannot in fact be distinguished" (VR 9).[6]

Armstrong and Tennenhouse's contention that all expression is acculturated and that therefore all discourse maintains "a pattern of dominance" (VR 25) itself suppresses crucial cultural/political differences. Their theory of representation elides the possibility of the Other speaking, as it "condemns" the *speaking* Other to power, which she really does not possess, that would wipe out her Otherness if she possessed it. Armstrong and Tennenhouse's theory prematurely elevates expressive otherness to a particularly insidious form of powerful sameness; the ubiquity of power that they assume suffuses discourse cancels their occasional nod of acknowledgment of variable positions. Their opening claim that the topics of class, race, and gender "have lost their oppositional edge," now that they have been cannibalized by literary critical studies, can itself be seen as blunting that sharp edge (VR 1). Perhaps it is in the context of such assertions of centripetal sameness that Mae Henderson, around the same year (1989), felt compelled to propose a model of reading "that seeks to account for racial difference within gender identity and gender difference within racial identity" precisely in an effort to establish a more complicated paradigm of "otherness." Henderson plays out various kinds of relationships of otherness, in which the black woman writer participates from a privileged position: "The engagement of multiple others broadens the audience for black women's writing, for . . . black women, speaking out of the specificity of their racial and gender experiences, are able to communicate in a diversity of discourses."[7]

While it cannot be denied, as Elaine Scarry elaborates in *The Body in Pain*, that pain eludes, if not resists, language, and while pain is therefore especially amenable to appropriation by persons in power, nonetheless the artists who provide the focus of this essay manage unopportunistically to convey the plight and pain of battered women, to expose the complicity of various institutions with batterers, and to censure the insidious process of the social construction of the battered woman. Armstrong and Tennenhouse's theory refuses to distinguish between power congruent with the dominant ideology—including literature complicit in battering—and power on the side of the powerless—including literature that works on behalf of battered victims, literature that fights back. Not to make such a distinction is like equating batterers who destroy their victims with victims who defend themselves by destroying their batterers. Not to do so, in other words, is to theorize in sync with a court system (which still has not universally recognized battered women's syndrome) that has been one of the major institutions active in the construction of the battered woman.

In Zora Neale Hurston's short story "Sweat," Delia Jones's husband, Sykes, keeps a diamondback rattlesnake in their kitchen to terrify her, to incite her to leave their home, and perhaps in the hope that it will escape its cage someday and bite, even kill, her. But when Delia flees from the escaped venomous snake and in turn chooses not to warn her husband that he is walking directly into its path (Sykes for some reason assumes that the snake is too sick to harm him), her violence against him is hardly synonymous with his against her (for one thing, he has abused her for fifteen years). Hurston's achievement, in fact, is to present their *modes* of violence as reciprocal, so that we can distinguish between their *positions* of violence. And the idea of equating Sykes's violence against Delia with Hurston's writing—certainly meant to decry Delia's oppression by Sykes—only italicizes the crudeness of a nevertheless widely-subscribed-to theory of representation that remains too abstract, that fails (whether it intends to or not) to take into account the specific cultural positioning of the supposed perpetrator. The only violence in "Sweat," besides Sykes's, is Sykes's redirected.[8]

Literacy and culture (in fact) are themselves sufficiently hoarded values that to make a claim to them is not necessarily to join the dominant class but can be yet *another* mode of redirection. In *Specifying*, Susan Willis points out that literacy and education are vital to the black underclass, and that in the fiction of Alice Walker they are embraced as part of the very "process of liberation." Walker's "radical understanding of education lies at the heart of literacy campaigns from revolutionary Angola to Grenada and Nicaragua. Clearly, the ability to raise questions, to objectify contradictions, is only possible when Celie begins writing her letters. Similarly, for Meridian, education (*notwithstanding its inspiration in liberalism*) and the academic institution (*notwithstanding its foundation in elitism*) offer the means for confronting social and sexual contradictions that she, as a black teenage mother, would not have been able to articulate—either for herself or anyone else" (my emphases).[9] This statement manages parenthetically to preserve what is most shrewd in Armstrong and Tennenhouse's argument without annihilating its dialectical corollary: that there are narrative strategies by which certain artists—positioned in ways that enable them to counter the dominant ideology—evade, often to attack and undermine, the dominant power systems that may at the same time furnish them with their basic weapons. The "feminist subject," as Teresa de Lauretis proposes in *Technologies of Gender*, both inhabits and stands outside the dominant ideology (including the "ideology of gender")—women are "at once within and without representation."[10] Despite the inclusion of de Lauretis in Armstrong and Tennenhouse's volume, this statement on the doubleness of the feminist subject clashes with the editors' sense of the limitations of the "'female' position": "From such a position," they argue, "one may presume to speak both as one of those excluded from the dominant discourse and for those so excluded. But doing so . . . is no more legitimate than Jane Eyre's claim to victim status" (VR 10).

Insight into modern disciplinary power tends to be blind to the premodernity of the power of battering. Delia, in Hurston's story "Sweat," is situated within a world of power that, according to a Foucauldian taxonomy, is premodern, regressive, in which battles are fought by parties (husbands and wives) whose access to power is far from equal, in which the sovereign in the form of a husband still wields spectacular power over the (female) body. Bodies in the world of battering are flagrantly marked to signal the sovereign's power; rather than being ubiquitous, such power depends on untainted forms of powerlessness. Hurston depicts a regime in which everything is not complicit, in which some things are simply weak, in an effort to deploy her modern literary power for the sake of a woman who is merely abused—that is, who does not participate simultaneously in her own abuse. Monarchical power survives in the family, allowing us to distinguish between despotic and insurrectionary uses of power. With his emphasis on modern disciplinary power, Foucault has in fact been charged with blaming victims. What Nancy Hartsock says of Foucault resembles my response to Armstrong: Foucault ignores power differentials "while claiming to elucidate them." His "image of a network in which we all participate carries implications of equality . . . rather than the systematic domination of the many by the few. Moreover, at times Foucault seems to suggest that not only are we equals but that those of us at the bottom are in some sense responsible for our situations: Power, he argues, comes from below. There is no binary opposition between rulers and ruled, but rather manifold relations of force that take shape in the machinery of production, or families, and so forth."[11]

An analysis of contemporary battering does well to recuperate Foucault by drawing on his concepts of *both* modern and classical power. Considered from a cultural standpoint, the battered woman is produced by institutions such as those alluded to by de Lauretis, the police, the judiciary, and the medical profession; by our sources of entertainment and pleasure (including the arts); and certainly by the ideology of gender. Batterers themselves have picked up on the effectiveness of modern disciplinary methods. They typically install a system of surveillance of their victim's every move, designed to mold her into a voluntarily obedient individual. Battered women are pressured to internalize their batterer's projected image of them, so that a system of apparent self-governance emerges; to blame themselves for the rocky relationship with their batterer; and to blame their bodies for the injuries they receive and sustain. In offering her an identity—that is, insofar as she begins to conceive of herself as nothing more than "a battered woman" and of pain as her essence—he may come close to shaping her "soul." [12]

Yet in the old-fashioned or classical arena of violence and torture that the battered woman eventually enters, punishment erupts into spectacle, pain is inflicted, and the body is revealed to be the batterer's primary target. The batterer reverses Foucault's historical arrow: finally the victim is marked, branded with infamy, so that her tortured body reflects the "truth of the crime." [13] Like the public execution in Foucault's analysis of pre-nineteenth-century forms of punishment, the acute stage of battering restores "sovereignty by manifesting it" through "invincible force," bringing into play the dissymmetry between the subject who dared to violate the law and the "all-powerful sovereign" who flaunts his strength (DP 48, 49). Rather than the equal implication of all involved parties, here we have "imbalance and excess," the superior "physical strength of the sovereign beating down upon the body of his adversary and mastering it" (DP 49). Power, formerly hidden and disseminated, is recentered. Declining the medical profession's usual participation in the construction of the battered woman, a medical staff worker in Sandra Cisneros's "Woman Hollering Creek" exclaims, "I was going to do this sonogram on her—she's pregnant, right?—and she just starts crying on me. *Híjole*, Felice! This poor lady's got black-and-blue marks all over. I'm not kidding. From her husband. Who else?" [14]

"Panopticism," Foucault writes, "is the general principle of a new 'political anatomy' whose object and end are not the relations of sovereignty but the relations of discipline" (DP 208). But modern disciplinary power, although it may predominate, does not go unsupplemented in the modern, or post-eighteenth-century, world. Foucault's premodern power persists—as do victims (and their advocates) unimplicated in the forces that victimize them. Yet it is not merely a matter of the coexistence of two forms of power: while there may no longer be a supreme sovereign publicly marking bodies, thereby sanctioning such punishment, faceless systemic "battering" encourages and protects physical brutality on the part of "sovereigns" whose castles are their private homes. Premodern punishment does not grind to a halt as modern discipline spreads; rather it descends to the micro-level of society, to the level inhabited by women's bodies, where it is supported by, and in turn supports, all the subtleties of modern discipline that operate on souls.

My sense of the shortcomings of Armstrong and Tennenhouse's theory of representation is not meant to ignore or minimize the difficulty of developing strategies for speaking on behalf of the inexpressive subject without re-disempowering her, or of using literacy against those who have themselves used it for the sake of their empowerment without vouching for the exclusivity of that power. Foucault's monarch, like Scarry's torturer, like contemporary batterers—all thrive on the central problem of pain, that it is inclined to remain prelinguistic. We are thus led to the central problem of *women's* pain, to the muteness that cowers before the language of power that, in Armstrong and Tennenhouse as well as Foucault, is so widespread. Despite the liabilities of such expression, however, several literary texts may be invoked that—italicizing differences rather than suppressing them—share Wini Breines and Linda Gordon's notion that battering is a socially constructed phenomenon, and in turn illustrate specific Foucauldian disciplinary measures taken by institutions of modern power that produce "the battered woman," even as they publicize the misery of women brutally beaten, savagely tortured, in some cases eventually killed—texts that, in bell hooks's terms, "talk back." Providing our focus here, Drabble's *The Needle's Eye*, Cisneros's "Woman Hollering Creek," Naylor's *Linden Hills*, and Walker's *Third Life of Grange Copeland* expose subtle, modern disciplinary power (in the form of noncorporal systemic battering) as well as the grosser premodern spectacular power (in the form of literal confinement and physical torture of the female body), to which the former mode of power inevitably relapses.

JUDICIAL BATTERING

In *Violence against Wives: A Case against the Patriarchy*, Dobash and Dobash report that "In 1971, almost no one had heard of battered women, except, of course, the legions of women who were being battered and the relatives, friends, [etc.] . . . in whom some of them confided."[15] In 1972, Margaret Drabble was at work rectifying this obliviousness, publishing

The Needle's Eye, in which she castigates the legal system for its nonchalance toward the case of Rose Vassiliou, a badly battered wife—for its complicity with battering.

Beginning with the nineteenth century, "the sentence that condemns or acquits is not simply a judgement of guilt, a legal decision that lays down punishment; it bears within it an assessment of normality and a technical prescription for a possible normalization. Today the judge—magistrate or juror—certainly does more than 'judge' " (DP 20–21). When Rose Vassiliou, in *The Needle's Eye*, seeks a divorce from her batterer, the judge, who labels Rose "highly eccentric," is not at all subtle in exemplifying Foucault's point.[16] It is only due to a legal hitch that the judge rules in Rose's favor, granting her the divorce and custody of her three children: for "a passionate desire to rid oneself of one's money is *technically* not as grave a matrimonial offence as the inflicting of black-eyes, split lips, cuts and manifold bruises" (NE 52, my emphasis). Even as the law happens to favor Rose, the judge passes along his assessment of abnormality, which is echoed so pervasively (for giving away a substantial portion of her fortune, Rose is considered mad by her parents, her husband, her solicitors, even a few friends) that Rose—like a typical Foucauldian subject produced by subjection—begins to define herself as "hopelessly impulsive," "simply incapable . . . of behaving in a rational and considered manner" (NE 45).

Rose's virtues—for example, her altruistic desire to help African children by building them a school—are transvalued as the defects of her irredeemably irrational character, situating Rose on the verge of a nervous breakdown. Because Rose, prompted by a photograph of a naked African child plopped down next to its dead mother's corpse, "its face lost, its eyes sagging blank with nothingness, its mouth drooping slightly open" (NE 97), donates her money to African children, she is (needless to say, ironically) made to doubt her capacity to nurture her own children. Her husband, Christopher, turns her charity against her: "don't you expect me to sympathise with all the subnormal races of Africa, there's enough subnormality on the very doorstep here, . . . you histrionic bitch" (NE 77). And Rose caves in: "*I* believe it, that's the point, he's right, he's right. I'm a hopeless mother, I know I am, I'm mean and mad and selfish, he's *right* about me, how can I defend myself when he's right?" (NE 246). Rose starts to feel that she should have endured her husband's abuse, "ought to have gone on taking it" (NE 270). When Christopher rapes her a week after the divorce, Rose (adopting Christopher's attitude) "felt she had deserved it" (NE 279). And it is upon reading Christopher's affidavit describing her incompetence as a mother, a document that ratifies the collusion of the legal system with the batterer, that Rose turns temporarily into a madwoman: "she moaned, and started to toss her head about, and her hands flew to her hair, and started to tug at it. . . . [H]er arms were as stiff as sticks, her hair where she had pulled it stood in clumps, she was not there in the flesh" (NE 248). If a man pulls out a woman's hair enough times, pretty soon she pulls it out for him.

The later Vassiliou court case on Rose's competence to *retain* custody of her children swings in her favor again only on a technicality. The judge, who "had once given custody to a father ["a most unsuitable parent, a religious maniac, a vindictive and violent man"], because his wife was living with her lover" (NE 338), had been inclined to put the Vassiliou children in the care of Christopher (an undisputed wife beater), except that Christopher, to give Rose a fright, had threatened by telegram to remove the children illegally from the country. Both the judicial system and Rose's husband, who physically batters her for her "subnormality," do their best to collaborate in an art of punishment aimed at normalization, an art thorough and exquisite enough to elicit Rose's participation. Half the time Rose believes, "I must be mad. . . . I should see a psychiatrist" (NE 252).

The other half of the time Rose is sufficiently clear-sighted to grasp that "Christopher and God" have constructed her martyrdom for her (NE 253), although the emphasis of the novel would have us replace God with the British legal system. Batterers and the law are more than once paralleled, underscoring the hopelessness of turning to the law to clear up the quagmire of battering, since the law is essentially the batterer writ large. Rose gradually learns that the legal system is as much a "self-perpetuating" morass as her marriage, and equally in labyrinthine league with violence: "far from drawing ends and lines and boundaries," the processes of the law "answered nothing, they solved none of the confusions of the heart and the demands of the spirit, but instead generated their own course of new offences, new afflictions, new perversions" (NE 173).

Like Breines and Gordon in "The New Scholarship on Family Violence," Drabble focuses on "collective cultural meaning and community control of marital violence."[17] Drabble's narrative adumbrates the message of Breines and Gordon that battered women are doubly victimized: by batterers as well as agents of social control who put the blame on women. Male domination is seen, in both texts, as part of a complex system of social power relations, rather than as merely the result of sexist attitudes or reprehensible behavior of individual men (although individual men are still held accountable). When Christopher complains about the inexorability of the processes of law, which proceed "unruffled" and "unperturbed" (despite "what happens after the case is set in motion") "until they've ground up the last little bit," Rose, making Breines and Gordon's point boldly to the most conspicuous agent of her pain and distress, retorts: "in that, they rather strikingly resemble you" (NE 294). The partnership between batterers and the law is alluded to again when, pondering another woman's court case, Rose is "perplexed by the nonchalance with which abuse and blows had been disregarded" by a judge "who would consider it an act of violence, in his own domestic situation, if a guest were to put down a glass on a polished wooden surface, or drop ash upon a parquet floor" (NE 79). When Rose seeks an injunction against Christopher for threatening to kidnap the children, the legal authorities more than hint that they are inconvenienced. Although judicial authorities behave as if wife beating is outside their professional domain (a private matter between a man and his "property"), their behavior only means that wife beating is so much *like* their authority that to call batterers in would be redundant.

For of course when police or legal action is *not* taken against a batterer, that inaction indirectly sanctions the abuse. Dobash and Dobash point out that the indifference of many policemen, some of whom identify with batterers, is in general shared by judges who tend not to regard wife beating as "truly criminal behavior," and may even consider the perpetrator's attacks to be "somewhat justified by his wife's provocations" (VW 219). In *The Needle's Eye*, a judge presiding over a case in which the husband made "a regular habit of flinging things at [his wife], slapping her, punching her and so on," is inspired to speak of "things that any man might do under provocation." The judge assumes, too, "that a few blows one way or the other [are] the normal fare of married life" (NE 79). The disparity between the law's obsession with nonfamily violence and its apathy toward "family violence" is surely part of the legacy of the specific common law that honored the right of men to beat their wives. Husbands and wives were viewed as a single entity: since an individual cannot "offend against himself," it was considered illogical that a woman might take her husband to court for abusing her (VW 208). The concept of the sacrosanct home and the ideal of the family counter efforts to ensure the rights of especially married women as well as efforts to protect them. "Until the 1950s, in Texas, Utah, and New Mexico," husbands who found their spouses committing adultery and in turn committed homicide were "granted special immunity" (VW 209).

As *The Needle's Eye* testifies, such laws, though defunct, still infect the atmosphere. The novel demonstrates the irresistible force of the idea that the family ought to be saved no matter how extravagant and excruciating the cost in violence to the woman's body, mind, and soul. In graphically presenting Christopher's cruelty, Drabble underscores that price. The grounds of Rose's divorce are "physical violence (medical evidence produced, neighbour's evidence, and a permanent scar on Rose's wrist), abusive language, violent and unreasonable demands, incessant and unmotivated jealousy" (NE 64)—an appalling enough technical description necessarily cloaking details that the novel makes vivid. "Christopher had thrown the tomato ketchup bottle at her and it had broken and gone all over, . . . and Rose had gone on yelling these demented Biblical tags until Christopher, understandably beside himself with rage, had kicked over the table and grabbed at her and said (frightening her into silence), Don't you quote the fucking Bible at me" (NE 76–77). Christopher locks Rose up in her bedroom, locks her out of the house in her nightdress, beats her black and blue, and yanks her hair out in large patches. Rose feels sure that unless they part they will "kill each other, perhaps even literally" (NE 78); yet society wants this couple to remain intact.

What is more curious is that the novel appears, after all, to want that outcome too. In a politically and philosophically tricky ending, Christopher moves back into the house on Middle Road. Yet this apparent rapprochement is not what it may seem: for while *The Needle's Eye* concludes with Rose and Christopher's reunion, it does so out of a deep sense of the pathetic inadequacy of the law. On her own with the children, in a gratifyingly shabby neighborhood, Rose achieves "some inexplicable grace" (NE 141). She takes genuine pleasure in simple acts such as drawing curtains and shopping—"I do them all with love" (NE 95). She can rest in peace in bed at night, without fear of being disturbed by blows. Nevertheless, Rose takes back her husband—because her personal situation, a marriage that has spawned three children mutually loved by their parents, refuses to reduce to any of the reconfigurations into which the law could set it. It is unquestionably not that a self-destructive Rose has acquired an appetite for pain: "no ulterior weakness of her own, no sexual craving, had prompted her to [take him], she had done it in the dry light of arid generosity, she had done it for others" (NE 350). Rose submits herself to her husband by the same logic of charity that tore them apart in the first place.

Rose comes to realize the difficulty of building upon her victory in court: "She had resorted to the law, as her father had done before [against her], and now she was a victim of its processes. . . . a court's settlements could not end the confusion" (NE 172). An abundance of unclassifiable evidence constitutes the case, overflowing legal bounds: "the divorce court had been a game played by others, custody cases were nothing but a sketch, a diagram of woe, and the full confrontation would take place on other territory. The decisions of judges, even when in her favour, were irrelevant" (NE 174). Legal systems can think only in terms of the desirability of winning, can never understand the necessity of loss. The novel is quite forthcoming as to why for Rose "there was no exemption, no cancelling of bonds, no forgetting" (NE 174), and why therefore the law is finally so inadequate: "How dreadful it is . . . that children are born of two parents, that they are the property of two parents with equal claim, that they do not spring fully grown from the brain, as Athene sprang from Zeus" (NE 249).

In *The Needle's Eye*, Rose's batterer exerts a fierce effort to contain her through physical force. His effort is backed up, and reflected, by disciplinary social/legal attempts to quell Rose's desires for autonomy and custody of her children. But finally the power of love exceeds these two modes of Foucauldian power—the former premodern, indulging in spectacular physical abuse; the latter systemic—attempting to close in on Rose. Rose's head splits ("If someone had taken a hatchet and split my skull," she thinks, "I could not suffer more"); she feels blood running in her brain from an "internal wound"; her brain is "wet with blood" ("I bleed, I bleed, I bleed") (NE 250)—neither as a result of punitive acts of brute force (although Christopher certainly imprints the marks of his strength on Rose's tender flesh) nor because of the disciplinary measures of the judicial system (although it certainly tries to control and mold Rose), but because her children will cry if she leaves them and suffer if she divides them from their father. Rose Vassiliou eventually assesses her situation's vast complexity, its irreducibility; and so she is able finally to realize what in her demands expression. Rose imagines love "as some huge white deformed and not very lovely god, lying there beneath the questions and the formality, caught in a net of which points alone touched and confined him—points, blows, matrimonial offences, desertions, legalities, all binding love down though he shapelessly overflowed and struggled" (NE 80). Rose's final decision testifies to her unboundedness, in contrast to the fixity of the law, that keeps her (also shapelessly overflowing) uncontainable by that system. Yet, rather than winning Rose power, Rose's decision—not at the expense, but for the sake, of others—puts her again at the mercy of dominant power. *The Needle's Eye* suggests that, far from opening up a new front of power, expressiveness available to women—in particular mothers—can be entirely weak with respect to the traps into which women are typically lured.

Thus Drabble responds to the dilemma posed by Armstrong and Tennenhouse of the writer's difficulty in avoiding violence against others. Drabble lends all her sensibility to her heroine (who therefore is not re-disempowered) but without in turn finding that her heroine becomes the new oppressor. Rose is in fact sufficiently weak at the end to tempt readers to regard her reunion with her husband as part of a martyrdom generated by the disciplinary systems of Foucauldian modern power. But ultimately Rose is the agent of her repositioning within her family. She consents to pay "the price of her own living death, her own conscious dying, her own lapsing, surely, slowly, from grace, as heaven (where only those with souls may enter) was taken slowly from her, as its bright gleams faded" (NE 349). It may seem that Rose makes a conventional, socially controlled sacrifice, typically demanded especially of women by family discipline—except that the novel has been *dedicated* to showing that Rose constructs her self best of all by paying high prices for the sake of children, be they African, her own, anyone's. Rose carves out her self in the first place by bestowing her money on African children and, as a consequence, moving into a shabby district. Rose's self depends on doing what is "right" (NE 95): "She had been right to take him" (NE 350). Like the mass-produced lion, "crudely cast in a cheap mould," "a beast of the people" (NE 352–53), that Rose admires at the very end, she therefore "weather[s] into identity" (NE 353).

Drabble holds out here, in other words, for the possibility that a woman can make a sacrifice and not be a masochistic-subject, for the possibility that female care has a source other than the dominant power structure that, some might argue, manipulates that care into being (it is neither dupe nor ally). To perceive Rose's sacrifice for children as weak or foolish, as naive, is in this novel to perceive it with the profit-hungry eyes of Rose's violent husband, or in the commonplace terms of a bourgeois judge. In *doubling* Rose's act of generosity to children, Drabble has arranged her plot to show that female recalcitrance may take place within, but is not of, male hegemony, and thus does not lead to normal empowerment. The outcome of *The Needle's Eye* is neither subjection, whether external or internal, nor cooperation with the dominant power structure, but charitable agency.

HOLLERING PAIN

In "Woman Hollering Creek" (1991), Sandra Cisneros focuses on simple, private life, apparently uninvaded by complex, power-laden institutions such as Drabble's byzantine judicial system. Cisneros's main character, Cleófilas, however, cannot escape public institutions to the complexities of personal loyalties and obligations, to put Drabble's opposition too starkly, because a force probably more efficacious than the judicial system, police, or medical profession in constructing the battered woman worms its way into the Mexican woman's world in "Woman Hollering Creek." Cisneros looks at a particularly beguiling mode of Foucauldian modern power—the *telenovela*—which teaches that "to suffer for love is good. The pain all sweet somehow. In the end" ("WHC" 45), and *thus* confronts the violence of representation. "Woman Hollering Creek," in fact, links Foucauldian disciplinary power operating through soap operas to the success of Foucauldian spectacular power, such as that wielded by Juan Pedro Martínez Sánchez over Cleófilas. The story provides a narrative not only unimplicated in these forms of power but one that shrewdly assesses their daunting collaboration. Cisneros's challenge was to produce a nonsentimental, nonviolent narrative about a battered woman who is made vulnerable by soap operas to her husband's physical abuse, to produce something other than another soap opera about the violent effects of soap operas. The women's narrative conveyed by the *telenovela* naturalizes the sweetness of pain; Cisneros writes to denaturalize that oxymoron. The question is how to do that, how to give voice to Cleófilas's pain, without glamorizing it and without outvoicing Cleófilas.

Cisneros collapses the distance between silent Cleófilas and herself in part by collapsing the distance between Cleófilas and the narrator, who is capable of excitement over the mother's dress in last night's episode of *The Rich Also Cry*, because that is what the dress the narrator plans on wearing to Cleófilas's wedding will look like once it is "altered a teensy bit" ("WHC" 46). Cleófilas herself seems only to slip from being like the unbattered narrator (at least as she is presented in the story) to being a battered woman. "The first time she had been so surprised she didn't cry out or try to defend herself. . . . [H]e slapped her once, and then again, and again; until the lip split and bled an orchid of blood, she didn't fight back, she didn't break into tears, she didn't run away as she imagined she might when she saw such things in the *telenovelas*" ("WHC" 47). Cleófilas's second surprise is that she reacts no better than soap opera heroines who endure everything for love. (The very unnaturalness of her suffering pain all the more powerfully inserts the act into an artificial discourse.) Cleófilas is left "speechless, motionless, numb" ("WHC" 48), illustrating Scarry's point that "[i]ntense pain is . . . language-destroying,"[18] and as a result needs someone to speak for her who can avoid the temptation of turning her voicelessness (powerlessness) into that speaking subject's power. Cisneros's narrator, as steeped as Cleófilas in narratives of battering yet endowed by Cisneros with the cultural sophistication to produce a counter-narrative, is in a prime position to provide yet another alternative to what Hartsock identifies as the two "alternatives imposed by Enlightenment thought and postmodernism: Either one must adopt the perspective of the transcendental and disembodied voice of 'reason' or one must abandon the goal of accurate and systematic knowledge of the world. Other possibilities exist and must be (perhaps can only be) developed by hitherto marginalized voices."[19]

Muteness—Cleófilas "sits mute beside [the men's] conversation," waiting, nodding in agreement, politely grinning and laughing at the appropriate moments ("WHC" 48)—is now the stuff of the narrator's narrative, which has become, for the purpose, omniscient. The narrator conveys the widening gap that Cleófilas gradually apprehends between Cleófilas's fantasy lover and her husband Juan Pedro, who "kicks the refrigerator and says he hates this shitty house and is going out where he won't be bothered with the baby's howling and her suspicious questions, and her requests to fix this and this" ("WHC" 49). The narrator astutely picks up too on Juan Pedro's typical insistence on certain domestic patterns and typical disproportionate irritation, or even fury, when these patterns are broken: "each course of dinner [must] be served on a separate plate, like at his mother's, as soon as he gets home, on time or late" ("WHC" 49). (The batterer's pique is often focused on dinner; so it has been said that microwave ovens have helped cut down on battering.)

If Cleófilas exemplifies the voiceless victim, the narrator, at first not obviously distinct from Cleófilas, eventually aspires to the role of expert on battering. She seems to be aware, for example, of what Lenore Walker in *The Battered Woman* calls the "loving stage" (phase three), in which batterers endearingly seek forgiveness: Cleófilas "stroked the dark curls of the man who wept and would weep like a child, his tears of repentance and shame, this time and each" ("WHC" 48).[20] The narrator feels the special vulnerability of the body of the pregnant woman, who in this case knows that she must walk a tightrope between protecting her batterer, by deceiving her doctor about her wounds, and protecting her unborn baby, by making sure that she gets her batterer's permission to be examined. The text even raises the analysis of woman abuse to the level of Breines and Gordon by placing Juan Pedro's violence in a broader social context, by referring to Maximiliano (one of Juan Pedro's buddies) "who was said to have killed his wife in an ice-house brawl when she came at him with a mop" ("WHC" 51) and alluding to newspapers "full of such stories. This woman found on the side of the interstate. This one pushed from a moving car. This one's cadaver, this one unconscious, this one beaten blue. Her ex-husband, her husband, her lover, her father, her brother, her uncle, her friend, her co-worker. Always" ("WHC" 52). Woman abuse, this story implies, is a pervasive phenomenon; Juan Pedro is one cog in a vast piece of heavy social machinery.[21]

But inasmuch as it emblematizes the difficulty of translating the subjectivity of pain into discourse, "Woman Hollering Creek" yields more than cultural critique. The story presents toward the end one side alone of a phone conversation between the two women who help Cleófilas escape: Graciela calls Felice (to ask Felice to give Cleófilas a ride to the Greyhound in San Antonio), and all we are privy to are Graciela's words. The seeming lopsidedness of this phone conversation points to the expressive lopsidedness between the narrator and Cleófilas—whose direct speech barely appears in the story. Aware of the gap—that is, aware that the eloquent knowingness of the narrator might only suggest a disastrous contrast with surrounding silences—the story seems to struggle to approach asymptotically the prediscursive realm of women's pain.

"Woman Hollering Creek" pulsates on many borders—between Mexico and Texas, Spanish and English, the nonbattered and battered woman, narrative and a holler, the discursive and nondiscursive. As the story builds, it produces more and more language until language bursts into a shout that manages to be both tortured and triumphant, which in turn produces a gurgling that manages to be both infantilized (like a giggling) and knowing (like Cixous's Medusa's laughter). And by the time the reader has grasped the import of the holler, the story itself—another "Woman Hollering Creek"—assumes the status of the nondiscursive. It is as if the *narrative* eventually releases itself in a holler, a pure expression of female "anger or pain" ("WHC" 46) (this phrase alone signifies the story's Kristevan symbolic/semiotic balancing act), so that the usual power imbalance between narrative and the nondiscursive is corrected. We realize that the purpose of the narrative is to transport us to the holler, and then to implode into one. Pain is not appropriated here by agents of power—Cisneros reverses the usual pattern that Scarry highlights. Instead of moving from prediscursive pain—through pain— to discursive power, Cisneros works through the discursive to reach the painful muteness it is founded on.

"DREAMS OF DARK KINGS"

Foucault theorizes that with the advent of the nineteenth century "the great spectacle of physical punishment disappeared; the tortured body was avoided; the theatrical representation of pain was excluded from punishment. The age of sobriety in punishment had begun" (DP 14). If battering conformed to the history of power that Foucault traces, physically brutal battering would have declined and faded away, its imitation of despotic brutality to the tortured body a transcended anachronism, as noncorporal systemic battering became more and more pervasive. Drabble and Cisneros (as well as current statistics) suggest otherwise: if Drabble shows that male abuse of a woman's body is endorsed by assumptions almost too self-evident to require legal articulation, and if Cisneros shows that that abuse is the currency of narratives too widespread (literally in the very air) to be challenged within language, both writers demonstrate that the fine-tuning, disseminating, and internalizing of the ideology of abuse, rather than outmoding corporal battering, merely endorse it, duplicate it in a larger arena, stealthily or invisibly.

In her novel about an unmistakably abused wife, *Linden Hills* (1985), Gloria Naylor restores Foucault's pre-panopticon dungeon. Naylor lays out the double entrapment of the abused wife and thus offers an impressively full answer to the undying question (raised relentlessly by the prosecution during the Lorena Bobbitt trial) of why the battered woman fails to leave. *Linden Hills* illustrates how the domestic carceral (which points to women's incarceration in the home and away from a teleology that views home and marriage as sweet alternatives to an external gothic world of ghosts, robbers, and rapists) and the literal carceral reinforce each other's grip. The battered woman is caught in a vicious circle: the subtle punishment of her mind and soul primes her for the gross punishment of her body; the cessation of physical torture only releases her to a comparatively pleasant world in which her mind and soul are subtly punished.

Naylor therefore, in *Linden Hills*, takes on both centered and decentered power: her heroine is the product of "multiple mechanisms of 'incarceration' " (DP 308). Willa is tortured by a devilish man, who behaves quite like, and conceives of himself as, a king—in a line of "dark kings with dark counselors leading dark armies against the white god." [22] Surrounded by a moat with a drawbridge, Nedeed's home is his castle; he uses his morgue-basement as a dungeon to contain his disobedient wife-prisoner. He puts her down there, without food, with their young son—who predictably gets sick, shrinks, and dies—during the coldest week of the year. Invisibility too is a trap.

Yet the domestic carceral is by no means underplayed. The efflorescence of Willa's will at the end of *Linden Hills* occurs in part through her realization that she has been, "from the second she was born" (LH 280), the victim of disciplinary coercion in the service of femininity. Willa answers her self-posed question—"How did she get down in that basement?" (LH 278)—by rehearsing her cultural training in becoming a "good girl" (LH 277), "a good mother," and "a good wife" (LH 279). Tracing her own trajectory from domestic to literal incarceration, Willa recalls wanting to marry Luther Nedeed, take his name, bear his child, clean his home, cook his meals, and then (apparently) walk down twelve steps into a cold, damp basement as his prisoner. Willa testifies to the process by which she gradually assumed "the constraints of power," inscribed within herself a power relation in which she played the role of master and slave, and became "the principle of [her] own subjection" (DP 202–3).

The kitchen carceral, then, facilitates Willa's descent into the basement; the physically torturous basement carceral produces Willa's craving for the kitchen. Once freed from her literal imprisonment, Willa is obsessed with the desire to do housework. In a conversation with Toni Morrison in the *Southern Review*, Naylor curiously describes her own wrestling with her character over this matter. In rebellion against Naylor, who wanted Willa simply to emerge from the basement and dart out of the Nedeed house, all Willa wants to do is affirm her identity as "a conventional housewife." While Naylor would like to see housekeeping as "a creative statement," [23] it seems clear within *Linden Hills* that Willa's obsession with cleaning house only bears out Lester's fence theory: "Why fences? . . . To get you used to the idea that what they have in there is different, special. . . . Then when they've fenced you in from six years old till you're twenty-six, they can let you out because you're ready to believe that what they've given you up here, their version of life, is special. And you fence your own self in after that, protecting it from everybody else *out there*" (LH 45). Having been doubly fenced in—first by the domestic carceral (whose boundaries make domestic life seem special), then by the literal carceral (whose more pronounced boundaries serve as a foil to the less evident boundaries upstairs)—Willa now finds housecleaning immensely appealing.

Naylor had hoped that Willa would discover the desirability of completely walking out by reading the former Mrs. Nedeeds' various texts— diaries, cookbooks, and photographs—collecting dust in the basement. For they comment loudly on the carceral nature of Nedeed domestic life. But what they seem to teach instead is the fine art of self-abasement, featuring self-mutilation. Once caught in the double jaws of the domestic/ literal carceral, a woman is not only more likely to end up being physically attacked by her husband (rather than by a stranger), but she seems equally apt to attack herself. Luwana Packerville (who literally belongs to her husband, since he purchases her as a slave) marks (at least 665, possibly 666) lines on her skin with a pin and her own blood to record the number of times her husband and son speak to her after a year of excruciating silence. Evelyn Creton exhausts herself cooking vast quantities of food; she gains twenty-nine postnuptial pounds, takes up binge-purging, and commits suicide with prussic acid. Priscilla McGuire wipes out her photographed face, labeling the black space "me" (LH 24).

Disciplinary processes within a system of surveillance deeply ensconced in culture and heavily played upon by the Nedeed husband (no matter which avatar) are adopted by the Nedeed wife herself, so that she keeps herself in line, meting out self-punishment when she crosses over. Victimization thus begins to resemble, to *become*, female masochism; in this way, Naylor intimates, the female masochistic-subject is made. Insofar as the Nedeed wife generates her desire out of her incarceration—her only means of self-production, or of self-reclamation, is extravagance within her training, excessive self-discipline—her self-surrender can be written. But insofar as her incarceration provides the limit of her desire, agency, and subjectivity, she goes uninscribed, her desire, agency, and subjectivity unformed and unexpressed.

Perhaps this double bind is why Naylor has Willie (a young man) express, through the poetry in his head (he is averse to writing it down), the battered woman's pain. Created when he was five years old, Willie's first poem was a response to his question of "how can my mother love my father when he makes her cry?" (LH 275). Willie's last poem (number 666, aligning him with Luwana) is likewise inspired by a batterer and a battered woman's pain: "There is a man in a house at the bottom of a hill. And his wife has no name" (LH 277). Since Willie is not a woman, there can be no implication that a woman's pain is her subjectivity, all that she has to express; since he is not a writer (not Naylor), there can be no implication that he has founded a subjectivity on superiority to women's inexpressive pain. Hence he is free to disclose its horror: "My mom got beat up every night after payday by a man who couldn't bear the thought of bringing home a paycheck only large enough for three people and making it stretch over eight people, so he drank up half of it. And she stayed . . . because a bruised face and half a paycheck was better than welfare, and that's the only place she had left to go with no education and six kids" (LH 58).

Willie's family history allows him, at a funeral, to detect Willa's absence through the store-bought cake that Nedeed brings—said by Nedeed to have been made by Willa ("It was no trouble, my wife baked it" [LH 146])—implying that Willa's "identity" is the product of her domestic subjugation: home-baked cake defines her presence. Having grown up observing his mother being battered, Willie can imagine uncannily Willa's victimization to the point that he frees her at the moment she obtains the will to free herself. (Readers tend to interpret Willie's sliding of the metal bolt on the basement door as an accident sufficiently contrived to strain narrative credibility.[24] But Naylor's carefully worded description—"Since his arms were full, he braced the crate against the two doors. Reaching under it, he felt the metal bolt slide toward the left" [LH 297]—suggests an intentional act, since Willie has no cause to brace the crate otherwise.) It is striking that in an allegory of will—in which Willie helps Willa to will her exit—the mechanics are obscure. But Willa is silenced—she does not keep her own journal or weave any other sort of text—and Willie mainly thinks his poems, so perhaps Naylor hesitates to be overexplicit or overexpressive here out of respect for their distance from the written word. Or possibly the scene is an allegory in order to bring to self-consciousness the literariness of Naylor's own expression as opposed to the incapacity of especially her female characters.

Comparing Mahler with Bessie Smith, Billie Holliday, and Muddy Waters, all of whom try "to say something with music that you can't say with plain talk," Laurel's grandmother, Roberta, proceeds to comment that "There ain't really no words for love or pain" (LH 235)—which is why Willa (like the women in "Woman Hollering Creek") wails, cries, screams, and howls hers. Italicizing the ineffableness of Willa's pain (and love), Naylor uses myriad signifiers of semiotic sounds. Willie alone hears. Everyone else seems to be absorbed in living out the suburban dream of Linden Hills, occupied by the classiest, most sophisticated, best educated African Americans—where the literal carceral is unthinkable. Like Foucauldian critics, citizens of Linden Hills are attuned not to what is repressed (suppressed or oppressed) but to the expressive. While women (such as Laurel) actively battle against the domestic carceral, the literal carceral is assumed to be too primitive (pre-nineteenth century) to exist. Testifying to the underside of the domestic carceral, Nedeed nonetheless wields enough premodern power to kill his son and destroy, if not kill, his spouse.

At the end everyone in Linden Hills merely watches Mrs. Nedeed go up in smoke: "[T]ell me I'm dreaming—they're watching it burn," Willie, astonished, announces to Lester (LH 302). That theory can be as deaf to the victims of premodern power as the residents of Linden Hills is perhaps not to theory's total discredit, since the victims of modern power are all expression, and the victims of premodern power tend to be silent. Feminism itself is still evolving from a prehistorical stage, during which, to quote bell hooks, "women who are daily beaten down, mentally, physically, and spiritually—women who are powerless to change their condition in life" were "a silent majority."[25] Even Naylor cannot quite get them to speak. Her difficulty is the necessity of writing her way out of writing, which seems to entail extreme self-consciousness; for Naylor is writing about the task of writing about something that falls short of expression. All the subtlety of literary talent must be committed to ensure that female nondiscursiveness (maternal love and intermittent madness in Drabble, triumphant dehumanized howling in Cisneros, extravagant masochistic acts in Naylor) will be expressed, so that its energy can be harnessed in the production of a counter-hegemony.

THE SPECTACLE EFFECT

Following the pattern of individual battering, which tends to commence with subtle, modern disciplinary power but then yield to grosser forms of premodern spectacular power, this essay (itself) shifts its focus from literature that emphasizes noncorporal systemic battering to literature that foregrounds literal confinement and physical torture of the female body, inscribed with the mark of the sovereign's power. That trajectory is not meant, of course, to imply a neat division between the former and latter groups of texts, since those that stress the cultural construction of battered women also include abused bodies, while those that exhibit beaten bodies do not isolate them from cultural contexts. Moving, with that qualification, from one side of the continuum to the other: a novel that offers us a full-fledged portrait of the vicious batterer as well as of the unmediated material devastation that he wreaks is Alice Walker's *Third Life of Grange Copeland* (1970). Walker also contributes to the debate on the cultural production of battering by invoking throughout her novel the absolutely intertwined question of the social construction of the black batterer, and thus raises a key question that complicates the gender argument we have followed to this point. Noting the asymmetry of power relations between men and women is surely insufficient for comprehending relative positions of power in all situations of heterosexual violence. How does gender inextricably interact with other social categories that (over)determine discrepancies of power? (The O. J. Simpson case specifically poses relevant complications: how should his superior gender positioning be weighed against his weaker racial positioning?) Future analyses of violence need to gain their sophistication by examining in detail the interplay of multiple sociocultural determinants of power, rather than by means of a concept of oceanic complicity, based on the premise that all discourse is necessarily acculturated and therefore tainted with power.

The Third Life of Grange Copeland is a meditation on the relation of two points presented obliquely in the opening pages: Grange, Brownfield's father, works "for a cracker" and "the cracker own[s] him" (GC 4); Margaret, Brownfield's mother, seems like "their dog in some ways. She didn't have a thing to say that did not in some way show her submission to his father" (GC 5). White men beat down black men; black men, in turn, beat down black women, and black sons; black sons later beat down black women. At least in his first life, Grange fits the role of the batterer rather snugly: "Their life followed a kind of cycle that depended almost totally on Grange's moods" (GC 11); like clockwork, Grange returns home drunk each Saturday night, threatens to kill his wife and Brownfield, and then rolls out the door into the yard, "crying like a child" (GC 12). Each week the same dreary pattern unfolds, and then it unfolds again in the life of Grange's son, for Brownfield inherits the sins of his father.

Caught in the generational cycle, he too batters upon being battered. Like Elaine Scarry's torturer, Brownfield breaks down his wife, Mem, by attacking her speech, sarcastically urging her to "talk like the *rest* of us poor niggers" (GC 56). Also conforming with Scarry's paradigm, he targets the home, domestic pleasure and peace. Brownfield is especially apt to fly into a rage when supper is not on the table the minute he walks in the door. Although Mem comes close to killing herself to set up the family in a decent house, Brownfield transforms that reality back into a dream: Mem and her daughters are forced to live in a virtual pigsty. (Ironically, the family ideal upholds sexist law, which itself upholds the privilege of batterers, yet the home is exactly what batterers are compelled to tear down: the first right of ownership is the right to destroy.) Brownfield also typically accuses Mem of infidelity (with white men), a figment of his imagination; drunk, he beats Mem regularly on Saturday nights; holidays, especially Christmas Eve, are tough times for Mem (as they are for most battered women). One such night Brownfield beats

Mem "senseless," knocks out a tooth, and loosens more. In what seems like an unstoppable cycle, Brownfield (again typically) stoops to venting his anger on helpless animals and children as well, by pouring oil in streams to kill fish, drowning cats, beating his young daughters, and (prefiguring Nedeed) freezing to death his too light-skinned, infant son.

Walker's method of conveying the horror of Brownfield's treatment of Mem, her method of indicting him through representation, is to present his various acts of violence as spectacle; it might be said that, in a sense, she imitates the batterer whose violence against his wife, children, and home she depicts. Walker puts the gory details on display: unnuanced violence apparently deserves unnuanced representation. Literary representations of violence at times must rely on, as Tanner describes it, "a highly visual mode of narration . . . to direct the reader's gaze upon a scene in a manner similar to the enforced perspective of [a] camera's frame."[26] During one incident, "Brownfield's big elephant-hide fist hit [Mem] square in the mouth." He shakes her "until blood dribbled from her stinging lips. . . . [S]he just hung there from his hands until he finished giving her half-a-dozen slaps, then she just fell down limp like she always did." With his foot Brownfield gives Mem a kick in the side; he threatens to cut her throat; he finishes her off with a "resounding kick in the side of the head" (GC 90–91). And like so many of the domestic battles in *The Third Life of Grange Copeland*, this one is witnessed by the children: we watch Brownfield fire his gun into Mem's face through her two youngest daughters' terrified eyes. By building specularity into the text in this way, Walker offers a double dose of the pain.

To convey the ghastliness of Brownfield's spectacular punishment, Walker breathes into it a second spectacular life; to achieve the effect she wants, she mimics Brownfield's actions in words. Like the realist writer whose "reality effect" Barthes explains, she sets up a "*direct* collusion of a referent and a signifier," expelling the signified from the sign. Brownfield's violence is given no denotative significance—it does not mean anything beyond or different from itself—and so again Barthes's words apply: "a signified of denotation" is eliminated, and what slips into its place is "spectacle" as a "signified of connotation."[27] Just as Brownfield's violence marks Mem's body in an act of premodern power (the *mark*, in Foucault, that elides the signified is distinct from the later *sign* of punishment where the punishment fits the crime, so that Foucault's monarchical effect entails Barthes's reality effect), Walker stamps the page with the "truth of the crime," making homeopathic use of a reiteration of violence.

The technical issue, in short, is how to acknowledge violence without transmitting it, which is the *thematic* issue of *The Third Life of Grange Copeland* as well. For it appears that it is in the nature of violence to reproduce itself (like Grange Copeland himself, it has multiple lives). Gender ideology—the concept of manhood—is one reproductive form: Mem complains, "just think of how many times I done got my head beat by you just so you could feel a little bit like a man, Brownfield Copeland" (GC 94). Other social etiologies are identified, although masculinity/social castration still might seem to be the underlying sore spot: Brownfield's rage at "his life and his world . . . made him beat her," "blame everything . . . on her" (GC 55). For he "could not stand to be belittled at home after coming from a job that required him to respond to all orders from a stooped position" (GC 56). Walker wants to stress that racist socioeconomic conditions are responsible for the transmission of violence, that black men displace their quite justified anger against white men (and women) onto black women. (So does Toni Morrison: after "big, white, armed men," in *The Bluest Eye*, interrupt Cholly and Darlene and then sadistically force them to continue having, what can only at this point be simulated, intercourse, Cholly cultivates "his hatred of Darlene." Hating the more powerful hunters would have "consumed him, burned him up like a piece of soft coal," so he hates the "one whom he had not been able to protect, to spare, to cover from the round moon glow of the flashlight.")[28]

But Walker is equally compelled to qualify this point about displacement. Racial oppression is at the same time considered to be an excuse for black male violence against black women. In blinding the violent black male to his own responsibility, in providing a barrier to recognition of black agency, this line of argument only serves as another form of white corruption. "You gits just as weak as water, no feeling of doing *nothing* yourself," Grange pleads to Brownfield. "Then you begins to think up evil and begins to destroy everybody around you, and you blames it on the crackers. . . . Nobody's as powerful as we make them out to be. We got our own *souls*, don't we?" (GC 207). Walker presents, and in turn critiques, a constructivist explanation of the black batterer, since it attributes excessive force to the white, dominant power structure. Walker urges black men to claim their violence against women in an initial effort to reclaim their souls. In a chapter titled "Reconstructing Black Masculinity," bell hooks argues similarly that "black male agency," "salvation," and "growth" will become reachable goals once black men relinquish "phallocentrism" (inherited from white patriarchy) and "envision new ways of thinking about black masculinity."[29]

The reproduction of battering occurs then, in Walker, in two fields: whites batter black men who then batter black women, all of which is literarily recreated as counter-spectacle. Walker replaces the transitivity of battering with self-conscious literary theatricality, in a sense turning the batterer's spectacular punishment against him (and thereby transforming the subtitle of this essay, "Spectacular Domestic Punishment," into a pun). Which is not to say that just as whites beat blacks and black men beat black women, the black woman (novelist) verbally beats black men. For Walker's exhortation to black men that they retrieve their souls by taking responsibility for their lives implies the possibility of being something other than a link in a chain of abuse, of not being merely a fascinated transmitter of the spectacle.

The spectacle of power that Walker reproduces, as a reproduction of a reproduction of abuse, supplies a self-consciousness that is the verbal equivalent of "soul." By means of a literary performance, Walker reveals the performative aspect of battering that allows, paradoxically, for the idea of "soul" as a kind of self-fashioning or self-production, once the spectacle becomes self-conscious—once the spectacle of battering is reflected by the spectacle of the spectacle of battering. If battering, in other words, is no longer seen as a mechanical social inevitability, but as a fascinating spectacle, then other (more imaginative, less violent) spectacle effects become possible. Without letting the white, dominant power structure off the hook, Walker's writing performs black male violence to unhinge it from the social forces that seem to generate it, and in thus loosening it suggests the possibility of conversion. The homeopathic strategy is double: by reproducing the spectacle of power, Walker leaves women's pain in a state of opacity (refusing to usurp it for the sake of her own literate power), as she injects self-consciousness into theatrical male violence to enable its reinscription.

By exposing the cultural constructedness of battered women, by translating through minimal discursivity battered women's pain into language, and by literarily spectacularizing male brutality against women, in an effort to disrupt the transmission of violence, Hurston, Drabble, Cisneros, Naylor, and Walker circumvent Armstrong and Tennenhouse's insistence upon the essential violence of representation. As if addressing their theory, *The Third Life of Grange Copeland* invests its hope finally in Ruth, Grange's literate and educated granddaughter, oddly mentioning that, if Ruth were to be shipwrecked on a deserted island, the novel she would most like to have in her possession is *Jane Eyre*. These women writers, in other words, work toward producing the therapeutic political effects of the *publication* of woman abuse. They attempt what Homi Bhabha considers to be our political obligation: both to "realize, and take responsibility for, the unspoken, unrepresented pasts that haunt the historical present." [30]

This is the direction we must collectively move in, bridging the gap as best we can between academic feminism and women in pain, without fretting too much over our possible complicity with representational offenses. For as Scarry writes, "[t]he failure to express pain . . . will always work to allow its appropriation and conflation with debased forms of power; conversely, the successful expression of pain will always work to expose and make impossible that appropriation and conflation" [31]—a warning especially critical in this woeful political era when victim-phobia is emerging as a cultural pathology.

NOTES

1. Kathy Acker, *Blood and Guts in High School* (New York: Grove Press, 1978), 99.

2. Nancy Armstrong and Leonard Tennenhouse, "Introduction: Representing Violence, or 'How the West Was Won,' " in *The Violence of Representation: Literature and the History of Violence*, ed. Nancy Armstrong and Leonard Tennenhouse (New York: Routledge, 1989), 2, 7, hereafter cited parenthetically in the text as VR.

3. It may seem to my readers, as it did to one of the editors of *Genders*, that I might also take up here Susanne Kappeler's *Pornography of Representation*. While it is true that Kappeler ends her book with a plea for "communication, not representation" and basically sees representation(s) as "a crucial strategy in the supreme subject's endeavour to maintain his position of power and privilege and the social, political and economic organization that supports it," she repeatedly calls for a transformation of representation, away from a pornographic, subject-object, or master-slave, model and toward an intersubjective model, in which women would actively participate. To Kappeler, representation has been "the means by which

the subject objectifies the world," but it isn't intrinsically doomed to enact such cruelty forever. Kappeler acknowledges, in fact, that the feminist critique of the pornography of representation must operate within the realm of representation. Susanne Kappeler, *The Pornography of Representation* (Minneapolis: University of Minnesota Press, 1986), 165, 198, 222.

4. In *Allegories of Empire*, Jenny Sharpe offers a more nuanced and compelling postcolonialist critique of *Jane Eyre* that (in the spirit of Mae Henderson) underscores racial difference within gender identity. *Jane Eyre* may very well rely "on the figuration of various colonial 'others,' " as Sharpe asserts (she takes Spivak's point that the "native female" is "excluded from a discourse of feminist individualism" further in arguing that "the silent passivity of the Hindu woman is the grounds for the speaking subject of feminist individualism"), but it does not do so necessarily as a function of representation. Jenny Sharpe, *Allegories of Empire: The Figure of Woman in the Colonial Text* (Minneapolis: University of Minnesota Press, 1993), 33, 55.

5. Teresa de Lauretis, "The Violence of Rhetoric," in *The Violence of Representation*, ed. Armstrong and Tennenhouse, 241.

6. In *Intimate Violence*, after noting that "Armstrong and Tennenhouse risk obliterating any distinction between semiotic violence and its empirical counterpart," Laura Tanner suspends the reader of "a representation of violence . . . between the semiotic and the real, between a representation and the material dynamics of violence which it evokes, reflects, or transforms." Laura E. Tanner, *Intimate Violence: Reading Rape and Torture in Twentieth-Century Fiction* (Indianapolis: Indiana University Press, 1994), 6.

7. Mae Gwendolyn Henderson, "Speaking in Tongues: Dialogics, Dialectics, and the Black Woman Writer's Literary Tradition," in *Reading Black, Reading Feminist: A Critical Anthology*, ed. Henry Louis Gates, Jr. (New York: Meridian/Penguin, 1990), 117, 136–37.

8. Zora Neale Hurston, "Sweat," in *Spunk: The Selected Stories of Zora Neale Hurston* (Berkeley: Turtle Island Foundation, 1985).

9. Susan Willis, *Specifying: Black Women Writing the American Experience* (Madison: University of Wisconsin Press, 1987), 126–27.

10. Teresa de Lauretis, *Technologies of Gender: Essays on Theory, Film, and Fiction* (Bloomington: Indiana University Press, 1987), 10.

11. Nancy Hartsock, "Foucault on Power: A Theory for Women?" in *Feminism/Postmodernism*, ed. Linda J. Nicholson (New York: Routledge, 1990), 169.

12. Because cases of female batterers and male battered victims are relatively rare, male pronouns will be used to refer to batterers and female pronouns to refer to battered victims.

13. Michel Foucault, *Discipline and Punish: The Birth of the Prison*, trans. Alan Sheridan (New York: Random House, 1979), 35, hereafter cited parenthetically in the text as DP.

14. Sandra Cisneros, "Woman Hollering Creek," in *Woman Hollering Creek and Other Stories* (New York: Vintage Books/Random House, 1992), 54, hereafter cited parenthetically in the text as "WHC."

15. R. Emerson Dobash and Russell Dobash, *Violence against Wives: A Case against the Patriarchy* (New York: Free Press/Macmillan, 1979), 2, hereafter cited parenthetically in the text as "VW."

16. Margaret Drabble, *The Needle's Eye* (New York: Ivy Books/Ballantine, 1972), 43, hereafter cited parenthetically in the text as NE.

17. Wini Breines and Linda Gordon, "The New Scholarship on Family Violence," *Signs: Journal of Women in Culture and Society* 8 (Spring 1983): 515.

18. Elaine Scarry, *The Body in Pain: The Making and Unmaking of the World* (New York: Oxford University Press, 1985), 35.

19. Hartsock 171.

20. Lenore E. Walker, *The Battered Woman* (New York: Harper and Row, 1979), 65–70.

21. This level of the analysis of woman abuse that I attribute here to "the text" seems to be the complicated product of Cleófilas's indirectly expressed consciousness as well as the narrator's concern, an intermingling that once again collapses writer/narrator/character boundaries.

22. Gloria Naylor, *Linden Hills* (New York: Penguin Books, 1985), 10, hereafter cited parenthetically in the text as LH.

23. Gloria Naylor and Toni Morrison, "A Conversation," *Southern Review* 21 (July 1985): 572–73.

24. This is the trend in the essays on *Linden Hills* in *Gloria Naylor: Critical Perspectives Past and Present*, ed. Henry Louis Gates and K. A. Appiah (New York: Amistad, 1993).

25. bell hooks, *Feminist Theory from Margin to Center* (Boston: South End Press, 1984), 1.

26. Tanner 12.

27. Roland Barthes, "The Reality Effect," in *French Literary Theory Today*, ed. Tzvetan Todorov (New York: Cambridge University Press, 1982), 16.

28. Toni Morrison, *The Bluest Eye* (1970; reprint, New York: Penguin Books, 1994), 150–51.

29. bell hooks, *Black Looks: Race and Representation* (Boston: South End Press, 1992), 106.

30. Homi K. Bhabha, *The Location of Culture* (New York: Routledge, 1994), 12.

31. Scarry 14.

THREE

Resistant Silence, Resistant Subject: (Re)Reading Gayl Jones's *Eva's Man*

Janelle Wilcox

In an interview conducted in the spring of 1975, just after the publication of Gayl Jones's first novel, *Corregidora*, Michael S. Harper asks Jones if any of her work was autobiographical. Jones responds with an acknowledgment that despite her use of first-person narration, none of her writing was "strictly autobiographical." She names one story as a slight exception: " 'The Welfare Check' is only in terms of the woman's being like me." [1] Jones elaborates further on the function of the narrator of the story and the purpose the story served:

[T]he woman narrator, even though the details of her life were different, was me in the sense that I needed her to explain myself. There was no way I could explain who I was to myself or anybody else except that way. Particularly my silence. I had to say something about it some way. . . . And I felt that if people read the story or if I read it to them, they would feel less badly about my not talking and it usually worked that way. So I needed the woman to be me at that time. [2]

Jones's thematic exploration of silence is not limited to "The Welfare Check." Silences punctuate the narratives of her two novels, *Corregidora* (1975) and *Eva's Man* (1976), as well as several short stories in *White Rat* (1977). In fact, Mae Gwendolyn Henderson's 1991 introduction to the paperback edition of *White Rat* points to silence as the defining element of the collection: "Her stories both thematize and formalize silence as a strategem that reveals the discontinuities and breaks in the connections and bonds between individuals."[3] What interests me here is Jones's subsequent silence—her absence from textual production—what Henderson terms Jones's "rather sudden and mysterious disappearance from the public eye."[4] After only two novels and one collection of short stories, Jones has stopped publishing her fiction.

In conjunction with examining Jones's silence, both her textual exploration of silence and her subsequent absence from textual production, I want to look at the critical apparatus that affects the reception of texts. Jones's work stretches across both decades and genres from fiction published in the seventies, poetry in the eighties, and criticism in the nineties. But it is the reception of her fiction that functions as an illuminating example of the normalizing force of literary reviews and criticism. Despite early critical acclaim, she remains one of the lesser-known, lesser-read, and underappreciated contemporary African American women writers. *Corregidora* was greeted by reviewers with nearly unqualified praise. When her second novel was published the next year, however, the same reviewers who had seen the author of *Corregidora* as a promising young writer saw the author of *Eva's Man* as perpetuating stereotypes about black women[5] and promoting hostility toward black men.[6] Jones's collection of short stories was published the year after *Eva's Man*, but no other fiction has appeared since then.

In *Discourse and the Other: The Production of the Afro-American Text*, W. Lawrence Hogue contends that "criticism as practiced by editors, publishers, reviewers, and critics . . . is a preeminently political exercise that works upon and mediates the reception of literary texts."[7] Following Terry Eagleton's assertion that literature is a construction "fashioned by particular people for particular reasons,"[8] Hogue moves beyond the general field of the politics of literary theory and into an examination of the politics of racial construction in literary theory and criticism. Historically, ideological forces (using the universalizing discourse of aesthetic value) determined what African American texts were considered aesthetically compatible to texts in the (Euro)American literary canon. For example, Hogue points out that naturalist novels such as Richard Wright's *Native Son* (1941) were admitted entrance to the canon, though still in a token position, because literary study in the United States was dominated by naturalism for the first half of the twentieth century. It is Hogue's contention that the social movements of the sixties provided space for African American writers to more effectively challenge the stereotypes and images that had dominated and disciplined the production of African American texts.

Hogue's examination of African American literary production is explicitly informed by Michel Foucault's analysis of discursive formation. As Hogue explains, discourse naturalizes itself and thus conceals its discrepancies and silences; therefore "the archaeologist's function is to demask this process of naturalization."[9] Numerous critics and theorists in American literary study have undertaken the task of unmasking the ideologies that underlie the construction of an American canon of literature, and African American critics in particular have noted the silencing of African American texts that do not conform to mainstream literary aesthetics.[10] Barbara Herrnstein Smith argues that "literary value is not the property of an object or of a subject but rather the product of the dynamics of a system."[11] Furthermore, she contends that literary critics and reviewers are within the system and view texts from a particular perspective. The perspective from which a reviewer read Gayl Jones's fiction was affected by aesthetic and political ideologies, as well as his or her social positioning.[12] The discourses of the 1970s that influenced the evaluation of literary texts included not only those informed by "universal" values of a predominantly Euro-American male perspective, but also those grounded in oppositional values—literary and political—such as black nationalism and feminism.

Many critics specifically name the social movements of the 1960s and 1970s as the major influence on the literary production of African American literature. Mary Helen Washington calls both the civil rights movement and the feminist movement the "subtexts" of the stories by black women collected in *Black-Eyed Susans/Midnight Birds*. She particularly notes the connections between the social text and the literary text of the writers, contending that "[b]oth of these movements for political change in our society have revised the lives and the art of black women."[13] W. Lawrence Hogue also points to the liberatory effects of the sixties social movements. He argues that breaking away from the dominant literary apparatus "gave Afro-American writers, perhaps for the first time in American history, the opportunity to write for black audiences of similar ideological persuasions."[14]

In contrast to Washington and Hogue, Madhu Dubey looks more closely at the contradictions and tensions between and within the dominant discourses of the 1970s. Her study of black women novelists of the

1970s focuses on works by Toni Morrison, Gayl Jones, and Alice Walker, which she says "constitute themselves as novels by carefully navigating between two influential contemporary definitions of good fiction."[15] Journals such as the *New York Times Book Review* promoted politically neutral fiction, while black nationalist journals such as *Black World* and *Freedomways* valued work that was didactic and politically useful. In addition to negotiating between two opposing standards of literature, those upheld by the white literary establishment and those valued by the Black Aesthetic, black women writers questioned and undermined the gender assumptions of black nationalist discourse. Dubey argues, "The internal gaps and contradictions of black nationalist discourse, especially visible in its construction of black womanhood, opened the space for an alternative black feminist definition of womanhood."[16] Dubey contends that the novels written in the 1970s by Morrison, Jones, and Walker strain the limits of both feminist discourse and black nationalist discourse.

As Dubey points out, the two interpretive communities that were in a position to review Jones's novels were the white literary press and the black nationalist journals. Barbara Herrnstein Smith maintains that the two kinds of texts that appear in interpretive communities appeal to either divergent or convergent tastes. Divergent tastes, Smith explains, are resistant to cultural channeling, while convergent tastes are tractable to cultural channeling. When texts that do not yield easily to cultural channeling appear in an interpretive community, "institutions of evaluative authority are called in to validate the community's established tastes and preferences."[17] As a result, texts with divergent tastes are discounted or even pathologized by the persons or institutions with evaluative authority. Although the focus of Smith's examination of the contingencies of value is on mainstream Euro-American literary study, she contends that all interpretive communities engage in normative criticism, valuing some texts and devaluing others. Black nationalist critics—male and female—who reviewed *Eva's Man* found no sociological relevance or realistic representation in a text about a criminally insane black woman. Eva's story and her mode of telling it resisted Black Aesthetic cultural channeling. Eva's story also resisted cultural channeling by critics looking for "universal" or "apolitical" literature. Although for different ideological reasons, white reviewers joined black nationalist reviewers in their condemnation of Jones's second novel.

Several interviews with Jones appeared in print between the years

1977 and 1984. The 1975 interview with Gayl Jones was conducted by African American poet Michael S. Harper, Jones's "first reader" [18] while she was at Brown University. It was first published in the *Massachusetts Review* in 1977. [19] In August 1978, black feminist critic Claudia Tate interviewed Jones at the University of Michigan; the interview was published in *Black American Literature Forum* in 1979 and reprinted in Tate's *Black Women Writers at Work* (1983). Roseann P. Bell records her conversation with Jones about *Corregidora* in *Sturdy Black Bridges* (1979), but states that the interview took place before the publication of *Eva's Man*. A brief interview/essay by Jones appeared in Marie Evans's *Black Women Writers (1950–1980): A Critical Evaluation* (1984). In 1982, Charles Rowell conducted an interview with Jones by mail, which was published later that year in *Callaloo*. The information provided in and the tone of the interviews seem to indicate that reviewers and critics, performing their role as "institutions of evaluative authority," affected Jones's public discourse. In contrast to the Harper interview, which provided biographical information and personal anecdotes, subsequent interviews are marked by a greater reserve and reticence on the part of the subject/object of the interview.

The interview with Claudia Tate is the first interview that makes explicit Jones's decision to resist biographical or psychological interpretation. In the 1978 interview, Tate provides an overview of Jones's published fiction and introduces Jones to the reader:

Born in 1949 in Lexington, Kentucky, where she continued to reside until she first went to Connecticut College and then to Brown University, Jones is now Assistant Professor of English at the University of Michigan. She refuses to divulge additional biographical information, contending that her work must live independently of its creator, that it must sustain its own character and artistic autonomy. But while she will not discuss her private life, she did, in the interview that follows, share some insights into her artistic endeavors and about her perceptions of American literary history. [20]

In addition to establishing Jones's reluctance to provide personal details that might be used for interpretive purposes, the interviews also provide evidence of Jones's continued production of texts. In the introduction to her interview, Tate says that Jones told her she was working on another novel entitled *Palmares* and that Jones expected it to be published in the "not-too-distant future." [21] In other interviews and reviews of her novels, reference is made to work either completed or in progress. Roseann P.

Bell's introduction to her interview of Jones states that Jones had already completed three novels.[22] Margo Jefferson's review of *Eva's Man* indicates that Jones had completed four novels and was working on a fifth.[23] In the Charles H. Rowell interview, Jones talks about novels and short story collections she has written, referring to them by both title and content.[24] Despite the fact that the interview took place in 1982, none of the works ever appeared in print.

The interviews with Claudia Tate and Charles H. Rowell provide evidence that Jones was affected by the overwhelmingly negative response to *Eva's Man*. Toward the end of the Tate interview, Claudia Tate asks Jones if she is influenced by reviews and criticism of her writing. Jones responds, "As I write, I imagine how certain critics will respond to various elements of the story, and I force myself to go ahead and say 'Well, you would ordinarily include this, so go ahead and do it.' "[25] In the Rowell interview, Jones refers to a "double-consciousness" evoked in her whenever she writes anything about sexuality. She also discusses the way critical reception influenced her choice of subject matter. When Rowell asks her about her decision to write on the Afro-Brazilian slave experience after having written two novels set in the United States, Jones explains that the Brazilian history and landscape helped her imagination. But she further articulates the decision in terms of a distancing strategy:

I also wanted to write about someone and a time distant from my own. It was also a way of getting away from things that some readers consider "autobiographical" or "private obsessions" rather than literary inventions—that they don't accept as imagination from a black woman writing about black female characters in a certain American world.[26]

The sense of restriction Jones voices is not limited to one particular African American writer. Jones herself indicates her awareness that the limitations she feels stem in part from her subject-position as a black woman. The reception of Jones's second novel, however, provides a particularly apt example of the silencing and containment of counter-hegemonic writers.

RESISTANT SILENCE, RESISTANT SUBJECT

Jones's *Eva's Man* plays out textually the ways that knowledge and power are linked in discourse. Eva begins telling her story from the cell of a psychiatric prison where she has been incarcerated for five years for the crime of poisoning and castrating a man. At her arrest, at her trial, at her sentencing, Eva's silence had been her defense. Her refusal to talk, either in justification for or explanation of her crime, signifies a resistance to entering the dominant medical, juridical, and sexual discourses represented in the novel. Eva's discursive containment and simultaneous resistance function as a metaphor for the containment of the marginalized writer. In contemporary literary study, the dominant culture often mishears the marginalized writer who is resisting or revising the dominant discourse. Even more likely to be misheard is the voice different from the naturalized minority discourse. Eva's silencing within the novel textually prefigures Jones's silencing within African American literary study. Eva Medina Canada, the character in Jones's novel, exhibits a resistance to interpretation that is paralleled by Gayl Jones, the writer and creator of that character.

Despite the connection I draw between the fictionally represented silence of Eva and the literal silence of Jones, I wish to be explicit here that it is not my intention to psychoanalyze Gayl Jones's silence. In fact, I am very much arguing against interpretation that collapses the distinction between character and creator. Jones's refusal to authorially intrude in her fiction has placed her in the defensive position of being mistaken for the characters she invents. In Mari Evans's *Black Women Writers*, Jones says, "I think I have an unfortunate public image, because of the published work. People imagine you're the person you've imagined."[27] The violence of interpretation that *Eva's Man* metaphorically represents extends from readers of the text to readers of Jones herself. I am suggesting, however, that her silence can be read in two interconnected ways: as the result of the disciplinary function of institutions, in this case the hegemonic and ambiguously (non)hegemonic[28] critical apparatus made up of publishers, reviewers, and critics, and as a silence that resists and denaturalizes the universalizing tendencies of interpretive communities. Because of my reluctance to participate in further interpretive "violation" of Jones, I have chosen to read both Jones's silence and Eva's silence as strategies of resistance. The following reading of *Eva's Man* is informed by Foucault's theories of discourse and resistant subjectivity, especially as they have been appropriated by feminist philosophers.

While other feminist theorists have examined silence as resistance, my appropriation of Foucault here foregrounds my interest in the ways that both Foucault and Jones explore how the psychoanalytic situation works as discipline. Foucault's refusal of psychoanalytic paradigms is echoed in Eva's hostile relationship with psychoanalysis in Jones's text. In the 1982 interview with Charles Rowell, Jones stresses Eva's resistance to participating in the psychoanalytic relationship: "She doesn't talk to the policemen. Ideally—and the kind of character I imagine her to be—she wouldn't have even talked to the psychiatrist either. But to tell the novel I had to have her do that."[29] Because Eva tells her story and at the same time resists telling her story, the reader is put in an uncomfortably complicitous position with the prison psychiatrist of "knowing" Eva only through her distorted narrative. Jones connects the unreliability of Eva's storytelling with the ambiguous positioning of Eva's audience: "How much of Eva's story is true and how much is deliberately not true; that is, how much of a game is she playing with her listeners/psychiatrists/others?"[30] The ambiguous designation of "listeners/psychiatrists/others" as Eva's "audience" functions to situate the reader in the position of being a knowing, thus violating, subject.

Because Jones undermines the authority of psychiatric discourse, we cannot unproblematically read Eva as the object of the text. At the same time, neither can we read Eva as a rational subject. Consequently, we must learn to read her as a resisting subject. Susan J. Hekman explains that for Foucault, "the constituted subject is the subject that resists."[31] More important, Hekman stresses the implications of Foucault's thought for feminism: "[w]omen's resistance to the constitution of their subjectivity is the essence of the feminist movement. . . . The result of resistance is the creation of a new discourse—born out of resistance to the modes of discourse that have constituted the feminine subject."[32] What Eva resists are the ways in which she is constituted by and within discourse. To subvert these constructions of sexuality, gender, and race, Eva uses silence—what Foucault would call the gaps and discrepancies in discourse. Learning to read Eva's silence means learning to read Eva's resistance.

Jones's strategy of telling the story only through Eva's subjectivity confounds the reader's attempts to read Eva as the object of the story. Throughout the text, Jones calls attention to the dynamic between a knowing subject and a known object. The knowing subjects take the form of Davis in his sexual relationship with Eva, the police in their disciplinary relationship, the court in its juridical relationship, the psychiatrist in his medical relationship, and newspapers and readers who are looking for the "truth" to be produced about Eva, the object to be known. Eva uses silence to resist violation and definition by these knowing subjects. Her words, "I said nothing," become an ironic refrain, echoing in every conversation, in every relationship.

Because Davis "knows" Eva only as a sexual object, he ties together the themes of sex and silence in one of the opening scenes of the novel. After joining Eva at her table, he says that he can tell something about her: "You ain't been getting it, have you?" Eva says nothing—to which Davis responds, "I don't expect you to say nothing. I can read your eyes." [33] He combines assertion, question, and interpretation without needing a response from Eva herself. Yet Eva's resistant silence disrupts Davis's definition of Eva, and he seeks more information from Eva in order to know/explain her. During the five days that Eva spends with Davis in his hotel room, Davis makes various attempts to break through Eva's silence: " 'Eva, why won't you talk about yourself?' I said nothing" (67); " 'Why won't you talk to me, Eva?' 'There's nothing to say' " (101); " 'Why won't you talk?' I said nothing" (116); " 'How do you feel about it, Eva?' 'It doesn't matter' " (118); " 'Say something, Eva.' 'There's nothing' " (121). " 'What are you thinking? You're not talking.' 'Nothing.' 'Why aren't you speaking?' 'I don't have anything to say right now' " (126). By refusing to talk, Eva avoids containment within the category of woman as defined by Davis.

"THEY SAY THAT'S ALL RIGHT, TO GO AHEAD TALKING"

The other knowing subjects in the text, the police, the court, the psychiatrist, the newspapers, likewise demand discourse from Eva. In *The History of Sexuality*, Foucault contends that "one confesses—or is forced to confess." [34] In the opening pages of the novel, Eva says,

[P]eople come in here and ask me how it happened. They want me to tell it over and over again. I don't mean just the psychiatrists, but people from newspapers and things. They read about it or hear about it someplace and just want to keep it living. At first I wouldn't talk to anybody. All during the trial I wouldn't talk to anybody. But then, after I came in here, I started talking. I tell them so much I don't even get it straight any more. I tell them things that don't even have to do with what I did, but they say they want to hear that too. They want to hear about what happened between my mother and father as well as what happened between me and that man. One of them came in here and even wanted to know about my grandmother and grandfather. I know when I'm not getting things straight, and I tell them I'm not getting this straight, but they say that's all right, to go ahead talking. (4–5)

The relentless pressure upon Eva to talk about her crime can be illuminated through Foucault's discussion of confession in Western tradition as it moved from the church and into the scientific and medical discourses. Sex was and continues to be the privileged theme of confession, and confession in turn governs "the production of the true discourse on sex."[35] Because Eva has committed a crime of sex and violence in her murder and dental castration of Davis, she is exhorted to confess and thus produce the truth about herself. Foucault further explains the connection between power and knowledge that exists in the relation between the confessor and his/her audience:

The confession is a ritual of discourse in which the speaking subject is also the subject of the statement; it is also a ritual that unfolds within a power relationship, for one does not confess without the presence (or virtual presence) of a partner who is not simply the interlocutor but the authority who requires the confession.[36]

For the prison psychiatrist, Eva's story, her confession, her recounting of intimate moments, are necessary for him to evaluate and judge her, but at the same time, Eva resists and challenges his knowledge of her. Though she is denied a role as a knowing subject herself, through her silence, she refuses to be a known object.

Foucault contends that "[t]here is not one but many silences, and they are an integral part of the strategies that underlie and permeate discourses."[37] Silence, as Foucault understands it, is "an element that functions alongside the things said, with them and in relation to them."[38] The "things said" work in relation to one another to form a discourse, but they are only a part of that discourse. In his adaptation of Foucauldian thought, W. Lawrence Hogue considers the text a discursive field of facts existing in relation to one another. For example, in examining the feminist discourse that informs Alice Walker's *Third Life of Grange Copeland*, Hogue calls the image of the oppressed black male a repeated discursive fact that works in relation to other discursive facts, such as the submissive and loyal black woman, to form the text's feminist enunciation.[39] In *Eva's Man*, the repeated discursive fact of the male character who reads Eva only through her gender and sexuality is a part of the discursive field of the text but only as it exists in relation to Eva's resistant silences. Each of the male characters attempts to force Eva into a discursive relation. Each engages in the discourse of sex in an attempt to "know" Eva, to produce the "truth" about Eva. What bothers Eva, Jones says, is that "men repeatedly thought she was a different kind of woman than she actually was."[40] In order to challenge and modify these discursive relationships, Eva relies on silence. Her resistance exposes the gaps in the discourse of black women's sexuality as it is defined by the male characters in the text.

"I HAD NEVER SAID JOIN ME BEFORE"

In Eva's storytelling, scenes from her days with Davis in the motel room are intercut with scenes from her childhood. The relations between Eva and Eva's man are punctuated with Davis's probing and Eva's silence, with Davis's interpretations and Eva's resistance. She tells him nothing about herself, yet Davis "knows" what kind of woman Eva is. He tells her that "most women who look like [her] wear earrings" and that she has "the kind of ass that a woman should show off" by wearing tight skirts (18, 54). Davis's reading of Eva is informed by dominant cultural representations of women that are based on both a woman's looks and her actions. Eva retrospectively speculates on what Davis must have thought (what any man would have thought) of her because of her willingness to engage in sexual relations with him:

What Elvira said those people think I am [a whore], Davis probably thought so too. It's funny how somebody can remind you of somebody you didn't like, or ended up not liking and fearing—fearing is a better word—but . . . I hadn't said anything to any man in a long time. And I had never said Join me before. He probably thought I was in the habit of sitting there in that dark corner just so men would . . . Yeah, they'd come where I was. "Shit, bitch. Why don't you stay in the house if you don't wont a man to say nothing to you." "Where you from, sweetheart?" "Shit, I know you got a tongue, I ain't never met a bitch that didn't have a tongue." And then when I was standing at the corner that time that man drove his car real close to the curb and opened the door. I just stood there looking at him, and then he slammed the door and went around the curb real quick. "Shit, you the coldest-ass bitch I ever seen in my life." "If you don't want a man to talk to you you ought to . . ." (9, ellipses in original)

The above passage illustrates the way Eva makes connections between her time with Davis and her past experiences and impressions. Eva realizes that Davis probably thought she was a whore, or at least whore-like, even though Davis expected, even demanded, a sexual response from her. Davis's understanding of Eva as woman/whore echoes the voices from Eva's past, the same demanding and inscribing voices of men who defined Eva by her sexual function while simultaneously condemning her for it.[41] Jones sets up a narrative structure that conflates Eva's memories into a flattened representation of relations between Eva and all the men she has known. Yet as Eva recollects these men, each relationship is described in terms of Eva's resistance to imposed definitions and emphasizes her strategies to effect self-definition. In her relationships with Freddy Smoot, Tyrone, Alphonso, Moses Tripp, and finally Davis, Eva's (contra)diction and her silences undermine the totalizing male definition of her. Through dissent, silence, and violence, Eva produces an alternative discourse that competes with the circumscribing male discourse in the text.

Eva's first sexual encounter is with the neighbor boy Freddy Smoot. Eva and Freddy are playmates until Freddy initiates a sexual relationship; Eva participates in the sexual encounter the first time but then rejects further contact. Eva says, "After he had that popsicle up in me I wouldn't play with him anymore" (13). Keith Byerman suggests that Eva cooperates in the sex play, but has no desire to repeat it. Freddy's subsequent meetings with Eva focus on Freddy's request to repeat the play, setting up a demand and rejection pattern. Byerman argues that "[a]ll the other major scenes replicate this initial one. In each, a male attempts to dominate a woman through some forceful act. The woman responds with a combination of passivity and resistance."[42] I would add that Eva's silence is a combination of passivity and resistance, but that it is generally read only as a passive act by the other characters in the novel and by readers. By granting Eva agency as storyteller, in other words, by listening to her own construction of self, one can more easily read Eva's silence as a resistant act. When Freddy persistently attempts to engage Eva in sexual play again both verbally—"You let me do it once"—and physically— cornering Eva to rub up against her, Eva counters Freddy's continuation and interpretation of their play:

"You let me do it once."
"I ain't gon let you do it no more."
"When you gon let me fuck you again, Eva?"
"You didn't fuck me before." (14)

Although the five-year-old Eva refuses a continued relationship with Freddy, she learns that his interpretation of both his and her sexuality is the one condoned by society. When Freddy is with his friends, he initiates a sexual chase of Eva: "There's Eva, we can get some" (19). Despite this pursuit every time Eva is alone, Eva's mother's friend Miss Billie laughingly characterizes Freddy as "just a little banny rooster, all stuck out in front" (67), and Eva's mother simply calls Freddy and his friends who chase Eva "a bunch of wild horses" (20). Neither of the women questions the constructions of sexuality that generate predatory males and victimized females. Instead, they draw on animal imagery to further naturalize the relations between men and women as relations between predator and prey.

Eva's next entrapment into sexual discourse is with Tyrone, her mother's young musician boyfriend. Eva is twelve when her mother begins bringing Tyrone home, and Eva recalls, "I never would say anything to him, and he never said anything to me" (29). But Tyrone breaks the silence between the two of them with a sexual act, taking her hand and placing it on his crotch. Eva pulls away and the relations between the two lapse back into a strained silence, occasionally punctuated with Tyrone's references to the event. Eva refuses to talk to him or about his actions until Tyrone demands a response from her. Confronting her alone on the steps one day, Tyrone says, "You see me, you can speak" (34). He demands that Eva enter into a discourse that will define her through her sexuality. Eva refuses to engage with him either sexually or verbally, contradicting Tyrone's insistence that she is sexually attracted to him with her statement: "I didn't feel nothing" (34). The phrase is a modification of her "I said nothing" refrain and is used for a similarly resistant effect. Tyrone responds with a threatening gesture to Eva's rebellion against the ways that he defines her, and Eva runs to the safety of her house.

The next male character who attempts a sexual/discursive relation with Eva is her married cousin Alphonso, who begins taking Eva to bars when she is seventeen. Because they are related, Alphonso expects Eva to tell him things that she wouldn't tell other men, like whether or not she has "been getting it." Eva truthfully tells him no. Eva's response gives Alphonso the reference point he needs to define Eva as a woman, in other words, to make comparisons that inscribe her in terms of sexual activity. He tells Eva that most girls her age have had the "meat *and* the gravy"

(57, emphasis in original). Alphonso repeatedly tells Eva that she is "too old . . . way too old not to had the meat" (58). Like Tyrone, Alphonso collapses the discursive and the sexual, attempting to initiate Eva into both. When his verbal suggestions are repeatedly contradicted, evaded, or ignored by Eva, Alphonso resorts to a physical discourse, grabbing Eva's hand and placing it on his exposed, erect penis. Eva again runs from a forced sexual exchange. When she goes out to the bars again with Alphonso, he tells her that she is "hard on a man" (72). Eva contradicts his interpretation of her by reminding him of their family relationship: "I told you to tell people I'm your cousin. You haven't been telling yourself, have you?" (72). The relation that Alphonso had invoked in order to engage Eva in his sexual discourse is turned against him by Eva's use of it to reject a sexual relation with him. While Eva's discursive strategy is effective in avoiding sexual relations with her cousin, she is again confronted by the inscriptions of women—sweetmeat, bitch, hussy, cunt, whore—that men use to both describe and condemn women through their sexuality.

Although Alphonso continues to insist that Eva's reasons for going out to bars is because she is looking for the meat and gravy, Eva continues to insist that she's "not looking for nobody" (72). When Alphonso leaves Eva alone in the bar one night, Moses Tripp, a man Eva says looked old enough to be her grandfather, attempts to buy a five-dollar feel from Eva. She leaves the bar, enacting the flight strategy she had used with Freddy, Tyrone, and Alphonso, but this time Eva is followed. Eva explains:

I got up and went out. He followed me out. I was thinking I should've known he'd follow me out.
"Do it for me, huh? Come on, honey. This is my last five."
"Leave me alone."
"Least feel on it for me. That ain't fair. Five dollars for a feel, that ain't . . . Alonso ain't got nothing I . . . Let." He reached for me down between my legs, then he screamed and pulled his hand back. He called me "bitch." (98, ellipses in original)

With this exchange, Eva makes a transition from a discourse of contradiction and denial into a discourse of violence. Rather than subject herself to the sexual violence of Moses Tripp, she stabs him with the knife that Freddy had given her. The active use of the phallic gift initiates a rejection and subversion of gender roles that Jones carries through the rest of the novel. Eva's violence also initiates a more resistant and insistent use of silence against those who demand explanation of her actions. She refuses to enter the juridical discourse: "I didn't tell anybody. . . . I just let the man tell his side" (98). Eva's silence functions as a metaphor for the unhearing audience that confronts her. Her refrain of silence underscores the inadequacies of her contradiction: "I didn't answer . . . I said nothing. . . . Nobody knew why I knifed him because I didn't say" (99). What can a bitch-cunt-hussy-whore say that will counter what is inscribed in the dominant male discourse?

"IT WAS JUST THE THING ABOUT THE TELEPHONE"

In addition to emphasizing the pervasive sexual discourse of the male characters, Jones uses a combination of white woman and black woman stereotypes to reveal how Eva's gender identification is constructed. The woman that Eva comes to identify most overtly with is the queen bee. When she is a child, Eva overhears Miss Billie and her mother talking about a woman they call the queen bee because, as Miss Billie explains, "every man she had end up dying. I don't mean natural dying, I mean something happen to them" (17). Although Eva's mother suggests that such a curse would be harder on the woman than the man, since she would not be free to really love a man, Miss Billie and the rest of the community judge the queen bee on her destructive powers. Eva says that she "used to think the queen bee looked like a bee and went around stinging men," but when she sees her for the first time, Eva notes, "[s]he didn't look any different from Mama or Miss Billie or Freddy's mama" (44). As she gets older, Eva learns that in the universalizing discourse of the men, all women are indeed like the queen bee in their destructive capabilities. When Eva stabs Moses Tripp in the hand for reaching between her legs, she is literally enacting the sting of the queen bee. Eva's violence functions on two seemingly contradictory levels: on the one hand, she has become what the dominant discourse says she is—the castrating bitch—on the other, her action challenges the logic of a discourse that expects passivity and sexual victimization from what it fears.

Eva's transition from a discourse of denial and rejection into a discourse of violence both initiates and serves as metaphor for her overt efforts at self-construction. She assumes an active role in constructing an identity that is not imposed on her by men who demand whore-like behavior from her, and she rejects a passive role of victimization.[43] Instead Eva enters a discursive and sexual relationship based on tenderness. Eva marries James Hunn, a man three times her age, who had visited her while she was in the girls' reformatory for her knife attack. Eva moves to Kentucky with Hunn and attends Kentucky State, where their marriage is happy until Eva realizes that as a wife, too, she is limited to always already inscribed interpretations of female sexuality. She recalls, "I didn't know that anything was wrong with him until we moved in this house and there was a telephone there and he said he was going to take the telephone out" (110). When Eva says that she wants to keep the telephone, Hunn tells her no, he doesn't want her lovers calling her. Eva thinks he is joking at first; when she realizes he is not, Eva says, "I told him I didn't have any lovers. He said every woman had lovers. He said he wasn't going to have a telephone in the house so that my lovers could be calling me up and then meeting me some place" (110). Eva is again confronted by a universalizing discourse that overrides her individual identity and self-construction. Eva leaves Hunn after two years, in spite of his continued tenderness toward her. He never turned his temper on her, but "[i]t was just the thing about the telephone" (111). Eva rejects, again, a prescribed role, this time the unfaithful wife. Furthermore, Eva refuses to have her speaking self, symbolized through the importance of the telephone, restricted because of a discourse that conflates access to communication and access to sex.

"IT'S EASIER BEING A WOMAN AND ALONE IN DIFFERENT PLACES THAN IT IS IN THE SAME PLACE"

When Eva leaves Hunn, she constructs an existence for herself comprising work and travel, suggesting a play with and performance of gender roles that denaturalizes cultural codes. Eva spends all her life on the road "just like a man" (75). When Eva begins her recollections, her life is a catalogue of place-names:

I was in Upstate New York then. I've lived in Kentucky. I've lived in New York City. I been in West Virginia, New Orleans. I just came from out in New Mexico. I just up and went down to New Mexico after I got laid off in Wheeling. They've got tobacco farms in Connecticut. I been there too. I didn't travel so much until after I was married, and that went wrong, and then I said I would just stay alone. It's easier being a woman and alone in different places than it is in the same place. (5)

Eva's point that it is easier for her to be alone in different places than in the same place indicates her unwillingness to be circumscribed by boundaries either geographic or cultural. Yet it also recalls her strategy of flight from situations in which she is physically or psychologically threatened. Despite her subversion of gender codes, Eva is never far from the material reality of male discourse and oppression. At one of the tobacco factories that she worked in, Eva is offered money for information about whether the black workers were going to vote for a union. Eva refuses the foreman but is made a counteroffer:

I said that I didn't know how anybody else was going to vote. He asked me how I was going to vote. I said I knew how I was going to vote. He said he had some money for me if I wanted it. I said I didn't know how anybody else was going to vote. He said never mind that. He said he didn't mean that. He said he had some money for me. I said by the time the voting was over, it would be time for me to be back on the road again. He said I didn't seem like I belonged around there anyway. He said I could be on the road before the voting was over. He sent me out and called somebody else in. He said he didn't like people who didn't know how to be grateful. (75)

Racial and gender oppression intersect in this exchange—if the foreman cannot buy information about the black workers in the factory from her, he will accept sexual favors instead. Both requests stem from his reading of Eva as a black woman and from his assumption of a right to violation.[44] In Eva's telling of the story, she collapses the event with other (mis)readings of her. In this section of the narrative, Eva also refers to Davis's displeasure because she is "hard to get into" (76), to the psychiatrist's insistence that she "open up" so he can help her, to Alphonso's assertion that Eva "frustrates a man" (80). In each case, Eva's resistance is not seen as a strategy to construct a subjectivity in opposition to dominant gender roles but as an unnatural resistance to culturally condoned penetration.

Eva's subversion of gender roles is played out further in the five days she spends with Davis in his room. Jones denaturalizes and destabilizes both male and female roles. Eva and Davis share the role of sexual initiator, but the rest of their roles get mixed up, with slippage back and forth from traditional roles to a reversal of the roles.[45] In the five days Eva spends with Davis in his room, Davis does the domestic chores, refusing to allow Eva to either cook or clean the room. Yet when the landlord presses him for the rent money, Davis responds harshly to Eva's suggestion that she pay for the room. Money and control remain a male prerogative. Eva's looks, as interpreted by Davis, challenge gender codes—she doesn't wear earrings or tight skirts like other women who look like her do. And it is Davis who conflates, across gender lines, two images of destruction:

> You look like a lion, all that hair."
> "It's the male lions that have a lot of hair."
> "Then you look like a male lion," he said laughing, "Eva Medusa's a lion." (16)

As the narrative swirls into greater fragmentation, the irony of Davis's naming of Eva as a destructive force is matched by the literalness of Eva's interpretation. The images of debilitation conflate as Eva literalizes the metaphors of Eve—"I squeezed his dick in my teeth. I bit down hard. My teeth in an apple" (128), Medusa—"I'm Medusa, I was thinking. Men look at me and get hard-ons. I turn their dicks to stone" (130), and the queen bee—"The sweet milk in the queen bee's breasts has turned to blood" (132). Eva's denaturalization of the male discourse culminates in the very action that underlies the discourse. The discourse that constructs predatory males and devouring females is carried to its logical conclusion. It is consequently—and ironically—designated as madness.

"DON'T YOU EXPLAIN ME"

Keith Byerman contends that Eva's "madness" demands that we question not only the grounds upon which the judgment is made, but examine also how the designation of madness functions, particularly in the "judgment of madness as an act of domination."[46] Eva's actions, the poisoning and castration of Davis, together with her insistent silence suggest to the "rational" reader that she is insane. Byerman, however, proposes that we examine the implications of labeling Eva insane:

Eva must be declared insane so that the meaning of her act can be evaded and suppressed. Through the symbolic significance of her violence, she threatens to expose male domination for the dehumanizing and exploitive system that it is. She has challenged, in a primal way, the right of that system to be considered natural and rational. Both her crime and her silence call into question this particular universe of discourse.[47]

Eva's madness, then, denaturalizes both the dominant male discourse that relegates her to dual roles of whore and castrator and the logic that designates her mad for performing these roles.

In addition to challenging naturalized systems of domination, Eva's silences function to refuse validation of the psychiatric monologue generated about her. In the final pages of the novel, a long "dialogue" is recorded between Eva and the prison psychiatrist. The passage is marked by Eva's refusal to speak confessionally within the discourse of psychiatry. While the psychiatrist prompts Eva to tell him about herself, Eva consistently resists his violation and interpretation of her through silence, contradiction, and violence. At one point, Eva tells the psychiatrist, "Don't look at me. Don't make people look at me" (168). She echoes and expands her resistance a few moments later, saying, "Don't explain me. Don't you explain me. Don't explain me" (173). Despite her resistance, the psychiatrist continues to "explain" Eva. The passage ends with the suggestion that violence is again Eva's only recourse to resist interpretative violation:

> You thought you were a bad woman, so you went out and got you a bad man. Don't explain me.
> And then you . . . Matron? Matron! Hold her! Hold her! (174, ellipses in original)

In *Madness and Civilization*, Foucault contends that silence is the underlying foundation for discourse about the mad: the emergence of psychiatry as a profession "thrusts into oblivion all those stammered, imperfect words without fixed syntax in which the exchange between madness and reason was made. The language of psychiatry, which is the monologue of reason *about* madness, has been established only on the basis of such a silence."[48] The silencing of Eva is necessary for the discourse on madness; her resistant silence, however, counters and delegitimizes the psychiatrist's (as well as the reader's) interpretive authority.

Foucault's genealogies of madness, prisons, and sexuality reveal how power is deployed and subjects are created through discourse. As Jana Sawicki explains, "ways of knowing are equated with ways of exercising power over individuals."[49] In a similar fashion, Jones's *Eva's Man* reveals how the subject Eva Medina Canada is created by her resistance to power exercised through discursive and disciplinary institutions. Eva's silence can be read as an act of agency that denaturalizes and subverts imposed silences. Sawicki contends that Foucault's strategy of genealogical critique is offered as an alternative to traditional—and totalizing—revolutionary theories that posit an oppressive force and a subjugated victim:

[G]enealogy as resistance involves using history to give voice to the marginal and submerged voices which lie "a little beneath history"—the voices of the mad, the delinquent, the abnormal, the disempowered. It locates many discontinuous and regional struggles against power both in the past and present. These voices are the sources of resistance, the creative subjects of history.[50]

I would suggest that literary works such as *Eva's Man* also give voice to marginal and submerged voices.[51] Eva's voice, through its dissent, silence, and violence, is the source of resistance in the text that both constitutes her subjectivity and allows her to modify the power wielded over her. By creating a character revealed only through her resistant subjectivity, Jones refuses to allow Eva to be violated by either the knowing subjects *in* the text (other characters) or the knowing subjects *of* the text (readers). My reading of *Eva's Man* ultimately suggests that while Eva is "unknowable," the meaning of her silence is not inaudible.

(RE)READING GAYL JONES'S *EVA'S MAN*

The possibility I have been exploring here is that Jones's work and, to some extent, the writer herself, were silenced by the disciplinary function of the interpretive communities of the 1970s. Madhu Dubey's recent analysis of *Eva's Man* focuses on its utter incompatibility with the "functional reading codes" of the Black Aesthetic:

The most subversive moments of *Eva's Man* are shrouded in an incoherence that seriously jeopardizes the reader's interpretive function, and prevents us from distilling any clear meaning from the text. It seems almost as if the novel must disclaim its right to meaning altogether if it cannot posit the clear, didactic meaning required by the Black Aesthetic. *Eva's Man* renders itself unreadable, as it were, in order both to escape the functional reading codes of the Black Aesthetic and to obscure its own refusal of these codes.[52]

The text's resistance to reading codes—of the Black Aesthetic as well as the codes required by mainstream (white) literary audiences—is mimicked throughout the text by Eva's resistance to reading codes of both the hegemonic culture and the ambiguously (non)hegemonic culture of black male domination. At the time of its publication, this narrative and thematic strategy functioned to refuse the novel entrance into either feminist or black nationalist literary study. The text strained the limits of the oppositional discourses of the 1970s—*Eva's Man* presents neither a female subject achieving self-definition nor an African American subject breaking free of stereotypes imposed by the dominant white culture.[53]

My (re)reading of *Eva's Man* is intended to suggest that, at the present cultural/critical moment, it is both useful and desirable to open the novel to new reading possibilities. Certainly, one element of the value of Jones's novel is in its exposure of the gaps and inconsistencies in both the dominant and subdominant discourses of the 1970s. I would also argue, however, that it is important to reread *Eva's Man* through its resistance to and denaturalization of the silence and essentialism imposed upon black female subjectivity by hegemonic white patriarchal discourse and the ambiguously (non)hegemonic discourses of white women and black men. In the nearly twenty years since the publication of *Eva's Man*, African American women writers have generated formally complex and themati- cally compelling works in black women's poetry, fiction, criticism, and political and literary theory. Resistance to dominant and subdominant constructions of black female subjectivity has resulted in the creation of new discourses, through which African American writers, as well as critics and theorists, have problematized notions of an essential black identity in literary and cultural studies. While Jones has not produced any fiction for the reading public since the 1970s, recent paperback publications suggest the possibility that new audiences exist for her fic- tion.[54] If *Eva's Man* can be reassessed and revalued by present interpretive communities, perhaps there can emerge a receptive audience for more of Gayl Jones's fiction.

NOTES

1. Michael S. Harper, "Gayl Jones: An Interview," *Massachusetts Review* 18 (1977): 711.

2. Ibid., 712.

3. Mae Gwendolyn Henderson, foreword to *White Rat*, by Gayl Jones (Bos- ton: Northeastern University Press, 1991), xi.

4. Ibid.

5. June Jordan accuses Jones of reinscribing the " 'crazy whore'/'castrating bitch' images that long have defamed black women in our literature." "All about Eva," *New York Times Book Review*, 16 May 1976, 37.

6. Loyle Hairston calls *Eva's Man* an "awful little book" and interprets it as "a study in male hostility." "Repelling World of Sexual Violence," *Freedomways* 16 (Second Quarter 1976): 133. Though less judgmental than many reviewers, Darryl Pinckney also concludes that "Gayl Jones's novels are, finally, indictments against black men." Darryl Pinckney, review of *Eva's Man*, *New Republic*, 19 June 1976, 27.

7. W. Lawrence Hogue, *Discourse and the Other: The Production of the Afro- American Text* (Durham: Duke University Press, 1986), 5.

8. Ibid., 3.

9. Ibid., 6.

10. African American theorists and critics who have pointed out the exclusionary nature of American literary study and have offered alternative theories of literature include Robert Stepto, *From behind the Veil* (Urbana: University of Illinois Press, 1979); Houston A. Baker, Jr., *Blues Ideology and Afro-American Literature; A Vernacular Theory* (Chicago: University of Chicago Press, 1984); Henry Louis Gates, Jr., *The Signifying Monkey. A Theory of Afro-American Literary Criticism* (New York: Oxford University Press, 1988); and Michael Awkward, "Race, Gender, and the Politics of Reading," *Black American Literature Forum* 22, no. 1 (1988): 5–27. African American feminist theorists and critics who have pointed out the exclusionary nature of both mainstream literary study and the male bias of African American study include Barbara Christian, *Black Women Novelists: Development of a Tradition* (Westport, CT: Greenwood Press, 1980); Gloria T. Hull, Patricia Bell-Scott, and Barbara Smith, eds., *All the Women Are White, All the Blacks Are Men, But Some of Us Are Brave* (New York: Feminist Press, 1982); Deborah E. McDowell, "New Directions for Black Feminist Criticism," *Black American Literature Forum* 14, no. 4 (1980): 153–73; idem, "Boundaries: Or Distant Relations and Close Kin," in *Afro-American Literary Study in the 1990s*, ed. Houston A. Baker, Jr. and Patricia Redmond (Chicago: University of Chicago Press, 1989); and Nellie McKay, "Reflections on Black Women Writers: Revising the Literary Canon," in *Feminisms*, ed. Robyn R. Warhol and Diane Price Herndl (New Brunswick: Rutgers University Press, 1991).

11. Barbara Herrnstein Smith, *Contingencies of Value: Alternative Perspectives for Critical Theory* (Cambridge: Harvard University Press, 1988), 11.

12. By "social positioning," I am referring to how one's race, gender, class, and sexuality affect one's speaking position through degrees of privilege and/or marginality.

13. Mary Helen Washington, ed., *Black-Eyed Susans/Midnight Birds: Stories by and about Black Women* (New York: Anchor Press/Doubleday, 1990), 15.

14. Hogue, 55.

15. Madhu Dubey, *Black Women Novelists and the Nationalist Aesthetic* (Bloomington: Indiana University Press, 1994), 12.

16. Ibid., 15.

17. Smith, 40.

18. Jones uses this term while discussing her graduate study at Brown, where she had "time to write" and a "first reader" whom she admired and trusted. Charles H. Rowell, "An Interview with Gayl Jones," *Callaloo* 5, no. 3 (1982): 53.

19. The interview with Jones was conducted for inclusion in Michael S. Harper and Robert B. Stepto, eds., *Chant of Saints: A Gathering of Afro-American Literature, Art, and Scholarship* (Chicago: University of Illinois Press, 1979). The anthology initially appeared in two issues of the *Massachusetts Review* in the fall and winter of 1977.

20. Claudia C. Tate, "An Interview with Gayl Jones," *Black American Literature Forum* 13, no. 4 (1979): 142.

21. Ibid.

22. In discussing the chronology of Jones's publications, Bell misnames one of Jones's works as a novel: "Since the interview was conducted, she has published a second novel, *Eva's Man*, and a third, *Almeyda*, as well as a collection of short stories called *White Rat*." Roseann P. Bell, "Gayl Jones Takes a Look at *Corregidora*," in *Sturdy Black Bridges: Visions of Black Women in Literature*, ed. Roseann P. Bell, Bettye J. Parker, and Beverly Guy-Sheftall (Garden City, NY: Anchor Press, 1979), 282. Excerpts from a longer work appeared in *Chant of Saints* under the title of "Almeyda." The work was an early version of *Palmares*, which Jones had told Claudia Tate in 1978 would be published soon as a novel, but which appeared in 1981 in the form of a long poem, *Song for Anninho*.

23. Jefferson's review of *Eva's Man* ends with a comment by Jefferson about Jones's writing style and personal reticence: "Gayl Jones writes rapidly and obsessively: she has completed two more novels and is at work on a fifth. She will not discuss it, which is just as well. Her imagination seems to thrive on outstripping one's expectations." Margo Jefferson, "A Woman Alone," *Newsweek*, 12 April 1976, 107.

24. Jones names five works that she had written but not published at the time of the interview: *Palmares* (a "straight dramatic novel" from which *Song for Anninho* was adapted), a collection of short stories called *The Straw Woman*, a novel in which the main character is named after the Brazilian trickster turtle Jaboti, a novel titled *The Birdcatcher*, and a work (the genre is unspecified) titled *The Stone Dragon*.

25. Tate, 148.

26. Rowell, 40.

27. Gayl Jones, "About My Work," in *Black Women Writers (1950–1980): A Critical Evaluation*, ed. Mari Evans (Garden City, NY: Anchor-Doubleday, 1984), 235.

28. Mae Gwendolyn Henderson uses the phrase "ambiguously (non)hegemonic" to describe the discursive status of both white women, a group privileged by race and oppressed by gender, and black men, a group privileged by gender, and oppressed by race. It seems an appropriate description of the status of white feminist reviewers and black nationalist reviewers of *Eva's Man* in the 1970s.

29. Rowell, 33.

30. Tate, 143.

31. Susan J. Hekman, *Gender and Knowledge: Elements of a Postmodern Feminism* (Boston: Northeastern University Press, 1990), 73.

32. Ibid.

33. Gayl Jones, *Eva's Man* (New York: Random House, 1976), 7–8. Subsequent references to this work are included parenthetically in the text.

34. Michel Foucault, *The History of Sexuality: An Introduction* (New York: Vintage Books, 1990), 59.

35. Ibid., 63.

36. Ibid., 61.

37. Ibid., 27.

38. Ibid.

39. Hogue is adapting Foucault's concept of discursive relations as developed in *The Archaeology of Knowledge*. Hogue says that in a literary text, certain discursive facts are repeated "with the intention of generating what Foucault calls an 'enunciation'—the object or statement of discourse—within the text" (67).

40. Tate, 146.

41. The sexual discourse of the men universalizes all women into whores, but Eva maintains a sense of individual female subjectivity in her descriptions of the women she has known. Even though her mother's infidelity is treated by her father as whore-like behavior—"Act like a whore, I'm gonna fuck you like a whore" (37)—and Alphonso and his wife act out a beating ritual for Jean's infidelity, Eva distinguishes between behavior and identity—she says that Freddy's mother, a prostitute, was the only whore she ever knew.

42. Keith Byerman, "Black Vortex: The Gothic Structure of *Eva's Man*," *MELUS* 7 (1980): 95.

43. The significance of Eva's action is "unheard" by her family: her mother infantilizes her—"I thought it was a play knife, Mama said . . if she'd known it was a real knife she would have taken it away from me"; her father interprets her as passive and incapable of action—"Daddy said it all didn't sound like Eva"; and her cousin contends that Eva must have been physically violated—"Alphonso said Moses must've done something to me, but they gave me this test, and couldn't find that he'd done anything" (98–99). Eva refuses to say why she stabbed Moses Tripp, even to her family, because they too already have her limited to certain categories.

44. In "About My Work," Jones briefly discusses the theme that recurs in her writing—the complexity of the intersection of racism and sexism: "In terms of personal/private relationships I suppose I'm more besieged as a woman. In terms of public/social relationships I suppose I'm more besieged as a Black. Being both, it's hard to sometimes distinguish the occasion for being 'besieged' " (234).

45. Jones creates an equally interesting play with gender roles and gender performance when Alphonso points out a transvestite to Eva: "You see that bitch over there? That ain't really no bitch, that's a bastard. Dress up like a woman and then come in here. Shit. He don't bother the men that knows him. Most of us know what he is. He just pick up on the men that don't. Most of the ones that hang around here don't fool with him. Sometimes she makes pickups, drunks or strangers. They find out right quick, though. They start messing around her. Naw, I don't even git drunk when I come in here, cause I know how I do when I'm drunk. I wouldn't get mixed up with that bastard for nothing. Wake up the next morning and find *his* wig in my face. Shit" (78–79). The literal cross-dressing and linguistic slippage between gender pronouns signify the instability of gender as a fixed identity. Judith Butler notes that the notion of a primary gender identity is parodied through such performative acts as drag and cross-dressing: "As much as drag creates a unified picture of 'woman' (what its [feminist] critics often oppose), it also reveals the distinctness of those aspects of gendered experience which are falsely naturalized as a unity through the regulatory fiction of heterosexual coherence. In imitating gender, drag implicitly reveals the imitative

structure of gender itself." Judith Butler, "Gender Trouble, Feminist Theory, and Psychoanalytic Discourse," in *Feminism/Postmodernism*, ed. Linda Nicholson (New York: Routledge, 1990), 338.

46. Keith Byerman, *Fingering the Jagged Grain: Tradition and Form in Recent Black Fiction* (Athens: University of Georgia Press, 1985), 184.

47. Ibid.

48. Michel Foucault, *Madness and Civilization: A History of Insanity in the Age of Reason* (New York: Pantheon Books, 1965), x-xi.

49. Jana Sawicki, *Discipling Foucault: Feminism, Power, and the Body* (New York: Routledge, 1991), 32.

50. Ibid., 28.

51. In the concluding chapter of *Madness and Civilization*, Foucault suggests that our only confrontation with madness, since the rise of the psychiatric profession, comes through aesthetic representations and that "by the madness which interrupts it, a work of art opens a void, a moment of silence, a question without answer, provokes a breach without reconciliation where the world is forced to question itself" (288).

52. Dubey, 89.

53. The interpretive communities who reviewed *Eva's Man* were particularly disturbed by Jones's use of sexual stereotypes as well as her textual representations of black men. Jones's editor at Random House, Toni Morrison, said that publishing *Eva's Man* was an "editorial risk" because of the similarities between Jones's two novels. Morrison said she considered the possibility that readers might say that all of Jones's books were "about women tearing up men" (qtd. in Keith Mano, "How to Write Two First Novels with Your Knuckles," *Esquire* [December 1976]: 66). In the 1978 interview, after the initial furor over *Eva's Man*, Claudia Tate asks Jones to explain why she used three pervasive symbols— queen bee, Medusa, and Eve biting the apple—that have been "very detrimental to men in our cultural history" (146). Jones explains that she "put those images in the story to show how myths or ways in which men perceive women actually define their characters" (146). In the 1982 interview with Charles Rowell, Jones says that she has come to see sex, as subject matter, problematic for African American writers "because when you write about anything dealing with sexuality it appears as if you're supporting the sexual stereotypes about blacks" (47). As a counter to the negative criticism about Jones's use of stereotypes, Madhu Dubey contends that attention to the formal elements of Jones's fiction reveal that rather than reinscribing the stereotype of the primitive black, Jones is deconstructing stereotypes that represent black identity: "*Eva's Man* repeats and recycles a limited number of sexual stereotypes in a stylized manner that forces us to regard black sexuality as a textual fabrication rather than a natural essence" (95).

54. Deborah E. McDowell's *Black Women Writers Series* published *Corregidora* in 1986 and *Eva's Man* in 1987 through Beacon Press, while Northeastern University Press published a paperback edition of *White Rat* in 1991.

FOUR

"The Ballad of the Sad Café" and Other Stories of Women's Wartime Labor

Charles Hannon

When they first peered from behind the shutter of the second-floor window of the Sad Café, Amelia Evans's "two gray crossed eyes" were met by those of a wartime readership of middle- and upper-class women.[1] This readership was accustomed to stories in which a woman's labor responsibilities were the reverse of what they had been a decade before, and practiced in understanding this reversal as a temporary phenomenon of a wartime economy. American women of the 1940s might have identified with Amelia, whose professional success during the absence of her husband Marvin Macy corresponded with the developing myth of their own wartime fortunes. But Amelia's refusal to submit to her husband after his return contradicted both the promise and premise of postwar household consumerism displayed in other wartime fiction, and in the product advertisements and wartime announcements that appeared on the same pages of the August 1943 *Harper's Bazaar* as Carson McCullers's "The Ballad of the Sad Café."

This contradiction suggests two readings of Amelia's isolation after the demise of her café. In the first (and most familiar), Amelia's resistance to the "normalization" of labor, gender, and sexuality after her husband's return makes her a freakish, "grotesque" character, a frightening prophecy for readers unwilling to cooperate with the return to a masculinist economy after the war.[2] The market for women's labor did contract following the armistice, and it will be a simple matter to show how

"Ballad" would have struck McCullers's editor as a useful demonstration of thrift and resourcefulness as patriotic virtues temporarily required of American women. A second reading, however, would explore Amelia's parlor-exile as a private space of resistance to the ideological pressures that imposed monogamous heterosexuality as the primary model of peacetime labor under a capitalist mode of production. Certainly our knowledge of McCullers's personal disavowal of a feminine, heterosexual identity induces us to consider a horizon beyond which the temporariness of women's wartime labor opportunities does not necessarily translate into temporariness with regard to gender and sexual freedom.

The horizon posited by McCullers's story requires a distinction between "official" and "practical" consciousness, which was suggested by Gramsci as a model for individual agency, but rejected by Althusser in his concepts of interpellation and economic determination.³ Marxist-feminist critics have sought to revise Althusser's concept of the subjected subject, always already constituted or hailed by official ideological structures, by reconceptualizing subject-formation according to a psychoanalytic rather than economic model, and thus positing the space of Desire as one in which oppositional subjectivities might be more successfully engendered.⁴ In Žižek's interpretation of Lacan, Desire is the site "of an original 'trauma', an impossible kernel which resists symbolization, totalization, symbolic integration"—resists, that is, reduction to anything like a permanent narrative of subject-formation.⁵ The Žižekian "Real" suggests a realm in which there is a constant slippage between Desire and the subjectivity formed at any given moment of narrativization. This is not to suggest that Althusserian analyses of subject-formation must be replaced by the psychoanalytic. Rather, a paratactic relation between the economic and psychoanalytic models must be pursued. By recuperating Desire into the Althusserian narrative of interpellation, one releases Althusser from the fatalism of economic overdetermination, and opens to the subject a space of self-determination that is relatively autonomous from the social formation's "official" consciousnesses.⁶

A commercial magazine—such as the wartime issue of *Harper's Bazaar* in which "Ballad" was first published—forms the ideal field for this conceptual parataxis, because while it attempts to perform its official function of interpellating women as wartime laborers and postwar wives/consumers, it verifies Desire as an irreducible realm of oppositional subjectivity and practical resistance. Magazines are a portion of the communication-Ideological State Apparatuses (ISAs) that Althusser posits, along with Repressive State Apparatuses (RSAs) such as the military, the prison system, and the police, as the primary machinery of ideological reproduction.[7] Whereas RSAs use physical violence to reproduce the ideological needs of the social formation, communication-ISAs maintain "relative autonomy" with regard to other social structures, and operate primarily through ideology.[8] For Althusser, even these spaces of relative autonomy are determined by the economic "in the last instance."[9] In a strictly Althusserian analysis, therefore, McCullers's resistance to hetero-sexual norms of labor, gender, and sexuality in "Ballad" would have to be read as the expression of an interpellated subjectivity, since in 1943 such reversals were encouraged by wartime America's temporary manufactur-ing and military needs. Moreover, in this reading "Ballad" would be said to interpellate McCullers's readers—primarily women whose self-identification as workers was required by the state—by offering them, "as the position from which the text is most 'obviously' intelligible," the position of an interpellated wartime laborer.[10] While private magazines do seek to impose official consciousness in this manner, they also give voice to what Terry Eagleton has discussed as the "performative contra-diction" in Gramsci, which ascribes agency to subjects acting within official structures but at cross-purposes with official ideology.[11] To as-cribe Gramscian agency to McCullers, then, will require interpreting "Ballad" as an interventionary text that disrupts official ideology by looking beyond the immediate moment of its production, by cautioning women against the normalization of labor, gender, and sexuality certain to be imposed following the war.

Although the vicissitudes of Amelia's labor in the café correlate with specific propaganda policies of the Office of War Information that were communicated to magazine editors in the fall of 1943, her refusal to relinquish her status as an economic agent upon her husband's return is a clear act of resistance to labor policies that would reinstate a masculinist bias once the male labor force returned. Similarly, while the town toler-ates Amelia's masculinity as long as it is obviously a substitute for the phallic power of her absent husband, she must fight to retain her mascu-line gender identity after his return, and this act of resistance has obvious implications for both McCullers and her readers.[12] Finally, although Amelia's desire for Lymon, and Macy's rejection of him, seemingly re-produce the official, compulsory heterosexuality of pre- and postwar

America, a gender-conscious analysis of their respective relationships will reveal the instability of this reading—will, in fact, indicate McCullers's radical critique of heterosexuality's foundational premises. "Ballad" simply refuses to participate in the inscription of heterosexuality as a postwar norm, and even when heterosexuality is figured, it is always "undone" by homosexual desire. If Desire is not a realm that is ultimately apart from the determining forces of the economic or social (as it appears McCullers would wish it to be), it is at least a realm of excess where these forces are vulnerable and inefficacious.[13]

The full force of McCullers's model of practical resistance will be apparent only if we first recuperate the historical subtext of the pages of *Harper's Bazaar*, where Amelia's eyes called the attention of wartime women away from advertisers' promises of postwar femininity within a heterosexual, consumerist household, and into her own story of resistance and opposition.

RSAS, ISAS, AND IDEOLOGICAL REPRODUCTION

During World War II, an ideological accommodation was instituted between the material needs of the state and the cultural products of America's private magazine industry. As Maureen Honey has shown, one manifestation of this accommodation was the popular image of middle-class women as patriots willing to leave the domestic sphere to work in military and industrial factories.[14] The development of this image was accomplished through the collaboration of private and government agencies.

In 1944, for instance, the privately organized War Advertising Council (WAC) and the Roosevelt administration's Office of War Information (OWI) collaborated to promote a national campaign called "Women in the War." The OWI advised advertisers of its particular labor needs related to the war effort, and the WAC asked private advertisers to devote a percentage of their advertisements to the theme of working women. The WAC went so far as to distribute booklets with sample advertisements and outlines for possible use by advertisers (*CRR*, 34). The government benefited from the resulting solidification of popular support for the war, and the uninterrupted production of necessary military and industrial goods. Advertisers, in turn, benefited from the linkage of private industry with national security (particularly important given the widespread skepticism with which industry was regarded since the early 1930s), and through the development of a propaganda mechanism through which women could be encouraged, after the war, to leave the factories and become reliable household consumers (see fig. 1).

We should recognize this symbiosis between private and public institutions as the aftereffect of ideological reproduction, a relatively straightforward example of "mechanical" causality. Functioning as an agency of the military—an institution at the top of Althusser's list of RSAs—the OWI collaborated with representatives of the magazine industry to cause

FIG. 1. "Mother, when will you stay home again?" ADEL Precision Products Corp., *Saturday Evening Post*, 6 May 1944. Reprinted by permission of TransDigm, Inc.

private magazine advertisements to represent forces and relations of production favorable to the needs of both government and industry. Advertising executives, however, were only one mechanism by which the production needs of the state were reproduced in the popular media during World War II. Honey demonstrates that fiction editors were just as likely to be guided by the war effort. In June 1942 the OWI established a Magazine Bureau, whose officers "took an active role in ascertaining the publicity needs of war agencies, information about which was then sent out as suggestions for specific stories to individual writers" (*CRR*, 37). By July, the OWI was publishing the *Magazine War Guide*, a monthly serial communicating the government's wartime requirements to magazine editors, and suggesting plots for magazine fiction that would encourage women to meet those requirements. The Magazine Bureau was particularly effective in a fall 1943 campaign called "Women in Necessary Services," which was motivated by the OWI's concern that women were entering high-profile industries at the expense of "service, trade, and supply industries" (*CRR*, 39). As part of this campaign, the *Guide* suggested that editors publish stories that attached patriotic values to jobs perceived as menial or unimportant. In a follow-up survey, the bureau discovered that "146 magazines with a total circulation of more than eighty-seven million had elected to participate in the fall promotion by August 1943" (*CRR*, 41).

Again, it would seem that the ideological needs of the state were reproduced rather mechanically in the popular images of women in magazine fiction. Wartime fiction interpellated women as subjects who could recognize themselves in the revised relations of labor and gender necessary to maintain the war effort and the economy. In important ways, "Ballad" intervenes in this process of ideological reproduction, but before detailing its mode of intervention, we should recognize those elements of McCullers's story that would have satisfied Mary Lou Aswell, literary editor of *Harper's Bazaar* in 1943, as coinciding with the guidelines established by the OWI. Although the *Magazine War Guide* requested editors to publish fiction involving women in wartime industries, such a backdrop was not necessary: "Fiction stories which are written *war-mindedly*," read the guidelines of a 1943 campaign called "Toughening up for War," "even when dealing with non-war subjects, stories that accept the changed standards of living that war creates as part of the 'color' and 'background' of the stories, are particularly valuable, as many magazines have already proved" (qtd. in *CRR*, 53). Of particular value in such stories were women characters who exhibited the values of thrift, economy, and self-sufficiency, and these were just the traits Aswell might have found in the primary character of "Ballad." "With all things which could be made by the hands Miss Amelia prospered" (5), McCullers's narrator tells us. In a single, early paragraph we are introduced to Amelia through her skills at butchering, canning, curing, milling, carpentering, moonshining, doctoring, and even lawyering. Within the context of the OWI's guidelines, Amelia's self-sufficiency exemplified traits called for in the July issue of *Harper's Bazaar*, in such articles as "Women in Men's Jobs— Civilian" and "You Certainly Can Can." [15]

Moreover, as a Jane-of-all-trades, Amelia would have been a useful model for the fall 1943 "Women in Necessary Services" campaign, in which nonindustry jobs were celebrated as "vital national service" (*CRR*, 40). For this campaign, the *Magazine War Guide* for June-July 1943 requested editors to publish fiction in which women find self-fulfillment "behind counters in food or other vitally necessary stores . . . or perhaps acting as community leaders in solving local problems" (qtd. in *CRR*, 40). Amelia's café is an example of a nonindustry, yet necessary, service the OWI would have wanted promoted in these campaigns, and in the absence of the hypermasculine Macy, both the café and Amelia's other businesses thrive. Amelia sues less, doctors more, and moonshines better than ever. "The café itself proved profitable," the narrator says, "and was the only place of pleasure for miles around" (24). Obvious signs of expansion appear about Amelia's property, including a literal sign reading "CAFE" (38), fans to cool off customers, and a "new and bigger condenser for her still" (45). In addition to providing necessary, nonindustry services such as medical treatment and financial advice and assistance, Amelia's work boosts the morale of local mill workers who otherwise would have no place to socialize, no sense of community or common purpose: "the company was polite" on the café's first night, "for people in this town were then unused to gathering together for the sake of pleasure. They met to work in the mill" (22).

The café closes down after Macy's return, however, and it is possible that this too would have seemed natural to McCullers's editor, as an expression of the necessarily temporary demand for women's labor. Once Macy returns, Amelia ruins the café by pricing everything at one dollar. Her doctoring abilities evaporate, and her practice loses all its customers.

She secludes herself after her loss in the fistfight with Macy, diminishing to a single face, "sexless and white, with two gray crossed eyes which are turned inward so sharply that they seem to be exchanging with each other one long and secret gaze of grief" (3–4). Suggesting the sexist stereotype used against women who refused to leave the workplace and embrace a domestic, dependent lifestyle, the narrator says "the great muscles of her body shrank until she was thin as old maids are thin when they go crazy" (70).

The representation of wartime labor and gender politics in "Ballad" is based upon a series of substitutions, which must now be enumerated. In the first, Macy "stands in" phallically for all healthy male figures. As he is first described by the narrator, Macy exudes youthfulness, strength, and masculine proprietorship: "Marvin Macy was the handsomest man in this region—being six feet one inch tall, hard-muscled, and with slow gray eyes and curly hair . . . he needed to bow and scrape to no one and always got just what he wanted" (27). Macy's stereotypical masculinity, moreover, is enhanced by the age and relative infirmity of the town's other male inhabitants. Not coincidentally, since McCullers wanted to emphasize the untraditionally masculine appearance of Amelia, the above description might easily be applied to her. Therefore, Amelia's ascendancy into the dominant (male) position following Macy's incarceration can be read allegorically as the general substitution of women's labor for men's in the wartime economy.

A second substitution, based upon an equivalence between prisons and the military, relates Macy's incarceration to the wartime conscription of males in a more fundamental way. Althusser arranges both the prisons and the army under the category Repressive State Apparatuses. "Repressive," Althusser writes, "suggests that the State Apparatus in question 'functions by violence'—at least ultimately (since repression, e.g. administrative repression, may take non-physical forms)."[16] Unlike the ISAs, which are private, ideological, and relatively heterogeneous, the RSA is public, unified, and *disciplined*, in the Foucauldian sense of marking its purposes and requirements upon the individual body. Under this substitution, the chain gang that appears sporadically throughout "Ballad," and the song wafting from its laborers on the Forks Falls Road are traces of the repressive state that can display its power equally in peacetime (in the prisons) as in war (in the army). The common ground between the prisons and the military is therefore absence: just as the state can require the service of its male population in a time of war, it can command Macy's absence from the town for a period of time arbitrarily chosen to compensate for his crimes.

Moreover, Macy's love-hate relationship with Amelia can be read as a relay of the antiwoman rhetoric that attended the construction of masculinity in wartime propaganda. Sandra Gilbert and Susan Gubar have shown how wartime propaganda separated women from the homosocial sphere of the military and portrayed them as both the cause and the spoils of war. Antiwar posters and political drawings symbolized war as a whore seducing virgin soldiers; while even more ambivalently, the military portrayed women both as desired objects to be defended from aggressor-enemies, and as syphilitic threats to be avoided and feared by servicemen.[17] Wartime propaganda thus consecrated "bonds between men in a manner which isolated women," which made women insufficient love objects for men seeking confirmation of their masculinity.[18] During and after the war, women writers responded to this "blitz on women" by representing both fascism and Allied militarism as "a logical extension of misogyny."[19] In McCullers's story, the effects of antiwoman constructions of masculinity are represented in Macy's return from the homosocial environment of the prison and his subsequent aggressiveness toward both Amelia and Lymon.

"THE BALLAD OF THE SAD CAFÉ"
REPRODUCTION *AND* RESISTANCE

Propagating wartime opportunities for women laborers but also projecting "inevitable" postwar restrictions, "Ballad" can be read as reproducing propaganda from the OWI and elsewhere that interpellated wartime women as subjects who could value themselves as temporary sources of productive labor, but hate themselves as the cause of war and conflict in the first place. McCullers's story also resists this reading, however, by insisting upon the extension of women's freedom and economic opportunity beyond the war years. Following Macy's return, Amelia does not passively surrender her proprietorship of the café, and the implications of her resistance must be considered. Beyond her demand that women retain their economic agency after the return of the male labor force, however, McCullers sets forth an argument against the ultimate determination by economic forces of women's gender and sexual identities. In

Macy's absence, the town is unusually tolerant of Amelia's and Lymon's unconventional gender performances; for McCullers's readers, to whom the analogous permissiveness of the wartime context was both familiar and advantageous, Amelia's active resistance to Macy's attempts, following his return, to beat submissiveness into her and masculinity into Lymon would have had specific implications. Finally, McCullers's various representations of sexuality, based closely in her own conflicted experience with her husband, Reeves, and the woman she desired, Annemarie Clarac-Schwarzenbach, assert her objection to manufacturers' fantasies of a fully heterosexualized postwar America, and detail her own counter-fantasy of a postwar culture in which Desire is removed from the interpellative mechanisms of the social.

Despite the parallel between the rise and fall of Amelia's café and the fluctuation in the market for women's labor during and after the war, we should not ignore Amelia's real efforts to resist the "inevitability" of Macy's return, and therefore McCullers's opposition to the shift in American labor policy implied in so many of the womanpower campaigns of 1943–44. Unlike the woman in an advertisement for undergarments appearing in the same issue of *Harper's Bazaar* as "Ballad," who knows that "someday we'll all be lounging again" (see fig. 2), Amelia will not allow Macy to appropriate the café and pocket her rightful profits. Instead, following his return she calls a strike of one, closing down both the café and the community. Now, the narrator tells us, "there is no good liquor to be bought in the town . . . . There is absolutely nothing to do in the town. Walk around the millpond, stand kicking at a rotten stump, figure out what you can do with the old wagon wheel by the side of the road near the church. The soul rots with boredom" (71). Here McCullers's resistance consists of the articulation of a caution to women against men's plans to reclaim their positions of economic dominance after the war, as well as a proposal for organized, possibly preemptive protest.

The expansion of the labor market for women during the war coincided with an easing of restrictions concerning a woman's public appearance and communal participation. Women were performing "men's jobs," and therefore were relatively free of the sartorial restrictions of previously rigid gender categories. Lilian Faderman, for one, has shown how this easing of restrictions encouraged butch women to wear pants and cut their hair as they pleased, with decreased likelihood of violent, heterosexist reaction.[20] The wartime loosening of gender categories is figured in

FIG. 2. "This *was* me . . . Just look at me *now!*" Industrial Rayon Corp., *Harper's Bazaar*, August 1943. Reprinted by permission of Forstman Little & Co.

McCullers's story in several ways. Whereas the town had once been scandalized by Amelia's mannishness—her unusual height, her short hair, and her "bones and muscles like a man" (4)—it learns, during Macy's absence, to revere her powerful difference. And whereas Morris Feinstein's "prissiness" (and probably his Jewishness) had precipitated a "calamity" and then his expulsion from the town years before, Lymon, himself proclaimed a "Morris Feinstein" upon his first appearance, is accepted and eventually celebrated for his outlandish gender performances.

But the town's ready approval of a café operated by a masculine woman and a feminine man is threatened with disruption once Macy returns. Macy is quick to cuff Lymon for attempting to seduce him with eye glances and dance moves (50), and immediately after Macy's arrival, Amelia "put aside her overalls and wore always the red dress she had before this time reserved for Sundays, funerals, and sessions of court" (53). The narrator underscores this brief surrender to the polarization of gender according to a heterosexual paradigm as Amelia's great mistake: "Miss Amelia seemed to have lost her will; for the first time in her life she hesitated as to just what course to pursue" (53–54). But it is possible that Amelia's donning of her one dress is not a submission to Macy's reintroduction of a heterosexual order, but rather what Judith Butler would call a subversive repetition of that order, a way of bringing "into relief the utterly constructed status of the so-called heterosexual original."[21] Employing a number of strategies to combat the assumed consequences of Macy's return upon women's gender identities, Amelia eventually exchanges her dress for her old overalls, "rolled up to the knees" (66), and fights Macy for the right to maintain her hard-earned sense of self. Like her refusal to relinquish her claim to the economy, Amelia's insistence upon defining her own gender identity would therefore suggest another model of resistance to McCullers's readers.

Amelia's resistance appears more forcefully when viewed upon the same pages as advertisements promising a return to femininity after the war. In addition to the themes of "womanpower" and "necessary services" suggested by the OWI through the *Magazine War Guide*, the advertisements in *Harper's Bazaar* at the end of summer 1943 are obsessed with protecting a feminine identity for American women despite the temporary necessity of their performing masculine labor. Thus an advertisement for lipstick that appears in the same issue as McCullers's story celebrates, "as a reflection of the free democratic way of life," the idea that American women "have succeeded in keeping your femininity — even though you are doing man's work!" (see fig. 3). In a medium focused on the femininity of America's working women, McCullers's narrative of an "Amazonian" woman making the most of her masculine traits — and resisting any opportunity to exchange them for a more traditional gender role — introduces an enormous ideological contradiction.

This contradiction can be observed in a brief contrast between McCullers's Amazon and the best-known Amazonian heroine of the

FIG. 3. "War, Women and Lipstick." Tangee Lipsticks advertisement, *Harper's Bazaar*, August 1943.

1940s, National Comics' Wonder Woman. Created by psychologist William Moulton Marston in 1941, *Wonder Woman Comics* began publication in the summer of 1942 with plots closely related to the war, often pitting Wonder Woman against leaders of the Axis powers. Many of the themes of the OWI's womanpower campaigns can be seen in the early issues of *Wonder Woman*. In issue 2, for instance, Wonder Woman agrees to box Mussolini's giant, Mammotha, but only if the latter's Italian handler agrees to divide the proceeds, whoever wins, between the USO and the Red Cross.[22] Unlike McCullers's Amazon, however, who is obstinate in her masculinity, Moulton's Amazonian superhero is superfeminine. Decked out in a tiara, bracelets, and high-heeled boots, Wonder Woman is constantly pursued as an object of male heterosexual desire. "My beautiful Angel!" exclaims Major Steve Trevor in the final panel of the issue referred to above, "Why must you leave me? Your work is done since the god of war is destroyed—." Wonder Woman's answer, of course, is that a patriotic woman's work is never done when the nation is at war—but that is no excuse, insists the underlying message, for a woman to neglect her femininity. According to Honey, this message grew ubiquitous as the womanpower campaigns developed, to overcome fears that performing men's labor would detract from the femininity of American women:

A good example of [the OWI's] suggested treatment is a sample one-minute announcement advertising WAVES intended for radio stations as part of the "Women in the War" campaign. The male announcer assures listeners that servicewomen are not masculine: "The girls in the WAVES are real American women—the kind who love parties and pretty clothes, and who are good at cooking and sewing too. They're very feminine, and proud of it." (CRR, 113–14)

Wonder Woman might be determined to battle fascism alongside the forces of democracy, but the ideology of the time asked that she remember to check her face beforehand (see figs. 4 and 5).

Unlike McCullers or Amelia, Wonder Woman responded willingly to the ideological call to protect and maintain her femininity even when performing officially masculine duties. Wonder Woman's heterosexual allure helped construct a uniform and patriotic femininity that would be desirable to ex-servicemen working in factories and offices, who were themselves bombarded with messages to marry a "real" woman (in the language of the WAVES announcement), buy a house on time, and start furnishing it with durable goods.[23] Since it is clear that Amelia's insistent masculinity would have grated against advertisers' smooth image of postwar feminine women, McCullers's additional contemplation of lesbian and homosexual desire in "Ballad" must have disrupted their equally ubiquitous fantasy of a heterosexual, consumerist paradise following the armistice. Far from reproducing the heterosexual dreamland depicted in wartime advertisements, the sexual tensions and attractions between Amelia, Lymon, and Macy imagine Desire as a site of resistance to the processes of interpellation that would produce a heterosexual identity for all.

It is possible that the town knowingly enters into Amelia and Lymon's

FIGS. 4 and 5. *Wonder Woman Comics #2—"Great Comic Book Heroes"* Copyright © 1965 DC Comics. All rights reserved.

heterosexual charade, since everybody seems to know that "Miss Amelia cared nothing for the love of men" (4), and since Lymon hardly conceals his preference for other men. On the café's first night, Lymon "got his bearings in an odd manner. He regarded each person steadily at his own eye-level, which was about belt line for an ordinary man. Then with shrewd deliberation he examined each man's lower regions—from the waist to the sole of the shoe" (18). Lymon "cruises" the men at the café, "asking questions such as if a man was married, how old he was, how much his wages came to in an average week, et cetera—picking his way along to inquiries which were downright intimate" (20). Both Lymon's effeminate personality and his occupation of what, in a heterosexual economy, would be a woman's position of desire vis à vis the men in the café, make him a suitable "feminine" love object for what may be Amelia's first awareness of her lesbianism or bisexuality. At the same time, Amelia's mannish appearance presents Lymon with a "masculine" object for his more overt homosexual desires. But what is most significant is the extent to which these "hidden" sexual desires completely displace any "normal" heterosexual narrative in McCullers's text, especially since the heterosexual narrative *was* played out so insistently in advertisements and other stories in magazines like *Harper's Bazaar*.

The town's tolerance of Amelia's café, which was "never so gay" (40) as when Lymon was around, could be a simple reflection of the increased (although hardly total) tolerance of gay culture during the war, which several historians have written about.[24] It is certainly true that McCullers's own sexuality developed more openly toward bisexuality during the early 1940s, when she first separated from her husband, Reeves. She first fell in love with another woman in 1940, when she met Annemarie Clarac-Schwarzenbach, but it was during her residence at the house of George Davis, editor of *Harper's Bazaar*, that McCullers was fully immersed in an environment that was tolerant of sexual difference. According to her biographer Virginia Carr, McCullers thought the atmosphere at 7 Middagh Street "campy," and Louis Untermeyer, a frequent visitor of the house's residents (George Davis, W. H. Auden, Gypsy Rose Lee, and McCullers—what Untermeyer called "that queer aggregate of artists"), recalled to Carr at least one "gay (in both senses of the word) occasion at which Auden and Gypsy Rose Lee were present."[25] In the same way that Macy's temporary absence from the town allows Amelia to explore latent desires sparked by Lymon's effeminacy, then, McCullers's separation from Reeves during her residence at 7 Middagh introduced her to an openness about sexuality that had been missing from her earlier life.[26]

Her attraction to other women was a constant threat to Reeves, but Carr dismisses the possibility that he took the advice of a friend to "go see those females and tell them to get the hell out of your wife's life—and then pop 'em in the jaw if necessary."[27] This violent response to what Reeves's friend understood as an insult to Reeves's masculinity does seem to motivate Macy's aggressive behavior toward both Amelia and Lymon upon his return from prison, however. Projecting the postwar homophobia of American society, Macy bashes Lymon and tries to beat Amelia into submissiveness.

Nevertheless, the economies of desire McCullers constructs between Macy, Amelia, and Lymon eventually overwhelm the messages of compulsory heterosexuality in Macy's outward behavior. It is something of a mystery to the town that Macy would fall in love with Amelia when he can have his pick of all the women in the town, but his choice makes sense if we recognize her masculinity as the real object of his desire. Likewise, rather than rejecting homosexual desire in his repudiation of Lymon's advances, Macy may reject Lymon for not being masculine

enough, especially after his recent years of incarceration in the homosocial and hypermasculine environment of the prison. There is the added
possibility that the conspiratorial glance between Macy and Lymon upon
Macy's return suggests that the whole story of Lymon's kinship to Amelia
is a setup, hatched during their involvement with each other in prison
before Lymon's prior release. Certainly Lymon's alliance with Macy in
the fistfight with Amelia, and their subsequent fleeing together suggest a
close relationship between them, as do a number of cryptic hints inter-
spersed throughout McCullers's narrative—we are told, for instance, that
"sometimes they would be gone for hours together out in the swamp"
(56).[28] In sum, although the narrative structure of "Ballad" seemingly is
motivated by the conventional assumptions of a heterosexual love trian-
gle, McCullers actually takes every opportunity to disavow heterosexuality—by emphasizing the constructedness of its conventions, and by sub-
verting, through parody and exaggeration, its claim to represent a natural
or original order.

IDENTIFICATION AND DESIRE: LOOKING AT "THE BALLAD OF THE SAD CAFÉ"

By offering readers differently sexed and gendered subjectivities from
which its representations of desire would make sense, McCullers's story
undermined the "dominant fiction" of heterosexual femininity produced
by other wartime fiction and advertisements. Ironically, then, McCullers
utilized the same mechanisms of resignification that manufacturers used
to produce middle-class women as factory laborers and service personnel.
In the process, she made available to her readers gender/sexual identities
unintelligible within the exclusively heterosexual narrative produced by
wartime advertisers. I thus insist upon returning "Ballad" to the pages of
Harper's Bazaar, because the magazine apparatus—a site of economic
determinism for Althusser—provides such a useful bridge between
Gramscian agency and the Žižekian Real as the individual subject's irreducible kernel of resistance. I would not argue, as McCullers would
seem to wish to, that Desire is fully removed from society's official
consciousnesses. But it should be apparent, to paraphrase Althusser, that
the regulatory practices of the state cannot lay down the law within the
realm of Desire as effectively as it can in other regions.

We could say that McCullers competed with wartime advertisers over

the right to interpellate wartime women: like advertisers, McCullers re-
lied upon material and psychological mechanisms to produce subjectivities that wartime women could imagine themselves occupying after the
war. One locus of this competition would be the individual psyche undergoing re-interpellation and thus repeating the dialectic between identification and desire which, in the Lacanian narrative, propels an individual
into the symbolic world of subject/object relations. Whereas the advertisers' narrative of compulsory heterosexuality offered only a single combination of identification and desire to produce the official consciousnesses
necessary to their fantasies about the postwar economy, McCullers's
narrative disrupted this vision by making available multiple configurations of identification and desire. As I indicated in my introduction, the
excess identities produced by McCullers's narrative would have assisted
advertisers by making their temporary masculinization of women in the
womanpower campaigns of 1943–44 intelligible. However, I also want to
emphasize how McCullers's interventionary gesture was, in turn, made
more forceful by the magazine context, and in particular, by the advertisements alongside which her story appeared.

The masculinization of women in the womanpower campaigns was
accompanied by a simultaneous masculinization in women's fashion in
the early 1940s. Two fashion advertisements from the August and September 1943 *Harper's Bazaar* will illustrate this phenomenon (see figs. 6
and 7). Like many of the advertisements from these issues, the promo-
tional copy for a wool suit by Rosenblum announces that it is "man-
tailored every inch of the way." A similar masculinization is evident in
an advertisement for Swansdown coats, in which the photographer has
consciously manipulated the shadows cast by the model. The shadows,
in the form of classic male silhouettes, extend in two directions, as if to
accentuate the profile of the masculinized subject. Given the way today's
fashion industry plays upon conventional configurations of gender and
sexuality, these fashion photographs raise questions about how identification and desire operated within the context of the womanpower advertisements. How did advertisers expect women to consume these images,
and how did the presence of these images on the same pages of *Harper's
Bazaar* collaborate with McCullers's production of "unofficial" subjectivities?

Diana Fuss has posited a revision of the Lacanian narrative to explain
the disjunction between the presumably heterosexual market for today's

FIGS. 6 and 7. Fashion photographs from fall 1943. Swansdown coats, *Harper's Bazaar*, September 1943; Rosenblum suits, *Harper's Bazaar*, August 1943.

fashion magazines such as *Vogue*, *Elle*, *Glamour*, and *Cosmopolitan* and the formal construction of a lesbian subject position vis à vis the erotic images of women that appear in them. For Fuss, a heterosexual woman viewing an erotically charged image of a feminine model is momentarily homosexualized through the process of desire, while the process of identification produces or interpellates her as a subject who wishes to be desired by men. This "homosexualization" of the viewing position destabilizes "the grounds of a heterosexual identity formation" by undermining heterosexuality's claim to purity even as heterosexuality is reconstituted and secured.[29] Because fashion photography constructs an Other that women both desire and identify with, Fuss concludes that "heterosexuality, far from constituting itself through the simple sublimation of homosexuality, works through and by the dialectic of its continual activation and disavowal."[30] There is little reason to doubt that "desire operates *within* identification" in 1940s fashion photography also.[31] What, then, of those photographs that participated in the reversal of women's gender and labor identities as part of the wartime atmosphere?

Immediately we are confronted with a weakness in Fuss's model that she herself acknowledges: it assumes a viewer who has previously been produced as a heterosexual subject, an assumption McCullers consistently sought to undermine in her fiction. Moreover, the fashion photography Fuss analyzes always "models" a maternal/feminine identity for women, but women of the early 1940s were encouraged to identify with (and therefore also desire) women who had been masculinized through their dress and labor positioning. Recognizing these weaknesses in Fuss's model would enable us to interpret both the womanpower advertisements and the wartime fashion industry as temporarily producing subjects to whom McCullers's representations of gender and sexuality would seem perfectly natural. In other words, the effect of masculinization in these "official" revisions of women's subjectivity would have made it more possible for wartime women to identify with McCullers's representations of gender and sexuality. While many advertisers (and most wartime magazine fiction writers) resolved this ideological dilemma by positing a postwar return to the feminine/heterosexual ideal, McCullers insisted upon producing subjectivities from which this "normalization" would itself seem unnatural.

Implicitly, McCullers asked her readers to consider how Amelia would have consumed these images of masculinized women. How would Carson McCullers have consumed them, or Cousin Lymon? If it is impossible to map out the economy of identification and desire in each of these relations of gender and sexuality, is this not because Desire is a realm that is ultimately irreducible to narratives of interpellation based upon a heterosexual model? An analysis based solely upon the concept of economic determinism would resolve this dilemma by emphasizing the temporariness implicit in the masculinized images of wartime women. The possibility of same-sex desire leading in any permanent way to lesbian subject-formation would be contained, in this reading, by the advertisements' repeatedly emphasized "crisis" context. As I have argued, however, this movement to foreclose subversive subjectivity is itself contained by McCullers's proffering, through the narrative apparatus of her story, of a plurality of subjectivities—of multiple combinations of identification and desire—from which both her text and the womanpower advertisements are "obviously" intelligible. Based upon its own model of continual activation and disavowal, then, "The Ballad of the Sad Café" posits Desire as a realm of the psyche that, for practical purposes, is neither subject to nor the subject of official pronouncements upon the inevitability of heterosexual paradigms—of labor, gender, or sexuality.

NOTES

I would like to acknowledge Uma Satyavolu Rau, Carol Siegel, Lisa Walker, and an anonymous reader at *Genders* for their perceptive readings of early drafts of this essay.

1. Carson McCullers, "The Ballad of the Sad Café," in *The Ballad of the Sad Café and Other Stories* (1943; reprint, New York: Bantam Books, 1986), 3. Further references to this text are cited in parentheses. I cite this widely available edition of McCullers's stories because the text of "Ballad" in it is no different from that in the original *Harper's Bazaar* of August 1943.

2. Critics have followed the lead of Ihab Hassan ("Carson McCullers: The Alchemy of Love and Aesthetics of Pain," *Modern Fiction Studies* 5 [Winter 1959]: 311–26) in using 1951, the date of Houghton Mifflin's republication of "The Ballad of the Sad Café," as its original date of publication. Thus losing its wartime context, critics have tended to read Amelia's gender and sexual difference as evidence of McCullers's interest in the gothic and grotesque. For instance, Margaret Walsh has recently wondered "whether the dwarf [Lymon] represents the grotesque inner psychological life of Amelia." "Carson McCullers' Anti-Fairy Tale: 'The Ballad of the Sad Café,' " *Pembroke Magazine* 20 (1988): 48. For an attempt to liberate McCullers from the school of the grotesque, see Ann Carlton, "Beyond Gothic and Grotesque: A Feminist View of Three Female Characters in Carson McCullers," *Pembroke Magazine* 20 (1988): 63–71. And for a brief consideration of McCullers within a reconceptualization of the gothic as feminist discourse, see Claire Kahane, "The Gothic Mirror," in *The (M)other Tongue: Essays in Feminist Psychoanalytic Interpretation*, ed. Shirley Nelson Garner, Claire Kahane, and Madelon Sprengnether (Ithaca: Cornell University Press, 1985), 334–51.

3. I take these terms to describe the dualistic nature of Gramsci's concept of hegemony from Terry Eagleton, *Ideology: An Introduction* (New York: Verso, 1991), 36, 50.

4. For Althusser, "*all ideology hails or interpellates concrete individuals as concrete subjects*, by the functioning of the category of the subject." See Louis Althusser, "Ideology and Ideological State Apparatuses (Notes Towards an Investigation)," in *Lenin and Philosophy and Other Essays*, trans. Ben Brewster (New York: Monthly Review Press, 1971), 173. In her revision of the concept of interpellation, Catherine Belsey views subjects "perpetually in the process of construction, thrown into crisis by alterations in language and in the social formation, capable of change." *Critical Practice* (New York: Methuen, 1980), 65. Likewise, Judith Butler looks for "possibilities of resignification" in the "slippage between discursive command and its appropriated effect." *Bodies That Matter: On the Discursive Limits of "Sex"* (New York: Routledge, 1993), 123, 122.

5. Slavoj Zizek, *The Sublime Object of Ideology* (New York: Verso, 1989), 6.

6. Much of the project of recuperating Lacan's influence upon Althusser, and thus recognizing that "unconscious desire and identification do not always follow the trajectory delineated for them in advance" (2) by the social formation, was done by Kaja Silverman in *Male Subjectivity at the Margins* (New York: Routledge, 1992). For a "radical" critique of determination in the last instance by the economic, especially as this concept displaced Althusser's earlier concern with the psychoanalytic concept of overdetermination, see Ernesto Laclau and Chantal Mouffe, *Hegemony and Socialist Practice: Towards a Radical Democratic Politics* (New York: Verso, 1985), especially 97–99.

7. For the connection between Gramsci's hegemonic apparatuses and Althusser's Ideological State Apparatuses, see Christine Buci-Glucksmann, *Gramsci and the State*, trans. David Fernbach (London: Lawrence and Wishart, 1980), 63–69.

8. "The class (or class alliance) in power," Althusser writes, "cannot lay down the law in the ISAs as easily as it can in the (repressive) State apparatus." "Ideology," 147.

9. "Each instance, in other words, has a relative autonomy that is particular to itself but that has nevertheless been assigned a place and function within the complex unity of the social formation by the social formation itself." Robert Paul Resch, *Althusser and the Renewal of Marxist Social Theory* (Berkeley: University of California Press, 1992), 39. For Althusser's statements on relative autonomy, see Louis Althusser and Etienne Balibar, *Reading Capital* (London: New Left, 1970), 99–100.

10. Belsey, *Critical Practice*, 57.

11. Eagleton, *Ideology*, 118.

12. My interest in the wartime context of McCullers's story compels me to read Amelia's resistance more optimistically than Louise Westling, for whom "Ballad" depicts "a masculine Amazon whose transgression of conventional sexual boundaries brings catastrophic male retribution." "Carson McCullers' Amazon Nightmare," *Modern Fiction Studies* 28 (Autumn 1982): 472.

13. In Judith Butler's terms, "the paternal law ought to be understood not as a deterministic divine will, but as a perpetual bumbler, preparing the ground for the insurrections against him." *Gender Trouble: Feminism and the Subversion of Identity* (New York: Routledge, 1990), 28.

14. The details of this discussion come from Maureen Honey, *Creating Rosie the Riveter: Class, Gender, and Propaganda during World War II* (Amherst: University of Massachusetts Press, 1984); hereafter cited in my text as *CRR*. For more on the wartime roles of women in American society, see Karen Anderson, *Wartime Women: Sex Roles, Family Relations, and the Status of Women during World War Two*, Contributions in Women's Studies, no. 20 (Westport, CT: Greenwood Press, 1981).

15. Even Amelia's moonshining complements a brief story in the April 1943 *Harper's Bazaar*, which advises women to take charge of the liquor cabinet in their homes: "It's your job now to buy the liquor, to keep the makings for drinks on hand for friends who drop in, for menfolk back on furlough" (56).

16. Althusser, "Ideology," 143.

17. See Sandra Gilbert and Susan Gubar, "Charred Skirts and Deathmask: World War II and the Blitz on Women," in *Letters from the Front*, vol. 3 of *No Man's Land: The Place of the Woman Writer in the Twentieth Century*, ed. Sandra Gilbert and Susan Gubar (New Haven: Yale University Press, 1994), 211–65.

18. Ibid., 246.

19. Ibid., 213.

20. See Lilian Faderman, *Odd Girls and Twilight Lovers: A History of Lesbian Life in Twentieth-Century America* (New York: Columbia University Press, 1991), 125–26.

21. Butler, *Gender Trouble*, 31.

22. For the complete episode, see Jules Feiffer, *The Great Comic Book Heroes* (New York: Bonanza Books, 1965), 142–52.

23. Wonder Woman's heterosexuality was not obvious to conservative psychologist Fredric Wertham, who worried that the lesbian subtext of her story would have negative effects on the "psychosexual" development of American youths. See *Seduction of the Innocent* (New York: Rinehart, 1953), especially 192–93.

24. See, for instance, Allan Bérubé, "Marching to a Different Drummer: Lesbian and Gay GIs in World War II," in *Hidden from History: Reclaiming the Gay and Lesbian Past*, ed. Martin Bauml Duberman, Martha Vicinus, and George Chauncy (New York: New American Library, 1989), 383–94.

25. Virginia Spencer Carr, *The Lonely Hunter: A Biography of Carson McCullers* (Garden City: Doubleday, 1975), 126, 119.

26. For much of her life, McCullers's understanding of her own sexuality was tempered by her continued relationship with Reeves. Although they were often separated, and even divorced once (only to remarry), she seemed to want to hold on to her partnership with him and also to have the freedom to explore her desires for other women.

27. Carr, *Lonely Hunter*, 104.

28. In this, at least, there is a close connection between Macy and Reeves, whose relationship with McCullers's friend David Diamond is discussed by Carr. Ibid., 67–75.

29. Diana Fuss, "Fashion and the Homospectatorial Look," *Critical Inquiry* 18 (Summer 1992): 734.

30. Ibid., 732.

31. Ibid., 734.

PART TWO

Renarrativizing Embodiment in (Post)Colonial Contexts

E. M. Forster's Queer Nation: Taking the Closet to the Colony in *A Passage to India*

Elaine Freedgood

At a moment of extreme narrative frustration in *A Passage to India*, when the relationship between the two protagonists of the novel, Dr. Aziz and Cyril Fielding, reaches one of many moments of impasse, Fielding describes India as a "queer nation."[1] This highly overdetermined appellation suggests the complexity of E. M. Forster's covert mapping of a queer nation in his most canonical work. "Queer" began to mean homosexual in the 1920s, and was certainly the slang term used by Forster's contemporaries.[2] For a Briton to describe India as a "nation" during the same time period admits the specter of impending imperial defeat. For Forster, the separateness of a "nation" (as opposed to a colony) raises the possibility that India might become a place freed from the constraints of British authority, including those constraints that oppressed him, as a closeted homosexual, so acutely. India becomes a potential site for an eroticized and Orientalized all-male utopia.

Forster camouflaged this dream of an intercultural homoerotic community because of his own closeted sexuality, but even more importantly because the fact of empire, the security and privilege it offered to men like Forster (and Fielding), was precisely what made it possible to enjoy the fantasy of transcending it. Men like Forster could entertain the idea of comradely or even sexually subordinate relations with colonized men because, when it really counted, they would always be, as male, middle-class Britons, socially, politically, and economically "on top." In Forster's own life, the British Empire—in India and Egypt—provided employment, native lovers, and imperial prestige.[3]

It initially seems, in Forster's life, philosophy, and fiction, as if the "epistemology of the closet," with its strategy of circumventing power through secrecy, might challenge and even threaten the epistemology of the colony, with its strategy of consolidating power through public display. But the two epistemologies finally collude in *A Passage* to preserve "India" as a place where Britons might find sexual liberation without giving up their power and privilege. Accordingly, Forster directs his criticisms away from empire: Aziz and Fielding cannot finally be lovers, according to the narrative logic of *A Passage*, not because of the institutions and practices of the British Raj, but because of the self-involvement and cruelty of British women, because of the resistant and devouring landscape of India, and finally, because of the heterosexuality required by Indian Nationalism and the self-rule movement. These displacements and postponements make *A Passage to India* exemplary of the representational and political snares and the tragic collaborations produced by the closet in the colony.

The privacy, or virtual secrecy, in which Edwardian homoerotic relations had to take place seems impossible in the Chandrapore of *A Passage* because of the unstinting personal publicity that is required of the British colonizers of India. Mrs. Moore, "accustomed to the privacy of London, did not realize that India, seemingly so mysterious, contains none and that consequently the conventions have greater force."[4] Privacy is precluded by the need to enforce these conventions through a system of mutual and unsparing surveillance. The British must be on stage at all times enacting, through an ongoing display of superiority and solidarity, their claim to authority. "[O]ne's always facing the footlights," Ronnie explains to his mother. "They notice everything, until they're perfectly sure you're their sort" (49).

The conventions of the Anglo-Indian community—what separates the pukka from the not pukka—are produced by and rely on the "manichean oppositions" of the colony as formulated by Abdul JanMohamed, following Frantz Fanon: "white and black, good and evil, superiority and inferiority, civilization and savagery, intelligence and emotion, rationality and sensuality, self and Other, subject and object."[5] To be pukka is to conduct oneself in accordance with the social algebra dictated by these pairs: the first terms must be kept on the British side of the equation, in a state of pristine isolation from their opposite numbers.

Forster confronts the manichean colonial situation under the profound influence of Edward Carpenter, who believed that same-sex relationships might exert a positive social influence.[6] "Eros," Carpenter wrote,

is a great leveler. Perhaps the true Democracy rests, more firmly than anywhere else, on a sentiment which easily passes the bounds of class and caste, and unites in the closest affection the most estranged ranks of society. It is noticeable how often Uranians [homosexuals] of good position and breeding are drawn to rougher types, as of manual workers, and frequently very permanent alliances grow up in this way, which although not publicly acknowledged have a decided influence on social institutions . . . and political tendencies.[7]

Carpenter defined a form of resistance for Forster as a closeted gay subject: in Carpenter's utopian vision, cross-class and, by analogy, cross-cultural relationships might influence the political domain silently, not having to speak their name until it becomes safe to do so.

The intention and the weakness inherent in Carpenter's, and Forster's, ideas concerning the possible political and social efficacy of secrecy are elucidated in D. A. Miller's analysis of secret subjectivity. Secrecy, Miller writes, is the

spiritual exercise by which the subject is allowed to conceive of himself as a resistance: a friction in the smooth functioning of the social order, a margin to which its far-reaching discourse does not reach. Secrecy would thus be the subjective practice in which the oppositions of private/public, inside/outside, subject/object are established, and the sanctity of the first term kept inviolate.[8]

In Miller's description, the secret subject can conceive of himself or herself as a resistance only so long as the second terms of these oppositions can be kept at bay. But we know that without second terms, first terms can have no meaning; they can thus neither be kept entirely at bay nor fully embraced. The terms of binary opposition depend upon and resist each other; the two sets of oppositions brought together by the closet in the colony initially clash, but then settle down such that the private, inside, secret subject can remain on the same side of the colonial oppositions as whiteness, goodness, and civilization, and—a crucial addition to the lists of JanMohamed and Miller—masculinity.

Within Europe in the late nineteenth century, the rise and spread of nationalism and related ideas of racial superiority went hand in hand with the definition and control of homosexuality. George L. Mosse has described how, in this period, a sense of English national superiority was based on an ideal of manliness that defined itself against the threatening "effeminacy" of both homosexuals and men of color, in which "the stereo-typed depiction of sexual 'degenerates' was transferred almost intact to the 'inferior' races," who were said to lack manliness.[9] Nationalist defini-tions of appropriate sexual identity oppressed and excluded both the colonized and the homosexual man from normality and masculinity. Forster's inheritance of, and entrapment within, the dominant discourses of Victorian and Edwardian Britain—Orientalism, English nationalism, "biological" definitions of race, and punitive medical models of homosex-uality—made it impossible for him to deconstruct or reconfigure such designations as the "normal," the "masculine," and the "European" or "English."[10]

Instead of challenging this set of ideologies, Forster worked to change the moral valence of homosexuality, to bring it within categories that his readers could recognize and approve. He described homoerotic feelings as "primitive," but also as part of the "common stock" of human emo-tions.[11] Men who desire other men become homeless noble savages in the "Terminal Note" to *Maurice* (1913): "There is no forest or fell to escape to today, no cave in which to curl up, no deserted valley for those who wish neither to reform nor corrupt society but to be left alone."[12] Forster suggests that India might be a place where the "primitive" nature of homosexuality might flourish, where he and men like him could be left alone, and where sensuality might triumph over even the sturdy but constraining rationality of Englishmen:

The buildings of Venice, like the mountains of Crete and the fields of Egypt, stood in the right place, whereas in poor India everything was placed wrong. . . .
. . . The Mediterranean is the human norm. When men leave that exquisite lake, whether through the Bosphorus or the Pillars of Hercules, they approach the monstrous and extraordinary; and the southern exit leads to the strangest experience of all. (282)

In "poor India" everything is in the wrong place, but Forster implies that this anti-normative messiness may lead to a strange and perhaps liberating experience for one constrained by the "human norm" as it is defined by Europe. Such a formulation relies on Forster's construction of the East as inherently abnormal—as if the East, or that part of it that is India, does not have its own norms, and indeed its own sexual rules and regulations.

Moreover, Forster plays a conceptual shell game, moving homosexuality around under cover of two conflicting versions of the "primitive": the East can never be, in the Western imagination, "primitive" in the sense that the West has been primitive. For Forster and his readers, the Western primitive is an ideal, a prehistorical moment of noble savagery. The Eastern primitive, on the other hand, is what Forster continually refers to as a "muddle." The European can take advantage of this muddle, but he or she will never idealize or identify with it. Forster would bring homosexuality within the "human norm" through a momentary conflation of two versions of the primitive, versions that will never be lastingly interchangeable.[13]

Although the actual content of the "strangest experience of all" is left conveniently unspecified in this passage, Forster engages in the exploitation of India and Indians through involving himself and his readers in imagining a country and its people in ways that both suit and protect the specific content of needs that are forbidden overt representation in the West (and in the East, too—the lack of sexual constraint is a Western fantasy, after all). Forster thus takes up the terms of the dominant discourses of imperialism, including Orientalism, racism, and homophobia, the very discourses that the Carpenteresque practice of secret subjectivity was designed, however inadequately, to evade and ultimately transcend.[14]

Forster describes Fielding as having "no racial feeling . . . because he had matured in a different atmosphere where the herd instinct does not flourish" (62). The "different atmosphere" is England; Fielding "had been caught by India late" (61). He has not come out to India with any glorious notions of serving empire, but because he needed a job (112). Forster carefully constructs Fielding as more an urbane tourist than a vulgar colonizer, making Fielding a specimen of a special individualistic Englishness, a national identity posed as an alternative to the "herd-instinct" nationalism ascribed to the longtime British residents of India. Indeed, Fielding's observation that the "white races are really pinko-grey" scandalizes the Anglo-Indian characters in the novel: "he did not realize that 'white' had no more to do with colour than 'God save the King' with god" (62). "White" is the crucial first term in the Manichean oppositions of colonial epistemology, and the most important one with which to identify. Fielding's liberalism, including his putative indifference to race, separates him from the Anglo-Indian herd, but this characterization of him works to recuperate rather than criticize imperialism. If all the British in India were as friendly and sensitive as Fielding (as one Indian character after another muses regretfully), the British Raj would be a fine institution after all.

When Adela charges Aziz with rape, Forster describes the Anglo-Indian response as hysterical:

Nothing enrages Anglo-India more than the lantern of reason if it is exhibited for one moment after its extinction is decreed. All over Chandrapore that day the Europeans were putting aside their normal personalities and sinking themselves in their community. Pity, wrath, heroism, filled the air, but the power of putting two and two together was annihilated. (165)

With this charge of hysteria, Forster calls into question the very masculinity of the colonizers, who ought to be rational and manly, rather than emotional and "feminine"—the role given by the British to the colonized of both genders. Forster suggests that the truly masculine men are those who, like Fielding, are single, uninterested in women, and sympathetic to Indians. If the Anglo-Indian herd is effeminate, Indians are pushed even further away from the "human norm" of Europe; indeed, they may be more vilified by the liberal racism of Fielding than by the conventional racism of Turtons and Burtons.

Forster's criticism of the hysterical family-centered nationalism of Anglo-India also challenges the imperial assumption that heterosexuality provides the most politically stable form of personal life. Monogamous heterosexuality was thought to provide the maximum political security for imperialism, with its confinement and containment of intimacy and sexuality within marriage. Any variety of heterosexuality, however, was seen as more conducive to imperial interests than homosexuality, with its associations of "corruption and degeneration."[15] Before large numbers of English women came out to India, "making life on the home pattern yearly more possible" (63), the British government encouraged and regulated Indian female prostitution in an attempt to prevent homosexuality, which was "dreaded as a threat to military discipline."[16] Forster covertly suggests that homosexual men might actually provide greater political security for imperialism. The stabilizing and calming effect attributed to heterosexual domesticity in the official imagination is never evident among Forster's Anglo-Indians, who, in the aftermath of Adela's allegation of assault, started speaking of "women and children"—that phrase that exempts the male from sanity when it has been repeated a few times. Each felt that all he loved best in the world was at stake, demanded revenge, and was filled with a not unpleasing glow, in which the chilly and half-known features of Miss Quested vanished, and were replaced by all that is sweetest and warmest in the private life. (183)

The idea that a degree of political security is conferred by wives and children is seriously undermined: wives and children bring on a "glow" that might lead to ill-considered and inflammatory actions. The mathematical symmetry of JanMohamed's "Manichean oppositions," which predict, with fingers crossed, that white colonizers will be unfailingly cool and rational in their dealings with the hotheaded and irrational subject races, is thrown into a revealing disarray. It seems that Fielding is the only levelheaded human being in Chandrapore, and possibly on the entire subcontinent.

The emotional excess attributed to "private [heterosexual] life" leads the novel into a misogynist turning of the tables: it is women and domesticity that corrupt the imperialist venture. At the "Bridge Party," a gathering convened to introduce Adela Quested and Mrs. Moore to Indians and to help build sympathy between English and Indian people generally, "the Englishmen had intended to play up better, but they had been prevented from doing so by their women folk, whom they had to attend, provide with tea, advise about dogs, etc." (46). Women are explicitly blamed for the poor relations between the colonizer and the colonized; they are the ones "who make everything more difficult out here" (214).

Forster thus tries, following the twists and turns of a serpentine logic, to elide the glaring incompatibility of homosexuality with the requirements of empire by displacing this incompatibility onto the practice of heterosexuality, especially because of its unavoidable requirement of close and frequent contact with women. British women are represented as capable of undoing the manliness, and even the sanity, of the family men of Chandrapore. Rather than question "masculinity" as an oppressive social construction, Forster attempts instead to feminize heterosexuality and appropriate true manliness for an all-male community. This was a common strategy among Forster's contemporaries, particularly when an author who was a member of the British mainstream in other significant ways (in terms of his color, gender, and class, for example) tried to legitimate and normalize his own sexuality. John Addington Symonds, in

A Problem in Greek Ethics (1901), described ancient Greece as a place where military might and imperial achievement *depended* on the manliness generated by homosexuality. T. E. Lawrence, in *The Seven Pillars of Wisdom*, depicted Arab homoerotic practice as the "sensual co-efficient of manly militarism."[17] Richard Burton used himself as an example of the coexistence of manliness and homoerotic practice: a dashing and intrepid explorer of the world, he was also a fearless participant in its sexual possibilities. The "documentation" of these possibilities in the "Terminal Essay" of his translation of the *Arabian Nights* (1885) contributed greatly to the Western mythology of the East as sexually permissive, particularly about homosexuality. Such strategies had little impact, however, on the dominant sexual ideology of British imperialism, in which it was maintained that any variety of heterosexuality was preferable to homosexuality, which was and is so profoundly connected, in the Western imagination, with weakness, corruption, and decay.[18]

In the first half of *A Passage*, Forster distributes power among a seemingly symmetrical triad of British, Muslim, and Hindu characters. The representation of early-twentieth-century India as divided into three major ethnic groups with three sets of competing interests is, of course, accurate and avoids a monolithic and distorted rendering of unspecified and interchangeable Indians. It is in its nuances that Forster's triadic representation mutes the reality of the grossly binary power relations of imperialism, in which the fact remains that the British ruled Indians, of whatever religious affiliation. Forster attempts, through suppressing this binary of power, to represent individual agency as somehow liberated or separated from the dominant social structure, to allow, perhaps, for relationships in the colony that are not "colonial." This strategy, rather than representing individuals as able to transcend the plane of politics and history, propels the novel into what JanMohamed has defined as the "machinery of the manichean allegory," the effect of which is to

dehistoricize and desocialize the conquered world, to present it as a metaphysical "fact of life," before which those who have fashioned the colonial world are themselves reduced to the role of passive spectators in a mystery not of their own making.[19]

Forster's dehistoricizing and desocializing begin with his use of an omniscient narrator who hovers in the sky, seemingly divorced from the complications of subjectivity: "so abased, so monotonous is everything that meets the eye, that when the Ganges comes down it might be expected to wash the excrescence back into the soil" (92). The abasement and monotony are rendered as the objective report of "the eye," "the invisible eye/I which strives," Mary Louise Pratt writes, "to make . . . informational orders natural, to find them there uncommanded, rather than assert them as the products/producers of European knowledge and disciplines."[20] Indeed, it is not European knowledge and disciplines that seem to be at work in Forster's representation; in India, "the sky settles everything" (9). Human agency—and British responsibility—are conveniently effaced as the social is subsumed by the natural and the natural by the supernatural.[21] Mrs. Moore's emotional paralysis, and ultimately her death, following her experience in the Marabar Caves, epitomizes the force with which the very geography of India undermines human intention. "Human" intention and agency are decidedly the property of the English, who ride in the "triumphant machine of civilization," a machine, however, that

may suddenly hitch and be immobilized into a car of stone, and at such moments the destiny of the English seems to resemble their predecessors', who also entered the country with the intent to refashion it, but were in the end worked into its pattern and covered with its dust. (211)

English subjectivity, rather than refashioning its object, may itself be refashioned: imperial power is muted by being represented as subject to such mysterious metaphysical forces. Mrs. Moore's loss of Western notions of meaning, the working of her subjectivity into the pattern of the "boum" of the caves, prevents even her ghost from reentering Europe; it must be "shaken off" the ship before it leaves Port Said, the terminal point of the Orient (256).

The omniscience of Forster's narrator, like the omniscience characteristic of much Orientalist scholarship, knows no bounds: Forster is apparently entirely confident of his ability to "report on" (that is, create) a social gathering of Indians at which no English person is present. Hamidullah, Mahmoud Ali, and Aziz are busy essentializing the English and are thus portrayed as being very like (and no better than?) their oppressors: according to Aziz, the difference between Turton and Burton "is only the difference of a letter" (11). The narrator's explanation of Aziz's unfortunate typology (which the novel actually goes on to vindicate) is that Aziz "generalized from his disappointments—it is difficult for a subject race to do otherwise" (13).

The brutality of the British Raj is thus elided and the "disappoint-ment" of a "subject race" is attributed to unjustified self-pity. Forster's attempt at a fictional rehabilitation of the historical blight of the British Raj reaches its nadir after the arrest of Aziz for the rape of Adela Quested. In a scene at the Chandrapore Club, Mrs. Turton, after chastis-ing English men for their weakness, suggests that "natives" "ought to crawl from here to the caves on their hands and knees whenever an Englishwoman's in sight, they oughtn't to be spoken to, they ought to be spat at, they ought to be ground into the dust" (216). Mrs. Turton's ideas are represented as a hysterical outburst, which is part and parcel of the characterization of English women throughout the novel as more racist than the men. In Forster's Chandrapore, British men may feel violent but rarely *do* anything violent, even though their women wish they would. It is not the fact of imperialism that is called into question in scenes like this, but the manner of it, and Forster makes clear his belief that "one touch of regret . . . would have made the British Empire a different institution" (51)—a better institution, one supposes, even a good one.

Mrs. Turton's idea, which is represented as unthinkable, as a ridicu-lous outburst, is based on the very real "crawling order" issued by the British government of the Punjab in the aftermath of the Amritsar massa-cre of 1919, in which the British opened fire without warning on a public meeting of Indian Nationalists, killing 379 people and wounding 1,200. The order was in effect for one week, during which Indians were re-quired to crawl on all fours if they had to pass through a street in which an English woman lived who had allegedly been assaulted by Indian Nationalists.[22] Although the details of the Amritsar massacre and its aftermath went unreported in the British press, Forster received a first-hand account of it in a letter from his friend Malcolm Darling, a civil servant in the Punjab at the time.[23] What P. N. Furbank describes as Forster's "indignation" at the British government is translated, in *A Passage*, into a stinging critique of British women. This muting of the brutali-ties of imperial relations, and the transfer of aggression onto female characters, becomes the misogynist foundation for the furthering of the relationship between Aziz and Fielding.

Both Aziz and Fielding are portrayed as having very loose ties to both national and heterosexual identities. Aziz's primary identification is as a Muslim, rather than as an Indian—he is as yet untouched by the Indian Nationalist movement, which will figure so largely in his move to Mau after the trial. Aziz also lacks a pronounced heterosexual identity: he is reluctant to remarry; his relationship with his wife, who is dead, was not passionate, and he feels that "a friend would come nearer to her than another woman" (55).

Similarly, Fielding's marginality in the Anglo-Indian community is based on his lack of "racial feeling" and the fact the he takes "no notice" of English women: "He had discovered that it is possible to keep in with Indians and Englishmen, but that he who would also keep in with Englishwomen must drop the Indians" (63). Fragments of a utopian male community surface frequently at the beginning of the novel, part of the fantasy that an all-male India, with English women at home in England and Indian women at home in purdah, would make it possible for English and Indian men to "get along."

Aziz and Fielding negotiate their intimacy through homosocial triangles, triangles that are based not on a common desire for women, but on a common rejection of women. These triangles proliferate rapidly in the scene in which Aziz shows Fielding a photograph of his wife as a sign of his trust, a small bridge toward intimacy that is then kicked away: "Put her away, she is of no importance, she is dead . . . I showed her to you because I have nothing else to show" (117). The bond produced by this gesture is further solidified by Fielding's admission that English women are "much nicer in England. There's something that doesn't suit them out here" (118). Aziz asks Fielding why he isn't married, which leads Fielding to reject Adela Quested as a potential wife on the grounds that she's "a prig." Fielding then emphatically declines Aziz's offer to procure him a "lady with breasts like mangoes" (120). The scene ends with Fielding giving his "manifesto" against marriage. These methodical rejections of real and imagined women seem to set the stage for an admission of some other kind of desire, perhaps the desire of the two men for each other. It is Aziz, in an impassioned plea to Fielding for kindness, who is given the burden of coming closest to such an admission:

Mr. Fielding, no one can ever realize how much kindness we Indians need, we do not even realize it ourselves. . . . Kindness, more kindness, and even after that more kindness. I assure you it is the only hope. (116–17)

Fielding interprets Aziz's plea as a request for much more than kindness:

Kindness, kindness, and more kindness—yes, that he might supply, but was that really all the queer nation needed? Did it not also demand an occasional intoxication of the blood? (117)

An Indian—Aziz—becomes an intangible, literally untouchable "nation" in Fielding's abstract and abstracted response. This abstraction, this removal from the plane of possible physical contact, allows Fielding to wonder if India, the "queer nation," needs "an intoxication of the blood" from an English man. But what *is* an "intoxication of the blood"? Of what act or acts does it consist? What does it mean that India "demands" it? Does this absolve England, or an English man, from responsibility? The camouflage in which homoerotic desire must enshroud itself in a publishable fiction becomes a kind of endlessly echoing Marabar Cave all its own, into which an otherwise helpful and lucid narrator retreats and cannot be reached for further comment.

It seems that what prevents Fielding and Aziz from becoming lovers is *not* that they are the same in terms of their gender, but that they are different in terms of their blood. It turns out that because Fielding's blood is English, it is not given to intoxication: "[e]xperience can do much, and all that he had learnt in England and Europe was an assistance to him, and helped him toward clarity, but clarity prevented him from experiencing something else" (118). The "something else" that Fielding is prevented from experiencing has been alluded to, perhaps, in a scene in which Aziz plays an impromptu game of polo with an unnamed English subaltern:

They reined up again, the fire of good fellowship in their eyes. But it cooled with their bodies, for athletics can only raise a temporary glow. Nationality was returning, but before it could exert its poison they parted, saluting each other. (58)

Perhaps a sexual interaction could raise a more lasting "glow" than an athletic one, and could purify each of the "poison" of clashing national and racial blood. This possibility is defeated by the very reification, in this scene, of national and racial identities as biological realities, located in the blood, which cannot be washed away by the sweat of polo, or of sex. Forster's concurrence with a biological concept of race cripples the development of a critique he seems to have been on the verge of making in having Fielding make the potentially subversive observation that "white has no more to do with colour than 'God save the king' with god."

While Fielding is safely imprisoned in the "clarity" of his Englishness, Aziz's longing for him can barely be contained in the submerged narrative space allotted for it. The homoerotic is both readable and unreadable in this text because Forster exploits the stereotypes of Asian men as feminized or effeminate: Aziz's thinly veiled crush on Fielding can be read as a symptom of his being a stereotypically "feminine" "Oriental," *or* as a stereotypically "feminine" homosexual. Aziz must bear, in addition to the burden of brown skin in a British colony, the burden of homoerotic longing, which Fielding, as a white and English male, will not be caught carrying. The closet in the colony only has room for the colonizer; the colonized must find other accommodation.

The force of Aziz's longing for Fielding breaks through the calm surface of the text when Aziz is finally, during the Marabar Caves expedition, disburdened of Adela Quested, who has just asked him, to his horror, if he has more than one wife. This question propels Aziz to move quickly ahead and enter the next cave. Upon emerging from this cave, Aziz temporarily loses sight of Adela, but then sees that she has run down to see Miss Derek, who has just arrived along with Fielding. Aziz does not know at this point why Adela has run off; he is simply glad that she has gone. He returns to the picnic site:

the colour and confusion of his little camp soon appeared, and in the midst of it he saw an Englishman's topi, and beneath it—oh, joy!—smiled not Mr. Heaslop, but Fielding.

"Fielding! Oh, I have so wanted you!" he cried, dropping the "Mr." for the first time. (155)

The narrator carefully distances himself and Fielding from the passion of Aziz, noting with cool condescension that Aziz has dropped the " 'Mr.' for the first time." In the intensity of his desire, or in his relief at being able to turn from Adela's obtuseness to Fielding's sympathy, Aziz forgets his colonized status, and his ingrained habit of deference to colonizers.

Aziz's assertion of himself as a social peer harks back to an earlier scene, in which his eagerness to lend Fielding a collar stud creates what Sara Suleri has described as the "most notoriously oblique homoerotic exchange in the literature of English India."[24] An addition must be made to Suleri's remarkable reading of the anal-erotic symbolics of studs and holes in this scene: Aziz plays the *active* role. It is Aziz's stud that goes into the "rather small" hole at the back of Fielding's collar. A double scandal is perpetrated here: the scandal of the homoerotic is compounded by the scandal of a colonizer in the passive role.

The colonizer's fear, which is undoubtedly also a wish, of penetration by the colonized has often been contained in colonial fiction (including this fiction) through the figure of heterosexual rape. If the rapist is caught and punished, the fear of, or more precisely the fear of the wish for, such penetrations may be symbolically assuaged. In *A Passage*, not only is the perpetrator of the assault of Adela Quested left unnamed, the act itself is never decisively confirmed or denied. Indeed, Adela herself insists that whoever "assaulted" her never actually touched her, but only her field glasses. No one believes her; Forster creates a woman who does not even consider herself a reliable witness of her own experience—an experience that, in any case, is rapidly detached from her, and transformed into an insult to all English women. Forster, in refusing to resolve what, if anything, has really happened to Adela, focuses the reader's attention on the ongoing mystery of her victimization and thus distracts from the specter (and the promise) of the colonized penetration of the colonizer that Aziz and Fielding, as stud giver and stud-less receiver, enact.

There is another paradox that attends the incident of the stud giving: in giving Fielding his stud, Aziz unmans himself. Ronnie Heaslop remarks on the stud-less state of Aziz's collar not once but twice as a telling emblem of "the fundamental slackness that reveals the race" (82). Taking the active role doesn't work the way it should; Aziz, in penetrating the colonizer, has also had to insist that Fielding keep the stud (or else risk being seen as either embarrassingly poor or shockingly impolite); he has had to give away the instrument with which he has penetrated his friend, and thus makes himself appear slack. The passive colonizer remains a man, indeed becomes more of a man, because he gets to keep the stud that makes his collar, and his race, stand up.

A sexually charged engagement with a shirt, however, marks the upper limit of Forster's representational risk taking. The "mastery of fantasy" in this text requires that the presence of the homoerotic be limited to flickers of meaning that are intelligible only to the knowing reader, or to the reader who wants to know.[25] These readers are Forster's queer contemporaries, who had to be expert at reading through the veils that (almost) occluded the homoerotic in published, and therefore public, works. The title of *A Passage*, for example, is itself a clue to the initiated that sexual difference lurks within the novel. "A Passage to India" is also a poem by Walt Whitman, and the exchange of Whitman memorabilia, as Eve Kosofsky Sedgwick has noted, was used by British men in the late nineteenth and early twentieth century to signal their erotic interest in each other.[26]

The chronic disappointment inflicted by compulsory secrecy is repeated in, and evoked by, the narrative of *A Passage:* as a structure that is inherently on the move, it cannot completely contain the frustration that attends the stalling of the growing intimacy between Aziz and Fielding. Neither can it explicitly name and call into question the interconnected institutions (imperialism, racism, homophobia) that produce this stalling. Frustration is displaced onto India itself, rather than onto the narrative closet produced by the "human norms" of Europe. Once again human (read English) agency, this time in the form of Forster's plot, is nullified by India, who calls " 'Come' through her hundred mouths, through objects ridiculous and august. But come to what? She has never defined. She is not a promise, only an appeal" (136). India, and Indians, as "objects ridiculous and august" in Forster's deeply ambivalent portrayal, are thus figured as continually luring English desire to the brink of a seduction that is never completed. In his representation of this deceptive appeal, Forster tellingly consigns India and its "objects" to the semantic limbo of a *female* pronoun.

Although Fielding takes Aziz's side after his (Aziz's) arrest for the rape of Adela Quested, he is far from "going native" in this choice. Forster carefully represents his national and racial subjectivity as different from but no less durable than that of his countrymen: it remains intact and separates him from both the hysterics of the Anglo-Indian herd and the even more emotionally overwrought Indians:

At the moment when he was throwing in his lot with the Indians, he realized the profundity of the gulf that divided him from them. They always do something disappointing. Aziz had tried to run away from the police, Mohammed Latif had not checked the pilfering. . . . Are Indians cowards? No, but they are bad starters and occasionally jib. Fear is everywhere, the British Raj rests on it; the respect and courtesy Fielding himself enjoyed were unconscious acts of propitiation. (173)

The source of fear shifts and slides in this passage: are Indians innately fearful or is fear produced by the British? The origin of fear is left undefined, Fielding's thoughts wander among the racial banalities of the day, and he succumbs easily to the dominant discourse of race. He realizes, perhaps with guilt, but certainly with resignation, that the respect and courtesy he has enjoyed are produced by the fear—whatever its origin—that characterizes the dominant social order of the Raj and that they are not the result of any friendship or intimacy produced outside this order.

Although Fielding acknowledges a sense of the "profundity of the gulf" that separates him from Aziz, he continues to believe in Aziz's innocence. Fielding's plight increasingly resembles that of the liberal colonizer as described by Albert Memmi:

> It is not easy to escape mentally from a concrete situation, to refuse its ideology while continuing to live with its actual relationships. . . . Colonial relations do not stem from individual good will or actions, they exist before [the individual colonizer's] arrival . . . and whether he accepts them or rejects them matters little. It is they, on the contrary which, like any institution, determine *a priori* his place and that of the colonized . . . and their true relationship.[27]

Forster cannot defend his protagonist and his plot against the force of the colonial conventions. Fielding's actions and Forster's plot are at this point entirely overwhelmed by the publicly flourishing institutions of the colony. The Carpenteresque, utopian vision of the possibilities that secretly erotic male relationships might produce is thoroughly discredited. And this is no mistake: Forster does not wish, as Carpenter did, to overthrow the existing political order, but rather to soften its effects so that empire might become a more congenial institution for all concerned. We might read Forster's characterization of Fielding as an inadvertent and oblique answer to the question asked in the letter to the "Président du Conseil" that opens Gide's *L'immoraliste:* "En quoi Michel peut-il servir l'état?" How can a homosexual citizen of an imperial nation serve the state? Forster's answers are suggestive if nonspecific: "kindness, kindness and more kindness," aided, perhaps, by an "occasional intoxication of the blood." Officially, the British Empire reviled homosexuality; unofficially homosexuality and homosexuals were deployed strategically within empire, to build personal relationships that, in their intimacy and temporary equality, seemed to transcend the constraints and cruelties typical of other colonial relations. Men like Forster and Gide, T. E. Lawrence and Richard Burton, gave empire a more human face and form. But they did so at their own risk: their "contributions" would never be officially avowed.[28]

Indeed, Forster may be mourning, in *A Passage*, the British Raj, the passing of which, during the writing of the novel between 1912 and 1924, is becoming increasingly certain. Forster's disillusionment in regard to

India in 1924 is clearly registered in a letter to the friend to whom *A Passage* is dedicated, Sayed Ross Masood:

When I began the book I thought of it as a little bridge of sympathy between East and West, but this conception has had to go, my sense of truth forbids anything so comfortable. I think that most Indians, like most English people, are shits, and I am not interested in whether they sympathize with one another or not.[29]

Although Forster does not mention the political events that have intervened between 1912 and 1924, his new sense of Indians as "shits" may well be related to the increasingly apparent vitality of Indian Nationalism.[30] The Nationalist movement, with its focus on self-rule, provided serious obstacles to the pleasure seeking of "apolitical" Englishmen like Forster (and Fielding).

Indeed, the final breach between Aziz and Fielding is precipitated by the two men gaining both a solid sense of national identity and an active reinvolvement with heterosexuality. Two years have elapsed since the trial, and Aziz has gone to live at Mau, a princely state in the interior where no English influence is present. As a recent critic has noted in connection with Aziz's move, "in *Hind Swaraj*, Gandhi associated living in remote places with the development of a sense of patriotism and nationalism that could blossom into a legitimate desire for Home Rule or political independence."[31] Forster ridicules this movement in his depiction of Mau: the school (which was to have been based on the British model) has been turned into a granary, Fielding can get no eggs, and the mosquito net in the guest house is torn. These complaints are themselves ridiculous as a critique of a movement for independence, since what Forster describes as appalling is a lack of comforts for colonizers, the very people who are being invited to leave. And if self-rule is portrayed as impracticable, Indian Nationalism is portrayed as impossible because India is essentially and irrevocably divided:

The fissures in the Indian soil are infinite; Hinduism, so solid from a distance, is riven into sects and clans, which radiate and join, and change their names according to the aspect from which they are approached. Study it for years with the best teachers, and when you raise your head, nothing they have told you quite fits. (292)

The infinite fissures of the Indian soil notwithstanding, Aziz's tenure at Mau has turned him into an "Indian at last" (293). Aziz attributes his sense of national identity to the "Hindu-Muslim entente" that was produced by his rape trial (266). The effects of Aziz's development of a sense of national identity are perhaps just what Forster feared: Indian Nationalism (in Forster's representation of it), like the English variety, prescribes heterosexuality within a stable nuclear family. Aziz has married again, and his children from his first marriage are now with him all year round (293). He has taken to writing poems concerned with "one topic—Oriental womanhood. 'The purdah must go,' was their burden" (293). Women would thus enter the space in which men might otherwise be able to form an all-male community, blocking the formation of any future interracial, international communities of men.

Fielding's tenure in England has similarly procured for him both a wife and a more solid English identity; he can now throw in his lot "with the Oppressors of India" (307). Nonetheless, it is Aziz's new sense of identity that forecloses the possibility of any further intimacy between the two men. In their final meeting, Fielding makes an attempt to draw Aziz closer, asking Aziz why his (Fielding's) wife and her brother like Hinduism. Fielding wants Aziz to talk to them about this, because, "at all events you're Oriental" (320). The fact that Aziz is a Muslim and not a Hindu is easily forgotten or dismissed by Fielding. Aziz's delayed reply invokes and revokes their common past: "Clear out, all you Turtons and Burtons. We wanted to know you ten years back—now it is too late" (321). Although Aziz continues to carry the burden of alluding to their mutual desire to "know" one another, on this occasion he announces its definitive demise.

The concluding paragraphs of the novel make a final gesture at the possible transcendence of social reality by individual good will, sealing its impossibility with a false and self-serving veneer of regret. Aziz continues to order Fielding's departure, at the same time predicting that there will come a time for them to be "friends":

"Clear out, you fellows, double quick, I say. We may hate one another, but we hate you most. If I don't make you go, Ahmed will, Karim will [Ahmed and Karim are his sons], if it's fifty-five hundred years we shall get rid of you . . . we shall drive every blasted Englishman into the sea, and then"—[Aziz] rode against him furiously—"and then," he concluded, half kissing him, "you and I shall be friends."

"Why can't we be friends now?" said [Fielding], holding him affectionately. "It's what I want. It's what you want."

But the horses didn't want it—they swerved apart; the earth didn't want it, sending up rocks through which riders must pass single file; the temples, the tank, the jail, the palace, the birds, the carrion, the Guest House, that came into view as they issued from the gaps and saw Mau beneath; they didn't want it, they said their hundred voices, "not yet, " and the sky said, "no, not there." (322)

The half-kissing and holding, the wish to be friends—all are defeated by the landscape in which they occur. It is this landscape, and not Aziz, that is given the last word. Forster's fantasy of mastery continues to deny Aziz any narrative agency. In a rhetorical move that we have seen before, Aziz becomes India; he is transformed into a landscape that says "not yet," continuing to delay but not decisively deny the desires it so endlessly excites. In this fantasy, India will never be a nation with an independent existence, but Forster's own imaginary queer nation, a place over which he will always have dominion.

Forster preserves "India" as a site for the English homoerotic imagination precisely by veiling and postponing, in this publishable fiction, the sexual possibilities that might be available there. The representational exigencies of Forster's closet require that A Passage to India, as its title suggests, forestalls arrival in such possibilities. At the same time, the novel suggests, to the initiated, that imaginary and actual journeys to India might become, as in a line of the Whitman poem from which Forster surely took his title, "a passage to more than India." The burden of representing the possibility of homoerotic fulfillment, however, is placed squarely on the colonized. Aziz can "want" Fielding, as he admits after losing Adela Quested at the Marabar Caves, but Fielding cannot want Aziz. The closet, like the Chandrapore Club, is a British-only institution.

A Passage to India can accommodate readers who want a passage to more than India, or something considerably less. The achievement of this doubleness has been described by Edward Said as "intimate estrangement": "a specific encounter with the Orient in which the Westerner regrasps the Orient's essence as a consequence of his intimate estrangement from it." Said notes that for Forster, this sensation produced the "despondency . . . of personal failure." [32] But it produced relief as well: intimate estrangement may be the ideal relation of the closeted to the colonized man. Estrangement protects British male subjectivity from being overwhelmed by desire for and identification with the "East," while the irreducible remainder of intimacy preserves the East as a place where liberation can be imagined as possible. Intimate estrangement allows for a closeness that is safely distant, and a distance that is comfortingly close: it might be the credo of E. M. Forster's queer nation.

NOTES

I wish to thank Samir Dayal, Siobhān Kilfeather, Debra Roth, Carol Siegel, Gauri Viswanathan, and an anonymous reader at *Genders* for their generous and helpful readings of this essay.

1. In a telling textual instance of the avoidance or disavowal of intimacy, Aziz's first name is never given.

2. Eric Partridge lists 1920 as the date for the use of "queer" to mean "homosexual" in *A Dictionary of Slang and Unconventional English* (London, 1984).

3. Forster had a romantic, although probably not physical, relationship with Syed Ross Masood, a Muslim Indian, in England and India; he had a sexual relationship with Mohamed el Adl in Alexandria when he worked there as a colonial employee; and he had a relationship with an Indian servant, arranged and approved by the maharajah of Dewas Senior, for whom Forster worked as a secretary. The condition of the maharajah arranging this relationship was that Forster be in the dominant role; there is noticeably no indication that Forster explicitly agreed to this condition. See P. N. Furbank, *E. M. Forster: A Life*, 2 vols. (New York, 1977) for detailed accounts of these relationships.

4. E. M. Forster, *A Passage to India* (New York, 1954), 49. (Hereafter cited parenthetically in the text by page number.)

5. I am following Forster's usage of "Anglo-Indian" throughout this essay, which refers to the longtime British residents of India. Mrs. Turton, the collector's wife, describes Fielding as "not pukka" early in the novel, although she does not elaborate on the basis for her claim. Note that the British borrow a Hindi word to describe what is socially acceptable among themselves. Citation is from Abdul JanMohamed, "The Economy of Manichean Allegory: The Function of Racial Difference in Colonial Literature," in *"Race," Writing and Difference*, ed. Henry Louis Gates, Jr. (Chicago, 1985), 87. JanMohamed and Fanon emphasize the polarities of power relationships in the colonial situation; for an elaboration and deconstruction of this binary view of power, see, for example, Homi K. Bhabha, "Of Mimicry and Man: The Ambivalence of Colonial Discourse," *October* 28 (1984): 125–33.

6. Forster's first meeting with Carpenter and his lover, George Merrill, in 1913 inspired him to write *Maurice*. A diary entry summing up the significant events of that year concludes with the line: "Edward Carpenter! Edward Carpenter! Edward Carpenter!" See Furbank, *E. M. Forster: A Life*, 1: 256–58.

7. Cited in June Perry Levine, "The Tame in Pursuit of the Savage: The Posthumous Fiction of E. M. Forster," *PMLA* 1 (1984): 73–74.

8. D. A. Miller, *The Novel and the Police* (Berkeley, 1988), 207.

9. George L. Mosse, *Nationalism and Sexuality: Respectability and Abnormal Sexuality in Modern Europe* (New York, 1985), 36.

10. See, for example, Edward W. Said, *Orientalism* (New York, 1979); Tom Nairn, *The Break-up of Britain: Crisis and Neo-Nationalism* (London, 1977); Nancy Leys Stepan, *The Idea of Race in Science: Great Britain 1800–1950* (London, 1982);

Jeffrey Weeks, *Sex, Politics, and Society: The Regulation of Sexuality since 1800* (London, 1989).

11. E. M. Forster, *Maurice* (New York, 1987), 254.

12. Ibid.

13. I wish to thank Samir Dayal for helping me clarify this point.

14. Unlike Forster, who was a liberal, Carpenter was committed to sweeping change, and was a leading proponent of socialism and feminism in addition to homosexual liberation. See Weeks, *Sex, Politics, and Society*, 171–75.

15. Ibid., 107.

16. Kenneth Ballhatchet, *Race, Sex, and Class under the Raj: Imperial Attitudes and Policies and Their Critics* (London, 1980), 10.

17. According to Furbank, Forster's reading of a privately printed edition of Lawrence's work in 1922 helped him finish writing *A Passage* because it "supported him in a cherished belief, that sensitiveness and introspection could exist side by side with vigour, active heroism and largeness of vision." In other words, Lawrence supported Forster in his belief that homosexuality and masculinity, as traditionally defined, are not mutually exclusive. Furbank, *E. M. Forster: A Life*, 2:119–20.

18. See Weeks, *Sex, Politics, and Society*, 107.

19. JanMohamed, "Economy," 87.

20. Mary Louise Pratt, "Scratches on the Face of the Country; or, What Mr. Barrow Saw in the Land of the Bushmen," in *"Race," Writing and Difference*, ed. Gates, 144.

21. Kenneth Burke points out that "the presentation as whole involves a stylistic device whereby *social motives* are viewed in terms of *nature*, and nature in turn is infused with glancing references to realms *beyond*." *Language as Symbolic Action: Essays in Life, Literature and Method* (Berkeley, 1966), 227.

22. See Percival Spear, *A History of India*, vol. 2, (Harmondsworth, 1965), 191. For a reading of the novel in relation to the massacre, see G. K. Das, "*A Passage to India*: A Socio-historical Study," in *"A Passage to India": Essays in Interpretation*, ed. John Beer (London, 1985), 1–15.

23. Furbank cites the account given in the *London Times*: "At Amritsar, on April 13, the mob defied the proclamation forbidding public gatherings. Firing ensued, and 200 casualties occurred." Furbank, *E. M. Forster: A Life*, 2:58. Note the strategic use of the passive voice.

24. Sara Suleri, *The Rhetoric of English India*, (Chicago, 1992), 138–39.

25. In the essay "Dissemination," Jacques Derrida describes the "East" as that which "assures the West of all its fantasies of mastery (including the mastery of its fantasies)." *Dissemination*, trans. Barbara Johnson (Chicago, 1981), 352.

26. See Eve Kosofsky Sedgwick, *Between Men: English Literature and Male Homosocial Desire* (New York, 1985), 206–7.

27. Albert Memmi, *The Colonizer and the Colonized* (Boston, 1957), 20, 37.

28. Richard Burton recounts being ordered, unofficially, by the British army in Sind to investigate the male brothels of Karachi. His report was mistakenly sent to Bombay, and he was summarily dismissed from the army. See *Love, War*

and Fancy: The Social and Sexual Customs of the East, ed. Kenneth Walker (London, 1964), 174–75.

29. Cited in Furbank, *E. M. Forster: A Life*, 2:106.

30. Such events include the Rowlatt Satyagraha of 1919, and the first Non-Cooperation Movement of 1920. The Rowlatt Satyagraha was a nationwide, Hindu-Muslim protest of the repressive laws of the Rowlatt Bill. The Non-Cooperation Movement followed, as the Indian Nationalists became increasingly convinced of the bad faith of the British in regard to eventual self-rule. See R. Kumar, ed., *Essays on Gandhian Politics: The Rowlatt Satyagraha of 1919* (Oxford, 1971); Gyanendra Pandey, "Peasant Revolt and Indian Nationalism: The Peasant Movement in Awadh, 1919–1922"; and Shahid Amin, "Gandhi as Mahatma," both in *Subaltern Studies: Deconstructing Historiography*, ed. Ranajit Guha and Gayatri Chakravorty Spivak (New York, 1988).

31. Frances Singh, "*A Passage to India*, the National Movement, and Independence," *Twentieth Century Literature* 31 (Summer/Fall 1985): 273.

32. Said, *Orientalism*, 248.

Engendering the Armed Struggle: Women, Writing, and the Bengali "Terrorist" Movement

Purnima Bose

O. M. Martin, the Rajshahi District Magistrate, did not dare to move a step without a posse of armed guards around him. He lived in great fear of the woman terrorist in particular, who seemed to him to be deadlier than the male of her species. Donovan, the Barisal District Magistrate, left his post and quit the country in a hurry. A pretext was trumped up by the administrative personnel to save him from embarrassment but "it is perfectly clear," wrote Anderson (the Governor of Bengal), "that he had lost his nerve and was becoming hysterical."
—Tanika Sarkar[1]

INTRODUCTION: REENACTING THE EASTER RISING

In 1928 when Surjya Sen, Ananta Singh, and Ganesh Ghosh were released from detention under the infamous Bengal Criminal Law Amendment Ordinance, they returned to Chittagong in order to renew their struggle for Indian Independence.[2] They belonged to an organization loosely associated with the Jugantar party, one of the two major parties in Bengal engaged in terrorist activities. Up till 1928, Jugantar primarily carried out assassinations, while the other party, Anushilan, focused on fund-raising and the procurement of arms by banditry. Sen, Singh, and Ghosh, according to Kalpana Dutt, "had found that the British government could not be dislodged by the killing of a handful of government officials, a few Europeans or police officers."[3] The terrorist revolutionaries became overcome with "despondency" (Dutt 1). To break this "inertia," the group decided to engage the government in "open armed conflict" (Dutt 1). They planned "to raid the government armoury and seize arms, cut communications and prevent the government from

getting reinforcements" (Dutt 1). And if the British government attempted to take back Chittagong, then the terrorist revolutionaries vowed
to fight to the death. Dutt explains that "they thought their short but
heroic legend would be blazoned forth all over the land and inspire new
generations to fight for the freedom of their motherland" (1).

On April 18, 1930, the anniversary of the Easter Uprising in Ireland,
sixty-four members of this group, which called itself the Indian Republican Army after the Irish Republican Army, launched simultaneous attacks on the police armoury, the British Auxiliary Force Armoury, the
Telegraph and Telephone Exchange, and the European Club at Chittagong.[4] The terrorist revolutionaries succeeded in capturing a large number of arms consisting of pistols, revolvers, rifles, and a few Lewis guns,
though the Lewis guns were ineffective because the terrorist revolutionaries could not find ammunition for them.[5] They damaged the Post and
Telegraph Office—cutting off telegraph communication—derailed a
train, and paralyzed the armed police force.[6] For four whole days, the
terrorist revolutionaries controlled Chittagong. On April 22, 1930, British reinforcements arrived, and attacked them on Jalalabad hill. The
terrorist revolutionaries' rifles proved no match for the machine guns of
the army, and as a result a large number of Indian fighters died. At this
point, the terrorist revolutionaries changed their strategy, deciding to
carry on a protracted guerrilla struggle instead of fighting to the death.
They fled to the forests, where they continued the guerrilla campaign for
several years.[7] The terrorist revolutionaries' leader Surjya Sen eluded
capture till 1933; he was tried and hanged in 1934.[8] With the execution
of Surjya Sen and the imprisonment of other key leaders, the Indian
Republican Army, Chittagong branch, dissolved.

Kalpana Dutt chronicles these events in her *Chittagong Armoury Raiders
Reminiscences*, first published in 1945. Though the events she records make
for high drama, lending themselves to a paradigmatic linear narrative that
could build to a suspenseful climax, Dutt does not organize her story
around plot. Rather, she arranges it according to character; of the thirteen
chapters that constitute her tale, eleven take their names from individuals
in the movement. In addition to these chapters, an introduction outlines
the major events of the period, and two concluding chapters briefly touch
on Dutt's incarceration as a political prisoner on the Andaman Islands
from 1933 to 1939, her conversion to communism while in prison, and

her experiences as a communist organizer following her release. The organization of Dutt's book is entirely consistent with the implicit ideology informing the terrorist revolutionaries' strategy of foregrounding individual bravery, through highly visible public acts, over mass organization. Together, the minibiographies are less a collective narrative of group action than they are tributes to brave men and women.

As part of a general corpus of writing *on* nationalism *by* nationalists, Dutt's *Chittagong Armoury Raiders Reminiscences* belongs to a body of texts generally neglected by Western scholars working on the problematic of nationalism. As Laura Lyons notes, much of the "traditional work on nationalism has focused on illuminating the historical and material conditions that gave rise both to nationalist ideology and to conceptions of the nation-state in the period of the enlightenment. This work remains largely metacritical; that is, it takes as its object of investigation other theories of nationalism."[9] The neglect of such materials suggests that Western scholars have not taken seriously practitioners of nationalism as theoreticians in their own right.[10] While feminist scholars have examined writing by South Asian nationalist women, their accounts of this writing tend to focus overwhelmingly on the informational details of specific events, determining which nationalists were involved in what actions. Lyons's injunction to treat writing by nationalists as theory, in the South Asian context, runs up against the conventions of biography, the preferred genre of many nationalist women.

For example, Dutt's text is not overtly theoretical. The minibiographies of her comrades rely on personal experiences and are more descriptive than analytic. Since various communist thinkers such as M. N. Roy and Leon Trotsky had articulated well-developed criticisms of terrorism that were circulating internationally at that time, her later conversion to communism gives rise to expectations that her text will function as a prototype for writing about the collective aspects of struggles. Dutt's text, however, provides little explicit information on five major topics: the organization's strategies, the theoretical foundations of the organization, the structure of the organization, an analysis of women's participation in the organization, and the gender ideology of the movement. I attempt to fill in these lacunae in my reading of Kalpana Dutt's *Chittagong Armoury Raiders Reminiscences* in terms of three textual moments: the generic conventions of biography provided both *by* and *within* this work;

the text's silences necessitated by the context of its first publication in 1945; and finally, the significance of its republication on the fiftieth anniversary of the raid in 1979.

FROM BIOGRAPHY TO MYTHOLOGY: NARRATING THE STRUGGLE

Dutt's title itself, *Chittagong Armoury Raiders Reminiscences*, initially sets up two narrative expectations. First, the title establishes the Chittagong armoury raid as a central event, anchoring the setting in Chittagong during 1930. Second, it suggests that the story of this event will be narrated by actual participants. The title, then, constructs the text as an anthology that will consist of the narratives of the individual participants in the Chittagong armoury raid. But the book does not deliver on these conventional narrative expectations. Though the introduction focuses on the armoury raid, the rest of the text covers a range of events dating from the release of a number of terrorist revolutionaries from prison in 1928, to the Bengal famine of 1943, to the provincial elections of 1945. Kalpana Dutt mentions these events as anecdotes that bear on the moral character of the individuals she profiles. Moreover, she herself did not participate in the armoury raid, since she was studying in Calcutta at the time (Dutt 10). Dutt was not an active member of the terrorist revolutionaries until her return to Chittagong during her college holidays, some three weeks after the armoury raid. Contrary to the expectations set up by the title, *Chittagong Armoury Raiders Reminiscences* is a nonparticipant celebration of the experiences and characters of the individuals who took part in the armoury raid.

Dutt's narrative of these individuals breaks down the traditional dichotomy between history and myth, by refusing to acknowledge a difference between the two discourses. Her character sketches often include references to literature and popular culture, comparing particular comrades to fictional heroes. In one instance, she likens Surjya Sen to Doctorda, a terrorist in Sarat Chandra's novel *Pather Dabi* (12). In another instance, Ananta Singh becomes "Robinhood," "a legend, a symbol of freedom and fearlessness" (Dutt 17). Indeed, Dutt's first glimpse of Singh is narratively framed in terms of a gendered male legend:

The famous Ramamoorthy circus had come to Chittagong. I was a small girl then. The family went along to see it. Elephants walked over the chest of a giant of a man. A heavy, strong armed giant held back a car whose engine was running fullspeed. I used to get thrilled by it all. An Englishman broke a hefty set of chains tied to a car—they were thick and strong! Then the white giant threw out his chest—Tarzan-fashion—and challenged Chittagonians to dare come and repeat his performance. An unknown youth took up the challenge. He walked up and broke the chain while the audience watched with bated breath—was he not foolhardy to try? I had heard then that his name was Ananta Singh. (17)

This anecdote begins with examples of superhuman strength that seemingly defy rational explanation. It then introduces "the white giant," a veritable "Tarzan," as part of this superhuman continuum. The "white giant's" challenge sets up two notable oppositions. The challenger and his opponent embody differences in age and nationality. While the "giant" is an "Englishman," his opponent is an Indian "youth." In meeting the Englishman's challenge, the youth symbolically defeats Tarzan. This defeat can be read as a repudiation of the Tarzan myth, the ultimate white male colonizer's fantasy of "going native," where the native has been eliminated altogether in favor of the pristine innocence of nature.[11] Chittagong's own Ananta Singh, then, rises to challenge the physical supremacy of the Englishman, proving that the English can be beaten, even on their own terms.

At the same time, however, the incident links the young Singh with an Indian mythic past in which public challenges and displays of masculine strength loom large. Singh joins the youthful ranks of Rama and Arjuna. In the *Ramayana*, Rama rises to King Janaka's challenge, by lifting, bending, and stringing Shiva's enormous bow in front of an awed audience. Similarly, Arjuna, in the *Mahabharata*, is the only one who can meet the challenge of Draupadi's public *swayamwara* where competitors are required to "string a bow kept on a pedestal and shoot five arrows at a revolving target above by looking at its reflection on a pan of oil below."[12] Both contests reward the victors with marriage. Thus Rama wins Sita as his bride, and Arjuna gains Draupadi as a spouse (though he ends up sharing her with his four brothers, on account of filial duty and as a result of a semantic misunderstanding). The terrorist revolutionaries, as I explain later in this article, gendered India as a female. In Singh's case, the female prize becomes India herself.

The participants do not speak for themselves in these vignettes. Each of the minibiographies is mediated through Dutt, who narrates anecdotes about her comrades. The sections are organized according to character, with each of the chapters bearing a terrorist revolutionary's good (proper) name or pet (nick)name. Dutt generally gives anecdotes that emphasize the high moral caliber of her comrades. Observations on the individual by other important terrorist revolutionaries support these anecdotes. The narrative voice freely alternates between the first person and third person omniscient. For example, describing Ambika Chakravarty's injury during the battle of Jalalabad hill, Dutt writes,

He had been shot through the head. His comrades left him for dead. He fainted and then later the cool night breeze slowly brought him back to consciousness. He was still terribly weak, could not move an inch without howling with pain. He himself had grave doubts whether he was still alive. It was highly unlikely, perhaps he had become a ghost? He tried out experiments—moved his hand ever so slowly, touched his forehead and felt an acute pain. Ah! He still had a sense of pain! The pain was real all right and not at all ghostly—may be he was still alive. Then he tried to pick himself up, ever so cautiously. But then he tumbled downhill right into a pond below. He revived after gulping down some water and started walking towards the town, he hobbled along, stopping every now and then for breath. (32)

Dutt adopts Chakravarty's point of view in this passage, attributing ruminations to him on the supernatural that she cannot know from her perspective. In fact, she begins this section by admitting, "There were several leaders of the Chittagong armoury raid whom I had never actually seen. Ambikada was one of them" (31). If Chakravarty did not describe his ordeal to Dutt, then who furnished her with the details that figure in her account? Dutt does not say. Her narrative does not name the sources that ordinarily legitimize historical discourse. Dutt's lack of explicit sources, together with the ambiguity surrounding her use of voice, blurs the distinctions between history and myth in her text. The changes in narrative voice bestow upon her text the authority of an eyewitness account, by giving the impression that Dutt was actually present at the events she describes. Given these shifts in voice, together with the title of the work, it is not surprising that some scholars have mistakenly assumed that Dutt participated in the Chittagong armoury raid. Both Kumari Jayawardena *(Feminism and Nationalism in the Third World)* and Vijay Agnew *(Elite Women in Indian Politics)* incorrectly identify her as a partici-pant.[13] Agnew even claims that Dutt "lead the Chittagong Armoury Raid" when "she was only 18."[14]

Dutt's inclusion of local stories surrounding the terrorist revolutionaries contributes to the transformation of her comrades into regional myths. She often attributes stories about the terrorist revolutionaries to "the people," suggesting that her comrades have already attained mythic status. P. C. Joshi, the general secretary of the Communist Party of India from 1935 to 1947 and Dutt's husband, agrees with this assessment. In the preface to the first edition of the book, he claims, "To read these reminiscences is to understand what made the leaders of the group legendary figures and the humblest of them household names where they were born and worked" (v).

Many of these anecdotes thematize "escape." Escape occurs at two different levels: at one level, the terrorist revolutionaries escape from the authorities, by eluding capture, and at another level, they escape from death itself. In the section on Mani Dutt, who is also known as the "Lecturer," Dutt describes an incident in which three of the underground terrorist revolutionaries venture into town. Some cart drivers begin to harass them. Suspecting that an informant has betrayed them to the cart drivers, Lecturer decides on a course of action:

He challenged them [the cart drivers] and he started going at them with both fists. He held them at bay and asked us to run for it. It was awkward, we had to run down the main street with a torch [flashlight] in one hand and a revolver in the other. Meanwhile the cartdrivers started shouting: "thief! thief!" After we had got a good start on them, Lecturer let them go and sprinted to join us and started yelling "thief! thief!" himself. At this, people thought the "thieves" were ahead of us and tried to run further ahead and we were beyond suspicion ourselves. In the confusion, we struck down an alley and were safe. (57)

Anecdotes such as this one highlight the terrorist revolutionaries' ability to think and act under great pressure, thus emphasizing their cleverness. And in addition, these stories provide moments of humor in the narrative, typically casting the authorities and other native collaborators as comic dupes. Anecdotes of the second level, those that treat escapes from death—such as the one on Ambika Chakravarty quoted earlier—likewise have an important narrative function. They establish the terrorist revolutionaries' bravery and resilience in the face of extreme physical pain, setting the terrorist revolutionaries apart from ordinary people by giving them a supernatural mystique. All these factors help to mythologize the terrorist revolutionaries.

Dutt's emphasis on individuals seems at odds with her professed communist politics. The tension between individualism and collectivity mir-

rors that between terrorism and mass organization and resonates throughout the book. In the 1979 preface to the second edition of her book, Dutt
comments on the inappropriateness of the title *Chittagong Armoury Raiders
Reminiscences*. Pointing out that "Raids were only a part of the whole
programme," Dutt insists that "Reminiscences of the Chittagong Revolutionaries" would have been a more apt title for her narrative (xiii). By
identifying her group now as "revolutionaries," Dutt retrospectively challenges their characterization as "terrorists" by "British imperialists" and
"bourgeois historians" (xii).

The discourse of "terrorism," according to Richard Rubenstein, generally relies on either of two similes: terrorism-as-crime or terrorism-as-
war.[15] Rubenstein explains that "political terrorism is sui generis—a
specific form of violence distinguishable from both crime and warfare,
although bearing a family resemblance to both."[16] The terrorism-as-
crime simile denies the possibility that terrorism, armed struggle, and
mass violence are linked in a continuum under the assumption that terrorism will not evolve into mass struggle.[17] Rubenstein argues that "To
assert that a violent act is essentially criminal is to have concluded that it
is *not* integral to a process of legitimate political transformation."[18] The
use of the terrorism-as-war simile, in contrast, views terrorist activity as
a method of warfare. This view, Rubenstein notes, is actually a "predic-
tion": "it foretells the gradual transformation of irregular warfare, fought
by a vanguard with limited, largely passive civilian support, into a conventional war or revolution that mobilizes the masses to defend their
interests directly."[19] As the organization progresses from individualistic
violence toward armed struggle—also known as "sustained or escalated
terrorism" by those in power—the focus of rebel attacks may shift from
symbols of authority to more strategic economic, military, and political
targets.[20] The Chittagong terrorist revolutionaries' decision to conduct an
armoury raid instead of assassinating British officials signals such a shift.

In northern India, where the terrorist revolutionaries are highly re-
vered, people call them "terrorists." When the signifier "terrorist" is
applied to describe forms of armed resistance to British colonial rule, it
loses its pejorative connotations in India.[21] The terrorist revolutionaries
referred to themselves as "revolutionaries." Their use of "revolutionaries"
substitutes a simile of terrorism-as-war for that of terrorism-as-crime. In
the Indian nationalist context, both usages of "terrorists" and "revolutionaries" complicate the association of terrorism and crime so prevalent in

the West. While Dutt generally refers to the terrorist revolutionaries as "revolutionaries," she calls them " 'terrorist' revolutionaries" in one location (9). This term occurs in the context of a passage devoted to the conversion of individual terrorist revolutionaries to communism while in "the cold, silent recess of the prison-cell" (8). Dutt's term "terrorist revolutionaries" simultaneously challenges the simile of terrorism-as-crime while maintaining a distinction between terrorism and mass organization. I have chosen to follow Dutt's usage because it undoes the conventional dichotomy of terrorism as crime or war.

As I noted earlier, prior to 1928 Jugantar concentrated its efforts on targeting British officials, policemen, and collaborators for assassination. In these cases, the victims stand in as symbolic representatives of social groups or governments. Through the assassination of symbolic representatives, "terrorists" seek "to cause a society or government to take notice of the imminence of large-scale struggles."[22] But if their actions are aimed at the existing government, "terrorists" are just as concerned with alerting "people . . . that constituted authority is no longer entrenched and un-challenged."[23] These symbolic acts are developed with three groups of people in mind: the populace, the regime in power, and the terrorist organization itself.[24] Baljit Singh outlines the objectives that correspond to each group: "1. [to] gain popular support, 2. [to] disrupt and destroy the military and psychological strength of the regime, and 3. [to] achieve internal stability and growth."[25] Short-term objectives often include building morale within the organization, movement advertising, the psychological disorientation of the public, the elimination of opposition forces, and the provocation of the government.

Jugantar's political assassinations exhibit these characteristics. Reflecting on the assassinations that took place in Bengal during the nationalist period, Tara Ali Baig comments, "Looking at terrorism today, I can't help feeling that was a rather polite kind of terrorism. There was no question of bombing groups of innocent people. There were definitely targeted individuals."[26] Before 1924, most of Jugantar's assassination targets consisted of Indians.[27] The majority of these individuals belonged to the police department, which waged an active campaign against the terrorist revolutionaries.[28] Indians who were not officials of the government were also selected as targets if they fell into three categories: police informants, individuals who openly testified against the terrorist revolutionaries in court, and those terrorist revolutionaries within the organization who had betrayed fellow members.[29] Some of the terrorist revolutionaries, Shaileshwar Nath observes, conceptualized the assassination of these Indians as a form of "divine dispensation, inasmuch as, the English merely tried to serve their own country whereas the Indians were traitors to their Mother."[30]

After 1924, Jugantar decided to target Europeans, generally government officials, for assassination. From 1931 to 1932 a few of Jugantar's targets included police inspectors, district magistrates, and a sessions judge. Unsuccessful attempts were made on Dacca's divisional commissioner, the governor of Bengal, and the commissioner of police of Calcutta, Sir Charles Tegart, notorious for his torture of terrorist revolutionaries.[31] Nath describes another aspect of these assassinations: "most of the murders were committed in broad daylight and in the most crowded localities."[32] Bina Das attempted to assassinate the governor of Bengal, Sir Stanley Jackson, in broad daylight during Calcutta University's convocation ceremony. Santi Ghosh and Suniti Choudhury assassinated the district magistrate of Comilla on his verandah in the middle of the day. All three of the women were arrested immediately after their acts. A good deal of the power of these assassinations as symbolic acts derived from their public performance and the willingness of individual terrorist revolutionaries to take responsibility for them.

It is important to situate Jugantar's highly visible actions within the context of colonial racism against Bengalis. The highly educated Bengali community challenged the British conception of Indians.[33] The British attributed a childlike primitiveness to Indians and focused their attention on communities that seemed to fit easily into this category: the peasants, tribal groups, and the princely classes, who were viewed as childishly self-serving.[34] As Philip Mason, a former colonial official, admits, "British officers in colonial situations always do like the simple, unspoilt people."[35] The educated classes, especially Western-educated Bengalis, were dismissed as comic imitations of Westerners. They were virulently caricatured in the figure of the Bengali babu: a small, dark-skinned, effeminate male intellectual who had an imperfect command of English. *Hobson-Jobson*, the dictionary of British India's patois, defines a "baboo" as a term that "is often used with a slight savour of disparagement, as characterizing a superficially cultivated, but too often effeminate, Bengali . . . the word has come often to signify 'a native clerk who writes English.' "[36] In *Plain Tales from the Raj*, former colonial officials describe "the fashion" of denigrating "the *babu* type":

"We used to make fun of them, very unfairly, because they were interpreting rules which we had made." *Babu* jokes, based on the English language either wrongly or over-effusively applied, were a constant source of amusements for all "Anglo-India." Coupled with the denigration of the *babu* was a traditional distrust of the Bengali—"litigious, very fond of an argument"—who was frequently seen as a trouble-maker: "He doesn't appeal to many British people in the same way as the very much more manly, direct type from upper India."[37]

This stereotype is so pernicious that it exists even today. In an interview that appeared in the *Souvenir Chowkidar* (1986), Raj revival writer Pat Barr asks Geoffrey Moorhouse, the author of *Calcutta*, "whether some Bengalis might resent having the story of their capital so well told by a foreigner who never even lived there."[38] Moorhouse replies, "They disagreed with some of it naturally, *Bengalis always argue*. But they like the book" (my emphasis).[39] Several years later, the fall 1989 issue of the *Chowkidar* assures us that "A Bengali without a point of view is like a fish out of water."[40] The term "Bengalis" is a regional and cultural marker, signifying people whose ancestors are from Bengal and who share a common language and culture. In these examples, all Bengalis have been cast as babus, as highly opinionated and consequently slightly ridiculous individuals.

The representation of the Bengali as overly fond of litigation and full of contentious opinions contrasts with Kalpana Dutt's repeated references to the terrorist revolutionaries' clear use of language. Commenting on Ananta Singh's autobiography, she says,

I got to know him through his writings too. He wrote his life story in jail and sent it out to us. His writing was simple and straightforward. There were no fine phrases and complicated constructions. He put his heart into it and applied a keen mind, and the result made wonderful reading. You could almost sense the writer next to you and get carried off by his powerful, irresistible logic. It was after reading his writings that I had got to know that he who feels intensely and has a clear understanding can write well. Nothing else is required for writing pieces that hit the mark. (23)

Dutt describes another comrade's writing in similar terms: Ganesh Ghosh's writing, for her, has a "beautiful, easy style," in which "Every word was simple and clear" (26). Ghosh and Singh produced their writing within the prison for the consumption of their comrades outside prison. The writing helped occupy the prisoners, sustain morale among those outside by communicating information about the prisoners, and provide an inspiring impetus to new recruits. In order to fulfill these functions, the texts had to be accessible and clearly communicate their messages.

The style of the writing, notable for its lack of complex "constructions," was closely related to its political function.

Like Dutt, with her portraits of individual terrorist revolutionaries, Ghosh and Singh both favored autobiography and biography as their preferred genres. According to John Beverley, the autobiographical form has implicit within it an ideology of individualism, "that is built on the notion of a coherent, self-evident, self-conscious, commanding subject that appropriates literature precisely as a means of 'self-expression' and that in turn constructs textually for the reader the liberal imaginary of a unique, 'free,' autonomous ego as the natural form of being and public achievement."[41] The terrorist revolutionaries' choice of the biographical genre manifested several contradictions. While the biographies derived from an ideology of individualism—which works against mass organization and subaltern empowerment—they proved valuable as a tool of propaganda to mobilize support and new recruits for the movement. Moreover, the biographies and autobiographies intervened in the racist British discourse of the babu. By presenting the heroic actions of individual Bengalis, the portraits both established Bengali terrorist revolutionaries as effective political agents and inserted the names of individual terrorist revolutionaries into the historical record, a record dominated by colonial figures and the native Indian bourgeois elite.

The terrorist revolutionaries did not limit themselves to prose. Ghosh not only wrote "the history and activities of the Bengal revolutionaries and . . . the Chittagong heroes" in prose, he also committed these to verse. Dutt quotes sections of his "Chittagong Brigade" in her book. Though it is impossible to reconstruct Ghosh's original text from her fragments, we can arrive at the significance of the excerpts that Dutt quotes, and see how these fit into the larger project of mythologizing the terrorist revolutionaries. In the following passage, italics demarcate Ghosh's text from Dutt's. I have chosen to follow Dutt's format, instead of the standard block one, to convey the spirit of this part of her text.

> "*Steadily*
>   *Step by step*
>   *Forward marched*
>   *To the grave,*
>   *To the field of fame*
>   *Forward marched*
>   *The youths brave.*"

Then he wrote: *"The fifty-eight marched on for four days, over the hills—without food, without sleep—haggard but determined. They pushed on under the blazing April sun, without any cover—over the bleak, waterless hilly wastes. The water-bottles were hot like pieces of live charcoal. Couldn't shoulder the rifles. They were sizzling hot."*

Then—*"Tegra opened martyrdom's gate,"* he wrote. Tegra was the first to fall before machinegun bullets. He was Loknath Bal's younger brother. Then others—many others—were mown down. (27–28)

The excerpts that Dutt quotes focus on the physical elements: the blazing sun, the waterless hills, and the heat. This evocation of nature differs strikingly from the representation of nature in the Bengali folk tradition, where nature and natural elements are typically allegorical. The songs of the Bauls of Bengal, for example, function on three interpretive frameworks: the natural, the religious, and the sexual. However, in Ghosh's poem, nature begins to personify the enemy, by punishing the terrorist revolutionaries with dehydration and unbearable heat.

Written as it is in English, "The Chittagong Brigade" draws less on a Bengali literary tradition than on an English one. The poem echoes Alfred Tennyson's "Charge of the Light Brigade," written in 1854 to commemorate the deaths of English soldiers in the Crimean War. Because of a confusion over orders during this war, a brigade of six hundred British cavalry charged some entrenched batteries of Russian artillery. As a result, three-fourths of the horsemen lost their lives. Tennyson wrote the poem after reading an account of the battle in a newspaper.[42] He ends his poem with the following stanza:

> When can their glory fade?
> O the wild charge they made!
> All the world wondered.
> Honor the charge they made!
> Honor the Light Brigade,
> Noble six hundred![43]

Ghosh's last stanza is a creative transformation of Tennyson's piece:

> *When can their glory fade*
> *O, the brave fight they gave*
> *Honour the Chittagong brigade*
> *The noble fifty-eight.* (28)

Like Tennyson, Ghosh emphasizes the total number of men involved in action. Ghosh draws on Tennyson's vocabulary, using "glory," "honor," and "noble" in his poem. Ghosh's "Chittagong Brigade" relies on the audience's familiarity with "The Charge of the Light Brigade." Ghosh strategically borrowed from Tennyson's verse, in order to elevate the terrorist revolutionaries to the same status of national heroes as Tennyson had been able to do for English soldiers during the Crimean War. Paradoxically, Ghosh used an English paradigm for his text to establish the bravery of Indians resisting British colonial rule.

Dutt's repeated insistence on the clarity of the terrorist revolutionaries' use of language repudiates the stereotype of the Bengali babu as overly fond of contentious argument and effusive language. The stereotype of the Bengali babu belonged to a gendered colonial discourse of racial typologies. The British divided Indians into the martial and nonmartial races. In *Plain Tales from the Raj*, former colonial officers identify the martial races as the Gurkhas, Sikhs, Punjabi "Mohammedans," Jats, Dogras, Garhwalis, and Mahrattas.[44] Lewis Le Marchand's characterization of the Gurkha soldier is typical of the discourse on the martial races, emphasizing as it does the innate simplicity, blind obedience, and tremendous courage of these men. The Gurkha, in Le Marchand's view, is "very proud, very gay, very simple. He's as brave as a mountain lion and he'll obey any order you like to give."[45] While the British valorized the martial races, they denigrated the nonmartial ones such as the Bengalis.

Ashis Nandy argues that the British concept of the martial races — "the hyper-masculine, manifestly courageous, superbly loyal Indian castes and subcultures," which "mirrored the British middle-class sexual stereotypes" — resurrected "the ideology of the martial races latent in the traditional Indian concept of statecraft."[46] This concept of statecraft is closely linked to the ksatriya caste, whose duties traditionally included governance and the protection of the state. Aurobindo Ghose, who was a terrorist revolutionary before becoming a yogin in 1910, valorized the ksatriyas as the warrior caste who would be agents of Indian Independence. Ghose produced much of the ideological and cultural foundations of the terrorist revolutionary movement. He drew on Hindu literature, particularly the *Bhagavad Gita* from the *Mahabharata*, to legitimize the use of violence as a strategy of resistance. In his *Doctrine of Passive Resistance*, Ghose sanctifies violence as a ksatriya's dharma, or moral duty. He writes,

The morality of the Kshatriya justifies violence in times of war, and boycott is a war. . . . Aggression is unjust only when unprovoked; violence, unrighteous when used wantonly or for unrighteous ends. . . . The sword of the warrior is as necessary to the fulfillment of justice and righteousness as the holiness of the saint. . . . To maintain justice and prevent the strong from despoiling, and the weak from being oppressed, is the function for which the Kshatriya was created. "Therefore" says Sri Krishna in the *Mahabharata*, "God created battle and armour, the sword, the bow and the dagger." [47]

The terrorist revolutionaries' actions can be understood as an attempt to establish masculine notions of bravery through individual public acts of violence that accord with ksatriya martial values. Analyzing the data available for the first phase of terrorism in Bengal, Leonard Gordon notes that 90 percent of the terrorist revolutionaries came from high castes; they were brahmins, kayasthas and vaidyas. [48] Of the eleven individuals Dutt profiles, two are brahmins, five belong to the kayastha caste, one is a Sikh, and the caste of the other three is indeterminable.

By boldly assassinating Europeans in public settings with large Indian audiences, the terrorist revolutionaries challenged the British stereotype of the Bengali babu as cowardly and effeminate. The terrorist revolutionaries accepted the colonial culture's ordering of manliness as greater than womanliness, which was in turn superior to femininity in men. [49] To this extent, they did not break out of the binary logic of colonialism. When the assassins were women, however, binary notions of gender became more complicated.

If the public assassination of European men by Indian men established the manliness of the latter, the assassination of European men by Indian women theoretically served to undermine European manhood. Indian women had long been considered backward and submissive in comparison with their European counterparts. The female terrorist revolutionaries were potent examples that Indian women could challenge British authority, by inverting the colonial ordering that equated strength with the masculine and the colonizer, and weakness with the feminine and the colonized. The British government's treatment of women in the mainstream nationalist movement often emphasized this ordering. F. C. Hart, a former policeman who served in the Special Branch, describes one encounter with female satyagrahis:

a number of women laid themselves down on the ground right across the street and held up all the traffic. When the Superintendent of Police arrived on the scene he was at first nonplussed. If they had been men he could have sent in policemen to lift them out bodily, but he daren't do it with women. So he thought for a bit and then he called for fire hoses and with the hoses they sprayed these women who were lying on the ground. They only wore very thin saris and, of course, when the water got on them all their figures could be seen. The constables started cracking dirty jokes and immediately the women got up and ran.[50]

In this example, the superintendent of police has marshaled the Indian cultural concept of *sharam* to the authorities' advantage. *Sharam*, or shame, is a powerful concept used to control Indian women. It is closely linked to notions of sexual chastity and has come to signify sexual impropriety of some sort. The term can be employed to cover a whole range of behavior. By exposing the women's bodies to the public gaze, the British authorities violated traditional norms of female propriety, in which women covered their bodies as a sign of their chastity. The authorities' shrewd manipulation of *sharam* effectively quashed the women's political protest.[51]

Though the female terrorist revolutionaries' actions symbolically emasculated European men, they did not theorize their actions in feminist terms. For instance, Bina Das, who unsuccessfully attempted to assassinate Sir Stanley Jackson, the governor of Bengal, during the Calcutta University convocation ceremony in 1932, explains her act in the following manner:

I had been thinking—is life worth living in an India, so subject to wrong and continually groaning under the tyranny of a foreign government or is it not better to make one supreme protest against it by offering one's life away? Would not the immolation of a daughter of India and of a son of England awaken India to the sin of its acquiescence to its continued state of subjection and England to the iniquities of its proceedings. . . . All these [sufferings of the people] and many others worked on my feelings and worked them into a frenzy. The pain became unbearable and I felt as if I would go mad if I could not find relief in death. I only sought the way to death by offering myself at the feet of my country and invite the attention of all by my death to the situation created by the measures of the Government, *which can unsex even a frail woman like myself, brought up in all the best tradition of Indian womanhood*. (emphasis in original)[52]

Das's explanation does not describe the relationship between India and England as simply that of victim and victimizer. She holds both culpable for England's continued rule over India. By describing herself as a "daughter of India" and Jackson as a "son of England," she implicitly couches the relationship between both countries in a familial metaphor. As members of the same generation, Jackson and Das are siblings, whose deaths will become symbols that will "awaken" the English and Indians to the injustice of colonial rule. Das's use of the familial metaphor rewrites the relationship between the two countries implied by E. M. Forster's *Passage to India* in 1924. Forster's positioning of the colonial encounter within a perverse relationship—with its suggestions of sexual assault—between an Indian man and an Englishwoman became a trope for later writers of the Raj. Paul Scott literalized this trope by initiating *The Raj Quartet* with the rape of an Englishwoman by a number of Indian men. Scott's "story of a rape" is a symbol of "two nations in violent opposition . . . locked in an imperial embrace of such long standing and subtlety it was no longer possible for them to know whether they hated or loved one another."[53]

But the sibling metaphor, employed by Das, does not altogether break with the sexual implications of Forster's narrative. Das simultaneously envisions Jackson's death as well as her own demise by "immolation." This reference to immolation conjures up the practice of sati, the immolation of a woman on her husband's funeral pyre. Satis are venerated as minor deities for expressing the ultimate devotion to their *pati-vrata*, the husband-God. Lata Mani argues that the debate around sati was part of a larger process of "reconstituting" indigenous tradition under colonial rule: "in different ways, women and brahmanic scripture become interlocking grounds for this rearticulation. Women become emblematic of tradition, and the reworking of tradition is largely conducted through debating the rights and status of women in society."[54] Sati was prevalent among upper-caste Bengalis, who were major participants in the rearticulation of tradition. The area around Calcutta had the highest concentration of upper-caste satis in the early nineteenth century.[55] Das says that she has been "brought up in all the best tradition of Indian womanhood," a tradition that at one time included sati.[56] Das's subtle reference to sati metaphorically makes Jackson her husband. But if he is metaphorically her husband, he is also her brother. Their relationship is incestuous and, by implication, "unnatural." It is symptomatic of the perversity of the times, in which the repressive measures of the government have "unsex(ed) even a frail woman like" Das.

Das's assassination attempt, according to Geraldine Forbes, "was to rouse people to action because Bina was an Indian girl driven to an unnatural act by the British Raj."[57] For all of Das's protestations that the violence of her action is antithetical to female nature, her cultural background and that of the Bengali terrorist revolutionaries contains strong violent female figures. *Shakti* is the female power principle embodied in the Goddesses Kali and Durga, who are both manifestations of Shiva's spouse Parvati and highly venerated in Bengal. Joanna Liddle and Rama Joshi describe Kali as "a malevolent destroyer, the manifestation of a terrible sinister force, black anger, implacable and bloodthirsty."[58] The gods created Kali in order to save them from their more powerful enemies. After completing her task, she continued her rampage of killing until her husband Shiva appeased her, by lying down in front of her.[59] In her malevolent aspect Kali demands blood sacrifices.[60] The more benevolent Durga is figured as a female warrior riding a tiger, with a weapon in most of her multiple arms. *Shakti* came to symbolize the "Motherland in different stages and conditions."[61] V. D. Mahajan elaborates this point:

Jagatdhatri—riding a lion which has the prostrate body of an elephant under its paw, represented the Motherland in the early jungle clearing stage. This is, says Bankim Chandra, the Mother as she was. *Kali* the grim goddess dancing on the prostrate form of Shiva, the God—*Durga*, the ten-headed *[sic]* goddess, armed with swords and spears in some hands . . . riding a lion, fighting with demons . . . this, says Bankim Chandra, is the mother as she will be.[62]

The early terrorist revolutionaries drew on these potent symbols for inspiration. Barindra Kumar Ghose, the younger brother of Aurobindo Ghose, and Bhupendra Nath Dutt, the brother of Swami Vivekananda, started the political journal *Jugantar*, from which the later terrorist revolutionaries took their name. "Jugantar" literally means "a different age." In the context of the nationalist struggle, it can be translated as "a new age." (Indeed, the *Samsad Bengali-English Dictionary* adds "an epoch making revolution" to these definitions.)[63] Ghose and B. N. Dutt published the journal from 1906 to 1908, when the authorities shut it down under the Newspapers (Incitement to Offences) Act.[64] With a circulation of around seven thousand in 1907, *Jugantar* was taken seriously by the British, as the *Sedition (Rowlatt) Committee's Report* indicates: "Its character and teaching entirely justify the comments of the Chief Justice, Sir Lawrence Jenkins, quoting and adopting the following words of the Sessions Judge of Alipore. 'They exhibit a burning hatred of the British race, they breathe revolution in every line, they point out how revolution is to be effected.' "[65] *Jugantar* exhorted its readers to sacrifice themselves at the altar of India, to take a life before giving one's life. Some examples of their rhetoric include the following:

We will bathe in the enemy's blood and with it dye Hindustan.[66]

Look there, the terrible sword glowing with blood is swirling. Look there, the guerrilla bands are swarming the country; they are plundering the arsenals; there, the vacant throne of the demon is being washed away by the waves of the Bay of Bengal.[67]

Will the Bengalee worshipper of Shakti shrink from the shedding of blood? . . . The worship of the goddess will not be consummated if you sacrifice your lives at the shrine of Independence without shedding blood.[68]

India became the Goddess Kali herself who demanded a blood sacrifice. In constructing India this way, the terrorist revolutionaries sanctified— through Hinduism—the violence they visited on the English. The terror- ist revolutionaries' use of Hindu rhetoric paralleled Gandhi's mobilization of Hindu discourse in his campaign of nonviolence. And though unin- tended in both cases, this language had the effect of excluding Muslim participation in the movement. The Bengali terrorist revolutionaries counted few Muslim participants among them, even though Bengal had a significant Muslim population at the time.[69]

The apparent contradiction of having a strong, powerful Goddess represent a subjugated country was partially resolved by having India simultaneously figured as the "Mother." Poetry, prose, and popular songs invoked and addressed the motherland. This motif even appeared woven in the borders of dhotis, the garment commonly worn by Bengali and brahmin men. In 1910, English had to order the confiscation of dhotis that flaunted the following Bengali poem in their borders:

> Mother, farewell,
> I shall go to the gallows with a smile,
> The people of India will see this.
> One bomb can kill a man, there are a lakh of
> bombs in our homes Mother, what can the English do?[70]

In 1930, in the coastal districts surrounding Midnapur where the govern- ment monopoly over salt manufacture excited popular protest, India was often represented as a mother. "A nationalist song," writes Tanika Sarkar, "compared the salt-earth to the mother's breasts from which no one had the right to take the child away."[71] Nationalist pamphlets con- tained illustrations of "Mother India in chains and tatters with white men dragging off her rich attire and jewels across the seas."[72] The use of the India-as-mother simile implicitly gendered India's revolutionary subjects as male. Indian women typically accrue status and power as mothers through the birth of sons. India's male sons would liberate her and accord her the respect due her.

The Chittagong terrorist revolutionaries employed the India-as-mother simile too. Given the ideological gendering of India, the participation of women in the movement takes on a special significance. Prior to 1930, few women were admitted to Jugantar, while Anushilan prohibited their membership altogether. After 1930, however, women began to participate in all phases of Jugantar's activities, carrying out assassinations and sometimes even leading raids against colonial targets. For example, Preeti Waddadar led a raid on the Pahartali railway club on September 24, 1932. Though she was willing to participate in the raid, she expressed reluctance to lead it. Surjya Sen, the leader of the revolutionaries, convinced her that her role as a leader would be an inspiration to other young potential female recruits.[73] The terrorist revolutionaries defined the raid as a success, since one individual was killed and twelve others were injured. But Waddadar died in the effort. She took potassium cyanide outside the club. Her suicide, as Geraldine Forbes notes, has been read a number of ways:

Her sister claimed she was wounded in the attack and took cyanide to prevent her capture by the British. Others have seen her death as the act of a young revolutionary overzealous to sacrifice herself. She had carried with her a letter to her mother in which she said that she was going to sacrifice her life for "truth and freedom." The urge to become a martyr, a symbol of dedication to the country's freedom, has emerged as a strong element in the decisions made by these young women to participate in dramatic and violent acts.[74]

Like Preeti's sister, Dutt believes Preeti was wounded, and committed suicide to avoid detention by the British. But detailed accounts of Preeti's death by other terrorist revolutionaries interpret her suicide as the act of a political martyr. R. C. Majumdar pieced together this dramatic scene from accounts by Ananta Singh and Ganesh Ghosh. After the three-minute raid, one of the fleeing participants ran back to urge Preeti to hurry and join them. Majumdar describes the scene in this way:

Handing over her revolver to him, Pritilata said. "All of you escape, do not tarry. Hit the enemy time and again and try to overthrow them; this is my last request. Go with my good wishes to you all, give my respects to 'Masterda.' " Pointing above with her finger, she said "That is my destination, the martyrs are calling me." With that she swallowed some potassium cyanide and embraced death. Sewn inside her garment was discovered a picture of Srikrishna.[75]

Preeti was the first woman to die in action. The terrorist revolutionaries interpreted her death in terms of its symbolic value. Preeti became an example of the possibilities of Indian womanhood. "From Preeti's actions," claims Dutt, "people were convinced for the first time that Indian women can do what our men have done. They can give their lives for their country as easily as men can" (44).

Because of Dutt's recognition of the power of example for Indian women, it might seem odd that she does not engage the question of gender more fully. *Chittagong Armoury Raiders Reminiscences* makes little of the special hardships that women must have encountered because of their gender. Dutt does not allude to the prevailing attitudes governing the conduct of single females. Forbes explains how the risk of scandal made it "difficult to arrange meetings between members of the opposite sex."[76] Arranging a simple discussion between men and women terrorist revolutionaries could entail complicated maneuvers.[77] Few of the women were adequately prepared to use firearms because it was so difficult to arrange secret training sessions for women. Most of the women did complete a course in " 'revolutionary skills' which technically included physical fitness, ju-jitsu, daggers, fencing, motor-driving, and sharpshooting."[78] Forbes speculates that "the reason women were not utilized more frequently or in different ways was more a result of logistical problems in training and supplying weapons to women than due to either the reluctance of males to utilize women or the unwillingness of women to perform violent acts."[79]

In spite of these limitations, women were assigned many of the same duties as the men in the organization.[80] They helped manufacture, smuggle, and hide weapons. They acted as messengers. Women wrote and distributed propaganda. They "absconded," going underground when called to do so. They also concealed absconding comrades, sometimes providing cover for them by posing as wives.[81] They assassinated members of the British ruling elite. Women participated in all stages of action: planning, organizing, and leading raids on the government. They did not, however, assume the top positions of leadership or attempt to transform gender relations within the movement. "They did not even justify their revolutionary actions on grounds of equality in political choice and protest," Tanika Sarkar claims. "They sought to explain their unconventional behavior in terms of a religious sacrifice at a time of exceptional national crisis."[82]

Though the Bengali family plays an enormous role in circumscribing a single woman's action, Dutt is silent in this regard too. There are few references to her natal family in her narrative; the terrorist revolutionaries substitute for Dutt's natal family. She refers to her elder male and female comrades in kinship terms. Dutt calls her closest male comrades *da*, the abbreviated form of the Bengali *dada*, which denotes an older brother, and she calls her female comrades *di*, the Bengali abbreviation for *didi*, referring to an older sister. Kinship terms in Bengal, Ronald Inden and Ralph Nicholas remind us, "refer not only to kinship roles but to roles defined by sex, generation, and age as well."[83] Dutt's choice of sibling titles is significant. The relationship between siblings is one of the most important in Bengal.[84] The love between siblings of opposite sex is the most egalitarian relationship between men and women of the same generation and family.[85] Even so, Inden and Nicholas rightly observe that "Within the family the egalitarian love that siblings have for each other is supposed to be subordinated to hierarchical love, based upon the differences in their ages. The parental love *(sneha)* that unites elder siblings with their juniors and the filial love *(bhakti)* that unites younger siblings with their elders is modeled after the hierarchical love that parents and children have for each other."[86] I do not want to suggest that Dutt decided to call her comrades by the kinship terms of the patriarchal Indian family simply on account of her gender. Rather, the terrorist revolutionaries as a whole group employed them to refer to one another. Their usage of these kinship terms relies on the cultural definition of *atmiya-svajana*, used to demarcate "one's own people." "One's own people" does not have a fixed meaning, encompassing as it does both filiative and affiliative ties. "Under appropriate circumstances" it can mean anyone.[87] For example, *atmiya-svajana* can be blood relatives, "persons related by marriage, by living together in the same house, neighborhood, or village, by being members of the same school class, by working together in the same office, by taking instruction from the same guru, by going on pilgrimage together," and so forth.[88]

Gordon describes the organization of the terrorist revolutionaries into basic units of action known as *dals*.[89] Dals were grouped around a single *dada* and often bore his name.[90] "In addition to his primary function as a political leader," comments Gordon, "the *dada* seems to hold something of the neoparental authority which the older brother would exercise in a Bengali family."[91] His authority partly derived from his age, since the dada was older than his followers. Gordon also notes that the relationship between the dada and his follower reflected an important religious concept, the *guru-shishya* relationship, in which "the disciple is to give complete loyalty, devotion, and respect to (the) teacher."[92] Surjya Sen, the leader of the Chittagong terrorist revolutionaries, was known as "Masterda." The *guru-shishya* relationship was formally recognized in Sen's title and reflected his professional status as a schoolteacher. In this regard, the *guru-shishya* relationship between follower and leader may be closely related to two facts: first, many of the dadas were schoolteachers, and second, colleges and secondary schools provided the major recruiting grounds for terrorist revolutionaries. The large number of schoolteachers involved in the movement might be connected tangentially to the high incidence of unemployment among these classes at that time.[93]

Thus, though Dutt does not explicitly identify the criteria that determined the status of individual terrorist revolutionaries within the movement, we can speculate that gender, filial, generational, and educational hierarchies played some role in conditioning social relations. As a young female student, the gendered terrorist revolutionary was probably subject to the authority of older movement males, who were often professional educators.

FROM TERRORISM TO ELECTORAL POLITICS
(RE)PUBLICATION IN CONTEXT

Chittagong Armoury Raiders Reminiscences was first published in 1945, after Dutt's six-year incarceration as a political prisoner in the Andaman Islands and her conversion to communism during that time. Dutt's conversion to communism, as well as that of her colleagues, is one of the recurring themes throughout the book. In the preface to the first edition, P. C. Joshi links her conversion to communism to her participation in the Bengali terrorist movement: "To read her own story is to understand a living phase of our national movement, how was it that in the thirties the vast majority of the terrorist detenus and prisoners became communists. . . . These reminiscences reveal how terrorism was the infant as communism is the mature stage of their revolutionary lives" (v-vi).

The leitmotif of communist conversion forms the basis for one of the problematics of Dutt's memoirs: how to "commemorate" the activities of her comrades, while simultaneously presenting communism as the ideal. Her text was first published in 1945 by the People's Publishing House, which also published the *Documents of the History of the Communist Party in India*. The People's Publishing House published a second edition of *Chittagong Armoury Raiders Reminiscences* in 1979. A publisher's note to the second edition of the work explains the republication of the text in the following manner:

On 1930 entire India was rocked at the daring exploits of Surjya Sen and his comrades initiated by what is called Chittagong Armoury Raid. In the history of India's war of independence—the Youth Revolt of Chittagong is a glorious chapter written in the words of gold. They not only raided armoury and attacked the European club but also they faced the armed force of the mightiest imperialist power in direct confrontation, gave a fight which taught British imperialism a lesson. The People's Publishing House paid its humble tribute to the valiant heroes in bringing out a book containing their portraits from the pen of one of the legendary figures, Kalpana Dutt.

On the eve of the 50th Anniversary of the memorable event we are bringing out the second edition with a new preface from the authoress.

The republication of Dutt's text on the eve of the fiftieth anniversary of the armoury raid suggests that the People's Publishing House is engaged in the invention of a particular version of the past. In other words, since anniversaries typically commemorate important occasions, the linkage of the text's republication with the fiftieth anniversary of the event invests the armoury raid and its participants with a special significance.

This second edition appeared in 1979, the same year that the Janata Party started to dissolve with the resignation of Socialist leaders Raj Narain and George Fernandes from Morarji Desai's cabinet. The Janata Party had dealt Indira Gandhi a resounding electoral defeat in 1977, as a result of her authoritarian actions during the "Emergency"—more popularly known as "Indira Raj"—from 1975 to 1977. Indira Gandhi and the Congress Party to which she belonged had long dominated Indian politics. Gandhi herself could trace her lineage in nationalist politics back to her grandfather, Motilal Nehru. As the country's first prime minister, her father Jawaharlal Nehru was figuratively also the "father" of India. But if Nehru was the "father" of India, Gandhi became India itself. During Emergency, she adopted the slogan "Indira = India," which was written prominently on Delhi walls. (After her electoral defeat in 1977, Indians rubbed the "r" out of the slogan so that the walls read "Indi a = India.")[94] Both Gandhi and Nehru play a major role in bourgeois nationalist elitist historiography, which locates the origins of the creation of India in the actions of a few elite leaders. In 1979, Gandhi's relatively low profile and the impending dissolution of the Janata Party coalition created the discursive space for new narratives of national origin to appear. "In the Congress history," Dutt writes in the preface to the second edition, "the revolutionaries were mentioned as 'terrorists' it was only now we find that these revolutionaries are recognised as freedom-fighters along with their Congress counterparts" (xiii). Since most of the terrorist revolutionaries converted to communism sometime before India's independence in 1947, their addition to the mythology of national origin, through the republication of *Chittagong Armoury Raiders Reminiscences*, advanced the credibility of Indian communists.

Back in 1945, the publication of the first edition of Dutt's text had an explicit agenda, as the dedication makes clear. Dutt dedicates her book to

> *My dadas and comrades*
> *Who are still behind the bars,*
> *With the confidence that the people*
> *For whom they suffered and fought*
> *Will help us to get them out.*

Dutt's *Chittagong Armoury Raiders Reminiscences* had an overt political mission, to bring attention to the plight of political prisoners and to galvanize people into demanding their release. Dutt ends the biographies of those still detained by spelling out the effects of incarceration on their health and pleading for their release.

The publication of the first edition in 1945 also had a more covert political mission. P. C. Joshi concludes his preface to the first edition with the following proclamation: "In every Chittagong home Kalpana Dutt is called 'Amar Meye',—our daughter. This daughter of Chittagong will seek, once again, the verdict of her parents, the people of Chittagong, as the communist candidate in the coming provincial elections" (vi). Dutt, along with the other terrorist revolutionaries, had carried out the Chittagong armoury raid with a view to its propagandistic potential to inspire Indians with the confidence that they could defeat the British. Years later, as a candidate for the provincial elections, she could draw on her transformation into a regional myth to garner electoral support.

Dutt's electoral campaign informs her narrative in a number of ways. Though Dutt continuously refers to her conversion to communism, she fails to articulate any of the critiques of terrorism developed by various communist theoreticians. To do so might mean the "demythologization" of the terrorist revolutionaries and could ultimately cost her the support of potential voters. A guerrilla campaign should ideally be organized on two fronts: on the battlefront and on the social front.[95] On the battlefront, the rebel army "uses irregular tactics, including hit and run attacks, 'expropriations' of arms and money, and selective assassinations, to tie down the regime's forces and hamper its recruitment efforts."[96] On the social front the leadership should simultaneously set up institutions of "dual power," which are democratically representative.[97] These would consist of committees linked to a central political organization. The constitution of the committees would be subject to the needs and requirements of the people and determined by them. The committees could be organized around issues like health care, agriculture, and education. The organization of committees would establish an infrastructure, making the transition to democracy much smoother. In this regard, the organizing work of the Farabundo Martí Front for National Liberation in El Salvador and the Unified National Leadership of the Uprising in the Occupied Territories, during the Intifada, has been exemplary.[98] The Chittagong terrorist revolutionaries, however, never moved beyond the battlefront and into the social front. Their inability to organize alternative civil structures constitutes a major weakness, one that Dutt does not acknowledge.

Criticisms of terrorism were circulating internationally and in India during the mid-twenties and thirties. The July 1925 issue of the *Masses* included a manifesto by the Young Communist International (YCI) addressed to "The Bengal Revolutionary Organisation of Youth." Though no such organization by this name existed in Bengal, the article was probably produced in pamphlet form and smuggled to India.[99] It is reproduced in its entirety in the *Documents of the History of the Communist Party of India*. The manifesto recognizes the "heroic efforts" of the terrorist revolutionaries, but gently reminds them that they have been ineffective, unable "to obtain any considerable concessions."[100] The YCI locates this ineffectiveness in the terrorist revolutionaries' failure to understand that workers and peasants—rather than the intelligentsia—are the true agents of change. They urge the terrorist revolutionaries "to set to work

to organise and rally [these classes] on the basis of a revolutionary programme which would meet their economic and political needs."[101] Such
a program, the YCI believes, could be determined by the study of the
actual conditions of these classes.

The YCI also explicitly faults terrorism as a strategy for national
liberation. While acknowledging the revolutionary's "moral right to remove the executioners and the garrotters of the people," the YCI points
out the limitations of terrorism in no uncertain terms:

(1) a terrorist act directed against an individual does not remove the whole system:
in place of the one who has been removed the British imperialism will appoint
another; one official merely takes the place of another, but the system of oppression remains intact; (2) terror demands a tremendous expenditure of effort and
diverts attention from the fundamental tasks of rallying, organising and revolu-
tionarily educating the masses.[102]

In spite of her allegiance to communism and her insistence on the centrality of this ideology for revolutionary change, Dutt does not articulate
these powerful criticisms in her narrative.

Dutt does not refer to another important aspect of the organization's
plan to take over Chittagong. The original plan divided the terrorist
revolutionaries into four groups, which would attack different targets: the
Police Armoury, the British Auxiliary Force Armoury, the Telegraph
and Telephone Exchange, and the European Club. While the first three
locations are obvious military targets, Dutt does not mention the group's
decision to attack a civilian target. The fourth group, under the leadership
of Naresh Roy and Triguna Sen, had been instructed to attack the club
and kill the Europeans to avenge the Jallianwalla Bagh massacre.[103] This
massacre occurred on April 13, 1919, when a large peaceful crowd,
numbering about ten thousand, gathered at the Jallianwala Bagh, in
Amritsar, to protest the passing of the Rowlatt Acts. General Harry
Dyer led a regiment of Gurkha and Baluchi troops to the gathering,
blocked off the only entrance to the park, and ordered his troops to fire
without warning into the peaceful crowd. Dyer's troops discharged 1,600
rounds of ammunition; official reports estimate that 379 persons were
killed, and 1,200 wounded were left unattended.[104] Dyer later explained
his motives to the Hunter Commission, which was investigating the
massacre: "I had made up my mind, I would do all men to death. . . . I
was going to punish them. My idea from the military point of view was

to make a wide impression."[105] Dyer concluded his remarks by stating his conviction that he had done "a jolly lot of good."[106] The Hunter Commission reprimanded Dyer and asked him to resign from the army. But the government allowed him to retain full rights to his pension in spite of the reprimand.

Several factors help explain the terrorist revolutionaries' plan to attack a civilian target. Innocent Indian women, children, and men had been massacred at Jallianwalla Bagh. The assassination of British civilians would have established a terrible reciprocity between colonizer and colonized. Furthermore, British civilians had been complicit in the Jallianwalla Bagh massacre. Notwithstanding the guarantee of Dyer's full pension, "Anglo-Indian" women took up a collection for Dyer, amounting to £26,000, which was no small sum in those days, to show their appreciation and support for him in the face of the official reprimand.[107] Moreover, the club itself represented a site of humiliation and racial inferiority for Indians. They were excluded from its premises as members, but allowed entry as servants. The club served as a racist sanctuary for Europeans from Indians, and in cases of civil unrest—as Forster's *Passage to India* shows—as a physical refuge from danger. By 1930, six years after the publication of Forster's novel, the Europeans in Chittagong no longer regarded it as a reliable sanctuary; instead they sought safety in boats anchored offshore. In any case, the terrorist revolutionaries did not succeed in their mission, because the club was empty on their arrival. Dutt's decision to exclude this information again may be linked to her campaign for office. Massacre, albeit out of revenge, is not likely to go over well with voters. As a candidate, Dutt had to establish herself as an agent of peace and stability as opposed to violence and bloodshed.

Dutt's lament over the passing of what she calls "Chittagong's golden age," in which the terrorist revolutionaries were able to carry out their revolt, is similarly significant (25). Chittagong's people, she feels, have fallen under the rule of thugs. Dutt mentions the degenerate state of Chittagong at least six times. Some references read as follows:

The spirit of Surjya Sen is still alive in Chittagong. But it has to fight an uphill battle against corrupt elements in our society who have grown strong and powerful profiteers, war contractors, those who trade in destitute women on mass scale. Those of us who worked with him are filled with shame that Surjya Sen's Chittagong should be reduced to its present plight. (16)

Chittagong homes used to buzz with tales of . . . heroism—those very homes today have become dens of cowardice and iniquity . . . today Chittagong is under goondashahi [thug rule] . . . today women in Chittagong sell themselves to lustful soldiers and greedy contractors. (24)

The devastating changes that have taken place in the life of Chittagong in these years cannot be understood without seeing them. There is widespread despondency, rules of social behaviour have been flouted, women from all sections are leading a life of shame. (43)

While Dutt draws on a male "heroic" past to mobilize voters in her electoral bid to be a communist representative, she simultaneously genders the "degenerate state of Chittagong" as female. The urgency of her campaign derives from the rhetorical link of a moral fall with the sexual traffic in women. Women, specifically prostitutes, become a trope for the degraded condition of the region still under colonial rule. Dutt's election offers her, then, the chance to fight a new battle, the battle against corruption, which will "restore Chittagong to its former greatness" (43). The Communist Party will build a "bridge between the glorious past of Chittagong and the heroic future . . . across the decline of the present" (57). And Kalpana Dutt, as the party candidate, will be the chief architect of this project.

CONCLUSION: BRIDGING DISCURSIVE PARTITIONS

I have attempted to situate a discussion of women's participation in the Bengali terrorist revolutionary movement within the context of the organizational politics—the theories, tactics, structure, and gender ideology—that underwrote the Chittagong armoury raid. Women's location within organized armed struggle movements has been overlooked within many accounts of Indian women in general and Indian nationalism in particular.[108] For example, many studies mention the assassination of District Magistrate C. G. B. Stevens of Comilla, alluded to by Marjorie Cashmore in *Plain Tales from the Raj*. Noting that Stevens "was greatly loved by all the people of his district," who considered him their *ma-bap*, Cashmore muses:

He [Stevens] loved India, he was devoted to India and like so many other men he worked long hours for India, and yet he met his end at the hands of two girls in saris. They came along to his bungalow and told his servant that they wanted to see the judge-*sahib*, as they had a petition to present to him. The judge came out on to the verandah and directly he got close to the girls with his hand out to receive the petition one of the girls pulled a pistol from her sari and killed him.[109]

Given that there were other Englishmen, contemptuous of Indians, who might have been considered more suitable targets by the terrorist revolutionaries, Cashmore asks why Stevens was marked for assassination. Many accounts refer to this incident, giving the bare details of the assassination. They note that the assassins, Santi Ghosh and Suniti Choudhury, were quite young at the time, being sixteen and fifteen respectively. None of the accounts, however, raise Cashmore's question. Their failure to do so makes the assassination an arbitrary event, instead of a consciously planned action with a definite purpose.

Yet Jugantar's choice of Stevens as a victim was anything but arbitrary. In an interview about Bengali terrorist revolutionaries, Bibhuti Basu, who spent several months in prison because he was in the vicinity of the assassination, stressed the fact that Stevens was acknowledged by the terrorist revolutionaries to be a "very good man."[110] But since the British authorities had murdered one of their comrades in detention at Midnapur District Jail, the terrorist revolutionaries conceptualized this assassination as a way of avenging his death. Because their dead comrade had a wife and small child, the group chose a British man in a similar situation, to draw, in Basu's words, "a parallel" between both murders.[111] As in the terrorist revolutionaries' plan to attack the European Club, mentioned earlier, this assassination established a terrible reciprocity between the families of the colonizer and colonized. The decision to assign the assassination to female terrorist revolutionaries—we might speculate—helped displace sympathy from the dead adult male magistrate to the two living young girls. In addition, while male terrorist revolutionaries convicted of assassination were generally sentenced to death by hanging, women terrorist revolutionaries were given the more lenient sentence of life imprisonment on account of their gender and, quite often as was the case, their youth. Ghosh and Choudhury, perhaps because of their youth and gender, were sentenced to life imprisonment instead of death. Quite possibly, the movement considered the differential gender and generational consequences of terrorist revolutionary action when delegating tasks.

Jugantar's decision to choose Stevens as a target does not get explained in the pages of nationalist histories or studies of Indian women. The absence of this sort of explanation in Indian nationalist histories bespeaks the necessity of acknowledging that those engaged in nationalist struggles are both "thinkers as well as actors" and "that liberation movements have their own intellectual and political histories."[112] As Laura Lyons eloquently argues, "the 'theoretical partition' between writing *about* nationalism and writing *by* nationalists has erected blockades across our intellectual hinterlands which now must be dismantled" (her emphasis).[113] In the South Asian context, the project of dismantling such a partition would entail, as the interview with Bibhuti Basu indicates, both the reading of writing by nationalists and the supplementing of these accounts with oral histories of nationalists. The necessity of listening to nationalist accounts is even more imperative, given that these voices risk being lost to history on account of their advancing age. Kalpana Dutt passed away on February 8, 1995, at the age of eighty-one, and it is to her memory that I dedicate this article.

NOTES

I derive the title of this article from Barbara Harlow's *Barred: Women, Writing, and Political Detention*, which is an exemplary study of women's participation in organized resistance movements. In addition, I am grateful to Elizabeth Butler-Cullingford, Barbara Harlow, Richard Lariviere, Laura Lyons, Supriya Nair, and Sangeeta Ray for their helpful suggestions on earlier drafts of this article. I also owe much to discussions on the Bengali terrorist revolutionary movement with Bibhuti Basu and Samir Kumar Bose. Finally, audiences at the 1993 Midwest Modern Language Association meeting in Minneapolis, the fall 1991 "Women and War" conference, and the fall 1992 South Asian Seminar Series at the University of Texas in Austin—three venues where I presented excerpts of this article—have aided me in clarifying the political stakes in this kind of project.

1. Tanika Sarkar, *Bengal 1928–1934: The Politics of Protest* (Delhi: Oxford University Press, 1987), 149–50.

2. This ordinance allowed the government of Bengal to arrest and detain suspected "terrorists" without trial. It also permitted the government, according to David Laushey, "to try cases involving terrorists before a tribunal without jury and without right of appeal." For more information, see David Laushey, *Bengal Terrorism and The Marxist Left* (Calcutta: Firma K. L. Mukhopadhyay, 1975), 28.

3. Kalpana Dutt, *Chittagong Armoury Raiders Reminiscences* (New Delhi: People's Publishing House, 1945), 1. Further references to this work will be included parenthetically in the text.

4. Biswakesh Tripathy, *Terrorism and Insurgency in India 1900–1986* (New Delhi: Pacific Press, 1987), 46. The terrorist revolutionaries deliberately timed

their action to coincide with the Easter Rising. Lokenath Bal, one of the participants, writes, "The bloodstained memory of the Easter Revolution of the Irish Republican Army touched our young minds with fiery enthusiasm" (qtd. in Ramesh Chandra Majumdar *History of Modern Bengal 1905–1947* [Calcutta: G. Bharadwajand and Co., 1981], 263). In fact, the IRA was a major source of inspiration for the terrorist revolutionaries. Kalpana Dutt describes how Surjya Sen encouraged her to read Dan Breen's *My Fight for Irish Freedom*. She also mentions the influence of James Fintan Lalor. In addition, Sinn Fein leaders like Terence MacSwiney—who died on hunger strike in 1921 during the Anglo-Irish war—exerted a strong influence on the terrorist revolutionaries. C. Sehanabish reflects on the impact of MacSwiney's death:

> It was widely reported in our papers about this Irish revolt of 18th April— that Ireland, so near England, almost a stone's throw, but even then they could retain power. The hunger strike was a peculiar weapon used by both Irish and Bengali revolutionaries. Maybe we were influenced by them. MacSwiney died after 72 days of hungerstrike; and when Jatin Das died here after 63 days, one of the things I remember was the telegram from Mrs. Mary MacSwiney, wife of the great leader: "Ireland joins India in grief and pride over the death of Jatin Das. Freedom shall come." (Zareer Masani, *Indian Tales of the Raj* [Berkeley: University of California Press, 1986], 114)

Though the West generally equates hunger strikes in the Indian context solely with Gandhi, they were a popular form of resistance among terrorist revolutionary political prisoners. Dutt mentions that political prisoners in the Andaman Islands went on hunger strike in 1937 over three demands: "their repatriation from the Andamans," "the inclusion of all political prisoners in class two," and "general release for all" (71). According to Dutt, political prisoners all over India started hunger strikes as a mark of solidarity with the Andaman inmates (71). While the tactic was derived from Irish models (see Laura Lyons, "Writing in Trouble: Protest and the Cultural Politics of Irish Nationalism" [Ph.D. diss., University of Texas at Austin, 1993], for a thorough explication of this context), it also drew on Indian cultural practices and nationalist discourse. Married Hindu women traditionally fast on certain religious days in order to guarantee the health of their husbands and sons. The body of the hunger striker literally stood as a symbol of the body politic, ill and emaciated under colonial rule. Simultaneously, however, fasting became a ritual method of restoring the health of the body politic. And as in the discourse of nationalist politics, this tactic gendered India as a suffering woman.

The colonial authorities also seem to have recognized connections between the Indian and Irish struggles. In 1932, Sir John Anderson was appointed governor of Bengal. He earned the appointment on the basis of his experience in Ireland, where he had earned "a reputation of success in suppressing the Irish terrorists" (Majumdar, *History*, 262).

5. Majumdar, *History*, 273.

6. Tripathy, *Terrorism*, 46.

7. Leonard Gordon, *Bengal: The Nationalist Movement 1876–1940* (New York: Columbia University Press, 1974), 248.

8. Ibid.

9. Lyons, "Writing in Trouble," 10.

10. Ibid.

11. In "Taking Tarzan Seriously," Marianna Torgovnick charts the ways Tarzan solidifies his identity by subjugating African natives and white women in the twenty-four *Tarzan* novel series by Edgar Rice Burroughs. Torgovnick argues that the early novels "defamiliarize axiomatic Western norms and raise the possibility of their radical restructuring" by showing how values—such as standards of beauty—are culturally determined. For example, in the first novel of the series, *Tarzan of the Apes*, Tarzan finds his reflection in a pond ugly since he had been conditioned to accept the apes' aesthetics of appearance. "But such radical, relativistic moments are counterbalanced and finally overcome by others," writes Torgovnick, "in which [Tarzan's] self is increasingly defined, in ways that yield security and satisfaction, by comparisons with Others" (48).

The first novel of the series was published in 1912, while the earliest Tarzan movie appeared in 1917. Approximately fifty Tarzan films have been produced since then. The early novels were appropriately serialized in U.S. men's and boys' magazines (70). But the novels, comics, and films had an international audience that included Africans, Indians, and Middle Easterners (263). For more information on the series, see Marianna Torgovnick, "Taking Tarzan Seriously," in *Gone Primitive: Savage Intellects, Modern Lives* (Chicago: University of Chicago Press, 1990).

12. R. K. Narayan, *The Mahabharata* (New Delhi: Vision Books, 1978), 32.

13. Kumari Jayawardena, *Feminism and Nationalism in the Third World* (London: Zed Books, 1986); Vijay Agnew, *Elite Women in Indian Politics* (New Delhi: Vikas Publishing House, 1979).

14. Agnew, *Elite*, 63.

15. Richard E. Rubenstein, *Alchemists of Revolution: Terrorism in the Modern World* (New York: Basic Books, 1987), 22.

16. Ibid.

17. Ibid., 31.

18. Ibid., 33.

19. Ibid., 28.

20. Ibid., 29.

21. I want to stress that the simile of terrorism-as-crime also occurs in India, but in other contexts. For example, most Indians consider the violence perpetrated by Sikh separatists in the name of Khalistan a form of terrorism that demanded "law-and-order" type solutions.

22. J. B. Hardman, "Interpretations of Terrorism," in *The Terrorism Reader: An Historical Anthology*, ed. Walter Laqueur and Yonah Alexander (New York: NAL Penguin, 1978), 224.

23. Ibid., 225.

24. Baljit Singh, "An Overview," in *Terrorism: Interdisciplinary Perspectives*, ed. Yonah Alexander and Seymour Maxwell Finger (New York: John Jay Press, 1977), 8.

25. Ibid.

26. Quoted in Masani, *Indian Tales of the Raj*, 115.

27. Laushey, *Bengal Terrorism*, 24.

28. Shaileshwar Nath, *Terrorism in India* (New Delhi: National Publishing House, 1980), 39.

29. Ibid.

30. Ibid., 40.

31. Tripathy, *Terrorism*, 46.

32. Nath, *Terrorism*, 40.

33. Shamsul Islam, *Chronicles of the Raj: A Study of the Literary Reaction to the Imperial Idea towards the End of the Raj* (London: Macmillan Press, 1979), 7.

34. Ibid.

35. Quoted in Charles Allen, *Plain Tales from the Raj* (New York: St. Martin's Press, 1975), 199.

36. William Crooke, *Hobson-Jobson: A Glossary of Colloquial Anglo-Indian Words and Phrases*, 4th ed. (Delhi: Munshiram Manoharlal Publishers, 1984), 44.

37. Quoted in Allen, *Plain Tales*, 198.

38. Rosie Llewellyn-Jones, ed., *Souvenir Chowkidar* (London: Chameleon Press, 1986), 42.

39. Ibid.

40. Rosie Llewellyn-Jones, ed., *Chowkidar* 5, no. 4 (Autumn 1989): 81.

41. John Beverley, "The Margin at the Center: On Testimonio (Testimonial Narrative)," *Modern Fiction Studies* 35 (Spring 1989): 23.

42. M. H. Abrams et al., eds., *The Norton Anthology of English Literature 2*, 4th ed. (New York: W. W. Norton and Company, 1979), 1175.

43. Ibid., 1176.

44. Allen, *Plain Tales*, 199–200.

45. Quoted in ibid., 200.

46. Ashis Nandy, *The Intimate Enemy: Loss and Recovery of Self under Colonialism* (New Delhi: Oxford University Press, 1983), 7.

47. Quoted in Gordon, *Bengal*, 120. Though Ghose himself was probably a kayastha, a member of the scribe caste, he clearly identified with the martial aspects of ksatriyahood. In the nineteenth century, some kayasthas claimed ksatriya status (327).

48. Ibid., 146.

49. Nandy, *Intimate Enemy*, 52.

50. Quoted in Allen, *Plain Tales*, 206.

51. Mahasweta Devi's short story "Draupadi" rewrites the relationship between *sharam*, nudity, and political protest. In it, Draupadi confronts Senanayak with her bleeding, brutalized, naked body. This confrontation, according to Gayatri Spivak, challenges "the man to (en)counter her as unrecorded or misre-

corded objective historical monument" (*In Other Worlds* [New York: Methuen, 1987], 184). But, as Ramón Saldívar has pointed out to me in conversations, we can very well ask: what happens to Draupadi in the next frame after the story ends? Will Senanayak release her because he now recognizes her as a "powerful 'subject,' " or will he more probably have her killed in the manner of other tribal rebels?

The film *Mirch Masala* offers a better example of effective gendered resistance. In it, the female workers of a pickle factory use chili powder as a weapon against a feudal landlord who is attempting to exploit sexually one of them. This practice was actually used by peasant women against their feudal landlords in the Telangana struggle, as attested in some of the narratives in the Stree Shakti Sanghatana, *We Were Making History: Women and the Telanagana Uprising* (London: Zed Books, 1989).

52. Quoted in Geraldine H. Forbes, "The Ideals of Indian Womanhood: Six Bengali Women during the Independence Movement," in *Bengal in the Nineteenth and Twentieth Centuries*, ed. John R. McLane (East Lansing: Asian Studies Center, Michigan State University, 1975), 64.

53. Paul Scott, *The Jewel in the Crown* (New York: Avon Books, 1979), 1. For an excellent analysis of the rape metaphor in colonial discourse, particularly E. M. Forster's *Passage to India*, see Jenny Sharpe, "The Unspeakabe Limits of Rape: Colonial Violence and Counter-Insurgency," *Genders* 10 (Spring 1991): 25–46.

54. Lata Mani, "Contentious Traditions: The Debate on *Sati* in Colonial India," in *Recasting Women in India: Essays in Colonial History*, ed. Kumkum Sangari and Sudesh Vaid (New Delhi: Kali for Women, 1989), 90.

55. Ibid., 88.

56. I do not want to dismiss the hundred years or so between the high incidence of satis in Bengal during 1815–28 and Das's assassination attempt in 1932 as irrelevant. I do not claim that attitudes toward sati did not change in this period, because they did. The incidence of sati decreased significantly in this period. I do want to suggest, though, that a hundred-year period can be relatively short from an ideological perspective, if we reflect on the fact that it may cover just two generations of a family, the major transmitter of "tradition" and culture.

57. Forbes, "Ideals," 65.

58. Joanna Liddle and Rama Joshi, eds., *Daughters of Independence: Gender, Caste, and Class in India* (London: Zed Books, 1986), 54.

59. Ibid., 55.

60. Ibid.

61. V. D. Mahajan, *The Nationalist Movement in India* (New Delhi: Sterling Publishers, 1979), 223.

62. Ibid. Note that the reference to the "ten-headed goddess" in this quotation is probably an error and meant to read "ten-handed goddess."

63. I am grateful to Richard Lariviere for bringing these details to my attention.

64. Ramesh Chandra Majumdar, *The Revolutionary Movement in Bengal and the Role of Surya Sen* (Calcutta: Calcutta University Press, 1978), 7.

65. Quoted in ibid.

66. Quoted in Mahajan, *Nationalist Movement*, 232.

67. Quoted in ibid.

68. Quoted in ibid., 239.

69. So entrenched would differences be between the two religions by 1947, that the British partitioned the subcontinent into separate states for each one. East (now Bangladesh) and West Pakistan, with a Muslim majority, was created as a Muslim state; India, with a Hindu majority, was founded as a democratic secular state. Over a million people were murdered in the communal riots that accompanied partition.

70. Quoted in Mahajan, *Nationalist Movement*, 235.

71. Sarkar, *Bengal*, 80.

72. Ibid., 82.

73. Geraldine Forbes, "Goddesses or Rebels? The Women Revolutionaries of Bengal," in *Women, Politics, and Literature in Bengal*, ed. Clinton B. Seely (East Lansing: Asian Studies Center, Michigan State University, 1981), 11.

74. Ibid., 12.

75. Majumdar, *History*, 280.

76. Forbes, "Goddesses or Rebels," 9.

77. Ibid.

78. Ibid.

79. Ibid.

80. Ibid., 3.

81. Sarkar, *Bengal*, 152.

82. Ibid.

83. Ronald B. Inden and Ralph Nicholas, *Kinship in Bengali Culture* (Chicago: University of Chicago Press, 1977), 71.

84. Ibid., 5.

85. Ibid., 24.

86. Ibid., 28.

87. Ibid., 3.

88. Ibid.

89. Gordon, *Bengal*, 142.

90. Ibid.

91. Ibid.

92. Ibid.

93. Mahajan, *Nationalist Movement*, 224–25.

94. I am grateful to Anju Kapur for bringing this detail to my notice.

95. For example, during the Anglo-Irish War of 1919–20, Sinn Fein set up courts to administer justice, while the Irish Republican Army engaged in guerrilla tactics.

96. Rubenstein, *Alchemists*, 29.

97. Ibid., 30.

98. For information on the organizing efforts of the Unified Leadership of the Intifada, see Noam Chomsky, "The Trollope Ploy and Middle East Diplomacy," *Zeta Magazine*, March 1989; Moe Seager, "Eyewitness: A Process of No Return," *Zeta Magazine*, January 1990; and Paulo de Rooij, "Notes on the Intifada: Photo Essay," *Zeta Magazine*, July-August 1990. For more information on women's participation in the Palestinian movement, see Philippa Strum, *The Women Are Marching: The Second Sex and the Palestinian Revolution* (New York: Lawrence Hill Books, 1992); Joost R. Hiltermann, *Behind the Intifada* (Princeton: Princeton University Press, 1991); and Orayb Arej Najjar, *Portraits of Palestinian Women* (Salt Lake City: University of Utah Press, 1991). The following documentaries also include valuable information: Michal Aviad, *The Women Next Door*; Elizabeth Fernea, *Witness for Peace*; and Erica Marcus, *My Home, My Prison*.

For information on the Farabundo Marti Front for National Liberation, see Jon Reed, "Bringing the War Home: El Salvadoran Resistance Takes the Offensive," *Zeta Magazine*, May 1989; and idem, "El Salvador," *Zeta Magazine*, May-June 1992. For a discussion of the Salvadoran student movement, see Joann Wypijeewski, "El Salvador: Voices on the Winds of Fury," *Zeta Magazine*, April 1989. For a discussion of the civil war and its impact on writers, see Todd Jailer, "El Salvador: Writing and War," *Zeta Magazine*, December 1990.

In addition, Barbara Harlow, *Barred: Women, Writing, and Political Detention* (Hanover: Wesleyan University Press, 1992) includes detailed discussions of women's participation in both the Salvadoran and Palestinian contexts, among others.

99. G. Adhikari, ed., *Documents of the History of the Communist Party of India, Volume Two 1923–1925* (New Delhi: People's Publishing House, 1974), 463.

100. Ibid., 473.

101. Ibid., 476.

102. Ibid., 479.

103. Majumdar, *History*, 264.

104. Kalikinkar Datta, R. C. Majumdar, and H. C. Raychaudhuri, *An Advanced History of India*, 4th ed. (Delhi: Macmillan Company of India, 1978), 971.

105. Quoted in Alexander Cockburn, *Corruptions of Empire: Life Studies and the Reagan Era* (London: Verso, 1987), 310.

106. Quoted in ibid.

107. Ibid.

108. Histories of the nationalist period typically marginalize the participation of women, or they focus on the participation of a few elite women—such as Sarojini Naidu—from prominent nationalist families. For example, Stanley Wolpert, *A New History of India* (New York: Oxford University Press, 1977) mentions only Sarojini Naidu and Kasturbai Gandhi in several sentences in two chapters devoted to the nationalist movement. In *An Advanced History of India*, Datta et al. limit their discussion of women's participation to the detail that some women accompanied Gandhi on his famous salt march to Dandi in 1930 (974). (The inclusion of this particular detail seems odd, given that Gandhi had originally prohibited women from marching with him, exhorting them instead to

picket toddy shops. In fact, Margaret Cousins took him to task for this decision in the pages of *Stri Dharma*.) As Gayatri Spivak has demonstrated in "Subaltern Studies: Deconstructing Historiography," even the Subaltern Studies Group, which is sensitive to the marginalization of subaltern classes, has been remiss in acknowledging women's contributions to Indian Independence (*In Other Worlds*, 197–221). Tanika Sarkar, *Bengal 1928–1934: The Politics of Protest* is a notable exception to this general tendency. But, though her comments are helpful, they are generally drawn from readings of novels written by males who were not part of the terrorist revolutionary movement, like Rabindranath Tagore. Tagore's novels *Ghare Baire* and *Char Adhyay*, as Sarkar notes, trivialize political women by placing them in conventional love narratives; the women do not become politicized out of conviction, but fall victim to charismatic men. Once in the political arena, the women become, in the words of Tagore's character Atin, "unbalanced, unnatural" (qtd. in Sarkar, *Bengal*, 153).

Texts devoted specifically to recovering the history of Indian terrorist revolutionary movements fleetingly mention, but do not elaborate on, the contributions of women. The best of this genre—Leonard Gordon, *Bengal: The Nationalist Movement 1897–1940*, and D. M. Laushey, *Bengal Terrorism and the Marxist Left*—are further limited in scope. (There seems to be a significant amount of literature on the Bengali terrorist revolutionaries written by them. Since they are in Bengali and not available in English translation, I have not been able to draw on them. Readers fluent in Bengali might want to examine Ananta Singh, *Chattagram Yuba Birodh*, *Keu Bale Biplabi*, *Keu Bale Dakata* and *Agnigarva Chattagram*; Sachindranath Guha, *Chattagram Biplaber Banhisikha*; and Preeti Waddedar, *Chattogram Biplaber Bahnisikha*.) While both Gordon and Laushey have extended discussions of the structure and composition of terrorist revolutionary groups operative before 1919, they give little of the organizational details of groups after 1928, the period in which the Chittagong terrorist revolutionaries had shifted their strategies from assassinations to larger-scale offensives.

The majority of the historical writings on Indian women that I surveyed fell into a genre characterized by the Stree Shakti Sanghatana, in *We Were Making History*, as "compensatory history" (19). These histories "locate" "the great women" who have been " 'left out' of male accounts" and place them "alongside the great men of history" (19). They measure women's participation in social movements by the actions of a relatively small number of elite women. In this sense, compensatory history of the nationalist period is the female version of bourgeois nationalist elitist historiography defined by Ranajit Guha as "the prejudice that the making of the Indian nation and the development of the consciousness—nationalism—which informed this process were exclusively or predominantly elite achievements" ("On Some Aspects of the Historiography of Colonial India," in *Selected Subaltern Studies*, ed. Ranajit Guha and Gayatri Chakravorty Spivak [New York: Oxford University Press, 1988], 37). Kumari Jayawardena, *Feminism and Nationalism in the Third World*; Manmohan Kaur, *Role of Women in the Freedom Movement (1857–1947)* (Delhi: Sterling Publishers, 1968); and Jana Matson Everett, *Women and Social Change in India* (New Delhi: Heritage Publishers,

1979) share this view. Though the Stree Shakti Sanghatana acknowledges "the conscientizing force of such efforts," it argues that "the critique provided by compensatory history is obviously not radical enough" (20).

Both Vijay Agnew and Geraldine Forbes have written in some detail on women terrorist revolutionaries. Forbes' article "Goddesses or Rebels? The Women Revolutionaries of Bengal" places the women terrorist revolutionaries within the larger context of the Gandhian nationalist movement, insisting that Gandhi helped provide the "groundwork" "for the entry of women into" terrorist organizations, by making political participation for women socially acceptable (4). While Forbes carefully delineates the literary and ideological influences that shaped these young women, she does so within the framework of the natal family. The family becomes the primary unit of collectivity for Forbes. As a result, her analysis implicitly devalues the organization's role in motivating and theorizing the activities of the women terrorist revolutionaries. Vijay Agnew devotes a chapter of her book, *Elite Women in Indian Politics*, to terrorist revolutionaries and other women—such as Aruna Asaf Ali and Sucheta Kripalani—who made up the left wing of the Congress Party. But like Forbes, Agnew downplays the influence of terrorist organizations over female members, focusing instead on the women's religious and cultural backgrounds. Both Agnew's and Forbes's work can be considered compensatory history, since their articles profile well-known elite women without examining their relationship to the organizations to which they belonged.

109. Quoted in Allen, *Plain Tales*, 202.

110. Bibhuti Basu, personal interview, May 17, 1991.

111. Ibid.

112. Lyons, "Writing in Trouble," 10.

113. Ibid.

SEVEN

The Power in Written Bodies: Gender, Decolonization, and the Archive

Julia Emberley

THE LOGICS OF DISCOVERY

During the 1940s in the eastern sector of the North West Territories an investigation of a French Canadian trapper (hereafter referred to as A.) took place. The death of two of his children through separate drowning incidents and the disappearance of his Inuk wife and three-month-old son aroused the suspicion of the Royal Canadian Mounted Police (RCMP). The investigation is contained in a series of RCMP records submitted by local subdivision police inspectors at Eskimo Point, territorial and provincial commanding officers in Manitoba and Saskatchewan, and the commissioner of the Criminal Investigations Branch Headquarters in Ottawa, Ontario.[1] Out of the various missives exchanged among these men, exemplary of the symbolic order, over a period of ten years (the reports begin 4 July 1940 and end 5 September 1950) emerges a story of tragic proportions involving deaths, insanity, exhumed bodies, a disappearing wife, drowned, burned, lost, and cannibalized children: all the compelling subject matter of a good detective novel.

The story I am about to unfold is not a work of fiction—as in the narrow sense of when we understand fiction to signify an oppositional value of "nontruth." It is a textual formation designed to follow a logic of discovery: hypotheses, speculations, and presuppositions are put forth, all aimed at constructing, while seemingly in the process of discovering,

184

the "truth" about A.'s "doings," if not wrongdoings, in the north. In an effort to gather evidence in order to find a just cause to arrest A., the RCMP exhume the bodies of the drowned children. In one particular case, a mutilated body comes to occupy a significant place as a site of evidence. But when contested testimony as to the biological sex of this exhumed body leads to a crisis of unresolvability, the written inquiry ends. After ten years of investigation, resolved only that they will never sufficiently construct the truth about the mysterious disappearance of A.'s wife and child and the "true" sex of one of the exhumed bodies, the federal Criminal Investigations Branch commissioner, without explanation, deems further investigation unwarranted. Case closed.

This essay closely examines this RCMP file as an authoritative discourse that generates its investigative procedures through a process of negotiating the significance of the "disappeared" Inuk woman's body and the corpse of the sex-undifferentiated body.[2] Hillary Leone and Jennifer Macdonald describe the process of negotiating the significance of the corpse in the following useful terms:

The corpse, like the book, must be seen as a product of "progress"; as such, authorities— medical, ethical, judicial, religious—are charged with the task of negotiating its borders. They determine the moment at which body becomes corpse; they debate how and when and under what circumstances we should employ or deny life-prolonging medical technologies; they make fine distinctions between the living and the dead. The authorities provide answers, albeit conflicting ones.[3]

In the case of the RCMP file, the bodies of the absent Inuk woman and the sex-undifferentiated corpse are subject to the conflicts and trials of a definitive search for truth as to the cause of death. But when a body is subject to the inscriptions of an authoritative discourse, it becomes a "written body" capable of producing significations that cut against the grain of the meanings and values ascribed by an authoritative framing. In other words, not only do authorities negotiate the borders of the living/ dead body and, indeed, determine how the body will signify its corporeal status, the written body itself can signify a multiplicity of conflicts and contradictions that extend beyond those borders. The surplus of significations produced by the written body in a colonial text is not unrelated to similar questions of the territorial inscription of the land. For example, during the period in which this RCMP file originally circulated, the Canadian federal government actively set out to substantiate its borders in the north and lay claim to its sovereignty over potential American or Russian interests. The Inuit who occupied this vast territory were subject to a range of governmental strategies to aid the process, such as the introduction of religious, governmental, policing, and/or military presences as well as a series of disastrous "relocations" that resulted in extraordinary hardship for the Inuit, including, in some cases, mass starvation.[4] The RCMP file represents a small if not minor event in the context of this larger historical struggle, yet as a minor discourse it has the advantage of drawing our attention to the micrological texture of power (to borrow Gayatri Chakravorty Spivak's phrase), the site at which truth and reason can be seen to mediate the larger and seemingly ungraspable complexity of the macrological relations between postcolonial "nations," such as First Nations, Metis, and Inuit in Canada, and the nation-state of "Canada" itself.[5]

The emergence of the Indigenous women's movement in Canada since the late 1970s also provides a macrological political and social context in which to situate my reading of the multivocality of the written bodies that appear in the RCMP document. This struggle has brought political pressure to bear on feminist scholars in Canada to rethink our current theoretical practices, particularly the strategic use of the concept of "sexual difference."

When, in 1980s feminist theory, "sexual difference" came to function as a metonymic code with which to decipher the libidinal investments of global transactions, Chandra Mohanty and Gayatri Chakravorty Spivak, among others, argued that the value placed on "sexual difference" as an organizing principle with which to analyze the situation of women in a cross-global context contributed more to exacerbating the contradictions of neocolonialism than furthering our understanding of the intersections of gender, power, and knowledge in the struggles for decolonization.[6] The problem lay in the positing as universal the effects of sexual differentiation regardless of the history and contexts of imperialism in which gender as a mode of social differentiation represents a specific strategy of subordination for imperial practices. Nevertheless, this exacerbation of the contradictions of neocolonialism created a productive tension, in that our awareness as to the political stakes involved when sexual differentiation enters the macrological debates of decolonization is dramatically heightened. Take, for example, the recent challenge by the Native Women's Association of Canada (NWAC) and the Women of the Metis

Nation (WMN) to the Canadian constitutional reform debates culminating in the Charlottetown Accord in 1992. The NWAC, supported by the WMN, appealed to the Federal Court for their right to political representation in the constitutional negotiations, which included four nationally recognized Indigenous political organizations: the Assembly of First Nations (representing status Indians), the Inuit Tapirisat of Canada (representing Inuit), the National Metis Council (representing Metis), and the Native Council of Canada (representing non-status Indians).[7] The challenge, which they won on appeal, was based on the Charter of Rights and Freedoms, which was passed as part of the Constitutional Act of 1982 (although it did not take effect until April 1985).[8] The Charter of Rights and Freedoms, which guaranteed equality to women, already played a significant legislative role in the passing of Bill C-31 (1985), which removed those sections of the Indian Act (1876) and subsequent amendments (especially in 1951) explicitly discriminating against (status) Native women. Briefly, those discriminations included the subsuming of a Native woman's legal status under her husband's, the exclusion of Native women from inheriting land rights upon the death of a male spouse, the exclusion of Native women from holding political positions within their elected band councils, and, perhaps the most contentious discrimination of all, the determination of Native women's status through marriage (in other words, if a Native woman with "status" married a non-status Native man or non-Native man, she would be stripped of her status).[9] In the case of Bill C-31, Native women were opposed by several Indigenous political organizations, which argued that Native women's challenge to the Indian Act was of secondary importance to the greater question of the Indian Act as a whole and the Canadian state's control over determining who is and is not an Indian. In other words, the supposedly larger and more important "collective rights" of Indigenous peoples took precedence over the "individual rights" of Native women guaranteed under the Charter of Rights and Freedoms. In the more recent conflict over Indigenous women's rights to participate in the constitutional reforms, the same issue of competing collective versus individual rights stood at the crux of the problem. As Jo-Anne Fiske points out, the notion of "collective rights" clearly excluded Indigenous women.[10] This brief narrative of the current history of the Indigenous women's movement would seem to indicate that this political struggle constitutes part of the women's movement generally referred to as "the struggle for equal rights." Such would be the case if it were not for the transcultural discourse aboriginal women deploy in order to legitimate their place in the political arena. The discourse is one that emphasizes matrilineal descent, a gendered division of responsibilities, a metaphorical displacement in the "mother" as "mother-earth" and metonymic associations between body parts and functions and attributes of healing (breast-feeding), life giving (the womb), and so forth. I cite the following words by Marlyn Kane and Sylvia Maracle from a special issue of *Canadian Woman Studies/Les cahiers de la femme*, edited by Indigenous women, as an example:

In our community, the woman was defined as nourisher, and the man, protector, and as protector, he had the role of helper. He only reacted; she acted. She was responsible for the establishment of all of the norms—whether they were political, economic, social, or spiritual. She lived in a very co-operative environment, where power needed not be lorded over.

In our Nation, while there is no question that the woman is the central figure in the scheme of things, our official government leaders are still men. That is how our government was given to us, and that is what is in our KAIANERE'KO:WA (great law). They are called ROTIANE, the best translation being "good men." . . . These positions cannot be confused with the elected "Chiefs" positions as prescribed by the *Indian Act*. Too often we hear men protesting women's attempts to gain these positions by reminding us that, in our ways, the "Chiefs" are men. I, for one, have promoted women becoming involved in the Band Council system, not because I think it is a good one that should be perpetuated, and not because I think there should be "equal" representation of women to men. Rather I believe that women have a responsibility to make sure that we don't lose any more, that we don't do any more damage, while we work on getting our original government system back in good working order.[11]

It is tempting to view this reinvention of tradition or neotraditionalism as an instance of naive essentialism.[12] Jo-Anne Fiske notes the essentialist voice of Indigenous women's political discourse and summarizes it as follows: "While male [aboriginal] leadership goals emulate the masculinist nation-state (despite expressing a counterhegemonic resistance to state authority), female leadership imagines a neotraditional community for which essentialist womanhood stands as a metaphor. Whereas women conceive of a community in which the womb is to the nation as the heart is to the body, men envision an Indigenous nation whose drum beat radiates from the quasi-powers of a 'third order of government.' "[13] I do not think that such a simple distinction between a masculine/feminine notion of the nation can hold, particularly if we consider that Rosmarie Kuptana, president of the Inuit Tapirisat of Canada, herself opposed the court challenge led by the Native Women's Association in favor of the creation of a "third order of government." More to the point, I think Fiske falls into the trap of attributing essentialism to the Indigenous women's movement when what we are actually witnessing is an example of taking the risk of essentialism seriously. If, as Diana Fuss suggests, "the political investments of the sign 'essence' are predicated on the subject's complex positioning in a particular social field, and that the appraisal of this investment depends not on any interior values intrinsic to the sign itself but rather on the shifting and determinative discursive relations which produced it,"[14] then this strategically deployed essentialism can best be understood in the context of the discursive history of colonization, in particular the effects of the Indian Act, which explicitly stated, as one of its discriminatory clauses, that the government would recognize only an elected band council composed of and elected by adult males.

In the above statement, Marlyn Kane and Sylvia Maracle argue for women's participation on band councils; however, they insist that this move toward the representation of Native women as political agents does not contravene an already recognized "sexual division" of decision-making responsibilities. While collective representation is affirmed, the notion of "equality" based on individual rights is denied. Furthermore, such a move is couched in terms of the struggle to achieve self-government and reestablish "our original government system." What appears as a contradictory set of needs and demands, with conflicting values and meanings attributed to Native women's position within uneven and competing political systems, can best be understood, I think, in the context of "shifting and determinate discursive relations" among the regulatory functions of the Indian Act, equal rights legislation in the name of constitutional reform, and the production of a counter-hegemonic discourse of neotraditional practices including notions of "collective rights" and a "third order of government." In the final instance, it is the Indian Act that has created an oppressive political system that excludes Native women from representative political power at all levels of government. In a colonial political system where individual rights represent the dominant form of political representation, to be excluded from such a system is to be excluded from any decision-making processes. The use of neotraditionalism based in a sexual division of decision-making powers strategically allows Native women to legitimate their positions as already constituted political agents. As members of elected band councils, they bring this already known and recognized political positioning into the field of representative political power established by the dominant colonial political system. While the legitimacy of their representative political power can only be recognized by the Canadian state on the basis of the protection it offers for individual equal rights, Native women argue for this representative status in order to reaffirm that this is in the interests of the collective rights represented by a broader Native political struggle for self-government and self-determination. Why Native women must reaffirm their collective rights over individual rights is, in part, a result of the divisiveness of Bill C-31, a divisiveness that stemmed from the legislative authority of the Charter of Rights and Freedoms taking precedence over the Indian Act.[15]

The macrological legislative and constitutionally based struggle for equal rights and, on the micrological level, the reinvention of a traditional discourse, in which decision-making spheres are divided along the lines of sexual difference, coexist in Indigenous women's political discourse. The simultaneous yet discontinuous relation between these inscriptional spaces represents a contradictory moment in the Indigenous women's movement from which to clear a space in order to establish their decolonial positioning as gendered political subjects within their bands as well as at the level of constitutional decision-making practices. In other words, the strategic use of an essentialist configuration of a sexual division of decision-making powers produces a doubly directed effect. It allows for the inscription of a site in which Native women already have political power; hence, the move toward representative political power in the dominant colonial system can be situated as part of a continuum of Native women's already recognized decision-making role. It also affirms that the continuation of Native women's decision-making power is in the interests of the broader Native political struggle for self-government. As agents of their own historical making, Native women have made strategic use of a "sexual division" of decision-making power.

While the Canadian state has made specific use of sexual difference as a mode of social differentiation by which to subordinate Indigenous women, the Indigenous women's movement has redeployed the performative charges attributed to "sexual difference," the rhetorical force given to the discourse of sexual difference in both the Indian Act and the Charter of Rights and Freedoms, to achieve not only representative politi-

cal power for Native women but to do so in such a way that Native
women are inscribed in the process of achieving collective rights for
Native self-determination. The *specificity* of Native women's struggle is
such that they are doubly inscribed as "Native" and as "women." Therefore, sexual difference must be understood in relation to another social
mode of differentiation, the colonial marginality imposed by the Canadian state. The following reading of "written bodies" in an RCMP document is situated, then, in the context of the Indigenous women's movement's strategic deployment of "sexual difference" against a hegemonic
colonialist production of "sexual difference" by the Canadian state. In
relation to an RCMP document, part of a minor discourse of the Canadian
colonial state, such a deployment not only works to (re)territorialize the
borders circumscribing the identity of an Indigenous/woman/body, it also
extends to the contours of the collective body of Indigenous women and
their involvement in the struggle of Indigenous people to preserve land
ownership and usage. I take the risk here of taking seriously the essentialist trope of "mother-as-mother-earth" as a strategic move in rearticulating
the collective struggle of decolonization, with the Indigenous women's
struggle to be recognized as part of that collectivity. Such recognition
entails an analysis of "sexual difference" in relation to those colonial
strategies used to keep Indigenous women at a distance from political
decision-making practices and to deny them the specificity of their struggle as Indigenous people, as Indigenous women.

THE INQUIRY

By disclosing the gendered character of the textual strategies deployed in
this RCMP investigation, it is possible to denaturalize some of the colonial assumptions at work in the narrative structure of the Canadian state's
policing apparatus, in particular, those assumptions that, first, create a
phantasmatic representation of an Inuk woman—the disappearing wife—
and turn the moment of her vanishing into the central motivation for
investigation, and, second, transform the contested terrain of a body's sex
into an objective phantom of displaced imperial relations among the Inuit,
the state, and a French Canadian trapper. The disappearing Inuk woman,
whose body is never discovered, and the mutilated body of one of the
drowned children whose biological sex is subject to dispute become in
these RCMP reports an ideological terrain of contested meanings. Ques-

tions emerge concerning not only the phallocentric assumptions of the text but also the ethnographic alibis recalled to support a savage and demeaning representation of the lives of this trapper, an Inuk woman, and their children.

A summary description of this decade of police files includes mention of the deaths of four children, two from drowning, one, twelve hours after birth, and still another disappearing with his mother. There are several notable events involving (1) serious burns inflicted to the head and hands of a baby, resulting in amputation and some minor head surgery, both of which took place in a remote cabin and were performed by the child's father; (2) the father's discovery of his son's drowned body a month later with parts of its face and limbs eaten by wolves; (3) A.'s self-described insanity, potentially due to syphilis; (4) a series of grave exhumations, the contents of which bring to the fore a discrepancy between A.'s testimony and a pathologist's laboratory report as to the sex of one of the bodies; and finally, (5) the mysterious disappearance of A.'s wife, consistently referred to as Mrs. A., her Inuit name never given. The vanishing wife initially raises the suspicion of the RCMP that A. has committed an act of foul play. This suspicion comes to structure a broader terrain of distrust from which follows an allegation that not only did A. murder his missing wife and child but he also killed the two children who purportedly died from drowning accidents.

The following is a detailed analysis of the investigative report. Since the text I am working with is not readily accessible I find it necessary to reproduce as much of the original text as possible in order to preserve its narrative continuity. However, the following reconstruction is not without its own ideological investments in disclosing the phallocentric and ethnocentric assumptions taken on the part of the investigators toward their object(s) of analysis. My point here is precisely to demonstrate the constructedness of the narrative along these ideological lines.

The case built up against A. is massive. The first three documents of the file, each entitled "Infant daughter of A. (Trapper)—Burned in tent fire," contain information about a small female infant who received severe burns to her hands and face when the pipes from a camp stove collapsed on the inside of the tent. In the first two documents A. is said to have requested medical aid to be sent to his remote campsite, but, unable to wait for the arrival of a Hudson's Bay Exploration Company plane some days later, returned to his camp with the injured child and performed his own surgical operations (4 July 1940, 29 August 1940). The third report, dated some nine months after the incident, summarizes the event and A.'s emergency surgery:

It appears that the pipes from a camp stove collapsed on the inside of the tent and fell over on to the bed upon which the child was laying, together with a bundle of dish cloths which also caught fire. This burning mass dropped directly on top of the child and she was burned severely about the head and arms and hands necessitating the removal of the index finger at the first joint and the middle finger at the second joint (by A.) of the right hand and not the left as previously reported on. A. stated he used disinfectant after snipping the flesh of the fingers off with a pair of scissors, after having first twisted the fingers off at the joints and that no complications had set in afterwards, the stumps of the fingers healing perfectly.

A small piece of bone was also removed from the forehead of the infant sometime after the accident, this piece of bone being approx. 1" x ¼", and at this time the spot where the bone was removed is hardly noticeable, having healed very nicely. (21 April 1941)

The fourth document in the file, dated 29 November 1947 (almost seven and a half years after the "Burned in the tent fire" incident) begins a series of sixteen documents entitled "Bertha A.—Padlei, N.W.T.—Death by Drowning." This report contains a radiogram sent from the Padlei trading post to the nearest RCMP detachment at Eskimo Point. The radiogram documents that the same infant burned in the tent accident, Bertha, drowned 13 September 1947 when she fell through the ice while A. and his wife were absent hunting. (Subsequent reports conclude that the drowning occurred on 30 September). Aside from a note to defer an official account of the incident until an inspector can be detached to A.'s camp, this report also mentions the cancellation of Family Allowance payments in the name of this child.

In the fifth document (2 September 1948), dated almost a year later and entitled "A. and Two Children—Eskimo Point, N.W.T. Sick and Destitute—Churchill, Man.," A. is reported to have left his camp and taken his two remaining children to Churchill, Manitoba, ostensibly to receive medical treatment for what he claims is a deteriorating nervous condition due to syphilis. According to A., his illness renders him unable to care for his children and he requests that they be placed in an orphanage. After a Wassermann test produces a negative result for syphilis, A. is diagnosed with anxiety neurosis, given an ounce of castor oil and an enema, and discharged. The end of the report contains a brief mention that the mother of the children died last spring, the spring of 1948.

Documents six (8 September 1948) and seven (11 October 1948) return to the Death by Drowning incident. These documents record A.'s statements about how the drowning occurred, as well as information about where the body was buried, information which will take on a great deal more significance in later reports. It is in the context of these reports that a separate file is opened to investigate the disappearance of Mrs. A. Document eight (9 November 1948), entitled "Mrs. A. and Small Son Paul J. A.—Padlei District, N.W.T. *Enquiry Re: Disappearance of:*" is the first of another major series of documents. This series plus the "Death by Drowning" documents constitute the bulk of the file on A., with the exception of a pathologist's autopsy report on a body exhumed from A.'s camp.

The remaining twenty-nine documents date from 8 January 1949 to 5 September 1950. By the ninth document the mystery has begun to consolidate itself as such. Suspicion of foul play is openly acknowledged in the tenth document (14 April 1949), and the RCMP begin their investigation in earnest. It is interesting to note that suspicion arises not from the local detachment at Eskimo Point. Rather it is the commanding officer at the Criminal Investigations Branch in Ottawa who voices the first note of suspicion: "We have grave suspicions, as the result of recent investigations by Cst. C—— of our Eskimo Point detachment that the woman and her son met with foul play and suspect that A. is responsible. There are only suspicions so far" (14 April 1949). Further to this declaration of suspicion, the terrain of distrust is immediately expanded to include what were previously held to be accidental drownings of both Bertha and another child named John, whose death in 1942 was never officially reported: "Two other children of this family, namely, one girl named Bertha was drowned or allegedly drowned on September 30, 1947. . . . Another named John, is said to have been drowned somewhere near their cabin in 1942 being 9 years of age at the time." This drowning of John A. was never reported by the constable in charge of the Eskimo Point detachment at the time (14 April 1949). What were initially thought to be *accidental* drownings now constitute allegedly *intentional* drownings.[16]

In an effort to consolidate the RCMP's suspicions, a process of ethnographic reconstruction begins to take place: facts are dissected from the body of information gathered and then reconstituted into a barbaric and savage representation of A.'s life. The discursive construction of A.'s

savage existence emerges in two interviews held by the RCMP in order
to gather more information regarding A.'s relationship to his Inuk partner
and why she mysteriously vanished. The story of Mrs. A.'s disappearance is recounted by the subregistrar of vital statistics, Mr. V——, at
Padlei. V—— testifies that A. arrived at his place in the afternoon of
18 May 1948 so as to inform him that his wife has been missing for
four days:

> Apparently Mrs. A. had left their Cabin on May 14th. to take the Mail to Padley
> *[sic]* some 25 miles distance. She had taken a team of Seven Dogs and a tobogan
> *[sic]* and their small Son with her. A. went on to say, Mr. V—— stated, that
> soon after his wife left for Padlei a snow storm accompanied with high winds
> came up. He had been worried, he stated, regarding his Wife and Child but
> thought she would have no trouble. He gave her until the 17th. of May—three
> days—to return from Padlei. When she did not return at this time he started into
> Padlei to look for her. (4 January 1949)

The RCMP conduct interviews with two individuals who were perhaps
the last people outside her immediate family to see Mrs. A. before she
disappeared. One interview was taken from an aboriginal woman referred
to as "P—— E.——," an Inuk midwife who helped in the delivery of
Mrs. A.'s last child in the spring of 1948.[17] She is reported as saying
the following:

> Upon being asked P—— stated that she had been present at A.'s Camp when the
> baby was born, sometime in the Spring of 1948 she thought. (Baby was born
> March 18th. 1948) She stated that a few days after the baby was born she told
> Mrs. A. that she had to leave to go home. Mr. A. was not in the Cabin at the
> time. Mrs. A. immediately started to cry and asked her not to go. She stated that
> she was afraid to stay alone with A. as he might do something to her. Upon being
> further questioned P—— stated that she had never seen A. strike or beat Mrs. A.
> and she did not know why Mrs. A. should be afraid to stay with Mr. A. P——
> went on to say that Mr. A. himself had not spoken to her (P——) since she
> arrived at his place just before the Baby was born. P—— stayed at A.'s Cabin
> three days after the baby was born and then returned home. (4 January 1949)

In a second interview with Father D—— of the Roman Catholic mission,
the following information is also gathered:

> During one visit approximately two years ago, [Father D——] stated, Mrs. A.
> was at home alone when he arrived. When he tried to talk to her in the Eskimo
> language—which he had done many times previous—she would not answer or
> talk to him. When A. came home that evening Father D—— learned that he, A.,
> had forbiden *[sic]* his wife to talk to anyone, not even Eskimos. That night, while

he stayed in the Cabin, Father D—— stated that A. treated his Wife somewhat like a dog. He would not let her eat at the table but made her sit in a corner of the room and he threw scraps of food at her. Father D—— left the Cabin the following day. Being further questioned Father D—— stated that A. had told him in the Summer of 1947 that he would like to leave the North Country now as he had enough but he couldn't do this ashe [sic] was "tied down" with an Eskimo Wife and Children. (4 January 1949)

Both interviews confirm A.'s mistreatment of his wife; however, P——'s testimony appears as a somewhat unsympathetic response to Mrs. A.'s fearfulness and Father D——'s represents the voice of a sympathetic and objective observer who, although concerned to communicate with Mrs. A., does not intervene on her behalf to put an end to A.'s abusive treatment toward her.

As the narrative unfolds it is clear that the RCMP are engaged in a process of deductive reasoning designed to confirm their already presumed, however hypothetical, suspicions that A. has committed some acts of murder. On the basis of the interviews with P—— and Father D——, Constable C—— of Eskimo Point draws the following conclusion:

From the foregoing it is quite apparent and possible that A. may have disposed of his Wife and Child by foul play. There is no conclusive evidence of this fact however at the present time. Bertha A., who was badly scarred by being burned wasthe [sic] first Child to die after A. had stated he would like to leave the North. Then A.'s Wife and Child disappeared. Here again it seems rather odd that A. should suddenly let his Wife go to Padley [sic] when previously he had forbiden [sic] her to leave the Cabin grounds, and even forbid her to talk to other people. (4 January 1949)

In an effort to prove their hypotheses about the legal crimes of murder A. has committed, the RCMP investigators reconstruct the testimonies in a manner that overlooks and thereby sanctions the unrecognized crimes of "domestic violence" A. commits against his wife and family. Nevertheless these scenes of brutality play an important role not only in validating suspicion against A. but also in validating the conditions of his life generally that would give him a motive: "he would like to leave the North Country now as he had enough but he couldn't do this ashe [sic] was 'tied down' with an Eskimo Wife and Children." The RCMP use this latter statement to attribute a motive to A.'s actions. I would suggest that there exists an assumed disposition on the part of the investigators that corroborates A.'s reasons for wanting to leave: the "savage" life of the North Country. Indeed, the two interviews taken are as important for their construction of this "savage" existence as for the information they impart. If solving the legal crime of murder is at stake, the RCMP must reconstruct the viable conditions on which murder would be likely to occur. I am not convinced that it is solely A.'s mistreatment of his wife that gives the RCMP cause to suspect murder; rather, it is the brutal conditions under which he lives that sanction his desire to kill. Those brutal conditions are figured in the body of the Inuk woman as both the victim of a brutality that does not constitute a "legal crime" and the body that signifies brutality itself in being that victim. In other words, the figuration of the Inuk woman as a passive victim and helpless "dog-like" creature who submits to A.'s violence creates the very figure of savagery the RCMP are looking for in order to legitimate their suspicion of murder. The production of the woman as a figure of savagery in the document is necessary to the legitimation of colonial law and the circumscription of what constitutes legality or illegality. The savagery of A. as an individual capable of murder, then, is cathected through the othering of his Inuk wife as the authentic savage figure.

In P——'s testimony the emphasis is on visual, and hence "objective," proof as to A.'s treatment of Mrs. A. In the interview recorded, it is only "[u]pon being further questioned" that P—— states "she had never seen A. strike or beat Mrs. A." The sentence continues: "and she did not know why Mrs. A. should be afraid to stay with Mr. A." Since there is no visible proof to corroborate the (unacknowledged) crime of domestic violence, that violence itself becomes unknowable. This is one way the setup of the interview allows the RCMP to dismiss the domestic violence as the site of evidence on which to convict A. Domestic violence is not the crime under investigation. Indeed, it does not constitute criminal behavior at all within the discursive makeup of the inquiry. It is the textual modes of representation of the testimonies that delimit the field of criminality, thereby constituting the active relationship between the crime and the criminal. The information about A.'s treatment of his wife only serves to confirm his murderous intentions and the barbarity of his alleged criminal behavior. I would also suggest that A. is implicitly being held guilty of another sort of crime, an ethnographic crime of miscegenation, a "racially mixed marriage" between a French Canadian and Inuk woman and, as the RCMP refer to them, his "half-breed" children (17 August 1949): a marriage and family A. distances himself from in an effort to escape the difficulties of his life in the north.

The two interviews also tell us that Mrs. A. received no support from her own people because A. denied her access to them. Father D——'s support is well-intentioned, however limited to sanctioning the violence of a religio-patriarchal control in the "privacy" of the domestic sphere. Finally, and perhaps most important, the RCMP, from whom she also received no help, are interested in her only after her disappearance. The textual construction of these interviews inscribes a phallocentric ethnography and discloses the following contradiction: the colonial man, the French Canadian trapper, is held in an active and civil opposition of criminality and legitimation, while the Inuk woman, as a figure of savagery, mediates the hierarchical status of this individual man for the state's policing apparatus. The Inuk woman's textual position as the disappearing wife—if not the disappearing referent—adds to her construction as an ideological phantasm, there to breach the gap between the colonial state and the uncontrollable forces of nature, between the commanding officer at the Criminal Investigations Branch in Ottawa and the margins of Canada's northern territory, which the RCMP are designated to assert and protect.

Another instance of phallocentric ethno-graphy occurs following the RCMP's decision that the only way to gather sufficient evidence to convict A. must involve exhuming one of the bodies buried near his camp. The decision to investigate the contents of one particular grave emerges due to conflicting reports about the whereabouts of Bertha's grave. Initially A. stated that he buried the body "on a small hill fifty yards N.W. of the cabin" (8 September 1948). According to a police patrol sent to A.'s cabin on 12 December 1948, Bertha's grave had been moved from its original site:

Two graves were located some distance from the cabin. One grave was small and apparently belonged to John A., A.'s son who was drowned in 1942. The other grave was very large and was apparently not there when Cst. B—— and S/Cst. G—— had visited the Cabin in May of 1948 [just after the disappearance of Mrs. A. and her son], according to S/Cst. G——. S/Cst. G—— stated that Bertha A. had been buried closer to the Cabin and an old Canoe had been turned over the grave and partially covered with sand and rocks. This grave in question was not there at this time. It had apparently been moved by someone—the canoe was not present either. As A. is presently in Churchill no reason could be found at this time as to why Bertha A.'s body should be moved from one place to another. (4 January 1949)

This new and larger grave was located closer to two hundred yards away from the cabin and not fifty yards as originally stated by A. (as noted in a subsequent document dated 16 August 1949). The above report continues with: "It is not known who might be buried there. It is exceptionally large—approximately twice as large as any other grave the writer has seen in the N.W.T." (4 January 1949).

When RCMP attempts to exhume the body in the middle of an arctic winter prove futile—the hard frozen sand and rocks making the task impossible—instructions are then given to return the following September when the ground has thawed. (Another attempt was made 7 May 1949.) When the body was finally exhumed in August 1949, Dr. M——, the local coroner, noted "suspicious signs to warrant pathologist investigation" (17 August 1949). M—— describes the body thus:

[S]mall headless corps [sic], lying on abdomen, legs flexed on thighs and crossed on each other. Arms were not apparent but body was not moved to see if they were present under. Trunk and limbs were clothed. A stick was used to tear the rotten clothing down the back in order to note injuries, no wound was made with this. In the right scapular region near the vertebral column a hole was noted, and the ribs had detached from the spinal cord. The shoulder was jammed up against the top of the box and no head was in evidence in its normal position. Lying in the region of the upper right shoulder was the mandible which was attached to the ma[x]illa [jawbone]. The maxilla had been detached from the base of skull with some apparent fracturing. The temporal boned [sic] were lying separated in the box. The upper skull was lying on its dome about the middle of the back. There appeared to be an old bandage in the cranial cavity but no soft tissue. What appeared to be one of the forearm bones was lying on the right side—it was fractured at one end with parts missing. Impressions:—Maxillary, and basal fractures of skull—teeth missing Scalp or hair not present, skull and arm bones in peculiar position, indicate the possibilities of foul play. Due to degeneration it was decided to leave the determination up to a pathologist. (16 August 1949)

Having determined that Mrs. A. and her son were not buried in this grave, the RCMP then turn toward the mutilated body as potential evidence of A.'s wrongdoing. The official laboratory report contains the following summary:

Remains of human child, approximate age nine to ten years. Sex -female. In a fairly good state of nutrition at time of death. Remains show almost complete adipocere formation. Cause of death cannot be definitely stated. There is no evidence however, of any injury to the body skeleton with the exception of what apparently is post mortem destruction, of the right arm as noted, by some carnivora. There are what appear to be tool marks appearing on the right humerus. Date of death can be approximated as at least or over one year. (*Laboratory Report*, 2 September 1949)

Surprisingly, the pathologist concludes that "there is no evidence in the remains that is contrary to death by natural means, for example, by drowning" (2 September 1949). On the basis of the pathologist's report, the mutilated body of the young Bertha provides the RCMP with little evidence that might resolve the question of Mrs. A.'s disappearance, nor do the pathologist's findings lead to any further illumination as to the nature of A.'s suspicious conduct.[18]

The results of the pathologist's report would seem to suggest that the suspicions against him are insubstantial if not unwarranted. There are, however, two remaining threads dangling in the minds of the RCMP: the case of the drowned boy, whose death was never officially reported to the RCMP, and the reason Bertha A.'s body was removed from its original site and reburied *elsewhere*.

In order to tie up the details of his son's death, A., who until this point has remained at Churchill and unbeknownst to him been under the surveillance of the RCMP, is interviewed in connection with the death by drowning of his son John.[19] In a sworn statement given by A. of the events leading up to his son's death, he recounts a canoeing accident that results in his 3½ year-old-son never being recovered, although A. managed to rescue his wife, Bertha, and another daughter, Dianna. A. describes how he found the body a month later, by chance:

[I] could not find John, I searched the river and the lake, about a month later, I dont [sic] remember if I was looking for John or one of my dogs that had gone away from camp, when I noticed a head and then the body, it had been mauled, both arms were eat [sic] off and the face had been eating [sic] away, I took the boy to my cabin, where I buried him. (17 October 1949)[20]

Initially, the only apparent discrepancy noticed by the RCMP in A.'s statement concerns the age of the boy. A. says in his report that the child was 3½ years old, whereas the information recorded by an RCMP officer in a report dated 11 October 1948 is that John A. was born in 1933. At the time of his drowning in 1942, this would make him nine years old (1 November 1949).

In response to why Bertha's body was moved, the RCMP hypothesize that due to the tooth marks noted on the body's bones, perhaps the body could have been dug up by wolves, in which case A. had to rebury it.

This speculation is not merely inspired by the story of the mauled body of John A.; the suggestion is soon put forth that perhaps the body exhumed was, indeed, that of John A. and not Bertha. Subsequent discussions with A. reveal the following:

[D]uring a visit with A. the subject of his Wife's disappearance came up during the course of the conversation, when A. stated he wished the Police could find his wife's body or what would be left of it, as he A. would feel much better if it were found, from there the conversation was discreetly led around to the graves behind his cabin and in this connection the following information was ascertained; Bertha was buried about ¾ way up the hill behind the cabin and in Deerskins (caribou) and that the grave is marked with a stone at the head and feet and that the body has never been removed. John was buried at the top of the hill in a somewhat larger grave, and that he put John's body in his tool box as it had been badly decomposed and mauled by dogs or wolves and had been decapitated and that he, A. had gathered up John's remains with old rags which he put in the tool box with the body and the head he placed on top of the body, closed the box up and buried same on top of the hill behind his cabin. . . .

It would appear from this report that the body examined was that of John A. and not that of Bertha A., as first suspected. (6 December 1949)

The statements by A. concerning the death by drowning of his son would indeed seem to confirm that the body exhumed was that of John and not Bertha. Only one small problem remains: the discrepancy between A.'s description of John's burial and the conclusion of the pathologist's report that the sex of the body exhumed is female.

The pathologist's report clearly states that "On examination of perineal region there is no evidence of the scrotum or penis. The vaginal opening measures ½" in length by 1/16th" in width. The labia minora and labia majora are well defined and what appears to be the urethal [sic] opening can be seen" (*Laboratory Report*, 2 September 1949). In the face of such certainty, the RCMP insist that the exhumed body is "definitely that of a female" and that A. is "either lying or has forgotten details in respect to the mode of burial of his son John and his daughter Bertha, or has become confused as between the two." The report goes on to suggest that the latter speculation is not unreasonable since A. "was in a state of Mental unbalance and he may have been in that mental state for some considerable time during the last year or so of his life in the cabin near Padlei" (21 December 1949).

It is now the mystery of the sex of the dead body that needs to be solved, and the RCMP, already demonstrating their superior skills of deduction and still holding to the infallibility of the Crime Detection Laboratory results, decide that the only way to resolve the case of the dead body's sex is to dig up the other grave site. On 23 August 1950 another grave was opened up.

The body was covered with deerskins and when the deerskins were removed it was quite plain the [sic] see the body was that of Bertha A. She was positively identified by two Eskimos who were present. These Eskimos had known her personally. The Eskimos are S/Cst. G—— E.—— and K—— E.——. The body was in an almost perfect state of preservation and the writer could quite plainly see the scars on the girl's face where she had been burned as a child. Her nose too was partly burned off. There were no visible signs to show that death had been due to foul play. (5 September 1950)

The officer in Eskimo Point who wrote this report concludes by saying that he is of the opinion that Bertha's body should also be sent to the Crime Detection Lab in order to clear up the matter once and for all. The response from the commissioner in Ottawa (suffering no doubt from a major attack of castration anxiety) deems further investigation unwarranted and the case is closed (21 September 1950).

The definitive identification of the second exhumed corpse as that of Bertha A. plays a dual function of closure within the RCMP text. On the one hand, positive identification makes it possible for the RCMP to close the case; on the other hand, the second exhumed corpse solves the confusion of gender the first body comes to signify precisely because a positive ID can be made. The ability to restore truth to the domain of a positive identity quickly displaces the anxiety of gender unresolvability assigned to the first exhumed body. Positive physiological identification substantiates any metaphysical uncertainty that might otherwise disrupt a definitive reading of the female-sexed status of the body. On both the physiological and metaphysical levels the positively identified, female-sexed body of Bertha settles the problem of uncertainty the very logic of discovery sets out to resolve. What remains unresolved, of course, is the discrepancy between the pathologist's report of a female-sexed body in reference to the first exhumed body and A.'s own account as to this body's "sex." [21]

AN EPISTEMOLOGY OF THE GRAVE

The body, writes Foucault, "and everything that touches it: diet, climate, and soil—is the domain of the *Herkunft* [descent]. The body manifests the stigmata of past experience and also gives rise to desires, failings, and errors. These elements may join in a body where they achieve a sudden expression, but as often, their encounter is an engagement in which they efface each other, where the body becomes the pretext of their insurmountable conflict."[22] Foucault's inscription of the body as a *pretext* to insurmountable social and cultural antagonism is one site of contest Judith Butler can be said to problematize when she criticizes Foucault's genealogical history for positing a prediscursive notion of the body that assumes "a materiality prior to signification and form."[23] If history for Foucault is quintessentially "the creation of values and meanings by a signifying practice that requires the subjection of the body" (130), in the final instance, Butler argues, the body can only be figured "as the medium which must be destroyed and transfigured in order for 'culture' to emerge" (130). With specific reference to the sexed body, Butler suggests, the "production of sex *as* the prediscursive ought to be understood as the effect of the apparatus of cultural construction designated by *gender*" (7, Butler's emphasis). In other words, the shape of the body, its figural deployment as a sexed entity, constitutes a terrain of contested meanings and values that are not necessarily pregiven to a sacrificial act of destruction in the name of cultural sovereignty. The idea that the body must be offered up to a mode of sacrificial dismemberment in order for "culture" to emerge is itself a product of a gendered configuration of bodily regulation: one that awaits "the inscription-as-incision of the masculine signifier for entrance into language and culture" (147–48). The body may indeed subvert a formation of knowledge that, in Foucault's words, "is not made for understanding; it is made for cutting" (154).

In the RCMP texts the corpse does indeed become a site of resistance brought about by the crisis of uncertainty in the determination of its essentially sexed nature, which no amount of autopsic dissection and postmortem dismemberment will be able, finally, to resolve. There are at least two essential truths in need of confirmation in the text of the RCMP reports: the true biological sex of a mutilated corpse; and the truth about the disappearance of A.'s wife, an Inuk woman and the mother of the sex-undifferentiated, although presumed female, corpse. In the former truth, not only must a sexed body be determined, but the logical conditions of necessity for differentiating a body on the basis of a male/female biological polarity must be established and put into practice. Following Nietzsche, Michel Foucault tells us that "[t]ruth is undoubtedly the sort of error that cannot be refuted because it was hardened into an unalterable form in the long baking process of history" (144). Likewise, due to the intensity of freezing temperatures, the relatively well preserved condition of the dead body could also be said to preserve the physiological and metaphysical conditions for a hardened irrefutability in the pursuit of truth this body will be made to effect and produce.[24] But if we believe that "the body obeys the exclusive laws of physiology and that it escapes the influence of history" (153), then, Foucault warns, we continue to err on the side of undeniable falsity. For according to Foucault, "[t]he body is molded by a great many distinct regimes; it is broken down by the rhythms of work, rest, and holidays; it is poisoned by food or values, through eating habits or moral laws, it constructs resistances" (153). Not only will the corpse resist the certainty of a biologically formulated, sexed differentiation for the medico-juridical powers of scientific interpretation, as in a pathologist's report, it will also resist the feminist investigating subject's attempt to solve this enigma solely within the metonymically proscribed terms of sexual difference. To position the female body as the necessary ground on which to lay solid foundations for a critical investigation without attention to the larger historical context of colonialism will only exacerbate a serious displacement: to borrow Gayatri Chakravorty Spivak's dissociative phrasing, that "the woman's body is the last instance, it is elsewhere."[25] The Indigenous female body must be situated by the strategies of marginality operating in the RCMP file, which reinforce colonial marginality and the marginalization of the issue of colonialism.

The other truth in question is the account of A.'s wife's disappearance, the woman's body that, in the final instance, *is elsewhere*. It is this phantasmatic body that foregrounds the limits of a critical investigation based upon a paradigmatic subject of (female) sexual difference. The Inuk woman's vanishing and her subsequent rediscovery as a textual phantasm point to the degree of visible indifference on the part of the juridical investigators toward the Indigenous female subject; although the issue of sexual differentiation with reference to the mutilated corpse noticeably dominates the RCMP reports' construction of the case against A., also worth noting is the indifference manifested toward the brutality of the Inuk woman's treatment at the hands of A., recorded and documented in the two interviews. The lack of recognition of the violence done to the Inuk woman and her positioning as a figure of savagery are constitutive to the colonial marginalization of her subject position by the policing apparatus.

By disclosing the significance of gender to colonial marginality in this visibly indifferent space it is possible to resist the reproduction of the fetishistic investments of (hetero)sexual difference for the culture of imperialism. To track the surplus of meanings that exceed the colonial authoritative borders established to contain the corporeal status of the Inuk woman's body is also to contribute to decolonizing the genealogy of the conceptual figure "sexual difference"; a project to be furthered through a sustained engagement with the material effects of language—its truth games and logics of discovery—on the bodies of imperialized subjects.[26]

NORTHERN EXPOSURE

In the encounters between Europeans/Euro-Canadians and First Nations, writing plays a significant role: merchants have kept books, governors have kept diaries, ship's captains have kept logs, RCMP officers have kept reports. Inscription upon inscription inscribes many thousands of non-European people into a universal equivalent for the world's trade in people. Those records, reports, acts, and logs not only document particular events, as a minor discourse they also constitute a micrological historical narrative and act as a material force partially shaping the lives of people who are subjects of and to history: history, written history of this sort is the law, one kind of ideological apparatus working with its repressive cohort: the coercive arm of the state: the military: the police force.[27]

As the legal arm of the state, the RCMP exist to maintain the state's national directives to bring the territories of the North under its jurisdiction. Unfortunately for the Canadian state, the Inuit live on these territories. Cultural incorporation is neither desired nor contemplated; only assimilation—an attempt to obliterate all traces of a different mode of social, economic, and political life—is acceptable. Within this legal discourse we can trace the phallocentric ethnography that places a "mixed body" at the site of an immutable and intrinsic ideology of sexual difference. "Sexual difference" operates for the RCMP as a signifier of certainty in an otherwise uncertain realm of bio-logical instabilities.[28] However, the undifferentiated sexed body, a body that must be "sexed" but cannot be definitively differentiated as male or female, resists positive identification. Or, on another register: the written body resists the definitive inscription of meaning proffered by the colonial state. I have read this text in light of the Indigenous women's movement, which effectively renegotiated the significance of sexual difference for the purposes of achieving collective representative political power. Such a renegotiation of sexual difference, itself, represents a strategic use of the performative potential of gender to both display as well as displace the political stakes involved in the decolonial contest over territorial lands. Displacement is another name for that "elsewhere," the site of the colonial marginalization of Indigenous inscriptions of the land. Currently, the Indigenous women's movement has given a different symbolic value to territorial lands by strategically deploying the figure of the Indigenous/woman/body as a metonym for the Indigenous people's collective right to land usage. As this colonial archival document figures an Inuit woman's body as a central site with which to mark the colonial borders of juridical, medical, and legal determinations during the 1940s, the contemporary Indigenous women's movement—a collective political body—is making its political struggle central to achieving the collective right to Indigenous self-determination.

NOTES

My thanks to Jay Tribby, Ross Leckie, Elie Korkmaz, Rajani Sudan, Frank Tester, and Peter Kulchyski for their helpful comments and suggestions on this essay, parts of which were written during my postdoctoral fellowship at the Society for the Humanities, Cornell University, 1992–93. Carol Siegel provided invaluable direction in the final stages of rewriting, for which I am very grateful. I owe a special thanks to Frank Tester and Peter Kulchyski for sharing this archival source with me.

1. All documents from Public Archives of Canada, Record Group 86, vol. 920. All references to documents are contained in the text and indicated by date.

2. To maintain a rigid distinction between a sex-(un)differentiated body and a sexually (un)differentiated body would be to deny an irreducible linguistic slide in which the libidinal investments of the biological enterprise no doubt play a role in the ethno-pornography of imperial desire and its libidinal object-choice.

3. Hillary Leone and Jennifer Macdonald, "Passio Perpetuae," in *Incorporations*, ed. Jonathan Crary and Sanford Kwinter (New York: Zone, 1992), 596–97.

4. For a well-documented account of this history, see Peter Kulchyski and Frank Tester, *Tammarniit (Mistakes): Inuit Relocation in the Eastern Artic, 1940–50* (Vancouver: University of British Columbia Press, 1994).

5. See Gayatri Chakravorty Spivak, "Can the Subaltern Speak?" in *Marxism and the Interpretation of Culture*, ed. Cary Nelson and Lawrence Grossberg (Chicago: University of Illinois Press, 1988), especially 279.

While the discourse of postcolonialism in Canadian literary studies has tended to keep Euro-Canadian literature at the center of its critical inquiry, as if the contradictions of the colonial encounter primarily inhere between English or French Canada and Britain or France, it is continually important to point out that there is such a thing as Canadian imperialism within "Canada." For Aboriginal peoples their relationship to the Canadian state is far more of a direct concern than the now historical effects of European colonialism.

6. For an extended discussion of the problematic of "sexual difference" produced in and by cross-global First World feminist publishing and analysis, see Chandra Talpade Mohanty, "Under Western Eyes: Feminist Scholarship and Colonial Discourse," *Boundary 2* 12 (1984): 333–58, reprinted in *Feminist Review* 30 (1988): 61–88. A revised version of this essay appears in Chandra Talpade Mohanty, Ann Russo, and Lourdes Torres, eds., *Third World Women and the Politics of Feminism* (Bloomington: Indiana University Press, 1991), 51–80. See also Gayatri Chakravorty Spivak, "Imperialism and Sexual Difference," *Oxford Literary Review* 8 (1986): 225–40.

7. These distinctions need some clarification. The difference between status and non-status Indians was determined by the Canadian state in the late nineteenth century through an ad hoc process in which individuals were signed up, often given Christian names, and added to a registry. Metis constitute a cultural group of mixed Scottish/Cree or French/Cree descent. The Inuit are an independent cultural and linguistic group occupying what are now called the North West Territories, the Yukon, and the northern part of Labrador, in Canada. In 1993, the Canadian state recognized Nunavat, a third order of government constituted by the Inuit of the Eastern Arctic.

8. *NWAC et al. v Her Majesty et al.*, Federal Court of Appeal, 20 August 1992.

9. For a detailed discussion of the discriminatory clauses of the *Indian Act*, see Katheleen Jamieson, "Sex Discrimination and the Indian Act," in *Arduous Journey: Canadian Indians and Decolonization*, ed. J. Rick Ponting (Toronto: McClelland and Stewart, 1986), 112–36.

10. Jo-Anne Fiske, "The Womb Is to the Nation as the Heart Is to the Body: Ethnopolitical Discourses of the Canadian Indigenous Women's Movement" (paper presented to the Thirteenth World Congress of Sociology, International Sociology Association, Beilefeld, Germany, 18–23 July 1994). Many thanks to Jo-Anne Fiske for allowing me to read her work in progress, which has been invaluable to this discussion.

11. Marlyn Kane (Osennontion) and Sylvia Maracle (Skonaganleh:ra), "Our World," *Canadian Woman Studies/Les cahiers de la femme* 10, nos. 2–3 (Summer/Fall 1989) [Special Issue: Native Women]: 7–19, especially 12 and 14.

12. See, for example, Mona Etienne and Eleanor Leacock, *Women and Colonization: Anthropological Perspectives* (New York: Praeger, 1980).

13. Jo-Anne Fiske, "The Womb Is to the Nation as the Heart Is to the Body: Ethnopolitical Discourses of the Canadian Indigenous Women's Movement," 6–7.

14. Diana Fuss, *Essentially Speaking: Feminism, Nature and Difference* (New York: Routledge, 1989), 20.

15. For a more detailed account than I can provide here of the history of Bill

C-31, see Julia Emberley, *Thresholds of Difference: Feminist Critique, Native Women's Writings, Postcolonial Theory* (Toronto: University of Toronto Press, Culture/Theory Series, 1993), especially 79–99.

16. As we will see later, the suspicion on the part of this Ottawa bureaucrat stems more from his ignorance of the realities of northern life than anything based on sustained knowledge of what would constitute suspicious behavior and criminal activity within this environmentally "alien" context.

17. According to Vic Satzewich and Terry Wotherspoon, *First Nations: Race, Class, and Gender Relations* (Scarborough, Ontario: Nelson Canada, 1993), it was not until the federal government census of 1951 that each Inuk was assigned "a disc number" (xv). The consistent usage of a name/number combination format (also referred to as "E" numbers) in the RCMP reports suggests that some form of notation was in use before the census report systematized its usage. This systematic notation was purportedly initiated for the purposes of administering family allowance payments in the late 1940s.

18. During the course of the exhumation of Bertha's body and the exchange of reports between the various RCMP divisions on this topic, several other reports on the disappearance of Mrs. A. were in circulation. During the period from Mrs. A.'s disappearance (May 1948) to September 1949, two dogs belonging to A.'s team as well as an abandoned toboggan were found, although it was concluded that the toboggan was not A.'s after all (7 November 1949, 29 November 1949, 10 May 1950).

19. It would appear, however, that A. had some of his own suspicions about what the RCMP were making of his story. In what is an ironic, or at least reflexive, moment in the text of these reports, the following comment is recorded, with quotation marks, from A.: "it must look suspicious to you as a Policeman." When requested what he meant by this comment the following explanation is recorded: "he said two of my children meeting their death by drowning and my wife and other child disappearing somewhere between my camp and Padlei and were never seen again, he then stated that he had been accused of murder, and he enlarged on this by stating that one dinner hour at the Army Camp, where he is employed, he was telling one of the other workmen about his troubles and how he lost four members of his family and this workman told him '[A.] YOU MURDERED THEM.' A. could not recall the name of this workman, however, during our conversation A. did inform the writer that his son John was buried on the top of the hill at the back of his cabin and that Bertha was buried on the side of the hill and that another baby boy that died at childbirth was buried across the lake from his cabin" (17 October 1949).

20. The contents of the statement leading up to this excerpt is as follows: "Sometime in June, 1942, I was moving with my family, Bertha, John, Dianna and my wife from my tent which was approximately half a mile above my camp. On the way down with a canoe, a 16' Cruser Canoe, we hit fast water and it took the canoe towards a rock, where the canoe upset in the rolls caused by the fast water and the rock. As the canoe started to upset I jumped into the water, the first one of my family, I saw was Bertha, I then looked for my wife, who was

carrying Dianna on her back, I got hold of my wife and got her over to the canoe and told her to hold on to it, I then went to the other end of the canoe and started working it towards shore, when near shore the canoe hit another rock and righted itself, my son John was underneath the canoe, holding on to the thwart, John was about 3½ years of age, I told him to hold on we hit another rock and the canoe turned over and I managed to beach same, I could not find John when I righted the canoe, got my wife and child ashore and went out in the canoe to look for Bertha and John, I found Bertha, but could not find John."

21. I would suggest that the difficulty of positively identifying the originally exhumed body lies in the "normative" understanding that gender difference functions as a symmetrical mark of sexual identity. The unidentifiable, if not undecidable, body in this police inquiry could be said to mark an unstable continuity between the categories of sex and gender. Like the figure of the transvestite for Marjorie Garber, this mark of gender undecidability leaves its trace within the RCMP narrative as an indication of "category crisis." By category crisis, Garber means "a failure of definitional distinction, a borderline that becomes permeable, that permits of border crossings from one (apparently distinct) category to another. The presence of the transvestite, in a text, in a culture, signals a category crisis elsewhere. The transvestite is a sign of overdetermination—a mechanism of displacement. There can be no culture without the transvestite, because the transvestite marks the existence of the Symbolic." When the unidentified sexed body resists the authorities' attempt to definitively negotiate its borders, a crisis of unresolvability occurs in the RCMP's investigative procedures, a crisis precipitated, I would argue, by the slippage between the categories of sex and gender. If as Garber suggests a category crisis signals a crisis "elsewhere," I would locate that elsewhere in the geopolitical sphere. At the same time the Canadian state sets out to bring the north under its sovereignty and, hence, establish a borderland, it must cope with territorial borders already in existence between the Inuit and "Canada," borders the Canadian state does not wish to traverse or incorporate so much as obliterate: to make of Inuit culture a paper "cutout," something that can be reduced to paper, to the storytelling technologies of police documents and pathologist's reports. See Marjorie Garber, "The Occidental Tourist: *M. Butterfly* and the Scandal of Transvestism," in *Nationalisms and Sexualities*, ed. Andrew Parker, Mary Russo, Doris Sommer, and Patricia Yaeger (New York: Routledge, 1992), 125. For a revised version of this essay, see Garber's extensive study of the figure of the transvestite in *Vested Interests: Cross-Dressing and Cultural Anxiety* (New York: Routledge, 1992), especially 234–66.

22. Michel Foucault, "Nietzsche, Genealogy, History," in *Language, Counter-Memory, Practice: Selected Essays and Interviews by Michel Foucault*, ed. Donald F. Bouchard (Ithaca, NY: Cornell University Press, 1977), 148. Further references to this work will be included parenthetically in the text.

23. Judith Butler, *Gender Trouble: Feminism and the Subversion of Identity* (New York: Routledge, 1990), 130. Further references to this work will be included parenthetically in the text.

24. Constitutive to the logic of discovery in the scientific mode of investigation

is what Evelyn Fox Keller identifies as "the urge to fathom the secrets of nature." In her discussion of the place secrecy occupies in mapping out the interpretive domain of the discourse of science, Keller notes that "Secrets function to articulate a boundary: an interior not visible to outsiders, the demarcation of a separate domain, a sphere of autonomous power." The idea of an interior space that must be brought to the surface, as it were, in order to disclose for examination that which has hitherto remained unexamined, is, as Fox argues, conditioned by the gender hierarchy: "The ferreting out of nature's secrets, understood as the illumination of a female interior, or the tearing of Nature's veil, may be seen as expressing one of the most unembarrassedly stereotypic impulses of the scientific project. In this interpretation, the task of scientific enlightenment—the illumination of the reality behind appearances—is an inversion of surface and interior, an interchange between visible and invisible, that effectively routs the last vestiges of archaic, subterranean female power." The logic of scientific discovery, predicated as it is on an interpretive methodology "for 'undoing' nature's secrets," succeeds, in the pathologist's report, in mapping itself onto the logic of a medico-juridical construction of truth. What is discovered in the process is that the contours of these scientific and legal investigations are demarcated by the physiological imperatives of an Indigenous/woman/body, defined first and foremost on the foundational premise of a heterosexual difference. See Evelyn Fox Keller, *Secrets of Life/Secrets of Death: Essays on Language, Gender and Science* (New York: Routledge, 1992), especially 40 and 41.

25. Gayatri Chakravorty Spivak, "Woman in Difference: Mahasweta Devi's 'Douloti the Bountiful,' " in *Nationalisms and Sexualities*, ed. Andrew Parker, Mary Russo, Doris Sommer, and Patricia Yaeger, 101.

26. It is also, of course, possible to note the lost ground of heterosexual difference in producing such a genealogy. A colleague once mentioned that while visiting an Inuit family he noticed that one of a pair of twin boys was dressed as a girl. When he inquired as to why one child was dressed as a girl and the other a boy when their biological sex was male, the older brother to the children explained that the female child was named for his eleven-year-old sister, who died shortly before the twins were born; hence, the child bears her name. Well trained, as most of us are, in the protocols of heterosexual sex/gender symmetry, my friend asked an obvious question: What happens when the child gets older? In response to which he was informed that when the child is old enough he/she could decide as to whether to keep his/her older sister's name and identity or take a masculinized name and male identity for her/himself. The point is that the child will decide who he/she wants to be. In some Indigenous cultures transvestism acts as a spiritual force for transformation often linked to the desire for dissimilitude. For example, the ethnologist Valérie Chaussonnet discusses transvestism among Native peoples of the North Pacific as an agent of spiritual transformation between the human and the animal as well as between gender identities: "Both men and women wore jewellery, although the styles were not necessarily identical. Bogoras noted that many Chukchi men wore women's earrings, generally by the order of a shaman. By direction of the shaman, Chukchi men also wore

women's-style boots on occasion. This transvestism was a ploy to hide and protect the person from evil spirits, in the same way that sick people had their faces blackened so that the evil spirit would not recognize them as human. Transvestism in the shaman's garments represented his or her position between the male and female worlds. . . . The passage between gender identities and other passages throughout the lives and deaths of Siberian people were marked on clothing with the same care that the Alaskan Eskimo represented the transformational relationship with the animal world." It is a compelling thought that A. may not have known the gender possibilities underlying his own children's sexual status. It certainly did not occur to the RCMP officers to investigate the possibility and implications of "transvestism" within the spiritual and naming practices of the Inuit among A.'s and his Inuk partner's children. See Valérie Chaussonnet, "Needles and Animals: Women's Magic," in *Crossroads of Continents: Cultures of Siberia and Alaska*, ed. William W. Fitzhugh and Aron Crowell (Washington DC: Smithsonian Institution Press, 1988), 225–26.

27. Many acts of inscription take place, including a set of toboggan tracks and dog's footprints in the snow outside Eskimo Point and a set of graves placed in the earth, dug, undug, and redug, as if to expose earth's "mystery" and then smother it. For a suggestive—however "biased"—reading of narrative forms deriving from a process of deciphering animal tracks on the ground, see Carlo Ginzberg, "Clues: Roots of an Evidential Paradigm," in *Clues, Myths, and Historical Method*, trans. John and Anne C. Tedeschi (Baltimore: Johns Hopkins University Press, 1989), in particular, 102–3. While enamored of "man the hunter," Ginzberg simply forgets about "woman the gatherer," or "woman the hunter," for that matter. The essay is also problematic for its evolutionary and progressivist reading of footprints in the snow, read by Palaeolithic man, to written intellectual abstraction, read by postmodern (male) cultural historian.

28. The code of "racial difference" could also be misread as a symmetrical map of cultural difference. As another social mode of differentiation, "race" provides the authorities with a ground from which to inscribe an ideology of cultural difference. In this case, that ground is re-presented in the document's construction of savagery in the body of the Inuk woman.

EIGHT

Bad Canoes and *Bafalo:* The Political Economy of Sex on Daru Island, Western Province, Papua New Guinea

Lawrence Hammar

"Would you be inclined to kiss and tell?" [the TV host asks]
"Oh, we don't kiss . . . too many germs."[1]

Kath Weston recently asked in *Genders* why "gender relations," the stuff of two decades of feminist theory and practice, seems always to mean male-female relations. Since gender is not reducible to essential character(s) or performance, since gender "no more resides in gesture or apparel than it lies buried in bodies and psyches,"[2] she argues that gender *performance* is infinitely possible, but gender *categories* (e.g., butch/femme) are more stable: they *already* presume "male-female."

As an ethnographer still reeling from the effects of having done depressing fieldwork, I find Weston's approach—to examine stable categories, those less so, and the disjunctures between them—very useful. My topics of fieldwork, "sex," "prostitution," "the sex industry," are unstable analytically and empirically. Perhaps it is just the new, post-fieldwork, postmodern me, but concepts by which I learned my discipline—"emic" versus "etic," sex versus gender, social structure versus social agency—have blurred or crumbled altogether at my fingertips. Despite the epiphany induced by having data of my own, I no longer trust the reality of even body *parts.*[3]

Given my problems in configuring ethnographic data on unstable phenomena, I cannot trust the truism that prostituted women never kiss their clients, a truism expressed as commonly by Hollywood as by social scientists as by my students. Kissing is, of course, the subject of a certain disdain. "Working girls" in New York state categorically that "You don't kiss, that's disgusting." "I won't kiss any guy . . . just something in me . . . it turns my stomach." "In jail they talk . . . 'what do you do . . . you kiss 'em?' . . . who ever taught you to be a whore?" "[A]nd I said to this motherfucker, 'if you wanna kiss, go home to your wife.' "[4] A prostituted Englishwoman, "Barbara," says in a recent essay, "The worst thing is kissing: if you don't want to kiss them and they want to kiss you. Instinctively, you pull back."[5] "Pepper," a woman character prostituted in a tawdry Alec Baldwin vehicle, *Miami Blues*, turns away abruptly from his character's kiss, informing him that "nobody kisses us." (That she *does* kiss him signifies her descent into violent monogamy.) In a film that tugged much harder at American heartstrings, "Vivian," played by America's sweetheart, Julia Roberts, tired of her client's sexual disinterest, asks him, "What do you want?" "What do you do?," replies the silently grieving, corporation-raiding Edward, played by Richard Gere. "Everything," she replies, "but I don't kiss on the mouth." Neither does he, at least not until the end, when they promise, chauffeur and limousine waiting below, to "rescue" each other with kisses. But I thought prostituted women didn't kiss clients?

Well, they don't, so when they do, discursive hell breaks loose: sentimental misogyny, meet teen girl Julia Roberts wannabes, meet Hollywood formula, meet bodily fluid exchange, meet HIV transmission. These kisses followed a week's worth of un-"protected" sex, remunerated by a $3,000 check. That Vivian refuses to cash it, in fact tears it up in front of him, says something about the instability of yet another truism. Is that why *Pretty Woman* is shelved under "Comedy"? Thinking back to Weston's argument, is that why boundary instability has been shored up, to "protect" marriage? Is the gender performance (payment for sex) unstable while the gender categories (husband and wife, john and hooker) remain stable?

These border troubles suggest that to read subversively *Pretty Woman* and countless other insidious misrepresentations of prostituted women is to reveal blind spots about dangers of heterosexuality and prostitution and truisms about them. Pepper, Vivian, Barbara, and millions of other cases globally and historically[6] challenge us to rethink what we think we know about prostituted women, about the nature of "sex work," and about what "risky" versus "safe" sexual activities are. That we have insufficiently done so reveals an element missing in our theorizing of and our practice around prostitution, which continues to punish prostituted women with further stigma and risk of HIV transmission. It is not so much the falsification of the truism that prostituted women do not kiss clients that interests me. It is not that kissing does not signify a level of intimacy, desire, and gender democracy[7] too contradictory of prostitution—that appears empirically true. Nevertheless, we still founder on the shoals of the Self/Other dichotomy;[8] in anthropological practice, categories seldom come as neatly packaged as research on prostitution suggests.

I have essentially four aims in this essay. First, I present data from fieldwork I conducted on Daru, capital of Western Province.[9] I argue that "prostitute," "wife," "boyfriend," "customer," "marriage," "prostitution," and "husband" are categories insufficiently stable upon which to rely in HIV prevention work. Pretending unstable categories to be stable is dangerous in multiple ways, sort of like pretending that the *supply* of condoms is the answer to the AIDS pandemic when *negotiation* of their usage appears more fundamental.

Relatively few studies of prostitution go beyond recounting the parameters of its sociology or psychology. The few that do focus more acutely on sexual, relational aspects often impute a "deviance" from accepted cultural norms seldom demonstrated empirically. For instance, poor women in contemporary Zaire and Kenya often sell sexual services in order to keep themselves and their families together. In doing so they become, nominally and epidemiologically, "prostitutes," subject to inordinate linguistic, public health, and other surveillance activity.[10] They also provide other domestic services to neighborhood men and to more transient workers, such as cooked meals, bathwater, conversation, beds to sleep in, and clothes washing.[11] In short, they do things wives do everywhere. Slightly better connected women in Zaire, however, in order to capitalize marketing ventures, also trade in sex to "facilitat[e] favors by officials to obtain and move goods and to reduce or avoid customs duties and taxes."[12] These women are seldom as stigmatized as are their lower-class sisters, though both "exchange sex for money or goods." Another absent question in the literature is whether "pimps" do in fact batter, cheat, and otherwise exploit women more frequently and severely than do "husbands." My second aim is to scrutinize husband/ pimp and prostitute/wife dichotomies in view of ubiquitous forms of prostitutive sex on Daru and in terms of the sexual double standard in theory and practice. In a "sex industry" with so many patterns, participants, and punishments, when males pay females for sex, whether they be "husbands," "boyfriends," or paying "customers," they strengthen themselves and an already misogynous political economy.[13] Since most theorizing about prostitution neglects political economy,[14] in favor usually of medical consequences of and psychological precursors to prostituted women, my third aim is not to do so.

Fourth, I address implicitly key questions for feminist practice regarding "exploitation," "choice," and "victimization" in prostitution. Though difficult to parse, translate, and spell out the implications across time and space, clues to the meaning of these terms are provided when, how, and the extent to which women divide themselves behaviorally and linguistically.

SEX IN THE SOUTH FLY

No less than in many other Pacific island communities, real and imagined sexualities help represent Papua New Guineans by and to Westerners. They are (in)famous for the alleged "sexual excesses" of their "cargo" cults, for their (sexually) "flamboyant cultures" in the south coastal region, and for their "ritualized homosexual" cultures north, west, and east. Head-hunting and cannibalism tropes are no less *Bounty*ous, Cooked up by historical and anthropological misunderstandings.[15] Sex pulls people to the Pacific, though, be they painters such as Gauguin, novelists such as Stevenson, idealists such as Mead, would-be scientists such as Malinowski, or loyal readers of *National Geographic*, a media source remarkably culpable for its depictions of firm-breasted native women and penis-gourd-wearing native men.[16]

By contrast, Daru, situated close to the Fly River (forty miles across at its mouth!), which drains into the Gulf of Papua, just north and east of the northernmost tip of Australia, is neither really on the tourist map nor very similar to the remainder of Papua New Guinea. As an island only four kilometers in diameter, it is dwarfed by the island of New Guinea due north, the world's second-largest. In terms of nutrition, personal safety, and sanitation, Daru does not resemble any mainland villages nearby,[17] and is separated from its rural support base by water. Though it is the provincial capital, real power lies north at Kiunga, headquarters of the massive Ok Tedi copper and gold mine. Overcrowding is severe on Daru, poverty is increasing, and privacy is virtually nil. Though close by to each of the fifteen or so villages I had the pleasure of visiting briefly during my stay, Daru shares little in common with them.

Daruan living is thus somewhat antithetical to what are taken to be "Melanesian" values proper to the "Melanesian Way," glossed elsewhere throughout the Pacific as *Fa'a Samoa* (the Samoan Way), *Faka Tonga* (the Tongan Way), *Vaka Viti* (the Fijian Way), and so forth.[18] Daru has an intranational (and now inter-national, apparently)[19] reputation for drinking and for ubiquitous *pamukus* (a Melanesian Pidgin term for promiscuous women), referred to in the local Kiwai language as *uba pe* (bad canoe), a canoe/woman with holes in it/a loose vagina, a canoe/ woman who has been around the island/block too frequently. Another term adopted in the nation's capital, Port Moresby, is now used on Daru. *Pamukus* there use the term *bafalo* to refer to paying customers, a contraction of "*bucks/fire*," dangerous money, marking women thus as *bafalo soldes/bafalo gels*.[20]

Ethnically, linguistically, socially, and otherwise, Daru is as rich ethnographically as anywhere else in the country. It is also filled to the brim with wonderful people whom I love dearly and miss terribly. But Daru is not really a "culture" in the sense of a territorially bounded population speaking a common language, sharing symbols, practices, and beliefs, having some kind of empirical—not just ontological—status. Several factors mitigate against a stable Daruan culture, among them incredible human traffic, linguistic heteroglossia, ethnic heterogeneity, the proximity of Australian and Indonesian borders, theological contestation, and, accordingly, religious denominational competition.

One could perhaps talk about a Body Politic. Politically, demographically, linguistically, and socially, Kiwai are the ethnic majority on Daru, and have been so for a century. Demographically, sexually, and in terms of stigma, Bamu people are a major minority. Ignored by the national government, not contacted by Europeans early or in a sustained way, Bamu villages north and east of Daru are bereft of many aid posts, schools, churches, roads, and development opportunities. Already nomadic by "nature,"[21] Bamu have migrated in waves to Daru and to sawmills, mines, and timber camps elsewhere in the province. Many

Daruan Bamu subsist on a highly commodified form of prostitution, and Bamu women elsewhere string together various marital/sexual unions with *wokman* (salaried laborers), often supporting whole Bamu settlements thereby.

In my experience, the bulk of non-Kiwai and non-Bamu Daruans believe Kiwai and Bamu women to be hopelessly addicted to vice— Kiwai to drinking, card playing, and promiscuity, Bamu to the latter two—by a combination of economic exigency and, more so in the case of Bamu, custom and "tradition."[22] For Bamu women, firewood, empty bottle, and *bili*-leaf (used as housing thatch and in cooking) collection and sale generate some income. But few Bamu are "regularly" employed in town or intermarried with Kiwai. Even fewer have traditional rights of access to water, land, gardens, or *maza* (reef), so they link to the political economy primarily through the sale of sex.

Though Kiwai are the clear ethnic and political majority on Daru, men and women do not share equally.[23] Particularly for Kiwai women without husbands and families to support them, without the necessary skills, connections, and education to obtain and keep what few salaried positions there are for women, selling sex is their best link to food, shelter, and clothing. Men related to them, in addition, often arrange these women's sexual and alcoholic activities. Tenuous marriages point to the intimate connection between marriage and economics.[24]

Thus we come to the importance of sex in the regional political economy. Daru is where both villagers and *wokman* "come for spin"—for "R and R"—from timber camps, sawmills, mines, and villages. Workplaces have male/female ratios often approaching, sometimes exceeding, 50:1. Beer is often prohibited there by company dictate, but is available on Daru more cheaply. "Home"-cooked foods and other domestic symbols such as bundles of sago, betel nut, and tasty dishes made with seafood, banana, and coconut are also difficult to come by at timber camps, but are available at Daru's public market and via consanguineal, affinal, and sexual ties to female labor. Men who come to Daru recreate themselves, thus, by visiting, by eating and drinking, and by doing sex with Daruan women. In all-male labor camps, a man's heterosexuality is difficult to forge and maintain. This is not to argue that prostitution is somehow necessary, that it must occur to make them better workers and human beings, rather, that macro-sociological and -economic factors make little other allowance for less abusive gender relations. Daru is not, therefore, just the site of the refueling of fishing boats, cargo barges, helicopters, and airplanes, not just where expatriate fishing boat captains and crews disembark for days and weeks at a time, not just where research vessel crews restock for trips up and down the Fly River. Daru is also where village men can have secret trysts, where they can have sex again if their wives are pregnant or recently postpartum, where they can drink with women not related to them, and where they can do sex with relative impunity in ways they cannot in their home "villages," whether those be on the mainland nearby or in Cairns or Port Moresby or Thursday Island in Torres Strait. Daru is also the seat of the Fly River Provincial Government (hereafter FRPG), probably the biggest income-generating industry on Daru. Pay is dispensed there every two weeks, at which time beer drinking and female sexual exploitation are heightened. Daru is also the site of a fair amount of gun and drug smuggling; these informal sectors generate income, attract people, and also link with the sex trade. Finally, given the existence of many "modern" amenities and ideas provided by wharf, airport, telephone, hotel, bank, radio, and trade store, Daru is the center of a particularly dense set of social, sexual, and economic relations.

This is not to suggest that much of what follows—the parameters and implications of prostitution—is so obvious. Indeed, much of it is hidden morally and discursively. Both "bigshot" authorities and local "grass-roots" fear damage to what little tourism there is. Missionaries frequently deny any pre- or extramarital sexuality. Several Mormon mission representatives denied to me both the existence of the outdoor bush prostitution locale *(sagapari)* and the extent of their (largely Bamu) congregation's participation in it. I fear offending the missionized sensibilities of my Daruan friends and informants. I do not wish to berate a few hideously culpable health workers at the expense of the remaining courageous ones. I hesitate to criticize the (blatant-not-just-to-me) complicity of current and former FRPG members for fear of not being able to return to Daru. I do not want to send the wrong message.[25]

Less obviously, Daruan prostitution is hidden by a discourse on sexuality, shame, genitalia, poverty, promiscuity, and male violence. This discourse, too, prostitutes women; during the Scottish regulatory period in Europe, " 'prostitutes' [were] the product of discourses about them."[26] Robert Hughes, too, writing in *The Fatal Shore* about the transportation of despised English convicts to Australia in the eighteenth and nineteenth centuries, argues that though prostitution was not a transportable offense, many "unfortunate girl[s]," "poor unhappy" women of the towns, "lewd and immoral women," and women who cohabited without marriage became prostitutes by being transported to Australia.[27] Daruan women become *uba pe* by being labeled thus, men become *bafalo* by engaging these women sexually and economically, and women who engage *bafalo* sexually become "bad canoes."

As a concerned anthropologist, I am fighting several demons at once. High unemployment, low educational attainment, significant village-to-township migration, and low wages push women into prostitution, but cultural, linguistic, and social factors help keep them there. Once stereotyped as *uba pe*, as *bad* canoes, women must sell themselves sexually. Petrol, food, beer, and betel nut prices keep going up, and sea cucumbers are in decline. The Fly River is polluted by effluvia released at Ok Tedi,[28] and threatens the livelihood of several score thousand people. Timber camps and sawmills leave muddy rivers, naked hillsides, and cash-desperate people in their wake. Soon the FRPG may depart for the greener pastures of Kiunga, taking a lot of money and jobs elsewhere. Thus, sex is part of a declining political economy insofar as it, like labor, is exchanged for money, food, and alcohol, and primarily women supply it. But there is also a political economy of sexual and other domestic services women provide. Neither of these two claims, however, is understandable without reference to theories of prostitution that in effect preclude them, which I discuss below.[29]

EXPLAINING PROSTITUTION

"Functionalist" theories assume prostitution to evince a "permanent imperfection" in human existence or in women,[30] that it provides socioeconomic mobility for some women, that it is "the most convenient sexual outlet for an army, and for the legions of strangers, perverts, and physically repulsive in our midst."[31] Prostitution, proponents of functionalist theories say, functions to protect marriage and women's chastity: "Take away harlots from human society and you will have tainted everything with lust."[32] Prostitution is a necessary if regrettable development of civilization, "the creation of democracy" itself, "as old as civilization," a "social evil" attendant upon civilized, dense populations.[33] Prostitution allegedly manages and satiates greater male sex drive and provides a break from (even an improvement upon) the "monotony" of marriage and horrors of seminal backup.[34] To privilege male prerogative and reify the needs of Culture and Society—as functionalist theory must—is to ignore how tenuous are women's ties to political economy.

Psychoanalytic approaches often ignore them altogether, arguing instead that customers of prostituted women are the real victims. Prostituted women are purported merely to be acting out sinister fantasies of rebellion against parents, patriarchy, hetero-, bi-, and homosexuality, customers' wives, and penis envy. Prostitutes are "humiliating all men by having intercourse with any and all customers,"[35] behaving in a way "psychologically injurious" to men; even when women give money to pimps it represents "the desperate craving for oral gratification": prostitutes "get their only satisfaction out of hurting and deceiving men."[36] In an oft-cited essay combining both approaches, Davis argued that "sex freedom" will never replace prostitution because the latter "performs a function, apparently, which no other institution fully performs."[37]

By appropriating nominally the same term—function—feminist scholars such as Ruth Rosen have come to rather different conclusions. Prostitution is a source of income to many more than just women. It provides "object lessons" in the form of degraded women, it helps maintain the sexual double standard, and it justifies repressive economic and political measures.[38]

Five case studies drawn from a much larger sample of women selling sexual services with and without the aid of "sex brokers"[39] challenge the notion that women "choose" prostitution, that they are "voluntary prostitutes" who "bear responsibility for what they do tonight and tomorrow; no one is 'exploiting' them."[40] Meet "Erepai," "Tipia," "Nemeru," "Pare," and "Aberewame" (all names herein are pseudonyms).

Erepai

Erepai was already married and divorced four times when I met her while distributing free condoms. As mother to five and grandmother to several more, she supports her family partly by sponsoring *vidio pati* (video showings) for which she charges ten to fifty toea (roughly equal to American pennies). She also earns twenty to forty

kina (roughly equal to American dollars) each *pede fotnait* (fortnightly payday) for having sex with one biological and one classificatory uncle, the latter a Member for, the other a worker in, the
FRPG. Less frequently, under "high feelings," she engages in sex
for money with video patrons, with an ex-husband, who lives in a
nearby, mainland village, for food and money, and with an American accountant boyfriend, "Murray." He lives between the U.S.
and Cairns and comes to Daru twice yearly on business. She receives two to three hundred kina for a long weekend when she stays
and does sex with him multiple times. In addition, though she has
not been in touch with him for two years, she still believes that the
father of two of her children will return and take them all to Sydney
to his boat.

Erepai's story indicates the geographical spread of women's sexual
networks, in her case from the U.S. to local villages to Daru and on to
Australia. Her words also evince disjunctures between rules about condom usage and actual behaviors. She recounts here (from a tape-recorded
and transcribed interview) a day of sex and drinking at a well-known
private *pamuku haus* (place of drinking and sex):

> Erepai: And the only, the only thing I was listening [to] was the
> toilet [where sex takes place] going bang, bang, bang. And I thought
> "Oh God, I hope the wall doesn't comes down." [But with her ex-
> husband] I have to use condom. . . . I don't trust him. [L.H.:
> Umm, hmmm. . . . Does he have other girlfriends, do you think?]
> Yes, she, he does. But uh, he tells me not to use condoms, and I
> say "No." . . . He used to tell me, "I used to live with you before
> you got the son from me, you should know me very well. You
> know me and I know you, you trust me and I trust you." And I say
> "Yeah, yeah I trust you, you trust me, but yet I want you to use
> the condom." . . . He don't use those, forget it.

Erepai allows Murray (and other higher-paying customers) to "go skin-
skin" (*sans* condom) because she claims to "know his ways," but does not
allow her ex-husband to, though the latter lives only kilometers away and
the former thousands of miles away. The increased intimacy of "skin-
skin" enables her perhaps to press for the greater material support that
Murray and high-ranking FRPG workers can offer.

Tipia

Tipia is thirty-five and has three children. She was "pulled" from grade two by her family, and later from her only job by her first husband, whom she met the night that *he* pulled her. He abandoned her and her children later, and she stayed "quiet" until marrying a man with three nonresident wives whom I suspect she does not know about. He is a client of a sex broker—in fact, her own cousin's brother-in-law—who procures customers for her both partially against her will (to Malaysian and national businessmen) and partially with her consent (in the case of men she wanted to marry her). She does not know that he procures women for her husband (who does not know of the customers procured for his wife). Though married, Tipia and her husband neither eat, socialize, sleep, or live together, nor do they have sex together particularly often. She still suffers from an until recently unchecked-for-eight-years Lippes Loop, and from genital ulcers and inguinal lumps caused by a sexually transmitted disease (STD) and perhaps also by a lingering infection caused by a condom left inside her by a Malaysian sea cucumber buyer. According to her, STD clinic staff did not give her condoms and information requisite to their use even after her latest STD (to be fair, in order to avert violence, some female staff still request the husband's knowledge and permission to dispense condoms; his knowledge would be her tacit admission of extramarital sex). Though he is publicly acknowledged to be promiscuous, he is not stigmatized; his large salary allows him to pay for whatever he wants sexually for enjoyment, but her lack of regular salary necessitates that she exchange sex for survival.

Tipia's case illustrates categorical tensions between "husband," "boyfriend," and "customer." Tipia does perform sexual and other services for her "husband" in exchange for a portion of his wages, but seldom eats, sleeps, or socializes with him. Another "boyfriend" she has slept with only twice. Family members want her to marry a "customer" she slept with once who gave her money and food. I stood one day in a loose cluster of friends along Mangopari Road, telling stories and chewing betel nut, marveling inwardly at "Tunigi" the sex broker in front of me. With no one but me the wiser, he arranged encounters for both husband and wife, *uba pe* for the former, *bafalo* for the latter, without either apparently knowing: both knew that he was setting up something for someone, but it was not clear what or for whom.

Nemeru

Nemeru, a widow, twenty-eight, quiet and chain-smoking, is cousin and frequent housemate of "Koria," another woman prostituted "freelance," by her husband and by sex brokers. Nemeru married at twenty-three an unknown man who showed up at her house one day and took her away ("E showed me is face and e pulled me"), and lived with him in his village until he took ill, became covered in sores and died, allegedly due to a sorcery attack employing fish poison, made by villagers jealous of his fishing success. Now widowed, her two children live with grandparents to the north, at Kiunga. She lives between three households on Daru, depending upon her ability to manage tender consanguineal and affinal social relations, made the more tender by her overdrinking and *uba pe* status. Her sexual activities are arranged by Tunigi and others, by coresident females, and by other *uba pe*. Sometimes she also walks up to the hotel, sometimes by herself, accompanied sometimes by Koria and others, and to other private houses, accompanied by other *uba pe*. She has several "boyfriend"- or "husband"-customers who blow into town from village or work elsewhere, nominal designations that owe more to the frequency of payments they make to her than to the existence of sexual/affective attachments between them. Nemeru is rare for having worked for regular wages (only two others in my sample have ever done so), but only started doing so recently. Her employers, a married couple who own a trade store, do everything they can (except pay higher wages) to keep her from "drinking with the men." They have forbidden her to *pamuk* (behave promiscuously sexually) during the week or in front of their kids, but *Tesde avinun* (Thursday, the beginning of *pede*) blends easily into *Mande monin*. Her salary of forty to fifty kina fortnightly, though, does not support her adequately.

Nemeru's case illustrates several profound Daruan social contradictions. To *bafalo* informants, as a body, Nemeru is an attractive *pamuku*, is pliant sexually, and is large-breasted. As a woman, a person, a widow whose partner died suspiciously, suddenly, she is an unattractive potential spouse. Her "husband died out there" (in the village), leaving her without support, "no one to support me," and men on Daru already "know her way." Boyfriends who say they will marry her only support her to the extent she (a) *is pamuku*, that is, will do sex with them, and (b) appears to be "staying quiet," "sexing" only with them. But *bafalo* seldom marry *uba pe*, who therefore must have many *bafalo*. Having too many *bafalo*, though, makes women unattractive spouses.

Pare

> Pare is twenty-six, childless, and popular with men for her light skin and personality. She was once married to a high-ranking businessman (who she found out had two other wives back in the village) and counts among her current *bafalo* his brother. Her marital "status" fluctuates; she is now married to a man she detests and whom she does not consider her "true" husband. She initiated divorce proceedings and has even pressed charges against his beatings of her, but is still married to him legally. Being without much money or livelihood, too old to do much fishing or cray diving anymore, her father first encouraged her to work with Tunigi when she was about twelve or fourteen, until such time as she first married. Since trying to divorce her current husband, she has begun more frequently to "go up" (to the hotel) to "look for beer and the boyfriends," though he beats her for it. Her resultant *uba pe* status makes potential sexual contacts interested (but potential spouses wary).

Marital "status" thus fluctuates greatly.[41] Pare does not consider herself married to her socially and legally recognized husband, since he does not support her, being himself itinerant, uninterested in fishing, and unwilling even to help her family collect sea cucumber, and since he beats her. Nevertheless, he is her husband because they are not "divorced." The police to whom she complains tell her to go home (they are, after all, married), that this is a "domestic issue." Her husband's nonsupport, though, combined with her father's and family's needs, drives her ever further towards *uba pe* behavior, but it gives her husband ever more cause culturally to beat and otherwise abuse her: *uba pe!* (slut) and *auwo ai!* (big vagina, slut) often greet her when he is drunk. Theoretically and practically, then, marriage and prostitution belong on the same continuum, and are not logical opposites.[42] Her father pushed her into remunerative sexuality, then into marriage. Her first husband pushed her out of marriage by hiding his already doubly married status, and thus into the sex trade again. Divorced, and therefore unsupported, she found herself "going out with the men," "going up" to the hotel, and associating with Tunigi for several years. Her current "husband" took her out of the sex industry by "marrying" her, but his abuse of her (culturally sanctioned by marriage) and his failure to support her necessitate her further participation.

Pare's case illustrates well the implications of *uba pe* status. Though "wife" and "*uba pe*" belong on the same analytical and empirical continuum, and despite the fact that a given man can be husband, boyfriend, or *bafalo* to the same woman (much less to several different women), far stronger centripetal forces operate once a woman is stigmatized as *uba pe*. It has culturally a lower center of gravity; *uba pe* occasionally take on boyfriends and husbands, and their residential and economic dislocation may flatten out for a while, but socially they remain objects of much scorn. By local cultural logic, though Aberewame recently married a man not from the area, "she is still *pamuku*," and the marriage was not given much chance once he found out her "real" status.

Aberewame

Aberewame is thirty-two going on sixty-two, and lives between several households, among them those of other *uba pe*, of her cousin, and of her father, containing her mother and father, four of her five children, several children of assorted siblings, and a young man (her own son) raised by her mother as her brother. Her several husbands have each been abusive and nonsupportive, though they scorn her as *uba pe*. Aberewame's male relatives and husbands turned her into *uba pe* directly and/or by example. Her father used to sell or "lend" sexually her mother to his "mates" for beer and money. Two ex-husbands did the same to her. Her brothers arrange sex with her for their "mates" in exchange for beer (and tried to do so once for me). She is frequently taken advantage of, and gets paid for sex only about a fifth of the time, though she usually receives free beer and sometimes food. She drinks to "drunken sense," "full blast," or "conkout" about every third day.

Thus, Nemeru, Erepai, Pare, Tipia, and Aberewame have each been prostituted by family members. All but Tipia find sexual contacts on their own, but each have their sexual and drinking activities arranged by Tunigi, too. Aberewame's father has sold her mother, and her brothers her. Erepai's two classificatory uncles pay her, their own niece, for sex on some paydays. Koria has been made pregnant by her uncle, who gives money, beer, and food to her and her husband, with whom she no longer engages in sex, but who sold her previously. He rents bedsheet, mat, pillow, and the middle room of their house in exchange for five to ten kina, beer, and sometimes food given by crocodile-skin buyer/sellers, FRPG workers, cargo barge captains, and his wife's uncle. Tipia's "pimp" is thus affinally related to her, and her husband is one of his biggest customers.

THE POLITICAL ECONOMY OF SEX

As the above data indicate, female sexuality figures mightily in the local political economy, controlled by marital and familial relations in ways akin to ways in which workers are controlled by economic and bureaucratic relations. FRPG "bigshots" dominate prostituted women while drinking and doing sex with them as they wield power over constituents, reminding us "how difficult it is sometimes to map the boundaries between sexual relations and economics."[43]

In terms of a broader look at a ten-woman sample, I find several key social relations:[44] first, there is great residential dislocation, necessitating that women change residence (defined as where one sleeps) 100–150 times per year; second, few women generate income other than through selling sex; third, marital status fluctuates greatly—"yes, he is my husband, he is man I love" (Nemeru), "I am staying single now, my husband went to Kiunga" (Leona), "no, he is not my husband, he never buys food for my children" (Tipia), "my husband is married to another woman" (Aramia); fourth, few women can successfully press claims upon men to support their pregnancies and offspring, due proximally to the fact that they had only three pregnancies between them during my stay, due perhaps ultimately to untreated STDs or to contraceptive *kastom we* (custom ways). As *uba pe* they have little with which to manipulate men's financial interests. Only Koria (via her uncle) and Aramia (via the relatives of her child's father) can manipulate cultural expectations that men take care of children, whether suitable "fathers" or not.

Marriage and prostitution are thus bound inextricably[45] by a number of economic relations. Following Cynthia Enloe's provocative lead,[46] I would describe the political economy of sex on Daru as necessarily including, in addition to those I have mentioned directly: husbands and boyfriends who pay wives and girlfriends for sex directly with money and goods or less directly with food and gifts; small children on foot and bicycle (or female staff at the hotel, typically during FRPG meetings) who receive money and food for passing messages between prospective sexual partners; fathers and brothers who sell female relatives sexually for beer and money; bartenders and other male staff at the hotel who arrange rooms, privacy, and alcohol in return for money and sex; social clubs that facilitate the sex industry by selling beer and by making vehicles and telephones available; the FRPG itself, which owns the hotel, lounge bar, and public tavern, and thus benefits from all room, video, food, and alcohol purchases; and members of other political bodies (and their drivers, clerks, "houseboys," etc.) who use expense account money to drink and engage in sex with nonspouses.

Though the above list could be expanded greatly, my point has been to locate sex in the local political economy. Through Daru are smuggled guns and marijuana, linking Port Moresby, where *raskol* gangs are headquartered, to the highlands where high-grade marijuana is grown, to Daru, from which *raskols* operate to exchange money, marijuana, and guns to Torres Strait islanders and thence to Australia. One *raskol* also brokers sex for FRPG workers within his extensive friendship, familial, and criminal network. On behalf of one, he arranged once (for fifty kina) to bail Aramia from jail, who then had sex with the FRPG official. When either the FRPG or landowners' associations meet on Daru, for instance, representatives stay at the hotel and at other *pamuku haus*. Drinking and sex go up accordingly in view of cultural norms to "shout" oneself and one's supporters to beer and food. Money is thus diverted away from development, literally pissed away, and women's second-class status is further entrenched. How can women resist?

DIVIDING THE BODY

America's *Pretty Woman* does everything, but she does not kiss on the lips. Kissing is a manifestly "safe" activity, but she also has unprotected (i.e., *sans* condom) sex with Edward for an entire week, which is manifestly *un*safe. She will not engage in a risk-free activity with a man she does not (yet) love, but does engage in riskier activities with a man she (eventually) does come to love. Where, then, is her "risk" located, at "work" with "clients," or at "home" with "boyfriends,"[47] "outside" on the streets, where she is subject to police harassment, to sexual violence of unimaginable intensity, and often to exploitative pimps, or in the gold-fixtured marble bathtub, "inside" a posh hotel? Is there a difference between "client," "boyfriend," and "husband"? After all, Edward offers throughout the week (a) to pay her $3,000 for a week's worth of escort (including sexual) services, (b) to put her up in a fancy apartment as his mistress, and (c) (presumably, given the final scene) to marry her. In the crucial condom scene, Vivian reminds Edward that she is a "safety girl." As she unzips her boots, pulling out a fistful of protection, she tells him, "Alright, pick one, I've got red, I've got green, I've got yellow, I'm out of purple, but I do have one Gold Circle Coin left, the condom of champions, the one and only, nuthin' is gettin' through this [,?!] sucker, whaddya' say?" Edward responds coldly with an arcane verb form, "I *profane* of safety." To him, fucking hookers, in other words, is like raiding corporations—whatever, never mind.

THE BODY PROSTITUTE

But at least she tried. When Vivian attempts to put latex between body and client/boyfriend/potential spouse, she challenges public health writings about prostituted women and AIDS.[48] She evinces at least some social agency. Following her lead, I consider the Daruan Body Prostitute a site of multiple, conflicting discourses, not a mere empty container into which male domination is transcribed, not just a tangle of planes, curves, and orifices onto and into which men reach sexual gratification and express a (gendered) political economy. It also mediates symbolically between and sometimes overtly resists the contradictory forces of contemporary Daru. For instance, *bafalo* do not usually use condoms; distribution, price, and shame present barriers to greater condom usage, but even when condoms are made available, most men refuse to use them. Sometimes women want to use condoms but their partners do not. Some kinds of partners will use condoms, but others will not, since most men are not truly "partners." Condoms can protect, but can also "spoil" bodies and genitalia dermatologically. They can come off, too, and they can also link vaginas pathogenically, which only adds to, not stabilizes or decreases, extant fears.

TOP AND BOTTOM

First,[49] women divide their bodies into "top" and "bottom." Hilda says, "I want cash in my hand before I pull my pants down." Nemeru says, "Uh, some of the clothes. The skirt, only the skirt . . . never . . . my, what, bra and tins [things]." Pare does not let men touch her *susu* (breasts) unless she becomes "dead already," "conkout": "Normal sense [when I'm not drunk, it's] pants out [off] only." Breasts, face, neck, and mouth, in other words, are reserved for enjoyment and intimacy with/for boyfriends and husbands, whereas only *bafalo* have access to vaginas. Maureen says, "I'm not going to drop my pants unless you give me some money. My whole body feels, I feel it." Hilda also says adamantly, "[I just] pull my pants down and that's it . . . I don't take all of my clothes off to my *bafalo* friends, no . . . I pull my pants down and that's it, I have sex with him, later on I wash myself, my bottom, and put my pants on and I'm going." Leona does not allow *susu*-touching by *bafalo*, either: "He knows that he is not my husband. . . . That's my way, only pants out [off] because it's not Gary [her 'husband']."

Good Sex/Bad Sex

Sexual activities are also divided medico-morally by partner identity. Hilda says, "[I] didn't change any of my styles" (alter any sexual positions available for *bafalo*), "but it's just that, the same styles I have a limit of [limit to] *bafalo* friends, just pull my pants down and that's it." Aramia expressed great shame about having sex in the hotel with *bafalo*: "I'm feeling shame, yes, they ask if a lady can touch, but me, I feel shame. [Q: about what?] Oh, say, cock, something like that, pinch them, suck them, that's a shameful to me, I don't like that, [kissing] too [and] like, say, "bend down" [a sexual position], I mean, giving "backfire" [another], I feel shame, that's something [bad] or with both my legs up . . . if it's not my boyfriend."

Sexual activities are also divided linguistically. Fellatio is "really bad one," "no good one," done with *bafalo* only under physical force, but more willingly with boyfriends and husbands. Aramia says that, otherwise, "we used to get scared of sick": "beer liquid" of heavily drinking *bafalo* can lead to malformed fetuses and difficult pregnancies. Hilda says it is *sabi* (Kiwai, "forbidden") to touch a *bafalo*'s but not boyfriend's penis with her hand, "Yes, with boyfriend, it's okay . . . because I'm screwing, I'm having a screw with my [*bafalo*, "fuck friend"], but with my boyfriend, I'm just having sex [making love], just loving him, that's what."

Anal intercourse and cunnilingus, too, are at least possible with boyfriends but for *bafalo* a clear no-no. Hilda says that "Yeah, some *bafalo* friends have asked me to screw it from [in] my ass or put my leg up, from sideways, or whatever . . . but I don't accept it. [L.H.: Why not?] Well, like I said, I think I'll give myself in [my anus] for my boyfriend, but not *bafalo* friends." "[N]o, that's dirty [cunnilingus]," reported Maureen. "I don't like it but they force me, but I said no, I said no, and I keep on, no, no."

Seeing the Skin

Clothing removal is also optional, for reasons of cultural value, expediency, and protection. "Skin" reveals a degree of intimacy during sexual encounters, reveals nakedly the contingent nature of the top/bottom distinction. Hilda explains that her *bafalo* friends used to ask her " 'why can't you strip off,' something like that, but I don't feel it's okay . . . I don't like it. I used to tell them 'I got baby,' I used to tell them, 'I've got baby to feed with my breast, so I'm not giving it to you.' " When she encounters *bafalo* who want what *bafalo* cannot have, she simply reminds them, "you are not my boyfriend," or "you are not my husband." "We are only a fuck friend . . . so I only just pull my pants down, screw, wash myself, and then pull my pants up and that's it." Leona concurs: "I'm asking him for money so I don't like him to see most of my body you know, I don't take all of my clothes off to my *bafalo* friends, no; they will not see my skin. . . . I pull my pants down and that's it, I have sex with him, later on I wash myself, my bottom, and put my pants on and I'm going. . . . With my ["husband," Gary] yes, I can strip off and make love, but with my *bafalo* friends, no . . . they are only a fuck friend."

Kissing Bafalo

At the outset I noted the truism that "prostitutes" do not kiss "clients": "I see two or three punters [clients] a night. I won't kiss them,"[50] says an English woman. Fair enough. Prostituted Daruan women, too, sometimes kiss boyfriends but less often *bafalo*. Aramia says, "when I'm not really really going, I doesn't want . . . [if it's] not my boyfriend I used to feel shame." Julie concurs: "No, sometimes when a man I love I kiss with him, when I don't love I just fuck, but man I really love I kiss with them." Aniato agrees: "To me, the people I love I kiss them before I go, but if the people whom I don't love I don't kiss them . . . just take off."

Condoms and Germs

Condoms also divide women from *bafalo* and from their body parts.[51] When I asked Nemeru, for instance, what she thought about condoms, she said, "No, it's good. I don't want to get [a] sick [sickness, from *bafalo*], or that's why I like condom." When Leona agreed to go to room 6 at the hotel with a FRPG Member one night, she just "ask him then, 'can you have that, ah, what, condom with you?' And then he turned and said that 'No.' And then I just got up and said that, 'Well, it's fine for you but I'm having the condom with me, for my life' and that's all." Aramia says, "Condoms, that's for my protection, too, just to look after my body, to protect my body, not to have some sickness."

Many of these women are learning to negotiate condom usage more consistently and forcefully. Aramia asked a man "to use condom, but he scold me, he doesn't want to use condom . . . but he kept on forcing me . . . he told me he's tired of using condoms. I kept on asking him, so he [pushed] me on the bed." Pare adamantly scolded one customer: "I told him, 'if you want to have sex with your wife you are going to use the condom,' because I'm really scared of it [gonorrhoea] . . . [if you're going to sleep with the women who knock on your hotel door] 'you use the condom, you won't have sex without the condom,' that's what I said." Maureen does not trust her *bafalo:* "If he doesn't want it, well, stiff shit.

Force people to have a sex, well, I don't want to have sex, those ones that won't use condoms."

Barriers to Barriers

Despite this new adamancy, women still face numerous barriers to more frequent and consistent condom usage. For one, I am no longer on Daru distributing free condoms. For another, Daruan men complain of the foreignness of condoms, their cost, and their absence in biblical and tribal lore. Men also value impregnating women. Men speak equally of the lost pleasure of "going skin-skin" and of the dangers of seminal backup, via river metaphors: they want to avoid semen "blockage," to "shoot their sperms," to shoot them "straight to Kiunga [up the Fly River]." "They [men who pay for sex] want to go [ejaculate] in a straight line. . . . They are *spak* [drunk]. . . . They don't want to waste their sperms for nothing. They think, 'fuck, we already paid [for beer/women], we won't waste our sperms.' . . . They want their sperms to get full travel." Women, too, sometimes prefer going "skin-skin" to increase their own or their partners' pleasure, to avoid not becoming pregnant, and to avoid their own vaginal blockage.[52]

As elsewhere in the world, condom use on Daru is negotiated partly in terms of partner identity. For "Women at Risk" in Central Africa, condoms signify as much about morality as about disease or pregnancy. "Nsanga" rejects "this morally stigmatizing label [given to women with whom men fear to have unprotected sex] and, if a lover were to propose using a condom, she would be angry: 'It would mean that he doesn't trust me.' "[53] "Vumba" says that "Men won't use the things and the girls can't make them. Anyway, a young girl would be ashamed to ask her friend to use a condom. He would think she was a prostitute!"[54] Like all devices related to sexuality, condoms are multivalent and meaning-saturated. Minimally, condoms have "dual functions" as disease preventives and contraceptive devices, but as concerned social scientists and public health practitioners we must also be ready for discourses of condoms-as-disease-itself, for notions of condoms as the *agents* of infection, as the *causes* of promiscuity and moral breakdown,[55] as well as markers of heightened or greatly decreased intimacy, which may have serious implications for women medically. Hilda, for instance, uses condoms with *bafalo*, but "[w]ith my boyfriends [I don't] because when I ask my boyfriend they

don't accept condom, they will think I have a sick. . . . I don't want to
be put off or let down, [so] if they are my steady boyfriend, I just accept
them [without a condom]." Julie says that she might consider going "skin-
skin" if her sexual partner were a married man (who she knows full well
are among the island's biggest *pamukus*). Koria uses condoms with men
she does not have affection for (such as her husband), and does not
generally use them with those she does have affection for, such as an
uncle and another sex broker. Leona uses condoms with *bafalo*, but goes
"skin-skin" with two partners her father recognizes as her "husband";
once pregnant, she expects "Gary" to marry her. Aberewame routinely
left at home the condoms and condom purses I gave her, hoping to
become pregnant so that the men, as fathers, not necessarily husbands,
would thereby lift her out of her misery. The boyfriend that Aramia
wanted to "stick on" threw away two such purses, hoping to impregnate
her—I became in essence barrier-by-distributor. Gradually, my naive,
ego-centered stance—how dare they toss the very condom purses I paid
good money for—gave way to one more appreciative, both of the straits
even more dire than I imagined and of the social agency they directed
at it.

Thus, while bodily and behavioral divisions appear straight forward—
"prostitutes" don't kiss their "clients," and in doing so divide (or unite)
themselves (and their body parts) from (or with) those of their sexual
partners (or customers), minimizing (or maximizing) intimacy—in fact,
these divisions are difficult to maintain. The woman quoted above unable
to kiss punters, for instance, qualified her statement later: "With people
I've known [for four months] . . . then I will."[56] Nor is technology
stable. Condoms can break or remain inside women, turning barrier into
nightmare. They can be used between vaginas, and they preclude going
"skin-skin," an activity that produces pleasure, children, perhaps even
feminine pride.

This technological instability surely reflects social and cultural instability, too. Traditional sexual values, controls, and mores have been undercut by alcohol, Westernization, urbanization, and the cash nexus, each
facilitating practices unimaginable until recently. Mimi, for instance,
revealed of her uncle: "He's a Minister [in the Provincial Government]
and he always tells me to tell these girls [her girlfriends] to drink, and he
got a car, always go around drinking, having sex in front of me with these
girlfriends for money." Evelyn was given "blue books" (pornography):

"My *tambu* [brother-in-law] gave it to me . . . but I was trying to vomit [was really turned off by them, so] I gave them to my cousin brother. I was trying to burn it, and gave it to my cousin brother, so he is keeping it for me."

Such behavioral disjunctures indicate how little still social relations now hold. Men begin to relate to women first as customers and then later as boyfriends and husbands or vice versa.[57] But some pimps are also sex brokers (even for their own female relatives) or customers, when they "get free ones" by "going on top" after they have arranged encounters for friends. Women will kiss *bafalo* who promise to "stick on" them, but *bafalo* seldom do, at least not on *uba pe*. Women want *bafalo* to use condoms, but they cannot touch *bafalo* penis. Women want to protect their own bodies, but they cannot inspect their own genitalia.[58] Like most men, Daruan men love sex, but hate some combination of women, femininity, and female genitalia.

For reasons adduced immediately above, and because of boundary difficulties, I hesitate to express, therefore, as I am frequently asked to, "how many other" women, couples, families, households, and communities are involved in "prostitution," how representative, in other words, these women are of women "in the general population." I struggle to configure what real husbands are, how real boyfriends are supposed to treat their girlfriends, and what a real wife looks like. Perhaps those are not the best questions. To say that those about whom I have written above characterize as little as 10 percent of the Daruan female population (or as much as 90 percent) is to obscure the far more fundamental issue: men exchange money, alcohol, goods, and gifts for sex because they can, whereas women exchange sex because they must. This distinction has real implications; reducing, say, the number of "prostitutes" on Daru by some kind of public health or punitive action would not do anything to unravel the social relations that produce them in the first place. Sexual double standards, legal powerlessness, male violence, and coerced sex are far more fundamental to the problem than is the question of the number of women who deviate from respectability.[59]

CONCLUSIONS

The implications of my analysis are fairly simple. AIDS prevention messages that presume bodies and relations to stay still long enough to model are inadequate. Admonitions to "Follow God's Way," to refrain from "going around with *pamukus*," to "know your partner," and to "be faithful" are dangerous; people have sex with and exchange in the process bodily fluids with other bodies, not moral precepts. As the words and feelings of these women show so clearly, our bodies—of all and each of us—are not the stable, unmediated, fixed entities we often take them to be. Some here and in Papua New Guinea will claim that I have unnecessarily "muddied the waters," that I am talking about too few women (and not particularly "good" ones anyway). Why talk about prostitution instead of marriage, about prostitutes instead of wives? Why decry promiscuity instead of promoting chastity? Lest I be misunderstood, I am not suggesting—not here, anyway—that prostitution is the same thing as marriage, that it is the logical outcome of marriage, that all wives are prostitutes, or that all forms of sex on Daru are prostitutive. Nevertheless, by erecting analytical boundaries between women we ignore what unites them, their relative inability to negotiate activities they and their bodies and minds engage in. "Wives" and "prostitutes" face essentially the same drunken, often violent men, they suffer from the same psychic disjunctures and STDs, and they have essentially the same set of limited options. Being a good housewife does not protect them from HIV any more than being monogamous protects them from male violence. Women on Daru suffer *qua* women, because gender relations are by definition between unequals. By exaggerating differences between "prostitute" and "wife" and between "prostitution" and "marriage" we feel good, as if we have parsed the categories cleanly, established their essential difference. Neither pathogens nor sperm, though, are conscious of the marital, social, or ontological statuses of the bodies they inhabit and affect. "Good" and "bad" women, "wives" and "*pamukus*" are drawn together into the same sex/gender/ exchange system, a point that can be demonstrated easily.

First, though *pamukus* clearly have a "spoiled" status, like wives, they have value and are venerated somewhat. Their presence and actions raise alcohol sales, and they are acknowledged for their drinking stamina—one had a song written about her played over the radio. Many have more money in their pockets than do women not so prostituted. Some have a modicum of autonomy, due partly to their defilement; "spoiled" already, they cannot become any more so, and they walk around in some ways more freely than do "good" women without real or putative virginity for fathers and brothers to "protect." *Pamukus* are beaten sometimes for *not* engaging in sex with men who wish them to; non-*pamuku* women are sometimes beaten *for* engaging in sex—and *vice versa*.

Second, all women, *pamuku* or not, participate multiply in identity construction and maintenance.[60] *Pamukus* move between public drinking establishments patronized by "big shots" but closed off to "grassroots" (villagers, fishermen, and sea cucumber collectors) due both to inflated beer prices and to rules of proper attire (no T-shirts or bare feet). *Pamukus* simultaneously signify and reproduce emergent lines of class distinction and privilege, not perhaps in the same ways as housewives do, but perhaps with similar effects.

Third, these women help construct male sexuality and identity, individually, ethnically, and collectively. Though males in general—whether teens on bicycles or pilots spending the night on Daru—can and do pay for sex, when women "consent,"[61] become pliant sexually, they shore up individual masculine pride daily battered by unemployment, by cultural loss, by grinding poverty, and, to hear it from some men, by their wives' refusals to engage in sex. Even Bamu women toiling at *sagapari* are not allowed to have sex with fellow Bamu—at least not at *sagapari*. Some *bafalo* persuade *pamukus* to "stay quiet" until they next come to town, and, to the extent they are paid by them in money and beer to do so, some fathers have an interest in seeing to it that their daughters do so. Familial, kinship lines are thus more tightly drawn around or at least in view of control of female sexuality. Collectively, the androcentrism of the political economy is obvious—the provision of female sexual services helps to move goods and services around like money, petrol, and electricity do. But more fundamentally for me, for other concerned social scientists, for concerned human beings, sex *is* the political economy, the investment one gender makes in controlling the thoughts, bodies, and actions of another.

In the sense in which I (inspired by Rosen, Walkowitz, and other feminist scholars) intend the term "function," prostitution functions as prop to some and forge to other profound social contradictions. Prostitution does not just demarcate some social boundaries and blur others; it reveals the ubiquity and necessity of the sexual transactions in which women must engage to survive, it veils ethnic and socioeconomic distress simmering not far below the surface, and discourse about it masks the brutalizing conditions that so many women endure on contemporary Daru.

NOTES

I wish to thank the Wenner-Gren Foundation for Anthropological Research (Gr. #5250) for funding my research, as well as my parents, Lester Everett and Norma Rigby Hammar, and Shirley Lindenbaum, Mervyn Meggitt, Louise Lennihan, Glen Petersen, Jane Schneider, Sydel Silverman, Kate Riley, Arlene King, the Institute of Papua New Guinea Studies, the Papua New Guinea Department of Health, the Institute for Medical Research, the Fly River Provincial Government, and other Papua New Guinean friends too numerous to mention for getting me to, through, and home from the field. Niko Besnier and particularly Carol Siegel and an anonymous reviewer encouraged me helpfully to clarify certain important points regarding boundary troubles. Some of Niko's points will be taken up elsewhere—I promise. As a sensitive guy of the 1970s, too, I thank my anonymous reviewer particularly for perhaps the ultimate compliment.

1. Carol Leigh, "The Continuing Saga of Scarlot Harlot III," in *Sex Work: Writings by Women in the Sex Industry*, ed. Frederique Delacoste and Priscilla Alexander (Pittsburgh: Cleis Press, 1987), 59.

2. Kath Weston, "Do Clothes Make the Woman: Gender, Performance Theory, and Lesbian Eroticism," *Genders* 17 (1993), 1, 17. See also Thomas Laqueur, *Making Sex: Body and Gender from the Greeks to Freud* (Cambridge: Harvard University Press, 1990); Gilbert Herdt, introduction to *Third Sex, Third Gender: Beyond Sexual Dimorphism in Culture and History* (New York: Zone, 1994), 21–81.

3. Laqueur, *Making Sex*; Judith Butler, *Gender Trouble: Feminism and the Subversion of Identity* (New York: Routledge, 1990); Bernice Hausman, "Demanding Subjectivity, Transsexualism, Medicine, and the Technologies of Gender," *Journal of the History of Sexuality* 3 (2) (1992): 270–302.

4. Michele Shedlin and Denise Oliver, "Prostitution and HIV Risk Behavior," in *Advances in Population*, vol. 1, ed. L. Severy (London: Kingsley, 1993), 165; see also Laurie Bell, ed., *Good Girls/Bad Girls: Feminists and Sex Trade Workers Face to Face* (Seattle: Seal Press, 1987).

5. "Barbara," "It's a Pleasure Doing Business with You," *Social Text* 11 (Winter 1993): 11–22.

6. One in six persons are prostituted in Olangapo City; see Brenda Sturtevant, "The Bar Girls of Subic Bay," *The Nation*, April 3, 1989, 445.

7. See Cindy Patton, "Hegemony and Orgasm—Or the Instability of Heterosexual Pornography," *Screen* 30 (1–2) (1989), 109.

8. See especially Margaret Baldwin's trenchant essay, "Split at the Root: Prostitution and Feminist Discourses of Law Reform," *Yale Journal of Law and Feminism* 5 (1) (1992): 47–120.

9. Daru has an unofficial population of fifteen thousand. I was in Papua New Guinea for nineteen months, mostly on Daru, aided immensely by Adori Ganoi and Suli Malu. I used questionnaires, conducted censuses, made systematic observations, audiotaped and transcribed thirty "sexual life histories," and, once

I figured out how to do so, distributed twenty thousand condoms, demonstrated at "AIDS Video Shows" held for church congregations and other local groups.

10. I note here a piece exemplifying, then a model of the implications of, and third an extraordinary exception to such discourse: Francis Plummer and Elizabeth Ngugi, "Prostitutes and Their Clients in the Epidemiology and Control of Sexually Transmitted Diseases," in *Sexually Transmitted Diseases*, 2nd ed., ed. King Holmes et al. (New York: McGraw-Hill, 1990), 71–76; Alfred Fortin, "Ethics, Culture, and Medical Power: AIDS Research in the Third World," *AIDS and Public Policy Journal* 6 (1) (1991): 15–24; Brooke Grundfest Schoepf, "Sex, Gender and Society in Zaire," in *Sexual Behavior and Networking: Anthropological and Socio-Cultural Studies of the Transmission of HIV*, ed. Tim Dyson (Liege, Belgium: Derouaux-Ordina, n.d.), 353–75.

11. See Luise White, *The Comforts of Home: Prostitution in Colonial Nairobi* (Chicago: University of Chicago Press, 1990); Brooke Grundfest Schoepf, "Women at Risk: Case Studies from Zaire," in *The Time of AIDS: Social Analysis, Theory, and Method*, ed. Gilbert Herdt and Shirley Lindenbaum (Newbury Park: Sage, 1992), 259–86.

12. Schoepf, "Women at Risk," 274.

13. I have made three claims here. First, "sex industry" is perhaps marginally useful here. Some parameters are evident: locale, duration, and price of remunerated sex; those involved beyond the man and woman, the drivers, messengers, and bartenders. Still, the term overinstitutionalizes: telephones are involved, but sexual escorts are not advertised in a phone book. Also, referring to these women as "sex *workers*" strains the categories further. Perhaps discussing labor forms is more apt: (1) a "family" form in which females are sold sexually for money, beer, and food by male relatives; (2) a "freelance" form in which women sell sex and companionship to "boyfriends" and "husbands" and more anonymous partners for money and beer; (3) a "sex broker" form in which clients are found for women and vice versa; (4) *sagapari* (literally, mangrove garden), an outdoor, two-dollar form of bush prostitution known throughout Papua New Guinea as *tu kina bus;* and (5) a truly ubiquitous form in which acknowledged and anonymous sexual partners exchange money, cassettes, T-shirts, tobacco, food, and betel nut: for example, 43 percent of respondents to one questionnaire had given or received thusly during or following their most recent act of sex.

Second, two Daruan men are acknowledged to accept money and beer for sex, and no doubt younger males (sometimes boys) are engaged similarly, but this was not the focus of my research.

Third, Carol Siegel and an anonymous reviewer helped me clarify why I have such difficulty using such terms without quotation marks. Some husbands give money to wives for household items prior to asking them for sex so as not to be refused. Papua New Guineans already exchange everything. Boyfriends give girlfriends money, tobacco, cassette tapes, and so forth after sex (and receive photos, a letter, or another tape in return), as is done in the U.S. "Boyfriend," "husband," and "customer" can refer contextually to the same person at different times or to different women. There may be real boyfriends and husbands, but all activities have an exchange component. Category-parsers, beware!

14. But see Ruth Rosen, *The Lost Sisterhood: Prostitution in America, 1900–1918* (Baltimore: Johns Hopkins University Press, 1982); Judith Walkowitz, *Prostitution and Victorian Society: Women, Class, and the State* (Cambridge: Cambridge University Press, 1980); Saundra Sturdevant and Brenda Stoltzfus, ed., *Let the Good Times Roll: Prostitution and the U.S. Military in Asia* (New York: The New Press, 1992).

15. See Greg Dening, *Mr Bligh's Bad Language* (Cambridge: Cambridge University Press, 1992); Gananath Obeysekere, *The Apotheosis of Captain Cook* (Princeton: Princeton University Press, 1992).

16. See Bruce Knauft, *South Coast New Guinea Cultures* (Cambridge: Cambridge University Press, 1993); Gilbert Herdt, ed., *Ritualized Homosexuality in Melanesia*, 2nd, paperback ed. (Berkeley: University of California Press, 1993). In "Modern Primitives," Fakir writes, "And of course, like a lot of people, I grew up tempting my primitive lust by reading good old *National Geographic* . . . [but] since they finally got around to considering these 'natives' as human beings, they can't show them naked anymore!" See "Modern Primitives," *Re/Search* 12 (San Francisco: Re/Search Publications, 1989), 7.

17. While there are promiscuous men and women in villages who produce "fatherless children," "promiscuity" still belongs to the township.

18. See Vilsoni Hereniko, "Representations of Cultural Identities," in *Tides of History: The Pacific Islands in the Twentieth Century*, ed. K. R. Howe, Robert Kiste, and Brij V. Lal (Honolulu: University of Hawaii Press, 1994), 406–34; Nicholas Thomas, "Substantivization and Anthropological Discourse: The Transformation of Practices into Institutions in Neotraditional Pacific Societies," in *History and Tradition in Melanesian Anthropology*, ed. James Carrier (Berkeley: University of California Press, 1992), 64–85.

19. I just heard that an international agency will soon be studying child prostitution/exploitation on Daru.

20. To untangle the extent to which contemporary "prostitution" is merely transformed "traditional" sexual practices, I searched Melanesian literature and found "legendary prostitution," "hospitality prostitution," "war captive prostitution," "wife exchange," and so forth, fourteen "types" altogether. An anonymous reviewer's sound criticisms spark the following: first, Papuan peoples did engage in various ritualized and not-so-ritualized forms of "hetero-" and "homosexual" intercourse, many of which fit well "Western" notions of prostitution; second, yes, it is wrong to map "Western" notions of value and equivalency onto "indigenous" practices, and surely have those indigenous practices been altered greatly by the introduction of the cash nexus, urbanization, and Rod Stewart videos; third, nevertheless, it is potentially no less ethnocentric to suggest that prostitution in a "Western" sense can only occur following Euro-American contact — "new" social forms and relations must always have something "old" to take hold of. Pre-contact prostitution existed and was the fundament of at least a few local

economies. What I observed between 1990 and 1992 is either a "distilled version" of what was observable in the recent past, or what has been extruded by internal migration, wage labor, new media, and so forth.

21. At least according to Wilfred Beaver, in *Unexplored New Guinea* (London: Seeley and Service, 1920).

22. See James Chalmers, "Notes on the Natives of Kiwai Island, Fly River, British New Guinea," *Journal of the Royal Anthropological Institute of Great Britain and Ireland* 33 (1903), 124. In *Unexplored New Guinea*, Beaver writes of "public prostitutes" that Bamu kept for the purpose of exchanging for currency and food.

23. Laura Zimmer-Tamakoshi analyzes in great detail and with great insight this issue on a national level; see her "Nationalism and Sexuality in Papua New Guinea," *Pacific Studies* 16 (4) (1993): 61–97.

24. See also Christine Obbo, "Sexuality and Economic Domination in Uganda," in *Woman—Nation—State*, ed. Nira Yuval-Davis and Floya Anthias (London: Macmillan, 1989), 79–91.

25. My work was excoriated thusly by writers of letters to the editor of the *Post-Courier*, accusing me of having carried out some kind of sex survey that made Daruans out to be crazed "sex maniacs."

26. Linda Mahood, *The Magdalenes: Prostitution in the Nineteenth Century* (London: Routledge, 1990), 163.

27. Robert Hughes, *The Fatal Shore* (New York: Knopf, 1987), 71, 24, 102.

28. See David Hyndman, "Mining, Modernization, and Movements of Social Protest in Papua New Guinea," *Social Analysis* 21 (1987): 20–38.

29. See also the fine essay by Lyn Sharon Chancer, "Prostitution, Feminist Theory, and Ambivalence: Notes from the Sociological Underground," *Social Text* 11 (Winter 1993): 143–71.

30. See Lars Ericsson, "Charges against Prostitution: An Attempt at a Philosophical Assessment," *Ethics* 90 (3) (1980): 337. Schidloff writes in the less famous "Sexual Life of Savages" that prostitution "is inherent in woman and has nothing to do with civilization or its absence." See *Venus Oceanica: Anthropological Studies in the Sex Life of the South Sea Natives*, ed. "R. Burton" (a nom de plume?) (New York: Oceanica Research Press, 1935), 124.

31. Kingsley Davis, "The Sociology of Prostitution," *American Sociological Review* 2 (1937), 755.

32. St. Augustine, quoted in Jess West, *A Herstory of Prostitution in Western Europe* (Berkeley: Shameless Hussy Press, 1982), 20.

33. David Halperin, "The Democratic Body: Prostitution and Citizenship in Classical Athens," *South Atlantic Quarterly* 88 (1) (1989), 158; Ruth Morgan-Thomas, "AIDS Risks, Alcohol, Drugs, and the Sex Industry: A Scottish Study," in *AIDS, Drugs, and Prostitution*, ed. Martin Plant (London: Tavistock, 1990), 105; William Acton, *Prostitution*, ed. and with introduction by Peter Fryer (1857; reprint, London: Hogarth, 1968).

34. Havelock Ellis, "Sex in Relation to Society," in *Studies in the Psychology of Sex*, vol. 2 (New York: Random House, 1936), 225; Harold Cross, *The Lust Market* (New York: Citadel Press, 1956), 92.

35. Karl Abraham, "Manifestation of the Female Castration Complex," in *Selected Papers*, trans. D. Bryan and A. Strachey (London: Hogarth, 1945), 361.

36. Cross, *The Lust Market*, 93; Harold Greenwald, *The Call Girl: A Social and Psychoanalytic Study* (New York: Ballantine, 1958), 94; Libbey, quoted in Lewis Baker, *The High Cost of Living* (New York: Tower Books, 1966), 66.

37. Davis, "The Sociology of Prostitution," 755.

38. Rosen, *The Lost Sisterhood*, 6–7. See also Mary Hawkesworth, "Brothels and Betrayals: On the Functions of Prostitution," *International Journal of Women's Studies* 7 (1) (1984): 81–91; Cynthia Enloe, "It Takes Two," in Sturdevant and Stoltzfus, eds., *Let the Good Times Roll*, 23.

39. Briefly, I prefer "sex brokers" to "pimps" because the former exploit the earnings less, and generally have less control over women than the latter. "Sex brokers" are, though, more than mere "messengers," the little kids on foot and teenagers on bicycles who receive a few coins or a soda to pass messages between men and women. Sex brokers roam the town from market to hotel to trade store to settlement, taking requests from men to find women, from women to find men, or both, then coordinate the location and arrival thereto of parties and items of consumption (alcohol, tobacco, etc.) concerned, sometimes escorting the woman in question to and from. To the best of my ability to say, my primary sex broker informant had sex with the women in question only thrice during my stay, and ended up with 24 percent of the earnings of 25 women in my sample, spanning 247 instances.

40. William Vollman, "Sex Slave," *Spin* 9 (9) (1993), 76. This quote strikes at the heart of deep divisions within feminism regarding whether there is "choice" in prostitution and whether prostitution is "sex *work*" and its practitioners "sex *workers*." Ronald Hyams, in *Empire and Sexuality* (Manchester: Manchester University Press, 1990), 137, and Lori Rotenberg, "The Wayward Worker: Toronto's Prostitute at the Turn of the Century," in *Women at Work: Ontario, 1850–1930*, ed. Janice Acton, Penny Goldsmith, and Bonnie Shepard (Toronto: Canadian Women's Educational Press, 1974), 137, both argue that it is. Valerie Jenness, "From Sex as Sin to Sex as Work: COYOTE and the Reorganization of Prostitution as a Social Problem," *Social Problems* 37 (3) (1990): 403–20, Kathleen Barry, *Female Sexual Slavery* (New York: New York University Press, 1979), Marlise Simons, "East European Women Duped into Sex Trade," *Oregonian*, June 16, 1993, A3, and essays and statements by Scott, Miller, and Hotchkiss, by Participant #1, and by St. James in Bell, ed., *Good Girls/Bad Girls*, 207, 50, 82 indicate that it is otherwise.

41. See, for example, Marjorie Shostak, *Nisa: The Life and Words of a !Kung Woman* (Cambridge: Harvard University Press, 1981).

42. See Schoepf, "Women at Risk"; Margaret Jean Hay, "Queens, Prostitutes and Peasants: Historical Perspectives on African Women, 1971–1986," *Canadian Journal of African Studies* 22 (3) (1988), 435.

43. Enloe, "It Takes Two," 24.

44. I include here "Ogamea" (thirty-nine, married, five children), "Koria" (twenty-six, married, three children), "Leona" (twenty, single, but with three

"husbands," no children), "Aramia" (eighteen, divorced, one child), "Maureen" (forty-two, divorced, two children), "Hilda" (twenty-eight, "married" to two *raskols* [criminal gang members], one child), "Julie" (twenty-two, single, no children), and "Aniato" (twenty-eight, single, one child).

45. Maureen had sex with a customer for the use of his phone with which to call her brother-in-law working at a sawmill elsewhere in the province to request that he wire money back.

46. Enloe, "It Takes Two," 25.

47. See also Sophie Day, "Prostitute Women and the Ideology of Work in London," in *The Epidemiology of AIDS*, ed. R. H. Kaslow and D. P. Francis (New York: Oxford University Press, 1989), 100–101.

48. This is too large and complicated an issue to take up here, but consider the following: A London physician argues that "the only people with AIDS" (in his Krobo tribe) are "prostitutes," and that their one common feature is "perineal disintegration," "to which [they] subject themselves" by practicing "abnormal" sex (either anal intercourse or vaginal intercourse too frequently). They are thus "the major means of propagating AIDS." See F. I. D. Konotey-Ahulu, "AIDS: Origin, Transmission and Moral Dilemmas," *Journal of the Royal Society of Medicine* 80 (11) (1987), 720. The "female condom" is marketed under the telling names "Femidom" and "Reality" in the U.K. and U.S., respectively. Who controls such "barriers" and "barrier methods" is greatly contested in feminist circles; compare Beth Baker, "The Female Condom: Reality Is All about Women Protecting Themselves," *Ms.*, March-April 1993: 80–81; and Laurie Liskin and Chuanchom Sakondhavat, "The Female Condom: A New Option for Women," in *AIDS in the World: A Global Report*, ed. Global AIDS Policy Coalition (Cambridge: Harvard University Press, 1992): 700–707. Public health literature is often poised in the middle, aware of the efficacy of the condom as a device, but often seemingly less aware of its negotiated usage; see Erica Gollub and Zena Stein, "Commentary: The New Female Condom—Item 1 on a Woman's AIDS Prevention Agenda," *American Journal of Public Health* 83 (4): 498–500.

49. Gail Pheterson notes that while penile/vaginal intercourse "was the least intimate and most usual transaction" for most prostituted European women, another said that "I save my vagina for my lover," engaging in penile/anal intercourse with the remainder of her clients. See "The Whore Stigma: Female Dishonor and Male Uncouthness," *Social Text* 11 (Winter 1993), 41.

50. Day, "Prostitute Women," 99.

51. Erepai touches sheathed penises only with rubber gloves; condoms can be used doubly, and create suspicion in women of where that condom (i.e., penis) has been.

52. From one young woman's vagina was removed a rotting condom by her mother with the aid of bamboo tongs because neither she nor her mother (much less her sexual partner) could bear to touch her genitals.

53. Schoepf, "Women at Risk," 268.

54. ibid., 271.

55. See also Joshua Gamson, "Rubber Wars: Struggles over the Condom in the United States," *Journal of the History of Sexuality* 1 (2) (1990): 262–82. I heard about men punishing suspected adulterous wives by using a condom with a putative *pamuku* and then using it again on their wives.

56. Day, "Prostitute Women," 99.

57. See, for example, ibid., 101.

58. Witness new tampon and condom applicator technologies that give us the "choice" not to touch our own genitalia.

59. An anonymous reviewer helpfully asked me, "I find it hard to imagine that all people are forced to construct their sexuality in these terms. Is it that corrupt a society or is the concept of sexual transactions as prostitution over-drawn?" My response is perhaps "neither." "Society" (in a sociological sense) is not corrupt, but contradictory social relations are; one does not have to document empirically a male conspiracy in order to show that male violence and payments for sex are ubiquitous. "Society" does not need fixing, but social relations do. *Uba pe* do not need reforming, but economic and political forces that impinge upon them do. Female condoms do not perhaps need so much promoting as does respect for the integrity of another's body and mind.

60. See, for instance, Floya Anthias and Nira Yuval-Davis, introduction to *Woman—Nation—State*, ed. Anthias and Yuval-Davis, 1–15.

61. See Nicole-Claude Mathieu, "When Yielding Is Not Consenting," pts. 1–2, *Feminist Issues* 9 (2) (1989): 1–50; 10 (1) (1990): 51–89.

Performing Masculinities

A Terrible Beauty Is Born: Henry James, Aestheticism, and Homosexual Panic

Leland Monk

Outing Henry James is all the rage these days, though it is a practice about which James himself would have expressed considerable outrage. He was aware, but also quite critical, of a thriving homosexual culture in his day, a culture I hesitate to prefix "sub-" because it was concerned more with culture in its exalted and rarefied forms than with a subterranean collective experience. As several critics have recently pointed out, James kept himself at some remove from the aesthetic movement in England in the 1880s and 1890s, in part because he associated it, especially in the figure of Oscar Wilde, with a decadent homoeroticism he found very disturbing.[1] He seems to have been repulsed by Wilde not simply on moral grounds (whatever those might be), but because the aesthete's public and flagrant suggestion of a homosexual life and style threatened to call attention to James's more private and discreet passion for members of his own sex. In this essay I will be analyzing the mechanisms of homosexual panic at work in James's response to the British aesthetic movement, not so much in terms of his relation with Wilde, which has been fairly well covered, but in his attitude to John Addington Symonds, a writer who was known both for his aestheticism and for his extensive homosexual adventures. I will focus in particular on James's 1884 story "The Author of *Beltraffio*," about an aesthete modeled on Symonds, in order to explore the ways James's writing allowed him to play out, safely and at a distance, the simultaneous fascination and repul-

sion he apparently felt in response to Symonds's embodiment of a homosexual culture. In "*Beltraffio*," the prophylaxis of fiction, with its multiple
identifications and displacements, carefully disposed within the heterosexual matrix of marriage/family/children, allowed James both to explore
intensely eroticized male bonds and to repudiate those desires as perverse
and pathological. There is then an ambivalent and finally deadly circuitry
of homophilia and homophobia wiring the narrative of this lurid little tale
about a specifically homoerotic love of beauty.

The titles of J. A. Symonds's two privately printed studies of same-
sex desire in the past and present, "A Problem in Greek Ethics" (1883)
and "A Problem in Modern Ethics" (1891), indicate that such matters
were for him always both a problem and a matter of ethical concern.
When Henry James was asked to write an appreciation of Symonds after
his death, the novelist found there were "insurmountable" difficulties; by
way of explanation, James invoked the titles of Symonds's homosexual
pamphlets in his refusal. There was an aspect of Symonds's life that was,
he said, "strangely morbid and hysterical and which towards the end of
his life coloured all his work and utterance. To write of him without
dealing with it, or at least looking at it, would be an affectation; and yet
to deal with it either ironically or explicitly would be a Problem—a
problem beyond me."[2] If homosexuality was a problem in Symonds's life
and work, James emphatically felt that it was *his* problem. Unable to
"deal with it," James himself seems rather "hysterical" in his aversion to
Symonds's "morbid" obsession that "coloured all his work and utterance."[3]

In an 1884 letter to Symonds, James was much less standoffish. He
sent Symonds a copy of an article he had published on Venice after
reading some of Symonds's own writings about Italy. The article was
meant to be

> a constructive way of expressing the good-will I felt for you in consequence of
> what you have written about the land of Italy—and of intimating to you, some-
> what dumbly, that I am an attentive and sympathetic reader. I nourish for the
> said Italy an unspeakably tender passion. . . . [I]t seemed to me that the victims
> of a common passion should sometimes exchange a look.[4]

James's biographer Leon Edel, a master at raising a sexual possibility only
to dismiss it, allows no innuendo in James's acknowledgment to Symonds
of "a common passion." In a shrewd reworking of James's phrase that

changes the meaning of "common" from "shared" to "vulgar," Edel writes, "Symonds was concerned with a different level of 'common passion.' "[5] James, on another level entirely, he implies, was never *that* common. Like his subject and Master, Edel would distinguish James's pure and elevated homosocial enthusiasms from the coarse and vulgar homosexual indulgences of Symonds and Wilde by stigmatizing the latter. In defense of the apparent homoeroticism in James's affection for Dudley Jocelyn Persse, for instance, Edel writes, "We must remind ourselves that if on the one hand there was a buried life of sexual adventure among some Victorian men, as evidenced by the Wilde case and the more recent evidence in the papers of John Addington Symonds, there were also many friendships which were romantic rather than physical." He then predictably concludes that such affection in James's case was safely and sanitarily narcissistic: "It was the love of an aging man for his lost youth, and the evocation of it in a figure of masculine beauty."[6]

Edel notwithstanding, the look of common understanding James conveyed to Symonds about the "unspeakably tender passion" they shared in their love of Venice seems provocative, especially given the "aura" surrounding that city. If in the public consciousness at the end of the nineteenth century "Oscar Wilde" became the *name* of the love that dare not speak its name, Venice was more discreetly the *place* of homosexuality, the literary traces of which appear in Mann's *Death in Venice* (1912), Baron Corvo's (F. W. Rolfe's) wonderful *Desire and Pursuit of the Whole* (written in 1909, though not published until 1934), and Waugh's backward-looking *Brideshead Revisited* (1945). The Italian city at the turn of the century was known to be a place of venereal pleasures where generous gentlemen could escape for a while the constrictions of a more puritanical homeland and indulge their love of male beauty.[7] Such a "common passion" may well have been suggested in the sympathetic look James meant to exchange with Symonds via his writing. In a revealing slip of the pen, James seems to acknowledge in his letter a profound sympathetic identification with Symonds: in the closing, he mistakenly wrote not "I shake hands with you" but "I shake hands with me."[8] Meeting Symonds over a mutual passion for the beauties of Venice, James's confused gesture of greeting and farewell also momentarily put him in touch with himself.[9]

The two writers never again corresponded, and James—as he did with Wilde—kept his distance from Symonds, preferring to gossip with Edmund Gosse, who was friendly with both men, about Symonds's homosexual pursuits. When Gosse loaned him a copy of "A Problem in Modern Ethics," James said he was grateful for the opportunity to read "those marvelous outpourings"; when Symonds died in 1893 James praised him to Gosse as a "passionately out-giving man"; and when Gosse during the Wilde trial loaned him some of Symonds's papers to read, James referred to them as "the fond outpourings of poor J. A. S."[10] For Henry James, the effusively outpouring, outgiving Symonds was a little *too* out.

It was a remark by Edmund Gosse about the problems of Symonds's married life that became the germ for James's short story "The Author of *Beltraffio*." Just two months after his friendly letter to Symonds, James wrote in his notebook, "he [Gosse] said that poor S.'s wife was in no sort of sympathy with what he wrote; disapproving of its tone, thinking his books immoral, pagan, hyper-aesthetic, etc." James noted the dramatic potential inherent in

the opposition between the narrow, cold, Calvinistic wife, a rigid moralist; and the husband impregnated—even to morbidness—with the spirit of Italy, the love of beauty, of art, the aesthetic view of life, and aggravated, made extravagant and perverse, by the sense of his wife's disapproval.[11]

The seed Gosse planted in James's imagination about a writer "impregnated—even to morbidness—" with a love of Italy, beauty, and art gone perverse itself resulted in a morbid tale the catastrophe of which, James worried, might be too gruesome and "unnatural."

"The Author of *Beltraffio*" is the story of a quiet but fierce struggle between Mark Ambient, the novelist modeled on Symonds, and his wife for possession of their beautiful young son. In the story's climax, Mrs. Ambient reads her husband's work and, horrified at what she finds there, allows their son to die of a serious illness rather than subject the boy to his father's corrupting influence. Mark Ambient is the leading practitioner of an "art for art's sake" aestheticism best represented by his masterpiece *Beltraffio*, the publication of which was "a kind of aesthetic war-cry."[12] In the portrait of Ambient the aesthete, who resembles Symonds, James also incorporated some aspects of Oscar Wilde and his aesthetic program, cannily anticipating the direction of, and backlash against, the aesthetic movement's association with decadence in the next decade.[13] Ambient's aestheticism is defined in opposition to his wife's moral didacticism (Mrs. Ambient thinks "a work of art should have a 'purpose' " [328]);[14] it departs from current realistic practices ("People had endeavored to sail nearer to 'truth' in the cut of their sleeves and the shape of their sideboards" [303]);[15] and it is distinguished from the pre-Raphaelite art that it resembles but surpasses (Ambient's sister is repeatedly associated with a pre-Raphaelite sensibility but, we are told, "[h]e was the original, and she was the inevitable imitation" [319]). The generally "profane" (310) nature of his work—*Beltraffio* caused something of a "scandal" (303)— makes Ambient's work "offensive to many minds" (331), including that of his own wife. Her sense of their opposition, Ambient observes, is "the difference between Christian and Pagan" (334). Her husband and his art, she is convinced, are "immoral" (335).

What morality Ambient expresses is subordinated to and determined by his art; "the highest social offense," deserving of capital punishment, he says, is neglecting to find and use the best word in his writing. To do so is "very bad" (333). He is more concerned about literature being corrupted by lax expression than he is about its power to corrupt with lax morals. Asked whether reading novels might be bad for youthful readers, he replies, "Bad for *them*, I don't say so much! . . . But very bad, I am afraid, for the novel!" (334). Ambient's aestheticism has a distinctively Nietzschean cast, as in his reformulation of what he considers "bad," which goes beyond the moralistic sense of good and evil as his wife understands them, effecting a revaluation of values. For the artist, it is beauty that determines the power, worth, and efficacy of all human endeavor. Ambient is obsessed by beauty: "I delight in it, I adore it, I think of it continually, I try to produce it, to reproduce it," he says (335). Ambient practices a kind of gay science in the exactitude with which his prose appreciates and expresses what he grandly calls "life," meaning the joy and suffering of *this* world rather than the consolations of the next to which his conventionally religious wife looks forward. The birth of the Ambients' son, who comes to embody the terrible beauty loved by Mr. Ambient and dreaded by Mrs. Ambient, becomes the birth of tragedy for the married couple when they engage in a battle to the death—not their own—for the body and future of their boy.

"The Author of *Beltraffio*" is told in the first person by the overly enthusiastic unnamed narrator, one of the "worshippers" (312) of Mark Ambient, the novelist who so masterfully practices and preaches "the gospel of art" (303). While the Ambient character is treated with considerable respect, James directs his most devastating satire of the aesthetic movement at the American narrator, whose effusive rhetoric is cleverly parodied. In his emulation of Ambient, the narrator sees and experiences *everything* as a work of art. Anticipating Wilde's "life imitates art" dictum, the narrator observes,

That was the way many things struck me at that time, in England; as if they were reproductions of something that existed primarily in art or literature. It was not the picture, the poem, the fictive page, that seemed to me a copy; these things were the originals, and the life of happy and distinguished people was fashioned in their image. (307)

The disciple's most comical travesty of his master's aestheticism appears in his hypersensitive response to "the literary allusions of the landscape" during a pastoral country walk with Ambient: they "breathed the same sweet air as the nibbling donkeys"; the whiteness of "the big, bandy-legged geese . . . was a 'note,' amid all the tones of green"; "I was forever stopping," he enthuses, "to say how charming I thought the thread-like footpaths across the fields, which wandered, in a diagonal of finer grain, from one smooth stile to another" (330). The pun on "smooth stile," like all of the narrator's "nature" descriptions in their rural tour of beauty, is completely, laughably "artistic."

Everything Mark Ambient has created is a thing of beauty for the narrator, not just his books but his boy. The narrator's most rapturous response to an aesthetic object (after *Beltraffio*) is his fascinated attraction to the angelic beauty of the Ambients' son, Dolcino. More than once, the narrator expresses his deep regret that he never got to hold or touch Dolcino during his visit. Even so, he describes in detail what it feels like to kiss the beautiful boy (310), which registers his powerful imaginative desire to do so. He senses from the first, even before Dolcino falls ill, that the boy is too beautiful to live. And as the child's illness progresses he becomes in the narrator's eyes more and more beautiful.

Mark Ambient's natural and literary creations are repeatedly conflated in the story, to the point that Dolcino and the writer's new novel seem interchangeable. "He's so beautiful—so fascinating. He's like a little work of art," the narrator exclaims about the boy (316). While Mrs. Ambient carries the sick child in her arms and then off to his room (in part to prevent her husband—and the narrator—from coming near him), the narrator describes himself "nursing" the proof-sheets of Ambient's new book under his arm, exclaiming to Mrs. Ambient, "Fancy my satisfaction at being allowed to carry them to my room!" (327)—which is just what he would like to do with Dolcino. When Mrs. Ambient for the first time takes up her husband's writing, the pages take the place of her (at this point bedridden) son—"she tucked the little bundle under her arm" (346). On discovering that his wife has taken the proofs of his new book to read, Ambient worries that "she would burn up the sheets, with his emendations, of which he had no duplicate" (347), instead, she allows their only child to be consumed by a deadly fever. Ambient's sister reports that, when she visited the sickroom the night Dolcino died, he was "quiet, but flushed and 'unnatural,'" with his mother sitting beside the bed. 'She held his hand in one of hers,' said Miss Ambient, 'and in the other—what do you think?—the proof-sheets of Mark's new book!' " (350). In this peculiar inversion of the Solomon story, the *mother* is pulled in two directions at once, finally allowing the son she holds in one hand to die rather than permit him to become altogether "unnatural" like the sick brainchild she clutches in the other. As she reads, her son becomes sicker and (at least to the narrator's way of thinking) still more beautiful. Reading her husband's work as her boy lies dying, Mrs. Ambient experiences firsthand a morbid beauty that only becomes more ravishing as it becomes more pathological, culminating in the final corruptions of the flesh. A terrible beauty indeed.

When exposed to the dazzling artistic talk of Mark Ambient, the narrator is "subjected to a high aesthetic temperature" (321), which is just what Dolcino contracts. The diphtheritic fever that rages in the boy and intensifies his beauty finds bizarre sartorial expression in the flagrant costume he wears during his last appearance in the story:

He had been dressed in his festal garments—a velvet suit and a crimson sash [with knee breeches and matching crimson silk stockings (342)] and he looked like a little invalid prince. . . .

Mark placed him on the ground; he had shining, pointed slippers, with enormous bows. "Are you happy now, Mr. Ambient?"

"Oh yes, I am particularly happy," Dolcino replied. (340)

This happy prince dressed in a velvet suit with knee breeches, brightly colored silk stockings, and dainty shoes is indeed the offspring of an aesthete; Mark Ambient's son is also, clearly, a Wilde child. Dolcino is dressed in Oscar Wilde's famous signature costume, which he wore on his tour of America, during which he met Henry James (who referred to Wilde as "an unclean beast") in 1882.[16]

When Dolcino hears that his mother does not like his father's books, he asks the narrator,

"Won't you read them to me, American gentleman?"
"I would rather tell you some stories of my own," I said. "I know some that are interesting."
"When will you tell them—to-morrow?"
"To-morrow, with pleasure, if that suits you." (344)

What "suits" Dolcino when tomorrow comes is not another aesthetic fashion statement like his garish velvet outfit; he gets wrapped up not in the narrator's smooth style but in a winding-sheet. The dying boy, infected with a febrile aestheticism and seemingly interchangeable with Mark Ambient's literary production, is (at least until his mother permanently removes him from that economy of exchange) the beautiful and ephemeral object of desire for this storytelling art lover; in every sense of the phrase, *the narrator wants to have Mark Ambient's child.*

The different value systems at odds in "The Author of *Beltraffio*" are defined not just by the Pagan versus Christian opposition of husband and wife but by two different (and "bad"—though not equally bad) ways to *read*, represented by the narrator and Mrs. Ambient. Both types of reading make an absolute value judgment about Mark Ambient's writing that is taken to be the singular and ultimate meaning of his work; the master trope organizes all the twists and turns of the prosaic particulars and gathers them under the rubric of an all-resolving interpretation. This totalizing Truth is then read back into the author's life, providing a skeleton key that unlocks all closets.[17] What the narrator calls his "fanatic" (328) enthusiasm for Mark Ambient and his work is evident in his conviction that, about the great writer, he has nothing to declare but his genius: "I remember looking for the signs of genius in the very form of his questions—and thinking I found it. I liked his voice. There was genius in his house, too, I thought" (306–7; the narrator also invokes Ambient's "genius" at 316, 326, 336, 338, 350). All the signs of Mark Ambient's life signify the transcendental signifier of his work: "genius."

Mrs. Ambient's equally "fanatical temperament" (336) consists in her fixed conviction, in place long before she actually reads his proof-sheets on that fatal night, that "her husband's mind is a well of corruption." According to Mark's sister, Mrs. Ambient thought his writings immoral and his influence pernicious. It was a fixed idea; she was afraid of these things for the child. . . . It is as if [his influence] were a subtle poison, or a contagion, or something that would rub off on Dolcino when his father touches him or holds him on his knee. If she could, she would prevent Mark from ever touching him. (329)

When Mrs. Ambient finally reads her husband's work, those feculent sheets give her the "proof" of his depraved nature.[18] The signs of vice and immorality metastasize before her eyes such that the secret and singular Truth about the author infuses, determines, and explains every mark on the page: "It governs every line, it chooses every word, it dots every i, it places every comma," as is said about the secret governing the novelist's work in James's story "The Figure in the Carpet."[19] Mark Ambient's writing is made up of ambient marks; it is writing with an atmosphere (as Wilde would say), a penumbra (as Eve Sedgwick would say), an aura (as John Addington Symonds would say), which permeates, surrounds, and emanates from the marks on the page, marks that can be remarked, marks with a surplus of ambient meaning that calls out for a name.

Since it is never unambiguously named or definitely characterized (beyond the affective response it elicits), the depravity Mrs. Ambient discovers in her husband's writing may or may not be of a homosexual nature; but her extreme reaction to that writing is nonetheless and definitively a case of homosexual panic. What eroticism there is in "The Author of *Beltraffio*" is specifically homoerotic. Sexual desire operates in the story first in the aesthetic rapport of Ambient and the narrator, with its mutually thrilling initiations into the "innermost mysteries" (323) of art. As in all of James's artist tales, this master-disciple relationship is intensely charged, dramatizing the pleasures of reading and of being read, played out for the most part across textual surfaces, not bodies. The pleasures these men enjoy together are almost entirely mediated by their literary passions. The *im*mediate and irresistible attraction the narrator feels for the beautiful Dolcino is the other site of homosexual attraction in the story. It is not then simply her husband's immoral writing and corruptive influence that prompt Mrs. Ambient to let her child die. "The book gave her a horror, she determined to rescue him—to protect him from ever being touched," Mark's sister declares (353). But there is a more proximate and literal "touch" that Mrs. Ambient dreads. The chapters from

Mark Ambient's new book about the exotic East may in theory disclose to his wife's horrified eyes the depravity of her husband's nature; but, I would argue, her panic attack is also triggered by what her husband's writing has wrought and brought—the "depraved young man" (341) who is willing to put theory into perverse practice, a man enraptured with her son's beauty, who wants to look at him, touch him, hold him, kiss him, tell him stories. She would rather he died.

With his death, Dolcino joins the ranks of beautiful boys in James's fiction who have to die, it would seem, because of the homoerotic passions they elicit (not least, perhaps, in their creator).[20] The "innocence" of these children is maintained—though only just—by their premature death, which interrupts and preempts the consummation of an impending homosexual intimacy. Such innocence then is only established retroactively, as a post-mortem effect, elegiacally bestowed on the inviolate body of the still uncorrupted youth. These haunted, knowing, attractive, and attracted boys occupy the liminal position and peculiar temporality of the not-yet-sexual, trembling on the verge of its experience and expression; and that is precisely what makes them so ravishing to the men who want them. The fatality that cuts short the homoerotic narrative by hermetically sealing childhood in an innocent preserve also paradoxically infuses the fiction with an intense pedophilia—the love of children, objective and subjective genitive. When the man-boy love story becomes an inquest, the deaths of these lost boys are attributed not to their being the object or agent of illicit sexual desires but to the machinations of a monstrous maternal figure—the negligent and selfish mother in "The Pupil" (1891), who trades on her precocious son's charm and turns Morgan over to Pemberton for services rendered; the possibly psychotic governess (acting *in loco parentis*) of *The Turn of the Screw* (1898), whose passionate embrace would protect Miles from the depraved Peter Quint's efforts to "possess" him; and Mrs. Ambient, who allows Dolcino to die rather than see him completely transformed into an aesthetic object, under the influence of his father and to the delight of the narrator, by a homoerotically inflected and infected love of beauty.

The extreme measures to which Mrs. Ambient resorts to keep her son out of the clutches of aesthetes are incited by a hysterically paranoid case of homosexual panic, by which I do not mean (rather an absurdity in this case) the mortifying discovery of homosexual urges in one's own nature. It is certainly possible to argue that, in a complicatedly displaced way,

Henry James projected his own disturbing erotic feelings for his own sex onto Ambient and the narrator and then recoiled from them, disowning such feelings through Mrs. Ambient's desperate "sacrifice." "We skirted rank covers," the narrator says of his charming country ramble with Mark Ambient (330); and in a sense, that is just what James does when he misogynistically locates the virulent homophobia of the story in the woman (wife and mother) who repudiates the homophilia of men—not just Ambient and the narrator but those other corrupt and corrupting aesthetes, Symonds and Wilde, thereby providing a rank cover for feelings harbored by the author of "The Author of *Beltraffio*."

I do not, however, want to restrict the sense of homosexual panic so luridly dramatized in this story to a mere psychological mechanism reducible to its author's sexually conflicted nature. Nor do I exactly mean the term in the sense Eve Kosofsky Sedgwick uses to characterize the coercions and obfuscations of the double binds regulating male relations under the regime of compulsory heterosexuality.[21] Such powerful cultural pressures may ultimately be at work in Mrs. Ambient's fatal resolve, but what interests me most about the crisis of "The Author of *Beltraffio*" is its staging of homosexual panic in and as the critical scene of *reading*. I would therefore emphasize the etymological sense of "panic" to characterize a terror associated with what might be called hermeneutic satyriasis— a hypersexual interpretive mode for which knowing and being are reflexively determined, each conjuring up the other—associated with the incantatory power of homosexual cognition and recognition. The vicious onto-epistemological circle of homosexual panic turns vertiginously on the undecidability between "it exists, so I must recognize it" and "I recognize it, so it must exist." Coming face-to-face with the vices of her husband's nature writ large, Mrs. Ambient realizes with horror that seeing is believing. And vice versa.

The erotics of reading then, *pace* Barthes, do not always and necessarily yield the *pleasure* of the text. The provocatively ambient marks of an aura-infused writing can and do solicit a homosexual panic of murderous proportions (look again at what Edward Carson said about *Dorian Gray* during Wilde's libel trial) as readily as they do an amniotic flotation tank of connotative excess. What need to be critically examined are the mechanisms by which a form of reading collapses the manifold signifiers of a text into a monolithic, monologic, and monochromatic signified of sexuality. And this goes for the homophilic as much as for the homophobic mode of interpretation. Both Mrs. Ambient and the narrator in James's story respond fanatically and monomaniacally to the novelist's work and influence in terms of a singular, reified, and highly cathected meaning that carries over from his prose to his person. The overt violence of one form of reading, which terminates in Dolcino's death, calls attention to the violence of the other: the acolyte who proclaims with partisan fervor the "genius" of his oracle's every utterance, like the current critical frenzy to queer the universe, manages to confuse or conflate important distinctions between seeing and believing, the work and the life, cultural context and polemical advocacy.

Focusing an analysis of homosexual panic on the critical scene of reading highlights how, especially with pre-twentieth-century works, the reader is always more or less implicated in the production of meanings in and around a text that is both reticent and provocative about the valences of its desires. James's story is instructive about the mechanisms of homophobic interpretation not only in the lurid depiction of its deadly consequences but in the careful attention given to interpretive procedures whereby the particular ambivalences of a text are made to mean one and only one thing. The more pervasive and effective forms of gay-resistant reading operate not by a repressive silence, which only makes the repressed element return more palpably, nor by an overt and murderous violence, which is so easily condemnable by a smug liberal consciousness. Rather, the hermeneutics of homophobia generally work homeopathically by acknowledging, even affirming (though only the more effectively to dismiss) a potential homosexual meaning understood in advance to be altogether homogeneous, undistinguished, and univocal in its import. Such liberal concessions effectually foreclose discussion of exactly what and exactly how a possible homoeroticism might mean and matter in a literary work. It is a matter then of reading the erotics of a text, including the particular manifestations and displacements of same-sex desire, as a productively *open question* that does not relapse into the glass-closeted double binds of the open secret.[22]

Where then is John Addington Symonds in "The Author of *Beltraffio*"'s portrait of a marriage gone awry supposedly modeled on his domestic difficulties? Edmund Gosse found him on page 571 of the first installment of the story. The passage Gosse apparently had in mind characterizes Ambient/Symonds as a scandalous writer with an uncommon fear of scandal. In reply to Gosse's gossipy praise of his penetration into Symonds's nature, James played dumb:

Perhaps I *have* divined the innermost cause of J. A. S.'s discomfort—but I don't think I seize on p. 571 exactly the allusion you refer to. I am therefore devoured with curiosity as to this further revelation. Even a post-card (in covert words) would relieve the suspense of the perhaps-already-too-indiscreet-H. J.[23]

If his readers found some allusion to Symonds in his story, James implied, it was certainly none of his doing. "I am told, on all sides," he wrote to his brother William, "that my *Author of Beltraffio* is a living and scandalous portrait of J. A. Symonds and his wife, whom I have never seen."[24]

Notwithstanding the author's coy denials, Symonds—and his homosexuality—are suggested in the story in several ways. Ambient's religious wife considers her husband an immoral Pagan, "no better than an ancient Greek" (334); Symonds privately printed and quietly circulated his study of Greek love, "A Problem in Greek Ethics," the year before James wrote his story. The letter of introduction that gains the narrator entrance to Ambient's country home is from a great American poet whose relations with the novelist are "only epistolary" (563), which suggests Symonds's long correspondence with Walt Whitman and the way a shared passion for the latter's poetry worked to connect like-minded men of letters in England.[25] More generally, Symonds's uncanny ability to recognize others who shared his homoerotic interests is figured in the immediate but unspecified sympathy between Ambient and the narrator. When Ambient meets him at the station, the narrator recognizes the novelist from a photograph: "my heart beat very fast when I saw his handsome face." Ambient recognizes the narrator as well, though he does not quite articulate what exactly it is that allows him to do so. "He recognized me as infallibly as I had recognized him; he appeared to know how a young American of an aesthetic turn would look. . . . He took me by the hand, and smiled at me, and said: 'You must be— a— *you*, I think' " (305). Ambient's uncharacteristic inability to find *le mot juste* is not just a matter of forgetting the narrator's name, since the novelist twice repeats this particular form of speech impediment (stopping before a word introduced by "a—") in relation to the two men's profound mutual understanding (318). In these three instances of blocked speech, Ambient seems to be stopping before a locution that would identify the narrator as a sympathetic fellow spirit; the usually eloquent writer hesitates before an unsaid noun introduced by the indefinite article, pulling up short before denominating the common ground of their intimacy. This minor and local use of aposiopesis, a rhetorical figure for a sudden breaking off in midsentence as though the speaker were unwilling or unable to continue, is elevated to an aesthetic principle in many of James's fictions, which are organized around and by an unsaid, perhaps unsayable, something.[26] James developed to near perfection an aesthetic of perverse discretion, in two senses—the fiction perversely maintains an insistent discretion, and the fiction is discreet about matters that seem emphatically perverse.

To the modern reader there are other indications that the unspecified depravities of Mark Ambient have a specifically homosexual valence: "'And then, of course, we mustn't forget,' [Ambient's sister] added, unexpectedly, 'that some of Mark's ideas are—well, really—rather queer!' " (329). The story is an anachronist's delight; not only are Ambient's ideas "queer," he is "grave and gay at the same moment" (306) and even has a fondness for "fruit" (313). I mention these latter-day epithets from the gay lexicon not to adduce "evidence" of the author's homosexual "intentionality" but to remark how readily James's perverse discretion about Ambient's perversities invites a retroactively eroticized interpretation. As the narrator observes about the difficulty he has keeping his story straight, "[t]his later knowledge throws a backward light" (316).

What I think is the most intimate connection to John Addington Symonds and his homosexual exploits in "The Author of *Beltraffio*" is right there in the title. Ambient's life, as was Symonds's, is steeped in Italian culture, especially of the Cinquecento, the subject of Symonds's voluminous study *Renaissance in Italy*. Two of Ambient's early novels are set in Rome and Florence and, though the setting of *Beltraffio* is never specified, Venice is a good guess. Symonds developed the habit of visiting Italy regularly after he left England in 1880, eventually establishing a semipermanent home in Venice. That city became the place of sensuous pleasures for him, including a wide variety of sexual adventures. He took up with the gondolier Angelo Fusato in 1881 but, as his biographer Phyllis Grosskurth points out, "his experiences extended far beyond Angelo," including (as Symonds says in his *Memoirs*) "professional male prostitutes."[27] The obviously Italian title of Ambient's greatest work is a composite of *bel*, the masculine prefix for "beautiful," and *traffio*, which variously suggests *trafficare*—to deal, trade, traffic, or intrigue; *traffigere*—to transfix or pierce; and *trafficone*—busybody or meddler.[28] All of these possible senses of *traffio* are suggestive in and for the story; but I would want also to include on the list a colloquial sense of *trafficone*, since, after all, "*Beltraffio*" means, and is presumably about, some kind of traffic in masculine beauty. *Trafficone* is Italian slang for a hustler.[29] The title of Ambient's masterpiece then suggests in a condensed and bitchy form James's sense of there being something vulgar, venal, and venereal about the homosexual affiliations of John Addington Symonds's love of beauty.

It is of course impossible to determine how much Henry James knew or speculated about Symonds's experiences with male prostitutes in Italy; but there is some suggestion that James may have been aware of the young Venetians of his day who trafficked in male beauty with admiring aesthetes. In the article on Venice he sent to Symonds before writing "The Author of *Beltraffio*," meant to remark their "common" and "unspeakably tender passion," James describes his impression of the area around St. Mark's:

> The condition of this ancient sanctuary is surely a great scandal. The peddlers and commissioners ply their trade—often a very unclean one—at the very door of the temple; they follow you across the threshold, into the sacred dusk, and pull your sleeve, and hiss into your ear, scuffling with each other for customers.[30]

Henry James tried in his writing to free himself from the pertinacious hold sex and commerce had on him. He would escape with his fiction into the temple of art, the sanctuary of culture, a safe and sacred place where beauty is neither mortal nor fatal. But those solicitations continue even beyond that threshold, tugging at his sleeve, hissing in his ear. . . . "The Author of *Beltraffio*" suggests at what cost James shunned such terrible beauty.

NOTES

A version of this paper was presented at "Nativity and Narrativity: Multicultural Frameworks of Literature," the 1994 International Conference on Narrative Literature in Vancouver.

1. See Jonathan Freedman, *Professions of Taste: Henry James, British Aestheticism, and Commodity Culture* (Stanford: Stanford University Press, 1990), 168–74; Joseph Litvak, *Caught in the Act: Theatricality in the Nineteenth-Century Novel* (Berkeley: University of California Press, 1992), 271–78; and Fred Kaplan, *Henry*

James: The Imagination of Genius, A Biography (New York: William Morris, 1992), 245, 300–301. See also Eric Savoy's similar discussion of James's relation to Walt Whitman, "Reading Gay America: Walt Whitman, Henry James, and the Politics of Reception," in *The Continuing Presence of Walt Whitman: The Life after the Life*, ed. Robert K. Martin (Iowa City: University of Iowa Press, 1992), 3–15.

2. Henry James, *Selected Letters*, ed. Leon Edel (Cambridge: Harvard University Press, 1987), 286–87.

3. In describing Symonds's homosexual concerns as "morbid," James may be consciously echoing Walt Whitman's famous answer to Symonds's query about the possible physical intimacies of "Calamus," which the poet repudiated as "morbid inferences." James knew of Whitman's response, if only because Symonds himself quotes it in his "Problem in Modern Ethics," which James read.

4. Henry James, *Selected Letters*, 197. "Venice" appeared in *Century Magazine* 25, no. 1 (November 1882): 3–23 and is reprinted in James's *Italian Hours*. The article included illustrations of Venice and was followed by a flattering engraved portrait of James and an appreciation of his work by W. D. Howells (24–29). In the essay, perhaps the closest James's prose ever came to a Paterian lushness, he devotes two pages to an appreciation of the city's gondoliers (13–14)—certainly one of Symonds's passions—remarks the pleasing absence of morality there (15), and observes that "[t]he men throughout the islands of Venice are almost as handsome as the women; I have never seen so many good-looking fellows" (23).

5. Leon Edel, *The Life of Henry James*, vol. 4, *The Treacherous Years, 1895–1901* (New York: Avon Books, 1969), 124.

6. Leon Edel, *The Life of Henry James*, vol. 5, *The Master: 1901–1916* (New York: Avon Books, 1972), 190–91.

7. For a general account of the homosexual allure of Italy, see Robert Aldrich, *The Seduction of the Mediterranean: Writing, Art and Homosexual Fantasy* (London: Routledge, 1993). For a specific and vivid account of the homosexual idylls available to British gentlemen in Venice, see Baron Corvo (F. W. Rolfe), *The Venice Letters*, ed. Cecil Woolf (London: Cecil and Amelia Woolf, 1974).

8. Henry James, *Selected Letters*, 198.

9. I would argue that it was precisely this initial and disturbing dissolution of boundaries between the two men that motivated James's subsequent aloofness from Symonds. When the latter died, James remarked, "[i]t always seemed as if I *might* know him"; in the event, he chose to know him not in life but in and through his fiction, where he could both imaginatively identify with Symonds's Italian passions and keep himself at a comfortable remove from their erotic implications. Henry James, *Letters*, vol. 3, ed. Leon Edel (Cambridge: Harvard University Press, 1980), 409.

10. Quoted in Leon Edel, *The Treacherous Years*, 126–28.

11. Henry James, *The Notebooks of Henry James*, ed. F. O. Mathiessen and Kenneth B. Murdock (Chicago: University of Chicago Press, 1981), 57.

12. Henry James, "The Author of *Beltraffio*," in *The Complete Tales of Henry*

James, vol. 5, ed. Leon Edel (Philadelphia: J. B. Lippincott, 1963), 303–55; the quotation appears on page 330. The story was first published in two parts in *English Illustrated Magazine*, June and July 1884. I quote the original version rather than the New York edition because James's revisions eliminated some traces of the story's connection to Symonds that I will be highlighting here. Page numbers will henceforth appear in parentheses following the quotation.

13. Because of the aestheticism they shared, Symonds is often associated with Wilde and the writers of the 1890s, though he was certainly more a moralist than a decadent. When Wilde sent him *The Picture of Dorian Gray*, Symonds told friends that, as much as he admired its audacity and artistry, "I resent the unhealthy, scented, mystic, congested touch which a man of this sort has on moral problems." He shrewdly recognized that Wilde's provocative stance "will only solidify the prejudices of the vulgar—to wit, that aesthetics are inseparable from unhealthiness or inhumanity, & that interest in art implies some corruption in its votaries." In *The Letters of John Addington Symonds*, vol. 3, ed. Herbert M. Schueller and Robert L. Peters (Detroit: Wayne State University Press, 1969), 477, 479.

14. In "The Sources of 'The Author of *Beltraffio*,'" Samuel F. Pickering argues that Mrs. Ambient's attitude represents that of Walter Besant against which James (in the person of Mark Ambient in the short story, and in his essay "The Art of Fiction") affirmed his own aesthetic values for the novel. In *Arizona Quarterly* 29 (1973): 177–90. There is some reason to align Ambient's aesthetic ideas with James's, not least of which is the fictional novelist's elaborate figure, which compares his uncompromising work as a writer to the intricate artifice involved in crafting a golden vessel, anticipating *The Golden Bowl* by twenty years. But it is more accurate to say that, in the lurid melodrama of the Ambients' conflict, and throughout James's fiction, aesthetic principles and moral principles—especially about sex—get played off against each other.

15. In "'The Author of *Beltraffio*' as Theory," Lawrence R. Schehr identifies the shirt cuff and sideboard passage as a reference to Flaubert. In *Modern Language Notes* 105 (1990): 1011 n.

16. See Richard Ellmann, *Oscar Wilde* (New York: Vintage Books, 1988), 178–79. Although Wilde did not publish "The Happy Prince" until 1888, the coincidence here is remarkable.

17. This impulse to read backwards from a writer's work to his life is called attention to in a confoundingly opaque passage of "The Author of *Beltraffio*." What I think makes it *so* confounding is the way such slippages between author and work are such a naturalized part of the reading process. When Mark Ambient's sister describes Mrs. Ambient reading the proofs of his new book in one hand while holding her sick child's hand in the other, she exclaims:

> "She was reading them there, intently; did you ever hear of anything so extraordinary? Such a very odd time to be reading an author whom she never could abide!" In her agitation Miss Ambient was guilty of this

vulgarism of speech [the narrator observes], and I was so impressed by her narrative that it was only in recalling her words later that I noticed the lapse. (350)

The reader too might be so impressed by the narrative that (s)he does not notice this revealing slip of the tongue highlighted in retrospect. As best as I can make out, the vulgarism of speech consists in saying "*whom* she never could abide" rather than the more correct "*whose work* she never could abide." This minor grammatical lapse configures the major crisis of the story, when Mrs. Ambient equates the perversity she discovers in her husband's writing with his person.

18. Feculent sheets of a more literal sort were offered as "proof" in Oscar Wilde's criminal proceedings. A housekeeper at the Savoy Hotel claimed that, after a boy was seen visiting Wilde there, she found fecal stains on the bedsheets (mentioned in Ellmann, *Oscar Wilde*, 460). Such testimony likely evidences less the particular intimacies of the aesthete with a male prostitute than the culture's sodomitical fantasies about Wilde, since, at least according to Ellmann (275–76), he did not practice anal sex.

19. Henry James, "The Figure in the Carpet," in *The Complete Tales of Henry James*, vol. 9, ed. Leon Edel (Philadelphia: J. B. Lippincott, 1963), 284. Melissa Knox also quotes the "dots every i" passage in *"Beltraffio:* Henry James's Secrecy," which relates "The Author of *Beltraffio*" to other of James's stories about an earnest disciple who tries to discover the secret of a great writer; she concludes (though sad to say, in a simplistic and reductive way) that James was in this way both revealing and concealing his homosexuality. In *American Imago* 43, no. 3 (Fall 1986): 211–27.

20. In analyzing (with requisite irony) James's homoerotic relation to his "inner child" in the prefaces to the New York edition, Eve Sedgwick does not take note of how in the fiction those boys who come under the sexual sway of an older and desiring man are regularly and, it would seem necessarily, though of course lamentably, killed off. See "Queer Performativity: James's *The Art of the Novel*," *GLQ* 1, no. 1 (1993): 1–16.

21. See Eve Kosofsky Sedgwick, *Epistemology of the Closet* (Berkeley: University of California Press, 1990), 19–21, and her brilliant reading of homosexual panic in James's story "The Beast in the Jungle," 182–212.

22. See D. A. Miller's still fruitful analysis of the open secret in "Secret Subjects, Open Secrets," chap. 6 of *The Novel and the Police* (Berkeley: University of California Press, 1988), 192–220.

23. Quoted in Phyllis Grosskurth, *John Addington Symonds* (London: Longmans, 1964), 270, though she mistakes the page number as 57. In *The Treacherous Years*, 126, Leon Edel provides what seems to be the correct reading of James's handwriting.

24. Henry James, *Letters*, vol. 3, 71.

25. See in this respect Eve Kosofsky Sedgwick, *Between Men: English Literature and Homosocial Desire* (New York: Columbia University Press, 1985), 205–6.

26. See Eve Kosofsky Sedgwick's related discussion of preterition and periphrasis in James, *Epistemology of the Closet*, 201–212.

27. Phyllis Grosskurth, *John Addington Symonds*, 243; *The Memoirs of John Addington Symonds*, ed. Phyllis Grosskurth (Chicago: University of Chicago Press, 1984), 277.

28. These possible senses of *"traffio"* are itemized in Melissa Knox, *"Beltraffio: Henry James' Secrecy,"* 227 n. Another likely source for the title of Ambient's masterpiece is the name of the Italian Renaissance artist Giovanni Antonio Boltraffio, a student and disciple in the homoerotic circle of painters around Leonardo da Vinci. One painting in particular by Boltraffio may well have informed James's story: the *Madonna and Child with Book*, which hangs in the National Gallery, London, depicts a religious version of the story's "primal scene"—a mother who holds a book in one hand and her child (who will eventually be "sacrificed") in the other. The painter is mentioned once, glancingly, in Symonds's seven-volume study *Renaissance in Italy*, which James owned; the name is spelled there as in the story, "Beltraffio." See John Addington Symonds, *The Fine Arts*, vol. 3 of *Renaissance in Italy* (New York: Henry Holt, 1888), 484. I am grateful to Brian Williams for mentioning Boltraffio to me.

29. Robert C. Melzi, *The Bantam New College Italian and English Dictionary* (New York: Bantam Books, 1979), 344. This (admittedly tenuous) Italian usage was much more emphatic in contemporary English. Both "traffic" and the similar "trade" (used by James in a passage I am about to quote) were words for prostitution or a prostitute at the time James was writing. See Eric Partridge, *A Dictionary of Slang and Unconventional English*, ed. Paul Beale (New York: Macmillan, 1984), 1259, 1258. For example, the prosecutor in one of Oscar Wilde's criminal trials informed the jury that Wilde's fellow defendant Alfred Taylor "was familiar with a number of young men, who were in the habit of giving their bodies, or selling them, to other men for the purposes of sodomy. It appears that there were a number of youths engaged in this abominable traffic." Quoted in H. Montgomery Hyde, *The Trials of Oscar Wilde* (New York: Dover Publications, 1973), 169.

30. Henry James, "Venice," 8. In *The Venice Letters*, Rolfe/Corvo twice refers to *ragazzi* who worked the Piazza San Marco in search of interested *signori* willing to pay for the pleasures of their company (30, 41).

Music of the "Fourth Gender": Morrissey and the Sexual Politics of Melodic Contour

Nadine Hubbs

Morrissey is an artist who believes in the precious, life-sustaining, re-demptive power of pop music. And he scorns those who fail in their responsibility to that power: "Michael Jackson has outlived his usefulness. . . . Prince and Madonna are of no earthly value whatsoever. . . . Most records portray life as it isn't lived by people."[1] Or at least that's how he felt in 1985, and according to one interview.[2] Of course, one probably ought to exercise sufficient skepticism—toward the press, and particu-larly the pop star-making machinery—to question statements like these, with such obvious myth- and money-making potential.

But Morrissey has proclaimed the same sentiments in his music. "Rub-ber Ring,"[3] for example (excerpted below), is a homage to songs that have been cherished and faithful companions:

> But don't forget the songs
> That made you cry
> And the songs that saved your life
> Yes you're older now
> And you're a clever swine
> But they were the only ones who ever stood by you[4]

And in "Panic" Morrissey is joined by a children's chorus for the final statement of the refrain, a tunefully cheery declaration of war on the purveyors of pop irrelevance:

> Burn down the Disco
> Hang the blessed D.J.
> Because the music that they constantly play
> IT SAYS NOTHING TO ME ABOUT MY LIFE

Whether through his verbal or musical utterances, however, Morrissey may not be easily readable at face value. For he has shown himself to be an artist of rather complex and elusive subjectivity, whose regard for conventional categories of fixed, literal meaning often seems to resemble that of Oscar Wilde,[5] whom he cites as one of the heroes of his *tortured* adolescence. Tortured, reclusive, celibate, narcissistic, dour, droll, literate—these are some of the key words in the Morrissey mythology. The persona we're encouraged to construct is clear enough: a sort of rock Emily Dickinson, trapped in a James Dean-like body.

This is not to say that Morrissey's personal "authenticity" is somehow undermined by his Wildean sensibility. Morrissey is a star, and every star (Wildean or otherwise) is subject to interpretation—whether through song lyrics, performances, video images, or personal interviews—only in terms of his or her constructed image. As a star Morrissey is, in Julian Stringer's words, a "media sign."[6] It is difficult, if not impossible, to know the extent to which his constructed public image genuinely represents the private person. The question, in any case, is irrelevant for present purposes: my focus in this essay is on Morrissey's work and on his public persona (which may also be viewed as one component of his work—a crucial one), both of which I assume to be deliberately and carefully constructed. These, after all, are the signifying elements that audiences respond to and interact with, and thus that contribute to the discourses of culture.

Having said all this, nevertheless I cannot resist briefly remarking on what may be irrefutable evidence of Morrissey's genuine messianic devotion to pop music. At age thirteen, a decade before the birth of his star persona, Steven Patrick Morrissey was so enamored of his favorite band that he began to collect their every press clipping; by nineteen he had even written a book about them, which was published in Britain.[7] "They" were none other than the seventies' trash-transvestite, glam-rock, hitless cult-band the New York Dolls. For some of us who likewise grew up with the Dolls, Morrissey's labors may give documentary proof of his love and devotion to pop—indeed, this might seem the only possible explanation.

Whether or not one shares such passion toward popular music, its considerable cultural power and influence, by now multigenerational, can scarcely be denied. Of course since the earliest days of rock 'n' roll certain observers have been eager to credit this music with tremendous social power, of a destructive sort; this is still the case with heavy metal and rap, especially.[8] Such concerns are in a sense opposite to my concerns in these pages, however—which lie with a constructive function of pop music. Specifically, I shall examine some ways in which powerful regulatory practices of gender, sexuality, and desire are constructed by popular music, Morrissey's songs in particular, and music in general.

Some groundwork for such consideration has already been laid: Simon Frith and Angela McRobbie provided the first word with their 1978 article "Rock and Sexuality." Frith and McRobbie's central thesis still holds: in contrast with the common view of rock as a sexually liberating force, they argued that rock reinscribes conventions of masculinity and femininity—along lines of active participants and passive observers, respectively.[9] Subsequent examinations—scholarly sociological studies as well as journalistic criticism—have dissected sex and identity in rock's visual images, bodily displays, and song lyrics.[10] But, as I'm not the first to note, considerations of the music itself are conspicuously absent from most of these analyses;[11] I'll return to this point.

For the moment, however, I return to Morrissey. He arrived on the scene in 1983, as lead singer and co-songwriter (with guitarist Johnny Marr)[12] for the English postpunk band the Smiths. The band broke up in 1987, and since that time Morrissey has seen continued popularity as a solo artist, writing and performing music that is often much in keeping with the Smiths' work, in both style and content.[13] I should note, however, that the songs analyzed in this paper come exclusively from Morrissey's recordings with the Smiths, and thus from a five-year period, 1983–87.[14]

Considerable popular and critical attention has been focused on Morrissey since his debut with the Smiths. In particular there has been a great deal of fascination and speculation concerning his gender identity and sexual orientation. Press sources have reported variously that Morrissey is admittedly gay, that he denies rumors that he's gay, and simply that he evinces an "ambiguous sexual point of view."[15] The cherished artistic idols and role models he has cited as his sole companions in a distraught and isolated adolescence—Oscar Wilde, James Dean, and the New York Dolls—constitute a veritable who's who of gay-camp sensibility. Yet he also has appeared to collaborate with journalists who seek to explain his avowed isolation and celibacy in heterosexual terms of rejection and impuissance, supplying references to "dreadful, incredibly uninteresting [adolescent] episodes with girls."[16]

Morrissey's song lyrics are characterized by his singular first-person perspective: it is that of a self-loathing narcissist, according to some critics, or of "the greatest autobiographical songwriter of his age," according to others.[17] His narratives suggest a gay viewpoint in some instances, and a straight viewpoint in others, but every instance is fraught with ambiguity. This ambiguity, as I shall illustrate, manifests an intriguing and rather specific schema in the Smiths songs: that is, most often the identity of the male as object of desire is shrouded in mystery; the female object appears more clearly identified, but more ambivalently desired.[18]

Perhaps Morrissey's most candid confession concerning sexual orientation is his admission to cultivating a sort of obscurity, or indeterminacy, in this regard. A 1986 *Rolling Stone* article observed that

Morrissey claims the lack of specific boy-girl (or even boy-boy, girl-girl) references in his lyrics is quite deliberate. "It was important for me to try and write for everybody." Yet there is an implicit erotic quality to Smiths records . . . that is quite different from the explicit sexuality of most top pop platters. "I find when people and things are entirely revealed in an obvious way," Morrissey says, "it freezes the imagination of the observer. There is nothing to probe for, nothing to dwell on or try and unravel. With the Smiths, nothing is ever open and shut."[19]

Elsewhere, Morrissey has proclaimed himself "a prophet for the fourth gender."[20] Thus he evidently passes on not only the first and second, but skirts the "third gender" as well, that nineteenth-century sexologists' category of the gender invert—a female soul in a male body,[21] or vice versa. From such elliptical statements one point emerges clearly: that sex and gender ambiguity, a resistance to finite fixing of sexual or gender viewpoint, is not merely an aspect of style with Morrissey. It is, in fact, a primary substantive element of his stated artistic project.

And it is more substantive, I would argue, than the "gender bender" poses struck (especially in the early and mid-eighties) by such artists as Boy George, Michael Jackson, Annie Lennox, David Bowie, and Prince. The former two in particular make clear, with their shrill claims of heterosexuality and "real" manhood, a willingness to cash in on the style of gender transgression while disclaiming associations with any deeper substance, as it were. For all these stars, the potentially ruinous image-effects of transgendering are counterbalanced by public displays of "normal," heterosexual credentials—which may involve spouses and children, womanizing, or even wedding Elvis's daughter.

The "gender play" itself, among pop artists of this ilk, is signified primarily and sometimes solely by a "look"—which, essentially, occupies some point along a cross-dressing continuum. Morrissey's appearance, on the other hand, has always been rather conventionally masculine, and is quite possibly the least subversive aspect of his work and persona. This difference was characterized by one journalistic critic, writing in 1985: "Like their name, The Smiths don't exactly look outrageous, but listen to them for a bit: Frankie Goes to Hollywood begins to sound like a retread party and Boy George is revealed as a pleasant but altogether conventional crooner. However outlandish their get-up, none of these guys seem actively intent on rearranging our taboos. The Smiths on the other hand, [are]."[22] Of course sex and gender taboos are chief among those being rearranged here, primarily by means of Morrissey's renowned "ambiguous sexual point of view." And his construction of this viewpoint is distinguished by a reliance on textual, musical, and visual significations that exceed and exclude drag accoutrements and gestures.

Also notable, and somewhat paradoxical, is the fact that Morrissey advocates, simultaneously and with equal vigor, relevance and accessibility, indeterminacy and ambiguity. In the early days of the Smiths especially, he had much to say about the irrelevance of most pop music and his passionate belief in the power of that music—when it is attuned to people's real lives.[23] Significantly, Morrissey's lyrics, however sexually open-ended, are sung with perfect English diction and printed as liner notes in most of his recordings.

Hence Morrissey's position, as it emerges from the intersection of these elements, must be distinguished from one of merely noncommittal or undirected obfuscation (as I shall further explicate below). His "fourth gender" standpoint rests on a refusal of both heterosexual and homosexual classifications, and dissension from the binary genders that make these possible. The only banner that he willingly bears in this realm is one of personal celibacy, which he has claimed from the time of his earliest interviews up to his most recent ones. This celibacy manifesto, whether or not it is truthful (predictably, there are those who seek to disprove it), certainly constitutes a unique stance among pop-rock stars and, whether or not calculated, a stratagem seemingly ideal to purposes of Morrissey's sex-gender resistance: for thwarting the reigning binarisms, it's hard to imagine a better position than celibacy.

NOWHERE FAST: MORRISSEY'S MELODIC CONTOURS

Having addressed several of the more usual themes of Morrissey criticism, I'd like now to turn to a consideration of his music. It is ironic that the music receives less critical attention than any other aspect of Morrissey's work, for it is indeed the music that fosters audiences' most powerful connections.[24] But such silence remains the norm for popular music criticism in general. As Simon Frith observed in 1987, "We still do not know nearly enough about the musical language of pop and rock: rock critics still avoid technical analysis, while sympathetic musicologists . . . use tools that can only cope with pop's . . . least significant . . . qualities."[25]

What strikes me as one of the *most* significant qualities of Morrissey's musical language, particularly in the Smiths songs, is conspicuous in such passages as this one from "Still Ill,"[26]

this one from "Half a Person,"

and this one from "There Is a Light That Never Goes Out."

Take me out ———— tonight ———————— where there's
mu - sic and there's peo - ple and they're young and a - live ——————

The quality I find salient in examples like these (it may come as no surprise) has to do with melody: melodic contour in these excerpts (and their continuations, not shown here) is extraordinarily flat. And this is especially evident at the earlier foreground, a step removed from the surface ornaments—the trills, mordants, and grace notes—that characterize Morrissey's "idiosyncratic crooning."[27] Some melodic passages in Morrissey's oeuvre are more active than these examples, but overall it is very typical for his vocal melodies to present extended stretches of repeated pitch. When pitches do change they do so within restricted pitch space, and stick mainly to chord tones. Notably, what melodic motion is present at the foreground is not goal-directed: repetition of figures is common, and within such figures starting and ending points are often identical. Hence the flatness of melodic contour observed at the foreground is echoed at, continues through, the middleground.[28]

One important effect of such melodic inactivity is the declamatory emphasis it lends to Morrissey's distinctive lyrics.[29] An absence of motion represents an absence of new melodic information, as it were, and thus listeners' attention is "preserved" for the remaining components—lyrics and accompaniment. But the static melodic quality also garners attention in its own right: it functions, in relation to relevant melodic norms, as a mark of difference—specifically a difference of inactivity. Such difference arises, of course, by contrast with other singers' levels of rhythmic activity and melodic contours.

But it is also created by contrast with the level of activity of the other members—the instrumentalists—of Morrissey's own (all-male) bands. This is true with the Smiths, and equally so with the bands that Morrissey has worked with in his solo career. A vivid sense of such contrast is evoked by one *Rolling Stone* concert reviewer, who remarks that "[the band] rocked tough, their precise swagger and matching ducktails setting off the singer's idiosyncratic crooning and silver-lamé theatricality."[30] In this excerpt, as in the performances themselves, contrast and hence difference arises out of visual, bodily, dramatic, and musical signs and gestures, which simultaneously coexist, intermingle, reinforce, inflect, and oppose one another.

Of course, journalists write regularly and adeptly about the visual signs of style, drama, and embodiment that can construct difference. Even in the brief passage just quoted, the reviewer manages to provide powerful images in all these realms. There is also some suggestion (albeit vague) of aural, musical difference in the references to "rock[ing] tough" and "idiosyncratic crooning." I believe that a crucial component of the "idiosyncrasy," or difference, that audiences perceive in Morrissey's singing is the static quality of his melodies. And this quality constitutes an intersubjective mark of difference so potent, I shall argue, that it has even received comment in the pop press—one of those rare instances of musical structure attracting the notice of rock critics. To notice their notice, however, requires some translation and interpretation of the discourse of rock criticism—a discourse that supports a rich and constantly evolving vocabulary of musical, visual, and expressive style, and a virtually nonexistent vocabulary of musical structure.

In *Rolling Stone*'s first article on the Smiths, in 1984, the critic James Henke comments that Morrissey "doesn't really *sing* so much as he speaks the lyrics in an often droning monotone that can be irritating."[31] But in fact, Morrissey does really sing—every syllable; never in his career has he approached anything like a rock *Sprechstimme* (which exists, of course— quintessentially with Bob Dylan).[32] Though Henke purports to describe Morrissey's vocal technique in the early Smiths songs, I believe that his remarks are best understood as linguistically rough attempts to characterize their melodic structure. For this is indeed "droning," and literally monotonous—that is, static and nonteleological—whereas the singing is not at all speechlike.[33]

Thus in the annals of Morrissey press, alongside the ever-present ruminations over the singer's personal and lyrical peculiarities, some peculiarities of his musical structures are also perceived and noted—if inarticulately. But these discourses typically link Morrissey's celebrated sex and gender complexities exclusively with his words and his persona, leaving untouched the structural qualities of his music, and the signifying potential therein. Meanwhile in academic music circles, "perhaps the most burning question regarding gender," as Marcia Citron has recently remarked, "is whether it is present in a piece of music."[34] To prepare the ground for this "burning question" as it relates to Morrissey, I shall outline a few of my assumptions and premises about gendered meaning in music.[35]

First, I do not assume that any musical gestures are intrinsically gendered. But throughout history many aspects of music have been invested with particular meanings, including representations of sexuality and gender. These, in turn, are not intrinsic phenomena, nor eternal or universal: though gender and sexuality are naturalized in culture and thus made to seem inevitable, they have been variously constructed in particular cultures and historical eras. Of musical conventions for their representation, some endure, while others do not; some cross boundaries of genre, style, and so forth, while others apply only within one school, a single composer's oeuvre, or even an individual work. Any analysis invoking such conventions therefore must be grounded in a discriminating awareness of musical and sociohistorical particularities.

A good deal of theory and criticism has already deconstructed the myriad ways our cultural discourses are rooted in notions of dialectical gender. If I rehearse some of the well-worn facts of these genders—that the masculine is constructed in terms of primacy, strength, action, and independence, and the feminine as its opposite and Other, secondary and different, weak, inactive, and dependent—my litany is intended as descriptive (of long-standing, powerful, and constructed cultural products), and surely not prescriptive (according to essentialist or any other assumptions). Like gender, the very notion of sexuality, and its associated categories as well, are cultural constructions. These are of more recent vintage, however, according to Foucauldians.[36]

BOYS' SONGS, GIRLS' SONGS, AND MUSIC'S PRODUCTION OF GENDER

Deconstruction of gender and sexuality in musical texts has been contested, problematized, and generally slow in coming to music theory and musicology. It is indeed problematic to theorize musical signification in the concert hall canon, where instrumental music is the prime repertory.

Here, of course, there are no words—or pictures—to help us along. And, in contrast with some past eras (such as the Baroque), compositional and critical practices over the past century haven't provided much framework for understanding meanings in music: until very recently such a perspective has been overwhelmingly ignored by performers, critics, composers, and listeners of serious music.[37]

For present purposes, however, there's no need to take on music, and melody, in its most abstract, inscrutable incarnations. After all, my subject isn't just any melody; it's melody in the service of song. And in art and pop song alike, one usual function of melody, text, and other available means is to represent and characterize a narrating subject, embodied by the singer. The most emphatic proof of this function is perhaps found in the silent, empty spaces of performance practice. That is, Joan Baez proclaims, "Virgil Cain is my name,"[38] Ella Fitgerald covers "Caravan" and "Witchcraft," Bette Midler snarls her own version of Mick Jagger's "Beast of Burden." But has anyone heard Elvis doing "My Boyfriend's Back," Joe Williams singing "Can't Help Lovin' Dat Man," or Sinatra performing "Someday My Prince Will Come"?

These examples may push it a bit, but the point remains: there are boys' songs and girls' songs, and specific (though tacit) laws governing each. A female vocalist may, occasionally, cover a boy's song: she is understood to take on the purportedly neutral and universal masculine perspective of the song's first-person subject, and thus, as a stand-in of sorts, she may sing love songs to another "she." This is "allowable" partly because the singer's subjective identity, being feminine (and hence passive, nonpenetrating), is not so overpowering as to pose a threat to the understood, heterosexual arrangement. But clearly, a male singer is less free to sing girls' songs; pronouns are assiduously altered, or more often, this threatening situation is avoided altogether. For it places a man in position to assume the gender-marked, nonuniversal identity of the feminine Other—or even to sing love songs to another "he." The tabooenergy accrued at such boundaries is evident in those instances when they are transgressed, as when artists tap this power for parody or other humorous purposes, or expressly to shock, provoke, or titillate.[39]

But it's not only gendered verbiage that plays into the codes of subject performativity in song. Can we imagine a demure soprano performing Vaughan Williams's "Vagabond," or a brawny baritone singing Poulenc's

"Hôtel"? Of these two well-known twentieth-century art songs, neither is a love song; their texts both contain first-person references to a narrating subject, but no gendered references at all.

The Vaughan Williams is a rousing, cocksure, devil-may-care song of wayfaring. Of course, this is gendered subject matter, but surely the fact that this song is performed exclusively by male singers also has much to do with musical rhetoric: from its first notes the vocal melody cuts quite a swath through pitch space, scaling rugged triadic ascents within the phrases—each of which is pitched progressively higher—in pursuit of the climactic goal. The piano accompaniment also participates in subject construction, notably through the steady tramp-tramp-tramping of the left-hand part. Issues of embodiment loom huge here: women don't walk this way!—nor move through (pitch- or other) space with such rambling, boisterous freedom. To invoke the 1950s medicoscientific voice of authority: songs like this could harm a female singer's reproductive system!

Musical rhetoric is implicated more pointedly in the Poulenc, for the text's topic—idle smoking in one's hotel room—is not clearly gendered. But by the time Apollinaire's surrealist text is layered with Poulenc's musical setting we have indeed, in Glenn Watkins's words, "the perfect transformation of an art song into a torch song."[40] The mere presence of this last phrase, *torch song*, is worth several paragraphs' analysis and explication. The term is freighted with gender- and sex-coded meanings, as Harvey Fierstein illustrates via their deft co-optation in his play title *Torch Song Trilogy*. In relation to the musical rhetoric of Poulenc's song, "torchiness" inheres in harmonic inflections from jazz and the cabaret, as well as tropes of erotic seduction invoked by the voice and piano parts alike. Rhythm and melody throughout the song create a static wash, a languid inactivity, constructing a subjectivity that male singers have tended infrequently to take on.

We might further note a parallelism between the musical rhetoric of gender in these two songs and the gendered conception of sonata themes documented by A. B. Marx in 1845, and echoed by subsequent writers. The resonance of "The Vagabond" and "Hôtel" with Marx's contrasting (primary) masculine-"energetic" and (secondary) feminine-"supple" themes, respectively, suggests the presence of shared conventions across certain boundaries of genre and history within serious music practice.[41] More relevant to my immediate concerns is the possibility of shared conventions among songs by Vaughan Williams, Poulenc, and the

Smiths—hence, within a genre of song conceived across boundaries of popular and serious musical practice, and twentieth-century history. Whether or not such a conception is orthodox, its potential validity is implied by a remark from Poulenc himself: "From childhood onward I've associated café tunes with the Couperin Suites in a common love without distinguishing between them."[42]

THE MUSICAL RHETORIC OF THE "FOURTH GENDER"

Morrissey's songs, as the preceding examples may suggest, transgress masculine convention through identifications with feminine subjectivity, and with other distinctly unmasterful ways of being. Of course, popular music offers an established practice of gender transgression: as flagrant spectacle—sparing no eyeliner—that ultimately enhances a rocker's daring, bad-ass image. Morrissey's transgender identifications—frequently abstruse and spectacularly unprovocative—are thus doubly transgressive; they are cast, among other unglamorous subject identifications, in the construction of a bona fide misfit. The song "Bigmouth Strikes Again" (excerpted below) presents an intriguing instance:

> and now I know how Joan of Arc felt
> now I know how Joan of Arc felt
> as the flames rose
> to her roman nose
> and her hearing aid started to melt

The hearing aid image here lends a note of delicious absurdity, via obvious anachronism. But less obviously, it deepens and complicates Morrissey's identification with Saint Joan: she never wore a hearing aid, but as fans know, in public appearances since the early Smiths years Morrissey has often affected (a nonoperative) one.[43] Thus the boundaries between the singer and the (feminine) object of his vicarious focus are blurred. The hearing aid, one might observe, is not standard issue in studly rock-star accessorizing; still, Morrissey's wearing it was an exercise in semiotic power. "In the midst of all the glamour, light, and shallow veneer of pop," he has said, it was "a symbol that spoke for downtrodden and lonely people."[44]

Another Smiths song, "Sheila Take a Bow," seems at first glance a fairly conventional affirmation of boy-girl love. In its twice-occurring refrain, Morrissey sings:

Sheila take a, Sheila take a bow	5/13
Boot the grime of the world in the crotch, dear	6/14
And don't go home tonight	7/15
Come out and find the one that you love and who loves you	8/16

The impression of heterosexual normalcy endures undisturbed through the final refrain, and then receives amplification in its extension:

Take my hand and off we stride [la la la la la la la la]	17
You're a girl and I'm a boy [la la la la la la, la la la la la la]	18

Line 18, "You're a girl and I'm a boy," is delivered and left at that, as a statement gloriously and patently replete in its ramifications. It suggests the reassuring familiarity of every boy-meets-girl script: "You're a girl and I'm a boy"—there it is; enough said. The bawdy dance hall stride gives way to smiling, carefree skipping music, for which "la, la, la" now suffices as a lyric—after all, from this point presumably everyone can supply the rest for themselves. With the myth well in motion, there's no stopping the inevitable love and happy-ever-after; all we need now is to repeat and fade.

And Morrissey obliges, beginning a repeat with line 19. But at line 20, something goes awry:

Take my hand and off we stride [la la la la la la la la]	19
I'm a girl and you're a boy [la la la la la la, la la la la la la]	20

One hears the sound of a wrench being thrown—or perhaps it's the drop of a large hairpin. In any case, its reverberations are enough to call into question all that had seemed manifest in the preceding scenario: we might note now, in retrospect, the presence from the start of a certain tone in the narrator's orientation to the girl. Beneath the very overt positioning of the girl as object of desire is a subtler note of something like avuncularity—located in the repeated, somewhat stymied references to her youth; the indication that she is a schoolgirl (l. 22: "Throw your homework into the fire"), and that he is older; and in the chaste epithet *dear*. On closer examination even the name, Sheila, is subversive: in vernacular usage it refers generically to a woman or girlfriend, like "chick" or "broad."[45]

Clearly line 20 presents a small but resounding bump in the dramatic narrative, for which, it seems, the text is to blame. But the text doesn't act alone: the wry piquancy of this moment owes much to its setup in strophic musical patterning. Lines 5–8 and 13–16 present a parallelism both musical and textual—the song's refrain; then lines 17–18 extend the preceding refrain (ll. 13–16), with new text on the same musical framework (and "la la la . . ." filling in for the second and fourth lines of text). By the time line 19 begins just as line 17, we are thoroughly lulled into our expectations—for continued musical and textual parallelism in line 20. The music plays to these expectations; it extends the parallelism— and thereby redoubles our surprise at the text's detour ("I'm a girl and you're a boy").

A similar textual picture receives a different sort of musical frame in "Half a Person." From line 10 until the end of line 12, predictable patterning is created by rhyme scheme, melody, and harmonic progression:

Sixteen, clumsy and shy	10
I went to London and I	11
I booked myself in at the Y. . . . W.C.A.	12
I said, "I like it here—can I stay?	13
I like it here—can I stay?	14
And, do you have a vacancy	15
For a Back-scrubber?"	16

The material of lines 10–11 presents as an antecedent unit: textually and harmonically open-ended, it awaits completion by a closural consequent. And we get just that—or its beginnings, at least—in the music that follows: "I booked myself in at the Y" (l. 12) sets the stage for such completion, through its textual rhyme and musical parallelism with line 10. But then comes Morrissey's ellipsis . . . which leads into a gender-reversing twist of text (". . . W.C.A."), wedded to a reopening of the musical argument. That is, rather than the expected consequent unit and cadential closure, we get a deceptive cadence of sorts (at "W.C.A."); and this gives rise to an extensional offshoot (ll. 13–16) in which the nascent narrative queerness is embroidered unmistakably queerer ("I said: 'I like it here can I stay? / I like it here can I stay? / And, do you have a vacancy for a Back-scrubber?' "). Thus, in this case, an unexpected addition to the text and dramatic narrative is *mirrored* by its musical setting— painted, and hence amplified, by a melodic extension.

I have already discussed the presence and significance of Morrissey's melodic inactivity, in his work in general and three examples in particular, including "Half a Person." But melodic structure carries further, powerful connotations in the latter instance. For within "Half a Person," melody is not only static and nonteleological, but repetitive, and narrowly focused in both range and idea. Such melody is exquisitely commensurate with Morrissey's textual themes in this song and elsewhere: it is the melody of obsession. It sets its own narrow confines and paces back and forth within them, frequently retracing its own path—and thus acts as ideal musical counterpart to Morrissey's narratives of compulsion, with their *idées fixes*, and their voyeuristic and sometimes agoraphobic preoccupations.[46] And Morrissey provides still a further level of reinforcement of his themes of obsession—in his obsession with (particular) themes. One needn't possess an exhaustive knowledge of the oeuvre to observe that Morrissey perpetually "is still singing the same old songs."[47] Throughout his work Morrissey's concerns, fascinations, and fixations run less broad than deep, and he continually revisits his lodes—at times with delectation, at times with loathing, but always, time and again, returning for more.

The song "Sheila Take a Bow" was found above to present a clear feminine object, of subtly equivocated desire; in this respect it groups with a number of other Morrissey songs. "Girlfriend in a Coma" does the same thing, but with a greater reliance on the manipulation of musical rhetoric. The song's textual scenario is grave from the outset:

> Girlfriend in a coma, I know
> I know—it's serious
> ....
> there were times when I could
> have "murdered" her
> (but, you know, I would hate
> anything to happen to her)
> NO, I DON'T WANT TO SEE HER
> Do you really think
> she'll pull through?

By the closing lines, things have progressed from bad to worse:

> Let me whisper my last good-byes
> I know—IT'S SERIOUS

This text alone introduces apparent conflicts of feeling in the narrator, in his odd responses to the grim circumstances: he "know[s]—IT'S SERIOUS," but he does not "WANT TO SEE HER"; he expresses concern for her life, but the occasion of her mortality finds him musing over the times when he "could have 'murdered' her." This marriage of tragic seriousness with transparent artifice is characteristically Wildean and quintessentially camp, as is the peculiar usage of capitalization and quotation marks—just what does it mean to "murder" or "strangle" in quotes? Meaning is precisely indeterminate: Morrissey's caps and quotes cultivate enigma, like the italics used similarly by generations of campy writers.[48]

But the ironic clincher in this song is provided by the music, which from its opening notes is a banal cliché. It is the fifties rock 'n' roll of willful naïveté, and of bland sentimentality. This insipid music and Morrissey's vacant, pretty crooning in it are as remote as they could be from any authentic sympathetic response to the sorrowful goings-on in the text.[49]

In a number of his songs Morrissey presents the reverse dynamic of that seen here: thus, a highly charged situation of desire, and a masculine object of ambiguous identity and role. "This Charming Man" (excerpted below) provides the prototypical example:[50]

> Punctured bicycle
> on a hillside desolate
> will Nature make a man of me yet?
>
> then in this charming car
> this charming man
>
> why pamper life's complexities
> when the leather runs smooth
> on the passenger seat?

Questions around gender are introduced immediately in the first stanza of this song, when the narrator mocks his own masculinity ("will Nature make a man of me yet?"). In stanza 3, a second question is posed rhetorically ("why pamper life's complexities / when the leather runs smooth / on the passenger seat?"). Here Morrissey's last syllable, "seat," is melismatic.[51] He had sung melisma in one previous place: that is, where the words "charming man" liltingly trail off in midsentence. There follows a momentary descent into interiority (during one bar's vocal rest); the narrator seems to weigh his options; and he reemerges with a decision: "why pamper life's complexities when the leather runs smooth on the passenger seat?" The mind/body problem implicit here is something of a recurrent theme in Morrissey's lyrics;[52] in this instance the narrator decides it in favor of the body—his rhetorical question (st. 3) tells us that much. But Morrissey's prolongation and inflection of the melisma on "seat" tells us more: it seems a marked indulgence, and tantalizingly connotes (while the text denotes) a surrender to sensual pleasure.

Fans of *The Rocky Horror Picture Show* might compare this moment with one in Frank N. Furter's song and dance number, "I Can Make You a Man." Frankie (a transvestite alien scientist) sings the song to his newly unveiled human creation, Rocky (a tan, blond, muscular hunk). He breathlessly details what he has planned for Rocky's workout regimen, but nearly loses his bearings at the line, "With some massage, and just a little bit of steam. . . ." Tracing his gloved finger down the creature's magnificent, oiled pecs, and then abs, Frank's voice reaches the word "steam" just as his finger reaches Rocky's skimpy gold lamé trunks. He lingers there (faintly tremulous), melismatically drawing out the word before finally regaining self-control, and resuming progress toward the cadence. The *double entendre* potential of "steam" is close to the surface in this steamy moment; it is more buried, but equally present, in Morrissey's "seat."[53]

WHAT DIFFERENCE DOES IT MAKE?

As I stated near the outset of this essay, one of my primary aims is to illuminate some ways in which Morrissey's music, and music in general, can participate in the cultural production of sex, gender, and desire. Such interrogation might help us interpret, among other things, one rock critic's reference to the Smiths' music as "distinctly nonphallic rock & roll."[54] The locution may represent mere rock catch-phraseology, a coinage too hip to pass up; but it seems worth noting that its assessment is stated in terms of difference: "distinctly non"-anything invokes comparison with a prior, somehow normative standard—here, "phallic rock & roll," which echoes Frith and McRobbie's "cock rock" (and is to that extent transparent).[55]

Morrissey's work resists, subverts, and transvalues cultural terms of sexuality and gender on verbal, visual, and musical levels. I have argued that Morrissey's melodies signify difference, specifically a difference of inactivity. And if Morrissey's different, inactive melodies—doubly gendered feminine—attract the notice of pop critic Henke, they also, significantly, incur his disapproval: his reference was to a "droning monotone *that can be irritating*" (emphasis added). Such irritation may bespeak a cultural expectation articulated, in conspicuously gendered terms, by Charles Ives, that music must go "onwards and always upwards."[56] What, then, of music that doesn't? Well, perhaps this is how music comes to seem "distinctly nonphallic."

Recognizing and unpacking the musical component in Morrissey's rock discourses affords illumination on multiple fronts: it redresses the neglect of this component in existing criticism; and it distinguishes Morrissey's constructions from more conventional rock examples of sex and gender transgression, in which musical semiotics is often less a factor.[57] Further, analysis of this sort recovers for conscious reckoning a dimension of Morrissey's songs that is powerfully, viscerally meaningful: the music. Here as elsewhere, music possesses exceptional qualities as a signifier—being perceived as nonverbal and embodied, seemingly "natural" and unmediated by social structures. Such an experience is evoked poetically by T. S. Eliot:

> music heard so deeply
> That it is not heard at all, but you are the music
> While the music lasts.[58]

Morrissey's songs afford insights into the ways in which music, through forces as mysterious to most listeners as they are irresistible, presents constructions of sex, gender, and desire. Such constructions cannot be understood apart from any verbal and visual dimensions attending a musical activity, or from the larger cultural ecology that sustains them. Thus any assessment of Morrissey's artistic difference must be drawn in relation to its particular cultural and historical contexts.

Most specifically, Morrissey may be considered in relation to a recognized postmodern practice invoking "flexible" subjectivities, including sexual and gender identities, and its enactment in the realm of pop music. In recent popular-culture criticism such practice has elicited a good deal of comment, both admiring and detracting, of which Susan Bordo's astute feminist critique is especially relevant to my concerns. Bordo contrasts resistance that is "directed against *particular* historical forms of power and subjectivity" with resistance "imagined [by some postmodern theorists] as the refusal to embody *any* positioned subjectivity at all; what is celebrated is continual creative escape from location, containment, and definition." And she identifies examples of the latter in the "plasticity of Madonna's subjectivity," as embodied in her chameleon-like image transformations, and in certain of her music videos.[59]

Unlike some other critics, Bordo finds little liberation in such "*jouissance.*" Rather she perceives in the purportedly playful, tongue-in-cheek expressions of Madonna and some other artists (an example from Ice-T is also cited) an irresponsible disregard toward the oppressive and coercive powers of the images in which they commute. Bordo summarizes:

Turning to Madonna and the liberating postmodern subjectivity that [certain academic and popular-press critics] claim she is offering: the notion that one can play a porno house by night and regain one's androgynous innocence by day [as Madonna portrays in her video, "Open Your Heart to Me"] does not seem to me to be a refusal of essentialist categories about gender, but rather a new inscription of mind/body dualism. What the body does is immaterial, so long as the imagination is free. This abstract, unsituated, disembodied freedom . . . celebrates itself only through the effacement of the material praxis of people's lives, the normalizing power of cultural images, and the sadly continuing social realities of dominance and subordination.[60]

Perhaps Morrissey should be counted among such pop artists whose claims as "daring and resistant transgressors of cultural structures that contain and define" Bordo exposes as facile and false.[61] He alleges, after all, to have "no sexual standpoint whatsoever."[62] Undoubtedly he constructs a rather agile subjectivity in his work: it is readable sometimes in gay terms, sometimes in straight terms, and it involves feminine, cross-gender identification in multiple realms. He has also consistently evaded self-declaration along hetero- and homosexual lines. Morrissey's refusal to assert publicly any gay identification has drawn criticism from various sources—including some fans and press accounts, and at least one pop colleague (Jimmy Somerville, fellow falsettoist of Bronski Beat and Communards fame). But neither has he sought to establish a straight identity. Indeed, unlike so many other stars of speculative sexuality, Morrissey has never presented the kinds of public spectacle by which one presumably qualifies for membership in the Conspicuous Heterosexuality Club.

For purposes of historical contextualization, another factor demands notice. That is, more or less simultaneous with the appearance of the Smiths, and of public ponderings over Morrissey's sexuality, was that of the outing phenomenon. With its advent in the eighties, queer subjects could fear imposition of unwelcome containment and definition not only from outside, homophobic forces, but from their own avowedly queer-identified and -affirmative peers. The impetus came from a new political faction within the queer community, professing belief in the transformative potential and efficacy of coming out. This position, of course, was and remains anything but unanimous in a community that is far from monolithic. In fact, if there is any point of uniformity in queer lives, it lies in the continuing certainty of reduction (to the perceived terms of one's difference), marginalization, and oppression in a queer-phobic, queer-hating culture. Whatever the future prospects for social transformation via coming out, it is this present reality that greets those who do.

Against such cultural and historical backdrops, and from an artistic position of which arcaneness is a refined and defining feature, Morrissey has steadfastly refused to declare (or confirm) a gay subject position. But still he chooses to explore queer themes, in the most knowledgably "inside" of queer-insider language. This sign is abundantly meaningful to other insiders: for queer listeners, Morrissey's work is about queer erotics and experience. I know of no queer fan who perceives Morrissey's work or persona in terms at all straight. Ambiguous, yes—infinitely, ingeniously so; but ambiguity is not particularly confusing to queer subjects, to whom its utility and indeed necessity are intimately known. Even cultivated sexual ambiguity is not something that tends to jam or erase well-formed "gaydar" readings—to the contrary, it tends to reinforce positive readings.

I also know of straight fans who harbor no notion that Morrissey or his work has anything to do with queerness. This perspective (not so rare as it may seem improbable) is readily afforded by mainstream ignorance of queer codes, and supported by the economy of compulsory heterosexuality. Morrissey's international following is considerable, and includes an oft-remarked male majority, particularly in Britain, where the Smiths "became a fundamental part of male adolescence, alongside acne and soccer."[63] This following includes numerous straight-identified members (even, undoubtedly, homophobic elements). And these fans too feel that their idol is singing directly to them and their experiences. Thus the question may arise: is one or another constituency being deceived or manipulated? Is Morrissey therefore an artistic fraud?

My answer is that if Morrissey is a fraud, it's not on this account. Perhaps the real question here is whether one can effectively resist and destabilize the hegemonic forms of subjectivity, while refusing containment in any of them. In his acknowledged attempts to decentralize the control of gender and sexuality, Morrissey has indeed evaded subjective containment—but not through indiscriminate refusal of any subject position whatever. Other pop artists, displaying what Bordo has called "true postmodern fashion," may deny any serious artistic intent for their ironic and ambiguous gestures.[64] But Morrissey's renowned irony and ambiguity contravene contemporary fashion, situated as they are by his effusions on the importance of pop music and its message.[65] Surely there is a difference between the postmodern resistance that primarily expresses "rebelliousness and a desire to fuck with people"[66] and Morrissey's project of resistance directed consistently, for over a decade, toward particular historical forms of subjectivity.

One of these forms is conventional masculinity. Morrissey's cross-gender identifications depart, however, from the usual pop-rock strategies, pioneered by his beloved New York Dolls. His approach involves not visual signs of cross-dressing and -comportment, but the more subliminal means of musical rhetoric, and allusively sophisticated textual identifications with feminine subjects—heroized, feminist (or protofeminist) figures like Joan of Arc, Virginia Woolf, Molly Haskell, and Susan Brownmiller.[67]

Morrissey's resistance is also directed toward sexuality. Presented with the standard sexuality ballot, he selects "none of the above," and specifies a write-in choice: celibacy. It's an odd choice, and a unique self-designation among pop-rock stars; it places him in a category reserved for nuns, monks, and scattered, scarcely noticed pre-, post-, or asexual others, whose full subject status is rendered problematical by their membership here. Of course this conventional form of celibacy is weakened by Morrissey's presence, and the distinct erotics of his work and persona.

From both artistic and commercial perspectives, it's not difficult to imagine why Morrissey might wish to resist containment in the binary categories of contemporary sexual subjectivity—particularly when the one most eagerly offered (by the media) is that of homosexuality. Not all forms of subjectivity are equally containing, of course; such is the essence of difference, of Otherness. The neutrality that is ascribed to a normalized subject position (whiteness, maleness, straightness) carries with it the broadest range of possibilities for both empathic appeal and individual particularities. The Other's position is more circumscribed, and, significantly, less valent; such is the essence of marginalization and ghettoization. Straight experiences, concerns, loves are everyone's concerns, whereas gay concerns are presumed to be relevant only to gay subjects.

Some would argue for direct and explicit insurgency as the only appropriate response to such constrictive, coercive social structures. But the more circuitous route by which Morrissey's work is received offers some undeniable advantages, to his accessibility agenda and, hence, to subversion. He claims that he wants to "write for everybody," and in this he seems at least partly successful. His celibacy platform is strange, but not alienating; to an extent unavailable via homosexual or bisexual (even heterosexual) identification, it eludes foreclosure on the full range of themes and qualities in his work—including not only sex and gender issues, but loneliness, literariness, wit, dourness, irony, and so on. In this way his work and persona remain "relevant" and susceptible to the identification needs and desires of even widely divergent audiences.[68] Ultimately, however, Morrissey's work does not speak to "everybody." His most ardent devotees have been described as "[h]igh-IQ misfits and fervent introverts"—surely there are limits on such a fan base.[69] But if Morrissey's greatest appeal is to misfits and introverts, it appears, at least, to embrace misfits and introverts of all sexual and gender outlooks.

Thus in addressing signification in Morrissey's songs, I don't intend or hope to fix them with determinate meaning: neither to contribute to the already bloated discourses of sanitizing normalization, nor to "out" his work and thus reduce it from the opposite direction. Either choice represents a surrender to the tyranny of literalism, and a failure of imagination. Moreover, neither choice represents the work's actual reception. Even Keith Howes's recent book, an encyclopedia of homosexuality in the British media, defines the Smiths as a "pop band of the early 1980s, whose moody lyrics . . . could be interpreted in a number of ways."[70] And these measured (if suggestive) tones emanate from a volume entitled *Broadcasting It*, whose neon-pink cover features three men in high retro-drag—all bold eyeliner, blond beehives, and polka-dot minidresses.

Morrissey's music is rife with sex and gender anomalies, and traffics heavily in gay-insider-coded meanings—to an extent perhaps only hinted at by the limited examples given here. And these preoccupations surface even more strikingly in Morrissey's post-1987, solo work: viewed with any awareness of the insider codes, releases like *Viva Hate* (1988) and *Bona Drag* (1990), especially, seem positively like gay theme-albums. Both the title of *Bona Drag* and its first track, "Piccadilly Palare," use palari, an underground language of gay Londoners and lingua franca of "gypsies, tramps, thieves and chorus boys."[71] And song titles on the solo albums include "Hairdresser on Fire," "Billy Budd," "Lucky Lisp," and "I Am Hated for Loving"; significantly, however, and in classic Morrissey fashion, these flaming, flaunting titles are less amplified and clarified than coyly equivocated by the songs that follow.

Clearly, any listening or criticism of Morrissey's oeuvre that ignores the relevant codes and secret languages neglects a crucial part of the picture. But to ghettoize this music under some reductive rubric of "gay rock," as certain observers would have it,[72] is also to miss the point rather completely—as I hope my readings have suggested. Far more rewarding than either of these extremes is to claim all the potential resonances of the work, in its rich multiplicity and adroit resistance to univocal interpretation.

NOTES

Earlier versions of this paper were presented to audiences at the Seventeenth Annual Meeting of the Society for Music Theory in Tallahassee (1994), Feminist Theory and Music 3 in Riverside (1995), the University of Michigan School of Music, and Wayne State University; I am grateful for their input, some of which has been incorporated into the present version. Acknowledgment is due to two anonymous respondents and the editors of *Genders* for their astute readings and suggestions, by which the essay has benefited considerably. I'd like also to express sincere thanks to all my friends and colleagues who have lent their insights, support, and encouragement to this project, including particularly Lisa Bowersox, Robert Hatten, Kevin Kopelson, Angela Le Compte, Fred Maus, and Andrew Mead.

1. Quoted in Fred Hauptfuhrer, "Roll Over, Bob Dylan, and Tell Madonna the News: The Smiths' Morrissey Is Pop's Latest Messiah," *People Weekly* (24 June 1985): 105–6.

2. The same viewpoint is expressed in numerous interviews and articles, however.

3. I read the title as a reference (characteristically oblique) to the vinyl disc— equally, compact disc or record.

4. Line division, punctuation, and capitalization in all Morrissey's song texts cited here follow that given in the booklets accompanying *The Smiths Best . . . I*, and *The Smiths . . . Best II* (see discography).

5. A relevant observation is registered in Mark Peel, "Viva Morrissey," review of *Viva Hate*, *Stereo Review* 53 (July 1988): 85: "Morrissey is so accustomed

to writing in the first person that he ends up being a spokesman for views you can't quite believe he'd admit to."

6. Julian Stringer, "The Smiths: Repressed (but Remarkably Dressed)," *Popular Music* 11, no. 1 (1992): 15. Stringer opens his article with a fine critical analysis of star image and the representations of stars in journalistic biographical discourse.

7. This "slim volume" was published two years later, in 1981, as *The New York Dolls*, according to William Shaw, "Homme Alone 2: Lost in Los Angeles," *Details* (Apr. 1994): 107.

8. This is pointed out and variously illustrated in Robert Walser, *Running with the Devil: Power, Gender, and Madness in Heavy Metal Music* (Hanover, NH: University Press of New England, 1993), 147.

9. Simon Frith and Angela McRobbie, "Rock and Sexuality," *Screen Education* 29 (1978–79): 3–19, reprinted in *On Record: Rock, Pop, and the Written Word*, ed. Simon Frith and Andrew Goodwin (New York: Pantheon, 1990), 371–89.

10. See, for example, Simon Frith, "Afterthoughts," in *On Record*, ed. Frith and Goodwin, 419–24; and Jon Savage, "The Enemy Within: Sex, Rock, and Identity," in *Facing the Music: A Pantheon Guide to Popular Culture*, ed. Simon Frith (New York: Pantheon, 1989), 131–72. Offerings from the popular press include the Morrissey articles by Hauptfuhrer, Henke, Fricke, and Shaw cited here.

11. This has also been noted in Simon Frith, "Towards an Aesthetic of Popular Music," in *Music and Society*, ed. Richard Leppert and Susan McClary (New York: Cambridge University Press, 1987), 145; Susan McClary and Robert Walser, "Start Making Sense! Musicology Wrestles with Rock," in *On Record*, ed. Frith and Goodwin, 285–86; and Walser, *Running with the Devil*, xiv, 21, and 28. Walser's and McClary's work provides notable exceptions to this music-ignoring tendency.

12. The resemblance between Marr's name and the popular French idiom *j'en ai marre* (essentially, "I've had it up to here") seems uncanny, especially given the prevalence of the punk "no future"/on-the-dole outlook in early-eighties Britain. Apparently it is mere happenstance: according to biographer Johnny Rogan, the guitarist made only one change to his given name, in 1983 adopting the present spelling so as to distinguish himself from Buzzcocks drummer John Maher. See Rogan, *Morrissey and Marr: The Severed Alliance* (London: Omnibus Press, 1992), 163.

13. Morrissey's recurrent themes and charged images include dreams; despair; betrayal, beleaguering, and demoralization at the hands of one's intimates; bicycle mishaps; alienation; fat women; self-mockery and -deprecation; criminals; and dogged pursuit of a disinterested love object. This list is partial and selective, and undeniably reflects my own fascinations with Morrissey's creative fetishes.

14. All these songs can be found on two disc volumes, *The Smiths Best . . . I*, and *The Smiths . . . Best II*, in addition to their respective original releases (see discography). It seems both desirable and essential to define clearly one's historical frame of reference in this realm: things have changed pretty rapidly over the last decade vis-à-vis society's general awareness of issues of gender and sexuality,

and hence, meanings have shifted. Too, gender and sexuality have a very different presence in pop music today than in the mid-eighties. Queer presence in particular is radically redefined by k.d. lang, Indigo Girls, Melissa Etheridge, Erasure, and others who have appeared on the scene since that time. Surely it would be premature to proclaim any "death of the closet" in pop music, however; as the work of some of these very artists attests, coded meaning, and reliance on the mechanisms of insider/outsider perceptions, are alive and well.

15. Sources for these three viewpoints are, respectively, James Henke, "Oscar! Oscar! Great Britain Goes Wilde for the 'Fourth-Gender' Smiths," *Rolling Stone* (7 June 1984): 45; Hauptfuhrer, "Roll Over, Bob Dylan," 105; and David Fricke, "Keeping Up with the Smiths," *Rolling Stone* (9 Oct. 1986): 33.

16. Hauptfuhrer, "Roll Over, Bob Dylan," 106. A similarly ineffectual boy-girl scenario is depicted in the Smiths song "Half a Person." This quotation is, of course, one of those references that can be interpreted as proof of either heterosexuality or homosexuality. In the context of the mainstream media (and indeed, the article just cited pushes hard on the heterosexual interpretation) and compulsory heterosexuality, the reference is conventionally read as a statement of (distressed) heterosexuality. As always, however, particular subjects' situations will lead them to read against conventional norms, and Morrissey's words may also satisfy those seeking statements of homosexuality, or asexuality.

17. See Paul Evans, "Morrissey," *Rolling Stone* (21 Jan. 1993): 24; and Shaw, "Homme Alone 2," 102, respectively. Critics elsewhere have expressed views reinforcing each of these.

18. Among the Smiths songs, examples of the former type include "This Charming Man," "William, It Was Really Nothing," "Hand in Glove," and, arguably, "There Is a Light That Never Goes Out"; examples of the latter type include "Girlfriend in a Coma," "Half a Person," and "Sheila Take a Bow." Interestingly, the female object of desire seems to disappear from Morrissey's more recent solo work.

19. Fricke, "Keeping Up," 33.

20. Henke, "Oscar! Oscar!" 45.

21. The famous phrase is that of Karl Heinrich Ulrichs, from a book of 1868. See Gert Hekma, " 'A Female Soul in a Male Body': Sexual Inversion as Gender Inversion in Nineteenth-Century Sexology," in *Third Sex, Third Gender: Beyond Dimorphism in Culture and History*, ed. Gilbert Herdt (New York: Zone Books, 1994), 219.

22. Frank Rose, "The Smiths," *Nation* (3–10 Aug. 1985): 91.

23. See, for example, Fricke, "Keeping Up," 33; Hauptfuhrer, "Roll Over, Bob Dylan," 106; and Henke, "Oscar! Oscar!" 45.

24. An exception to this critical norm is provided by Stringer, "The Smiths," 15–26. The author examines several elements of the Smiths' image—English identity, white ethnicity, emotion, and sexuality—in connection with qualities of their music. I find his insights percipient, even if I am not always satisfied by his musical analyses, which indulge at times (like much journalistic rock criticism) in a pastiche-like rhetoric of unexplained catch-phrases and unsubstantiated semiotic characterizations.

25. Frith, "Towards an Aesthetic of Popular Music," 145.

26. The song transcriptions are my own.

27. The latter phrase appears in Evans, "Morrissey," 24.

28. The terms *foreground* and *middleground* originate in the work of the Austrian music theorist Heinrich Schenker (1868–1935). Schenker and his followers analyze tonal music in terms of hierarchic levels, namely, foreground, or actual musical surface; middleground, in which embellishing details are partially stripped away; and background, representing an ideal structural "skeleton" of the music.

29. Another structural and semiotic factor in these melodies, on which I'll comment only briefly here, is their rhythmic quality. In this realm, too, inactivity constitutes a salient feature and a mark of difference. But rhythmic inactivity in Morrissey's songs tends to work in its own rather specific way: that is, longer passages of rhythmic stagnation are followed by (indeed *answered* by) short bursts of rhythmic activity. An instance is found in "Half a Person" (see example): rhythm is sustained, widely spaced, and deferred by syncopation on "Call me morbid, call me pale / I've spent six years on your trail"; then, in a relative flurry of vocal and accompanimental rhythm, come the (musically and textually) amplifying lines, "Six full years of my life / On your trail." The opening stanza of "This Charming Man" is in some ways comparable, though here the answering rhythmic burst delivers a suggestive stroke that meaningfully inflects and augments (again, musically and textually)—rather than repeating or amplifying—that which precedes it. This little burst soon turns out to have been a mere foreshadowing, however, of the more climactic one comprising the whole of the third stanza.

30. The "silver-lamé" metaphor recalls an earlier reference to the shirt Morrissey wore on stage that night. See Evans, "Morrissey," 24.

31. Henke, "Oscar! Oscar!" 45. An apparently echoing reference, "his voice has been described as dronish," appears the following year in Hauptfuhrer, "Roll Over, Bob Dylan," 105.

32. *Sprechstimme* is a technique of half-speaking and half-singing introduced by Arnold Schoenberg in his *Pierrot lunaire*, op. 21 (1912). One could cite in comparison a number of pop vocalists, including not only Dylan but Leonard Cohen, Rickie Lee Jones, Tom Petty, Robbie Robertson, and Neil Young.

33. Every other popular-press characterization of Morrissey's singing known to me confirms my assessment here, and favors a "crooning" trope over anything involving speech. A sampling taken only from *Rolling Stone* yields references to "a choirboy's tremulous cry" (Fricke, "Keeping Up," 33); "Edith Piaf-on-the dole vocals" and "croons and hoots" (Mark Coleman, review of *The Queen Is Dead*, *Rolling Stone* [11 Sept. 1986]: 94; and idem, review of *Your Arsenal*, *Rolling Stone* [29 Oct. 1992]: 69); and "idiosyncratic crooning" (Evans, "Morrissey," 24).

34. Marcia J. Citron, "Gender and the Field of Musicology," *Current Musicology* 53 (1993): 70.

35. These run roughly parallel with those detailed more fully by Citron (ibid.); that she breaks such issues down to simplest, clearest terms is quite useful, given music scholars' widely varying levels of openness and sophistication toward

humanities critical and theoretical discourses (not to mention past polemics and misapprehensions arising therefrom).

36. By Foucault's well-known account, modern homosexuality was born in 1870 and heterosexuality created subsequently, in contradistinction. Michel Foucault, *The History of Sexuality*, vol. 1, *An Introduction*, trans. Robert Hurley (New York: Pantheon, 1978), 42.

37. Recent serious-music scholarship that does take up issues of musical meaning includes Fred Everett Maus, "Music as Drama," *Music Theory Spectrum* 10 (1988): 56–73; Susan McClary, *Feminine Endings* (Minneapolis: University of Minnesota Press, 1991); Robert S. Hatten, *Musical Meaning in Beethoven: Markedness, Correlation, and Interpretation* (Bloomington: Indiana University Press, 1994); and other examples, in growing numbers.

38. As the first line in her definitive rendition of the Robbie Robertson song, "The Night They Drove Ol' Dixie Down."

39. I find Prince's song "I Wanna Be Your Girlfriend" an excellent example in this regard; of course, many artists could be cited, including the New York Dolls, Madonna, David Bowie, and Mick Jagger.

40. Glenn Watkins, *Soundings: Music in the Twentieth Century* (New York: Schirmer, 1988), 275. Watkins's brief, eloquent discussion of this song invokes a number of the coded characterizations that accrue to it—including "languorous," "seductive," "torch song," and Pierre Bernac's reference to it as "the laziest" song ever written—and that confirm the conventionality and intersubjectivity of its sex-marked and gendered meaning.

41. It was Peter Bloom who identified the passage from Marx, *Die Lehre von der musikalischen Komposition* (1845) as possibly the first statement of thematic contrast in terms of a "masculine-feminine analogy." See Bloom's communication to *Journal of the American Musicological Society* 27 (1974): 161–62. I translate Marx's *schmiegsam* as "supple," whereas Bloom uses "flexibly" (and restructures the grammar a bit at this point).

42. Francis Poulenc, *My Friends and Myself* (1963), trans. J. Harding (London: Dennis Dobson, 1978), 31. Quoted in Watkins, *Soundings*, 274.

43. At the same time, incidentally, his eyeglasses, functional and corrective of nearsightedness, have tended to be worn only offstage and in private.

44. Hauptfuhrer, "Roll Over, Bob Dylan," 106.

45. The name is Irish, but this vernacular usage is now chiefly Australian and New Zealander; antipodal usages are widely familiar among Britons, however.

46. See also Morrissey's latest U.S. single (as of the time of this writing), "The More You Ignore Me, the Closer I Get," in which the narrator clearly is stalking the object of his second-person address. The narrating subject appears desperately consumed by obsession, *Fatal Attraction*-style, in songs like the Smiths' "What Difference Does It Make?" ("The devil will find work for idle hands to do / I stole and I lied, and why? because you asked me to / but now you make me feel so ashamed / because I've only got two hands / well, I'm still fond of you") and Morrissey's "Last of the Famous International Playboys" ("Reggie Kray—do you know my name? / don't say you don't / please say you do . . . but

I never wanted to kill / I AM NOT NATURALLY EVIL / such things I do / just to make myself / more attractive to you / HAVE I FAILED?").

47. The phrase appears in Simon Reynolds, "An Enigmatic Morrissey Still Battles His Demons," review of *Vauxhall and I*, *New York Times* (4 Apr. 1994): 34 (sec. 2).

48. A wonderfully insightful and entertaining recent discussion of camp signification (including typographics) and some related issues is found in Kevin Kopelson's review of Wayne Koestenbaum, *The Queen's Throat*. See Kopelson, "Tawdrily, I Adore Him," *19th-Century Music* 17, no. 3 (1994): 274–85.

49. If there are hints of intertextual paths leading into the song, there is also some path leading away from it: for reasons not entirely clear to me (except insofar as Araki has publicly professed admiration for the Smiths), Daryl Chin uses the title "Girlfriend in a Coma: Notes on the Films of Gregg Araki" for his contribution to *Queer Looks: Perspectives on Lesbian and Gay Film and Video*, ed. Martha Gever, Pratibha Parmar, and John Greyson (New York: Routledge, 1993).

50. The song was the Smiths' second single, and first chart hit, in 1983.

51. *Melisma* refers to a more or less extended melodic passage set to a single syllable of text, usually to expressive effect.

52. It is likewise, of course, in Wilde's writing. Another, quite explicit, occurrence in Morrissey's lyrics is the refrain of "Still Ill": "Does the body rule the mind / or does the mind rule the body? / I dunno. . . ."

53. Such *double entendre* may be more likely for listeners familiar with some of Morrissey's other references. In "Hand in Glove," for instance (a Smiths song explicitly about a socially taboo love; its specific makeup as male-to-male is not explicit but clear enough, the assiduous avoidance of pronouns notwithstanding— even *a fortiori*), posterior imagery is planted from the very first words: "Hand in glove / the sun shines out of our behinds."

54. Fricke, "Keeping Up," 32.

55. Frith and McRobbie define "cock rock," in contrast with "teenybop," as "music making in which performance is an explicit, crude and often aggressive expression of male sexuality" ("Rock and Sexuality," 5–8).

56. Charles Ives, *Memos*, ed. John Kirkpatrick (New York: W. W. Norton, 1972), 136. Ives (1874–1954) was an American composer with firm roots in New England and its Transcendentalism. That he also kept, throughout his musical career, firm roots in the New York insurance industry (as a successful fulltime businessman) had evidently to do with the gynophobia and homophobia that often attach, in our culture, to the identity "musician." His vehement expressions of such phobic attitudes are examined in some recent musicological discourse, including Maynard Solomon, "Charles Ives: Some Questions of Veracity," *Journal of the American Musicological Society* 40, no. 3 (1987): 466–68; Nora Beck, "An Examination of Gender in Selected Writings and Music of Charles Ives" (Paper presented at the conference "Feminist Theory and Music: Toward a Common Language," Minneapolis, 28 June 1991); Lawrence Kramer, "Ives's Misogyny and Post-Reconstruction America" (Paper presented at the conference "Feminist Theory and Music: Toward a Common Language," Minneapolis, 28 June 1991);

and Stuart Feder, *Charles Ives, "My Father's Song": A Psychoanalytic Biography* (New Haven: Yale University Press, 1992).

57. It is worth noting that rock performances in which "gender bending" is primarily a visual (or even verbal) affair often involve musical gestures, including virtuosic ones, undifferentiated from those of "gender-normative" performances. But virtuosity, which is conventionally gendered masculine, is not a feature of the inactive melodies cited above. See Walser, *Running with the Devil*, 126, for further discussion of the gendering of virtuosity in rock.

58. T. S. Eliot, "The Dry Salvages." Quoted in Kendall L. Walton, "What Is Abstract about the Art of Music?" *Journal of Aesthetics and Art Criticism* 46, no. 3 (1988): 351.

59. Susan Bordo, "'Material Girl': The Effacements of Postmodern Culture," *Michigan Quarterly Review* 29, no. 4 (1990): 669–75.

60. Ibid., 676.

61. Ibid.

62. Hauptfuhrer, "Roll Over, Bob Dylan," 106.

63. Ibid.

64. As does Madonna, according to Bordo, " 'Material Girl,' " 673.

65. This unfashionableness has been noted in the popular press. William Shaw, for example, in recalling his first meeting with Morrissey in 1983, remarks on his outpouring of "a giant love of pop music that none of his would-be cool contemporaries seemed able to match." See Shaw, "Homme Alone 2," 104.

66. Madonna, "White Heat," interview by Kevin Sessums, *Vanity Fair* (April 1990): 208. Quoted in Bordo, " 'Material Girl,' " 673.

67. The reference to Joan occurs in "Big Mouth Strikes Again," and the Woolf reference (invoking *A Room of One's Own*) in the title of the Smiths' "Shakespeare's Sister"; Morrissey claims important sympathies with feminist authors, including Haskell and Brownmiller, in a 1985 interview (Hauptfuhrer, "Roll Over, Bob Dylan," 105).

68. This phenomenon has been exposed and explored in relation to Elvis Presley and his differing audiences: see Sue Wise, "Sexing Elvis," in *On Record*, ed. Frith and Goodwin, 390–98.

69. The description is from Evans, "Morrissey," 24.

70. Keith Howes, *Broadcasting It: An Encyclopaedia of Homosexuality on Film, Radio and TV in the UK 1923–1993* (New York: Cassell, 1993), s.v. "Smiths."

71. Ibid., s.v. "polari." Variants of *palari* include *polari, parlari, palare*, and *parlyaree*.

72. For example, Henke ("Oscar! Oscar!" 45) claims at the outset of his 1984 article that Morrissey "admits that he's gay." He later writes, in discussing the songs, "it would appear that his is largely a homosexual viewpoint," and— coincidentally?—delivers a higher density of gay-cliché-loaded references than any other Morrissey commentator I've encountered (ascribing, within short space, an "upper-crust" English accent, tendency to extravagance, disinterest in teenage dating and sports, and great importance to Oscar Wilde and James Dean). One can only speculate as to the possible relevance of Morrissey's contemptuously

titled song "Journalists Who Lie" (on the 1991 CD maxi-single *Our Frank*, Sire/Reprise 9362–40043–2).

DISCOGRAPHY

Chronologically ordered, of Morrissey's albums (U.S., on CD) with the Smiths and as solo artist

Smiths. 1984a. *The Smiths*. Sire/Rough Trade 7599–25065–2. Reel around the Fountain; You've Got Everything Now; Miserable Lie; Pretty Girls Make Graves; The Hand That Rocks the Cradle; This Charming Man; Still Ill; Hand in Glove; What Difference Does It Make?; I Don't Owe You Anything; Suffer Little Children.
———. 1984b. *Hatful of Hollow*. Sire/Reprise 9362–45205–2. William, It Was Really Nothing; What Difference Does It Make?; These Things Take Time; This Charming Man; How Soon Is Now?; Handsome Devil; Hand in Glove; Still Ill; Heaven Knows I'm Miserable Now; This Night Has Opened My Eyes; You've Got Everything Now; Accept Yourself; Girl Afraid; Back to the Old House; Reel around the Fountain; Please, Please, Please, Let Me Get What I Want.
———. 1985. *Meat Is Murder*. Sire/Rough Trade 7599–25269–2. The Headmaster Ritual; Rusholme Ruffians; I Want the One I Can't Have; What She Said; That Joke Isn't Funny Anymore; How Soon Is Now?; Nowhere Fast; Well I Wonder; Barbarism Begins at Home; Meat Is Murder.
———. 1986. *The Queen Is Dead*. Sire/Rough Trade 7599–25426–2. The Queen Is Dead; Frankly, Mr. Shankly; I Know It's Over; Never Had No One Ever; Cemetry [sic] Gates; Bigmouth Strikes Again; The Boy with the Thorn in His Side; Vicar in a Tutu; There Is a Light That Never Goes Out; Some Girls Are Bigger Than Others.
———. 1987a. *Louder Than Bombs*. Sire/Rough Trade 7599–25569–2. Is It Really So Strange?; Sheila Take a Bow; Shoplifters of the World Unite; Sweet and Tender Hooligan; Half a Person; London; Panic; Girl Afraid; Shakespeare's Sister; William, It Was Really Nothing; You Just Haven't Earned It Yet, Baby; Heaven Knows I'm Miserable Now; Ask; Golden Lights; Oscillate Wildly; These Things Take Time; Rubber Ring; Back to the Old House; Hand in Glove; Stretch Out and Wait; Please Please Please Let Me Get What I Want; This Night Has Opened My Eyes; Unloveable; Asleep.
———. 1987b. *Strangeways, Here We Come*. Sire/Rough Trade 7599–25649–2. A Rush and a Push and the Land is Ours; I Started Something I Couldn't Finish; Death of a Disco Dancer; Girlfriend in a Coma; Stop Me if You Think You've Heard This One Before; Last Night I Dreamt That Somebody Loved Me; Unhappy Birthday; Paint a Vulgar Picture; Death at One's Elbow; I Won't Share You.
Morrissey. 1988. *Viva Hate*. Sire/Reprise 9362–25699–2. Alsatian Cousin; Little Man, What Now?; Everyday Is Like Sunday; Bengali in Platforms; Angel,

Angel, Down We Go Together; Late Night, Maudlin Street; Suedehead; Break Up the Family; Hairdresser on Fire; The Ordinary Boys; I Don't Mind if You Forget Me; Dial-a-Cliché; Margaret on the Guillotine.

Smiths. 1988. *Rank* (live album). Sire/Rough Trade 7599–25786–2. The Queen Is Dead; Panic; Vicar in a Tutu; Ask; Rusholme Ruffians; The Boy with the Thorn in His Side; What She Said; Is It Really So Strange?; Cemetry Gates; London; I Know It's Over; The Draize Train; Still Ill; Bigmouth Strikes Again.

Morrissey. 1990. *Bona Drag*. Sire/Reprise 9362–26221–2. Piccadilly Palare; Interesting Drug; November Spawned a Monster; Will Never Marry; Such a Little Thing Makes Such a Big Difference; The Last of the Famous International Playboys; Ouija Board, Ouija Board; Hairdresser on Fire; Everyday Is Like Sunday; He Knows I'd Love to See Him; Yes, I Am Blind; Lucky Lisp; Suedehead; Disappointed.

———. 1991. *Kill Uncle*. Sire/Reprise 9362–26514–2. Our Frank; Asian Rut; Sing Your Life; Mute Witness; King Leer; Found Found Found; Driving Your Girlfriend Home; (I'm) The End of the Family Line; There's a Place in Hell for Me and My Friends.

———. 1992. *Your Arsenal*. Sire/Reprise 9362–26994–2. You're Gonna Need Someone on Your Side; Glamorous Glue; We'll Let You Know; The National Front Disco; Certain People I Know; We Hate It When Our Friends Become Successful; You're the One for Me, Fatty; Seasick, Yet Still Docked; I Know It's Gonna Happen Someday; Tomorrow.

Smiths. 1992a. *The Smiths Best . . . I*. Sire/Reprise 9362–45042–2. This Charming Man; William, It Was Really Nothing; What Difference Does It Make?; Stop Me if You Think You've Heard This One Before; Girlfriend in a Coma; Half a Person; Rubber Ring; How Soon Is Now?; Hand in Glove; Shoplifters of the World Unite; Sheila Take a Bow; Some Girls Are Bigger Than Others; Panic; Please, Please, Please, Let Me Get What I Want.

———. 1992b. *The Smiths . . . Best II*. Sire/Reprise 9362–45097–2. The Boy with the Thorn in His Side; The Headmaster Ritual; Heaven Knows I'm Miserable Now; Ask; Oscillate Wildly; Nowhere Fast; Still Ill; Bigmouth Strikes Again; That Joke Isn't Funny Anymore; Shakespeare's Sister; Girl Afraid; Reel around the Fountain; Last Night I Dreamt That Somebody Loved Me; There Is a Light That Never Goes Out.

Morrissey. 1994. *Vauxhall and I*. Sire/Reprise 9362–45451–2. Now My Heart Is Full; Spring-Heeled Jim; Billy Budd; Hold On to Your Friends; The More You Ignore Me, the Closer I Get; Why Don't You Find Out for Yourself; I Am Hated for Loving; Lifeguard Sleeping, Girl Drowning; Used to Be a Sweet Boy; The Lazy Sunbathers; Speedway.

———. 1995. *World of Morrissey*. Sire/Reprise 9362–45879–2. Whatever Happens, I Love You; Billy Budd; Jack the Ripper; Have-a-Go Merchant; The Loop; Sister I'm a Poet; You're the One for Me, Fatty; Boxers; Moon River; My Love Life; Certain People I Know; The Last of the Famous International Playboys; We'll Let You Know; Spring-Heeled Jim.

ELEVEN

Lost Boys and Angry Ghouls: Vietnam's Undead

Amanda Howell

[W]ar . . . requires both the reciprocal infliction of massive injury and the eventual disowning of the injury so that its attributes can be transferred elsewhere, as
they cannot if they are permitted to cling to the original site of the wound, the
human body.

—Elaine Scarry, *The Body in Pain*[1]

Myth deprives the object of which it speaks of all History.

—Roland Barthes, *Mythologies*[2]

After her husband, an Air Force colonel, was declared missing in action
in 1967, Emma Hagerman became one of the first members of the National League of Families of American Prisoners and Missing in Southeast
Asia. In 1976, she testified before the House Select Committee on Missing Persons in Southeast Asia as to the effect of the POW/MIA issue on
American families who wait and watch for the return of lost husbands
and sons. She commented bitterly on both the power and strange logic of
images that deny the effects of war and time on the body: "we families
have become emotional cripples . . . some families . . . no longer look for
an accounting, but are waiting for a resurrection."[3]

In the horror films *Deathdream* (1972),[4] *House* (1986), *Jacob's Ladder*
(1990), and *Universal Soldier* (1992), dead, missing, and imprisoned American soldiers *are* resurrected, and they return to the United States as

monsters. These films privilege states of bodily dissolution disavowed by the persistent belief in living POWs. Yet one can learn a great deal from these horror films about the fears and desires that animate the POW/MIA fantasy—the fantasy of the always-imminent-yet-deferred return. These films are symptomatic of not only the desire to disown the injuries of Vietnam but also the fascination exerted by those losses and the compulsion to repeat them.[5] Focusing on the undead body, a body that is at once KIA, MIA, and POW, these films dramatize the voyeurism and fetishism that structure public fascination with the missing.[6] Popular narratives (including but not limited to film) constructed around the POW/MIA clearly objectify that figure: they make the missing the center of a mystery, the object of obsessive and inquiring looks. The POW/MIA is the focus too of fetishistic adoration—in the marketing of bracelets, and more recently, in the search for bones and relics of American dead in Southeast Asia. These films serve as further evidence of our cultural fascination with the missing, even as their strikingly paranoid narratives deal thematically with the objectification and fetishization of the POW/MIA. In so doing, these films negotiate anxieties about masculinity and material history, representation and the control of perception.

In what James Donald would call their "lurid obsession with archaism and liminality," these films suggest the fragility of the masculine ideal constructed and the national identity supported by fantasies of the missing.[7] These horror films figure troubled masculinity in terms of bodies that are out of control: bodies at the mercy of their own inscrutable cellular workings, the nefarious plots of the military and government, and the instability of their own perceptions. These depictions of Vietnam's undead undercut the traditional coherence of cinematic masculinity and thus call into question the model of masculinity in use by feminist film theory over the last twenty years—a model centered on the male voyeur and fetishist, on the white male prerogative of vision and power, on the control of the male body and its foreclosure as an object of vision. Fictions constructed around the missing focus on a male—rather than a female—body that is the object of fetishizing or punishing looks. Thus what Donald notes as the central generic trope of the horror film, an obsession with "the instability of culture, the impossibility of its closure or perfection" (247), appears in these films as a disruption of classic cinema's scopic regime and the gendered division of its narratives. However, to simply reverse the terms of activity and passivity (proposed most notably by Laura Mulvey's "Visual Pleasure and Narrative Cinema"),[8] to discuss, for instance, the "feminization" of the missing on film, does not seem particularly useful. Such a move would only confirm and further mystify the gendered divisions of the patriarchal nation/family by which these texts are organized. Feminist theoretical accounts of unconscious fantasy, however, provide the means to consider how the POW/MIA fantasy works—that is, how the viewer/believer's desires might work through its scenarios—to both resist and support patriarchal dominance. At the same time that horror films imagine the missing as pursued, penetrated, abject, and objectified, they also facilitate the disavowal of war's injuries. This apparent contradiction is not accidental, but is central to the appeal of the POW/MIA and of the fantasies constructed around him.

MISSING MEN

Every war has had missing soldiers; only with the Vietnam War have the missing become the focus of so much popular concern and debate. Narratives constructed around the missing are central to America's understanding of Vietnam (both the war and the country) and how the public negotiates its wartime losses. Under the Clinton administration, most official discussion of the American missing in Southeast Asia centers on the recovery of remains. Yet even with the move toward normalization of United States relations with Vietnam, the language to discuss the recovery of the missing is sufficiently ambiguous to allow for the possibility of bringing home not only bones and fragments, but live POWs as well. The April 1994 advertisement for the "It's Time—Bring Them Home!" watch (figure 1) is a literal rendering of the POW/MIA fantasy, notable in that it not only presumes the existence of living POWs of the Vietnam War, but also extends that belief retroactively to the missing of the Korean War as well. The double image of the commemorative color print adopted as the official symbol of the Live POW Lobby in 1993 depicts Vietnam as a land outside time, still war-torn, and covered in barbed wire—even as the hourglass indicates that time is running out for the aging, but still alive, American POW.

However fantastic such a representation might seem, official origins of the belief in living POWs are clear enough: in the late 1960s the Pentagon created a category that mingled internal classifications of MIA and POW,

FIG. 1. "It's Time—Bring Them Home!" (advertisement), *Vietnam*, April 1994, 74. By permission of Financial Services of America, Inc.

and thereby suggested that any American whose body is missing in Southeast Asia is in fact a living prisoner of war.[9] Popular concern over and awareness of the POW/MIAs were the result of the efforts of several groups working independently to educate and agitate the public on their behalf. The first of these groups was the League of Families, which currently serves as an official liaison between the Department of Defense and the American public on all POW/MIA matters. The league originated in 1967 as a sorority of POW/MIA wives who worked to increase public and government awareness of the plight of their husbands; by 1969, the issue of the POW/MIAs had also been taken up by a number of more overtly political right-wing groups, formed by concerned citizens like Ross Perot. For such groups, the POW/MIAs were a rallying point for anti-antiwar fervor and a focal point for the so-called silent majority. In 1968 and 1969 Americans had seen filmic and photographic evidence of the brutality of America and its allies to their enemies: the massacre at My Lai, the cruel conditions of Saigon's prison camps, the tiger cages of Con Son Island. From 1969 to 1973, however, through publicity campaigns funded directly and indirectly by the government,[10] the image of the missing American soldier supplanted other images of the war's violence, as the POW/MIA issue allowed Nixon to represent the United States as the victim, rather than the aggressor, of the war in Southeast Asia (Clarke 29–37; Franklin 49–54). Jonathan Schell observed in the *New Yorker* that, by 1972, "many people were persuaded that the United States was fighting in Vietnam in order to get its prisoners back."[11]

The only organization with authority to speak for POW/MIA families, in 1973 the league opened its membership to "professional philanthropists" (including Carol Bates, the originator of the POW/MIA bracelet) who proclaimed themselves the "adopted" families of the missing (Clarke 37–43; Franklin 54–87).[12] While by the mid-1970s it had become clear to many wives of the missing that the government had used its obligation to them to prolong the war, the league's new leadership strongly protested status changes and argued that only the addition of new information could justify a change to KIA (Clarke 39–46).[13] Resistance to status changes persisted even after 1976, when G. V. Montgomery, formerly VIVA's and the league's champion in Congress, released to the public the final report of his House Select Committee on the issue:

the results of the investigations and information gathered during its 15-month tenure have led this committee to the belief that no Americans are still being held alive as prisoners in Indochina, or elsewhere, as a result of the war in Indochina [and that] because of the nature and circumstances in which many Americans were lost in combat in Indochina, a total accounting by the Indochinese Governments is not possible and should not be expected.[14]

Despite this conclusion, Carol Bates, executive director of the league, responded with outrage to President Carter's 1977 approval of the military's request to resume changing the status of the missing when judged appropriate: "[the president's] decision to administratively 'kill-off' the remaining POW/MIA's by declaring them all legally dead is the final blow . . . in a long list of broken promises" (qtd. Clarke 109). Thus, the missing who were a rallying point for the Nixon administration subsequently become a site for voicing dissatisfaction with and mistrust of the government.[15]

In the first chapter of *Mythmaking in America*, Bruce Franklin notes the "religious nature" of widespread belief in living POWs, the power of which derives from "its defiance and transcendence of perceived reality and ordinary thinking" (8–9). The belief in living POWs of the Vietnam War is all the more striking when one considers the relatively small number of missing, 2,546, just over 5 percent of the total losses. By contrast, 5,866 men were listed missing (BNR—body not recovered) after the Korean War (over 25 percent of the total losses), and 78,794 after World War II, which is just over 22 percent of total losses (Clarke 7). Yet even into the 1990s, belief in living POWs persists, as evinced by the "It's Time—Bring Them Home!" watch, whose sales will benefit the Live POW Lobby of America. Moreover, the belief in living POWs is not limited to activists, special interest groups, or traumatized families of the missing; as of 1991, the *Wall Street Journal* reports that 69 percent of Americans surveyed believe that there are still prisoners of war alive in Southeast Asia and that 52 percent of those believe that the government is not doing enough to get them back (Franklin xi).

The significance of belief in living POWs is suggested by interviews conducted with dependent parents of POW/MIA servicemen by the Center for Prisoner of War Studies after the 1973 POW release. These interviews led sociologist Hamilton I. McCubbin and psychologist Philip J. Metres to conclude that "the ambiguity of the situation . . . left these parents in a state of limbo as to the finality of their losses . . . the work of mourning had been aborted or suspended and might, over time, cause psychological complications." Among the most notable effects of this "limbo" is the inability to imagine the future: "When asked by another group member, 'What would your plans be should your son not return?', a mother, who expected her son to return replied, 'My mind is made up; don't confuse me with the facts.' " [16] The image of a family in suspended animation as it waits for the missing to return is borne out by a Veteran's Day 1969 advertisement that offers clues to the persistence of belief in living American POWs of the Vietnam War and a schematic model of the POW/MIA fantasy. Placed in newspapers nationwide by Ross Perot's organization United We Stand as part of its public awareness campaign, the advertisement (figure 2) proclaims the organization to be the voice of America ("The Majority Speaks, Release the Prisoners") and represents the POW/MIA in terms of Cold War images of the family—contained and isolated. It features a photograph of a mother and two children kneeling at the edge of a bed in prayer, with the caption "Bring our Daddy home safe, sound, and soon." The caption is, presumably, the unspoken words of the family's prayer, but it is also an appeal to the reader, who can do his or her part to "bring our Daddy home," by filling out the attached application and becoming a member of United We Stand. [17] In both the image of the family and its address, the ad constructs a supportive home front, imagined in terms of the patriarchal family. In its portrayal of and appeal to a united home front, the ad not only reaffirms a national identity guaranteed by history as it recalls images of past wars, but offers—despite the image of body bags on foreign airfields that was all too familiar by 1969—the possibility that the missing might return "safe, sound, and soon." Images of the physical waste and horror of war are replaced by that of the family coalesced around the missing father—an absent center, an abstracted and perfected patriarch.

Considering the nature of this image, it becomes clear why the POW/MIA issue has persisted long after "Operation Homecoming" in 1973 and why the missing have haunted succeeding administrations. Ideologically overdetermined to say the least, the missing patriarch is at once beyond corrupt institutions and evidence of institutional corruption. The missing are both a site where hegemonic masculinity [18] and the institutions predicated upon it can be reaffirmed *and* a site where fear and dissatisfaction with those institutions can be expressed. At the same time that the missing serve as focal point for a nation imagined as an ideal family, they

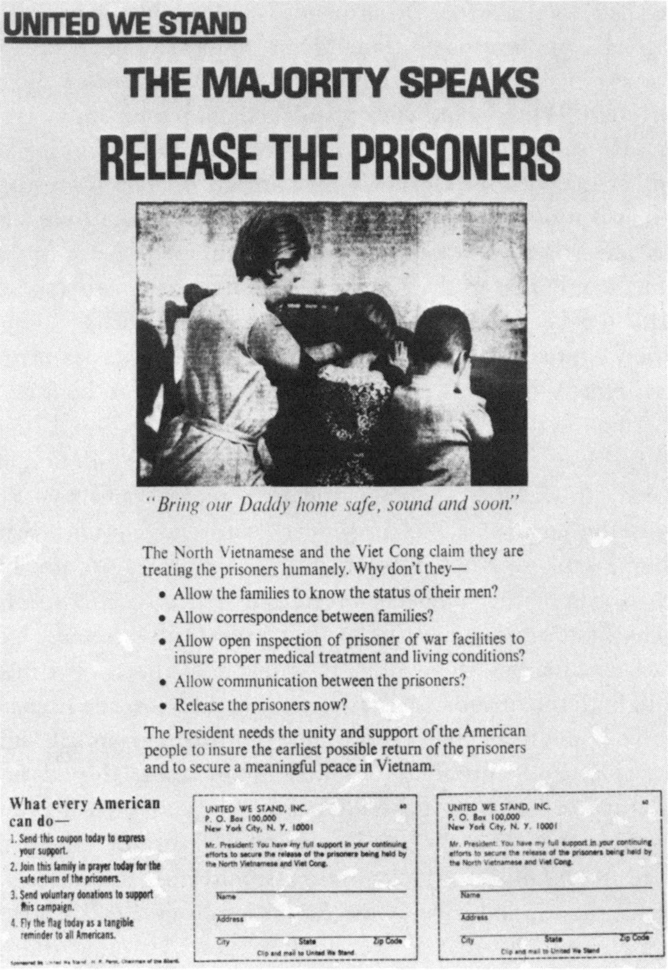

FIG. 2. "Bring Our Daddy Home Safe, Sound, and Soon" (advertisement), *New York Times*, 9 Nov. 1969, 73.

also serve as a reminder of one of the most important lessons of Vietnam (especially after the release of the *Pentagon Papers* in the early 1970s)[19]— that the government lies. At the same time that the missing facilitate a continuation of Cold War international policy—with, for instance, the embargo against Vietnam—they also serve as an emblem of domestic strife, political impotence, fear, and rage.[20]

In the context of "live sightings" in the 1980s and the search for remains in the 1990s, the missing are imagined in a scopic field of inquiry as (ever-receding) objects of vision. The potential aggressivity of looks directed toward the missing, looks whose object is both to find the missing and confirm the criminality of the Vietnamese government, becomes clear in rescue films of the 1980s where discovery of live POWs precedes the punishment of their captors. In the horror films discussed in this essay, however, the missing *themselves* are the object of the aggressive and controlling looks—of the media, police, government, military, and other mysterious powers. *Deathdream, House, Jacob's Ladder*, and *Universal Soldier* all focus on masculine identities reduced to their corporeal horizons and on male bodies out of control. The later three films draw on a rich tradition of conspiracy theories popularized through the 1980s and 1990s. (For instance, William Stevenson and Monika Jensen-Stevenson, in their 1990 *Kiss the Boys Goodbye: How the United States Betrayed Its Own POWs in Vietnam*, describe a shadow government that blocks POW rescue attempts in order to cover up clandestine operations still conducted in Indochina.[21] In 1992, Ross Perot contended that the U.S. government has been lax in investigating POW/MIA reports because of the CIA's involvement in heroin trafficking in Southeast Asia.)[22] All four films suggest an affinity between those anxieties addressed by belief in the missing and the generic concerns of contemporary horror, with its "unquestionable obsession with the physical constitution and destruction of the human body; a paranoid or conspiracist tendency in social and political thinking and a complex of negative images which inform popular attempts to address the problems of death and of dying—especially insofar as they are subject to the influence of medical technology and institutional bureaucracy."[23] In the 1972 film *Deathdream*, for example, a soldier is literally called back from the grave by his mother's prayers for his safe return. His body self-destructs; in so doing it mocks the expectations placed on it by patriarchy. In the other films, not only bodies but their perceptions are out of control, as unseen forces manipulate vision and temporality, representation and history. In the 1986 horror-comedy *House*, an old mansion haunts its new owner with his own memories of the Vietnam War. In *Jacob's Ladder* and *Universal Soldier*, the white male body and its perceptions are at the mercy of those governmental, medical, and military organizations that would ordinarily support, maintain, and give meaning to them.[24]

BODY HORROR

The contemporary Horror film tends to play not so much on the broad fear of Death, but more precisely on the fear of one's own body, of how one controls and relates to it.

—Philip Brophy, "Horrality—The Textuality of Contemporary
Horror Films"[25]

What is *abject* . . . the jettisoned object, is radically excluded and draws toward the place where meaning collapses.

—Julia Kristeva, "Approaching Abjection"[26]

In *Deathdream*, Andy, who by all accounts was a perfectly nice boy before he left for Vietnam, returns to his family and community abject and monstrous, a murderous corpse. The film is deeply critical of how patriarchal power is maintained in both the family and community and darkly humorous in its portrayal of the public's denial of the violence and abjection central to war. When faced with the results of Andy's nocturnal feedings and news reports of a mysterious soldier who is the prime suspect in recent murders, citizens are shocked ("Can't believe a soldier'd do a thing like that"). Little boys from the neighborhood are eager to hear about Andy's exploits as a soldier ("Did ya see any action?" "Did ya kill many guys?") and to display their own skills in martial arts ("They teach you karate? I'm learning it. Watch this!") but back away in terror when the veteran demonstrates his prowess by strangling the family dog, Butchy.

The story of *Deathdream* is a variation on that in which a monkey's paw has the magical ability to make wishes come true for its possessor but at terrible, unforeseen cost: after a nice poor old couple's wish for money causes the death of their beloved only son, the parents wish for his return. The story ends with his ominous, shuffling, muddy step, *just outside the door.*[27] In *Deathdream*, the power that brings Andy (Richard Backus) back from the dead is his mother's obsessive love and denial of his death. The film opens with a brief, confusing scene of a firefight: a soldier falls and another soldier, Andy, tries to reach his friend. A freeze-frame captures the moment when Andy is also shot. Opening credits roll over this still and out-of-focus image of the moment of death; on the sound track we hear a woman calling for Andy. The credits end and Andy falls as the woman's voice gives way to sinister demonic voices. In the first scene of the film, Andy's family (mom, dad, sister Cathy) is having dinner when an officer comes to the door with news of the young man's death in Vietnam. That night, Andy's mother (Lynn Carlin) holds a vigil; alone in a candle-lit room, she whispers, "They lied. They lied. You'll recover." Meanwhile, a truck driver picks up a mysterious hitch-hiker—a soldier, as he tells his friends when he stops at the local diner for two coffees—who doesn't have much to say. Later that night Andy's family is awakened by a noise; they come downstairs (father armed with a pistol, ready to shoot) to find Andy, pale but whole. Over the next three days, he appears clearly changed by his war experience: he is reluctant to participate in celebrations and strangely reticent about his war experiences; he spends much of his time alone in his room, is prone to lonely nocturnal wandering and fits of violence. Meanwhile, the truck driver is found murdered and an investigation ensues. As rumors begin to circulate that a drug-crazed soldier is sought in connection with the truck driver's murder, Andy's father (John Marley) becomes suspicious of his son. He enlists the advice of their family doctor, who, when told of Andy's behavior and his murder of their dog, agrees that it sounds "pretty bad" and stops by the house to see the young man himself and to offer a free checkup as a welcome home gift. Later that evening, Andy visits the doctor at his office for his "checkup," murders him, and drains his blood. After the doctor is killed, Andy's father is convinced that his son is a murderer and goes to the police—ostensibly to throw them off the trail. Meanwhile, Andy has gone out on a surprise double date with his ex-girlfriend JoAnn, Cathy, and her boyfriend Bob. While Andy and his father are out, Andy's mother sees a television report of the murders and realizes that Andy is the killer. Determined to save him, the mother tries, unsuccessfully, to stop her husband when he later leaves to find and warn the teenagers. Andy's father is too late. Andy wreaks havoc at the drive-in and comes home with the police in pursuit. When the father sees what is left of his by now quite decomposed son, he shoots himself. Andy's mother tries to drive him to safety, but they only get as far as the graveyard—where Andy has prepared a marker for himself: Andy Brooks, 1951–1972.

On one hand, *Deathdream* is—like Elia Kazan's film of the same year, *The Visitors*—an example of how, as Rick Berg puts it, "the massacre at My Lai had infected the image of the vet": "The vet is pictured as an ominous threat to the living room, sign of the home and place of the family. Like their VC counterparts and those other outlaws, the bikers, vets are rapists, the irrepressibly uncivilized who violently intrude on our peace and quiet. They have crossed over the threshold, and violated the sanctuary of the American dream."[28] Rereading the United We Stand image of the family in terms of what Berg calls the "Vet Cong," the vulnerability of the mother and her children praying for a soldier's return takes on a new significance. Clearly, what Andy's mother's prayers have called back from the grave no longer fits into the family and is, in fact, a threat to it. But *Deathdream* is a significant representation of the returned veteran due not only to its violence, but to the way that monstrosity and aggression come from both outside the family and community and from within. Ultimately, fictions of mother love, civic duty, and self-sacrifice through which war disowns its violence and injury appear to be themselves aggressive, literally "consuming passions."[29]

The representation in *Deathdream* of the undead soldier's relation to his community and family resonates with the American public's fascination with the POW/MIAs in 1972. The American public was eager to consume the missing, especially through purchase and possession of POW/MIA bracelets, then reaching the height of their popularity. VIVA wholesaled the bracelets to groups like the National League, United We Stand, and Junior Chambers of Congress, and by early 1972 was distributing more than five thousand bracelets a day. By midsummer the number reached eleven thousand per day (Franklin 54–57). This consumption of the POW/MIAs and—by extension—of all that the missing had come to represent through the efforts of groups like United We Stand gives credence to Judith Williamson's observation that "passions are themselves consumed" and her interpretation of the way that, in consumer culture, passions are "contained and channeled into the very social structures they might otherwise threaten" (11).

Deathdream vividly depicts the return of the threat (of loss, death, dissolution, violence) contained by the popular constructions of the missing and by fetishization of the bracelet. In particular, the tie between mother and child that is central to the United We Stand image of home front solidarity and "meaningful peace" is itself a source of horror in *Deathdream*. Because Andy's gruesome return is the direct result of his mother's obsession with him, the film typifies the way that, according to Kristeva, rituals of defilement and rites of abjection converge on the maternal, a site of monstrosity. Both the film's obsession with Andy's body and the mother's obsession with her son bear out Kristeva's thesis that the abject is "the place where meaning collapses" (2). The film's narrative is entropic: we watch the family and community fall apart as Andy's body decays. Moreover, Andy's mother, if not actually outside meaning, becomes progressively more alienated from its institutional forms. Even in the first scene of the film, during which the mother maintains a self-absorbed monologue at the dinner table about the meal and her missing son, her enthusiasm is clearly in excess of her proper role as linchpin of domestic comfort and solidarity. Her obsession and her self-absorption—foreshadowed by the repeated plea of her voice during the opening credits ("Andy, you can't die, you promised me you'd come back. You *promised* me")—emphasize the terrible isolation and vulnerability of this family, whom we first glimpse in a long shot through the lighted window of the otherwise darkened home and street. The low-budget aesthetic of the film—rudimentary lighting (and its tendency to wash out or obscure the actors), cheap props, bare interiors, and wooden performances—confirms the bleakness of this family's life. Although the family is provisionally unified by a common loss, Andy's return will expose its fragility. In the course of the film, we find that Andy's mother is bitter toward institutions of patriarchal power that would separate her from her son—just as she is derisive of its representatives, especially the military and her husband. Soon after Andy returns, she accuses her husband of forcing him to enlist and not wanting him to return. His father retorts, "he enlisted 'cause he didn't want you to turn him into a goddamn mama's boy and he was right." The couple's argument over Andy, who sits alone in his room upstairs, is conducted on the threshold of the kitchen and den, their respective territories. Mother seldom leaves the kitchen, and exercises her power solely through the regimentation of meals that shape the family's interaction. ("You all have a lovely picnic, I'm going to go in and clean up the kitchen . . . if you need anything, just *call* me.") Ultimately, however, the mother's obsession with her son envelops the entire household: it is, after all, her candle-lit vigil and whispered plea that draw the demonic Andy from his grave. Subsequently, the horrific results of maternal desire pervade the film through its depiction of the corpse and corporeal alteration, cannibalism, and murder, as well as the inability of the family and community to understand these horrors.

In her discussion of the cultural significance of soldiering and mothering, Jean Bethke Elshtain points out that both are liminal or "boundary" experiences: "Soldiers, like mothers, are involved with food, shit and dirt

. . . similarly immersed in worlds revolving around stomachs, bodily harm or well being, the search for protection." [30] If one applies Kristeva's formulation of the abject to Elshtain's observation, one can see how maintaining the mythic power of both the soldier and the mother depends upon managing the liminality of their experiences—whether through containment, as in the United We Stand image of the family, or exploitation, as in the body horror of *Deathdream*. In addition to showcasing the physical effects of death and dissolution, *Deathdream* foregrounds the problem of meaning raised by the abject. For example, of particular importance to the maintenance of suspense in the film is the family's inability to recognize Andy for the zombie-killer that he is. Narrative tension accrues around the question of whether we are witnessing the dawning realization of Andy's monstrosity or the growing inability to deny what was known all along. And the problem of interpretation is not limited to the family. The film also shows the television's obsession with the abject and horrific as well as its tendency to dull the edge of violence and death. The media's role in *Deathdream* echoes contemporary criticism of television coverage of the Vietnam War that focuses on both its sensationalism and limitation. In his 1969 collection of essays, *The Living-Room War*, for example, Michael J. Arlen describes television's portrayal of the war as both horrifying and normalizing. [31] Like the nightly coverage of the war, Andy's nocturnal activities are reported regularly; the media attention attests both to a lascivious interest in and civic concern with the gruesome details of his murders. However, even as television shows Andy's mother what her son has done, it falls short of explaining what he has become. Andy's murders are reconstructed and contained as a crime spree. This representation of television confirms both Margaret Morse's assertion that "news in the West is about the anormal. . . . about challenges to the symbolic system and its legitimacy" [32] and Nick Browne's conclusion that television "helps produce and render 'natural' the logic and rhythm of the social order." [33]

The role of television in *Deathdream*—to reassert patriarchal law and the symbolic order even as it attests to public fascination with the abject—is similar to television's role in George Romero's *Night of the Living Dead* (1968). In *Night of the Living Dead*, besieged survivors of a zombie plague eagerly turn to the evening news for an official account of their plight. In Romero's film, the newscast reestablishes the borders between the living and the dead, the human and the not-human in its explanation of the catastrophe. Yet even as the newscast provides helpful hints for the extermination of the zombies and features footage of newly deputized citizens who pick off zombie prey, embattled survivors in the viewing audience are also positioned as consumers of death and violence.[34] Similarly, in *Deathdream*, fascinated spectators pictured at the scene of the doctor's murder attest to public interest in violence and the appeal—as well as the horror—of the abject.

In *Deathdream* the media's representations and the mother's desires are ultimately portrayed as mutually sustaining systems, both of which feed off Andy. In its portrayal of Andy as the (rapidly dissolving) locus of their respective desires, the film dramatizes the public's voyeuristic and fetishistic investments in the missing. The media, official vehicle for ghoulish public curiosity, avidly searches along with the police for clues and evidence that will lead to the identity of the mysterious killer-soldier. Meanwhile, Andy's mother persists in her obsession with her soldier-son and denies growing evidence of death and decomposition, as she lives vicariously through the power of a patriarch-to-be. As a result, one has a strong sense of Andy's being consumed by his family and community, even as he cannibalizes his friends and neighbors. This effect is heightened by the structural organization of the film. Scenes alternate between domestic and public spaces, Andy's home and the local diner, bar, police department, city morgue, and doctor's office. Characterization of the family and community is dominated by images of eating and gossip, as these spaces are linked by consumption of Andy and his violence, through the media of radio, television, newspaper, police reports, and hearsay. For instance, the film cuts from a shot of the corpse of Andy's first victim, the truck driver—who sprawls over his front seat with his throat slashed, his truck open in a pasture, cows mooing in the background—to Andy's family surrounding him at an impromptu backyard picnic. Later in the same sequence, the film cuts from the coroner, who inspects the truck driver's body and discusses the possibilities of the case while eating a sandwich, back to the family picnic, where the mailman stops for a sandwich and attempts to reminisce with Andy about war. The mailman, a World War II veteran, muses on the necessity to "clean it up, for public consumption," and the film cuts to the diner, where waitress, cook, and customers eagerly eat and discuss with the police the murder of their friend the truck driver. The first indication of Andy's abnormality after he returns from serving his country is that he refuses to eat and to offer his story back to the community. Instead, he sits in his room or in the backyard all day, says nothing, and only feeds on members of the community at night. Andy's alienation from the community is most luridly suggested by his fastidious habit of employing a syringe to drain his victims' blood and inject it into his own body—an image that at once recalls the soldier-addict and refuses the messy orality of both the traditional vampire and Andy's family and neighbors.

While accounts of and speculation about the recent series of murders fascinate the community, most of the horror for the viewer of *Deathdream* centers not on witnessing Andy's murders, but on the fact that one knows—even before Andy's body begins to leak—that the nice, silent, sad young man sitting out back in a lawn chair not eating egg salad sandwiches and not telling his family and neighbors stories about his war experience is slowly rotting inside. Yet, although much of the film's horror emanates from this knowledge, Andy's violence is portrayed not so much as an extension of a bodily necessity (as in the case of Romero's zombies) as an extension of and ironic commentary on his fulfillment of, as a soldier and son, the expectations of patriarchy. As Robin Wood points out, Andy is "a figure quite inadequate to sustain the ideological burden he is meant to carry."[35] As he is both a son and a future patriarch, the dissolution of Andy's body—a body central to narratives of family, nation, and war—suggests that he has literally given way under ideological pressure; his body cannot contain its decay any more than the family can contain its aggression. Thus, Andy's monstrosity is not the product of the Vietnam War alone. Significantly, Andy never attacks his parents: rather, they self-destruct when faced with the emptiness of their expectations. After Andy strangles the family pet, his father spends much of his time closeted in his room, drunkenly mooning over family albums, consumed with nostalgia, until finally he kills himself. His mother slowly goes insane; her obsession with her son—her desire to keep him safe—only increases as his criminality and monstrosity become impossible to ignore. She forfeits the rest of her family for her son and releases him only after she literally drives him to his grave.

In Romero's zombie trilogy, each film focuses on a particular group or institution: the family (*Night of the Living Dead*), the media and consumer culture (*Dawn of the Dead* [1978]), and military and medical institutions (*Day of the Dead* [1985]). As a decadent past feeds on the present, zombie

consumerism and zombie aggression highlight those aspects of contemporary society that make any sense of the future untenable. The horror in
Deathdream, by contrast, focuses on the destruction of *past* ideals concerning family/community, media/consumer culture, and the police/military.
As ex-girlfriend JoAnn says to Andy during their ill-fated double date at
the drive-in, what she really wants is to "pick up where we left off."
JoAnn's wish is cut short when Andy's face starts to ooze—after which
he attacks her in a parody of backseat lovemaking (literally "eating face"),
strangles Bob, and runs down Cathy with the car. Likewise, later films
featuring Vietnam's undead—*House, Jacob's Ladder*, and *Universal Soldier*—
will also struggle with a nostalgic desire for the past and a desire to "pick
up where we left off."

In the way *Deathdream* savagely attacks both the family and its ideals,
it exemplifies what Robin Wood, in his study of contemporary horror
films, calls the "crisis in ideological confidence of the 1970s" (162). By
contrast, the horror films of the 1980s and 1990s that feature Vietnam's
undead attempt nostalgically to recall a time before Vietnam. In their
portrayal of the family especially, the later films demonstrate the way
that, with the election of Reagan in 1980, "the cold war and the call for
domesticity became fashionable again."[36] Yet these films, like *Deathdream*,
also focus on the damaged male body as a site of cultural negotiation.
This body is at the mercy of its own corruption and/or is victimized by
shadowy conspirators. Thus, at the same time that the later films provide
nostalgic fantasies,[37] they also manifest a striking uneasiness with regard
to the male body and subjectivity that suggests the complexity of the role
the POW/MIA still plays in American culture.

While the eruption of Andy's body in *Deathdream* vividly figures the
return of war's waste and violence, its abjection also presents a problem
of interpretation—thematized by the role of the media and news in
the film. Such problems of understanding and representation also figure
centrally in Vietnam horror films of the 1980s and 1990s, whose narratives focus in different ways on the quest for truth concerning the past.
Unlike *Deathdream*, however, it is not only interested onlookers, the
media and police, but the soldier/veteran himself who pursues the mystery of past events and present identity, and is thus both subject and
object of these strikingly paranoid fictions.

HISTORY IS WHAT HURTS: *HOUSE, JACOB'S LADDER,* AND *UNIVERSAL SOLDIER*

The dialectic of repulsion and fascination in the monstrous reveals how the apparent certainties of representation are always undermined by the insistent operations of desire and terror.
—James Donald, "The Fantastic, Sublime and the Popular; Or, What's at Stake in Vampire Films?"[38]

Hysterics suffer mainly from reminiscences.
—Joseph Breuer and Sigmund Freud, *Studies on Hysteria*[39]

The POW/MIA rescue films of the Reagan eighties—*Uncommon Valor, Missing in Action, Rambo: First Blood Pt. II*—make good the losses of Vietnam and turn defeat into victory; racist and phallocentric, they reinvigorate an American identity predicated on the power and strength of the individual white male.[40] They represent Vietnam as a frontier, primitive and primal, removed temporally and spatially from a decadent American society that has forgotten its heroes. As Jeanine Basinger points out, these films allow Americans to "go back in and rescue ourselves—a convenient way to make a new Vietnam war—one in which *we* are victorious."[41]

In their "lurid obsession with archaism" (Donald 247), *House, Jacob's Ladder,* and *Universal Soldier* show the nightmare logic informing belief in live POWs and MIAs still being held in Vietnam. These films depict Vietnam as ever present, outside history, in stasis. It lurks in haunted non-spaces—the skin of a house and the undead space of the soldier-body—ready to be fought again and again. Moreover, these films portray history, memory, and the past as aggressive forces, to be struggled against within paranoid fantasies about brainwashing and surveillance. Fredric Jameson characterizes contemporary paranoid fictions as a "privileged representational shorthand for grasping a network of power and control too difficult for our minds and imaginations to grasp . . . conspiracy theory (and its garish manifestations) must be seen as a degraded attempt—through the figuration of advanced technology—to think the impossible totality of the contemporary world system."[42] In these three films about conspiracies, surveillance, and mind control, the body—missing, returned, and manipulated—is a site for working against and through institutions of power and knowledge, especially knowledge of history and of Vietnam.

In the horror-comedy *House*, Roger Cobb (William Katt) is a successful writer of bad horror novels; when he inherits his Aunt Elizabeth's house after her apparent suicide, his personal life is in disarray. He is recently divorced and his young son has been missing for a year. (As in the case of Vietnam's missing, there are hints of conspiracy surrounding his son's absence, and the FBI is on the case.) When he moves into the old house, he begins work in earnest on his new book, a memoir of his tour in Vietnam—despite his agent's warning that no one wants to read about the war anymore. Roger finds that his memory and writing are blocked. Meanwhile, the house manifests symptoms that he traces to repressed memories of the war. Every time Roger sits down at his computer to write, the house comes alive—big game trophies wriggle on the walls and tools escape their shed to fly around with murderous intent. His first night in the house, his aunt appears to him with the warning that the house had "tricked" her and it would trick Roger too. "It knows everything about you." And indeed, many of the house's disturbances seem directly motivated by his various losses and traumas: as memories of Vietnam slowly emerge, he sees and hears traces of his son, and a shapeshifting ghost appears to him in the form of his ex-wife (only to mockingly revert to grotesque, purple-faced obesity). Thus the house serves as a quite disturbing model of therapeutic remembering. Roger solves the house's mysteries as well as that of his son's disappearance when he follows the clues offered by his aunt's surreal paintings and ventures through the bathroom mirror, into the house's haunted skin—into the past and Vietnam. Deep inside the house, Roger confronts the past, embodied in the reanimated corpse of his old army buddy "Big Ben" (Richard Moll), who seeks revenge for Roger's having "abandoned him to the Cong." Ben is one of the imprisoned/missing, abandoned by his buddy and country; as a POW, he has suffered a "fate worse than death" and is hot for revenge. The film concludes when Roger discovers that Ben is the one who kidnapped his son; after Roger rescues the little boy, escapes with him from Vietnam/inside the house, and destroys Ben, his wife returns as well. Thus, the past is put to rest and the family is reunited.

In *House* the idea of the POW/MIA is distributed over several characters: Big Ben, Roger's son, and Roger himself. Ben is the stereotypical Vietnam soldier-psychopath, as commonplace by 1986[43] as the horror films that *House* parodies.[44] Played by Moll, who is best known at this time for his role on the sitcom *Night Court*, Ben is the maladjusted soldier who is entirely insufferable in any context except combat, when he shows himself to be fierce, brave, and exceptionally violent. Like Andy, when he returns as a corpse he is bent on revenge; but unlike Andy, Ben is a comic figure. The mystery of the disappearance of Roger's son Jimmy is portrayed with more seriousness than that of Ben's grudge against Roger. We learn of the circumstances of his abduction, like the circumstances of Ben's abandonment, through Roger's flashbacks: at his aunt's house a year earlier, Roger is outside clipping hedges as Jimmy plays nearby. He looks up and the boy is gone: he runs to the front yard too late to stop a car speeding away, then glimpses a figure in the swimming pool that disappears when he dives in. While memories of Vietnam focus on Roger's failure to act, memories of Jimmy's abduction center on his inability to understand what he has witnessed firsthand. After moving to his aunt's house, it seems that the old lady's original assessment of the situation—that the house took the boy—is right. Yet clues in the house, like his own visual evidence, are impossible to communicate to anyone outside the house. Roger is thus imprisoned by its reality.

In the baroque way that the haunted house is identified with Roger's haunting past in Vietnam, the plight of the POW/MIA separated from home and family figures the extraordinary dysfunction of an otherwise ordinary and happy contemporary American family. That is, by attributing this family's difficulties to Roger's wartime past and to the house, its essential viability is guaranteed. Governing this representation is the motif at work in the "It's Time—Bring Them Home!" watch advertisement, wherein the United States' past in Vietnam appears as a sinister reflection or double of American culture in the present.[45] In the haunted house, Roger's son is lost, his wife is demonic, and Roger himself is maddened and pursued by his past; once he destroys the house's secret that haunts him, son, wife, and Roger return to normal and are reunited. The image of Roger venturing into a mirror in order to return to Vietnam and find his son is also characteristic of the occult film with its language of portals and openings; according to Carol Clover, while the occult film is obsessed with female bodies in crises, it is also centrally concerned with men who emerge as "new men" or die.[46]

In *House*, as in *Jacob's Ladder* and *Universal Soldier*, the horror of war is characterized in terms of a fear of being watched and a loss of control over representation, the powers of vision and understanding: most strikingly, Roger glimpses his son in the windows and in the television and hears his voice coming from deep inside the house. Like the house in *Poltergeist* (1982), this interior is suffused with a troubled history, in sharp contrast to the ordinary (and rather dull) suburban life outside. The secret literally underlying the paranormal disturbances in the earlier film is that developers have built over an ancient Indian burial ground, which causes angry spirits to possess the house and harass its occupants. By contrast, it is Roger's own past that has been covered over in *House*— partly because of his guilt concerning Ben, but partly too because, as Roger's agent tells him, no one wants to hear about Vietnam anymore. If Roger is going to write about Vietnam, he will have to do so on his own. Yet, at the same time that the film makes fun of horror fans and of the difficulty Roger has in escaping his own notoriety as a horror novelist in order to pursue more serious interests, it also energetically conflates horror fiction and Vietnam "fact" in its combination of haunted house and haunted vet genres. Most interesting in terms of contemporary representations of the missing—especially the importance of high-tech surveillance equipment in gathering evidence[47]—is the way Roger's paranoia and epistemological obsession—so characteristic of gothic horror with its insistence on and fear of seeing—is portrayed in terms of military reconnaissance. After his first encounter with the creatures living in his aunt's bedroom closet, he orders an entire truckload of surveillance equipment. He dons his old uniform, he sets traps—cameras and floodlights—to capture evidence of the house's supernatural activity as martial music plays on the sound track. The most comic sequences of the film focus on Roger's frenzied attempts to capture, record, and represent the disturbances he sees in the house.

Just as history lives in Ben's desiccated form as well as in the haunted skin of a malevolent old building in *House*, in *Jacob's Ladder* and *Universal Soldier* history is contained by the bodies of the missing and resurrected. Jacob Singer (Tim Robbins) is missing in the sense of having lost his sense of place and time: he is resurrected to the extent that we discover, in the finale, that all the events that take place in post-Vietnam New York have been in fact the "death dream" of a mortally wounded soldier in Vietnam. Thus, *Jacob's Ladder* renders in a particularly complex way the same temporal relation depicted in *House* and the "It's Time" advertisement, whereby war-era Vietnam persists parallel to postwar America. The "surprise" of *Jacob's Ladder* is, of course, that it is not Vietnam but the United States that is a dream, a memory, a delusion. At the same time that we see Jacob haunting a postwar landscape in which he has no place because he is for all intents and purposes already dead, he is also (like Roger Cobb) haunted and pursued by demons. *Universal Soldier* takes up far more literally the idea of the missing having been resurrected as monsters and let loose on post-Vietnam America: MIAs frozen in 1969 are thawed out and reconstructed as super soldiers in the nineties.

In the first sequence of *Jacob's Ladder*, a battalion of American soldiers in the Mekong Delta on 6 October 1971 is attacked, and Jacob Singer is downed by a bayonet. The film cuts from his cry of pain and look of confusion to his waking with a start, in a subway train. This beginning, strikingly similar to that of Brian De Palma's *Casualties of War* (1989), appears, like the earlier film, to mark Vietnam as a dream and as a memory. Unlike *Casualties of War*, however, the train does not take us back into Vietnam but apparently forward, into Jacob's life in New York after the war. The action of *Jacob's Ladder* appears to be divided among three periods of Jacob Singer's life—before, during, and after Vietnam—and between two spaces—Vietnam and New York. The film is highly discontinuous, as Jacob is plagued by spatial and temporal shifts. The film marks the hellish urban landscape of post-Vietnam New York as "present" in the opening sequence; but the New York that Jacob has awakened to is a sinister dreamscape of inexplicable circumstances and visual effects. Jacob's relationship with this terrain is genuinely paranoid, much like Roger Cobb's relation to his aunt's house, as the city manifests symptoms of what appears to be Jacob's war trauma. Jacob's perceptions are fragmented in a way that makes him a truly liminal figure; he is uncertain whether he is dreaming or awake, alive or dead, and the audience shares his confusion. The associations by which one maintains identity in life—human contacts, institutional connections and documents, linear time and coherent space—are either absent or shattered. In the absence of a coherent sense of the present, Jacob's body and its pain are the only constants in the film. Starting with the bayonet wound that cuts from Vietnam to post-Vietnam New York, Jacob's physical pain marks the spatial and temporal shifts in the film, transitions into the future, the past, and the more distant past.

Tormented by the sense that he is being watched, pursued, and manipulated, Jacob Singer becomes obsessed with finding the source of his torment. He not only reads about witchcraft and demonology, but consults with medical, military, and legal authorities, to no avail: institutionally, he does not exist; his files are gone, and his past is erased. Ultimately, Jacob's nightmarish lives turn out to be fantastic flashbacks and flashforwards on the part of a dying soldier in the hands of military doctors. And what at first appears to be a story of war trauma or demonic possession concludes as a story of government conspiracy and surveillance and military experiments with hallucinogenic drugs. In Jacob's "death dream" an informant, Michael, tells Jacob about "the ladder," a hallucinogen he helped the military synthesize in 1968, in order to tap into "base anger" and "primal fear." The firefight whose "memory" has tormented Jacob was the result of the military's decision to test the drug on American soldiers on the eve of a major offensive in 1971. The informant, Michael, tells him, "You killed each other, brother against brother, no discrimination." A final black screen informs us that the conspiracy theory developed in Jacob's "death dream" is based on a reportedly true event, the government's experiment with the hallucinogen BZ. Ironically, the conclusion of *Jacob's Ladder* and the affirmation of the drug-test conspiracy depend on precisely those medical and military authorities whose credibility is undercut in the course of the film: doctors proclaim the soldier dead, the military makes official record of his name. Thus, the most problematic aspects of the film devolve on one purely organic source: the war-torn and chemically altered body.

In *Jacob's Ladder* the cinematic apparatus appears as an instrument of torture, capable of wresting Jacob and the viewer from one world into another. Prior to the film's ending, Jake is genuinely hysterical in his relation to time and space; and, because the discontinuity of the film requires a close identification with his confusion, the viewer's relation with time and space is hysterical as well. Jacob's hysteria associates memory flashes and temporal transitions with pain: editorial cuts from one time and space to another are marked by bodily torture and penetration—whether the "deep adjustments" of Jacob's chiropractor, the rib-cracking embrace of his amorous girlfriend, the plunging of his fever-wracked body into an icy tub, or the insertion of a needle into his brain by a nightmare hospital staff. Only in retrospect does it become clear that the only temporally coherent (though brief and fragmented) narrative in the film is Jacob's "flashbacks" to Vietnam—the sequence of his injury, rescue, treatment, and death in the Mekong Delta. Only at the end of the film is the viewer placed outside Jacob's confusion and pain, as the ending of the film reasserts the authority of the cinematic apparatus (as well as that of the military and doctors) to represent the past truthfully and transparently.

While the government's attempt to create super soldiers in *Jacob's Ladder* destroys a soldier's body and transports him fantastically into postwar America, a similar government conspiracy in *Universal Soldier* wipes out a soldier's memory and revives his body to use it as an antiterrorist weapon in postwar America. Like *Jacob's Ladder*, *Universal Soldier* focuses on the white male body at the mercy of medical and military institutions, which transform American war dead into genetically altered super soldiers. After an entire platoon is wiped out by its own sergeant in 1969, the incident is written up as "MIA" and ten bodies are collected from the field and packed in ice. Twenty-five years later the platoon is regenerated as "Unisols," whose efficiency depends primarily on the suppression of their memories through drug therapy and the replacement of their vision with the controlled and simulated point of view of the military. Just as Jacob Singer's body and perceptions are taken out of his control, those of the Unisols are regulated and mediated by the military, through genetically reconfigured and drugged bodies in which surveillance technology is literally embedded. Yet memories of Vietnam emerge; and when they do, Unisols GR 44 (Jean-Claude Van Damme) and GR 13 (Dolph Lungren) run amok, repeating in present-day America the scenario that led to their deaths in Vietnam. In Vietnam, Sargeant Scott (Lungren) had gone insane and wiped out a village of unarmed Vietnamese civilians as well as most of his own platoon. A lone survivor, Luc Devreaux (Van Damme), refused to kill the last two villagers, a young boy and girl; Devreaux and Scott shot one another and died simultaneously. Seeing two Asian youths held hostage by terrorists at the Hoover Dam awakens fragmentary memories of this event in the newly transformed Unisols. Memories return again when Veronica "Ronnie" Roberts (Ally Walker), a journalist, trespasses on the Unisols' top-secret mission and is caught by 13 and 44 along with her cameraman. When Ronnie's cameraman is killed by GR 13, Ronnie uses GR 44 to escape from the Unisol complex. The journalist and the Unisol are pursued by the military and, later, by GR 13, who reverts to his past identity as Sergeant Scott and seeks revenge against GR 44, the "traitor" Private Devreaux, and Ronnie, a "female POW." Ronnie takes GR 44/Devreaux home to Louisiana, where he has his final battle with 13/Scott at his parents' farm.

In *Universal Soldier*, as in *Jacob's Ladder*, the male body is the site of governmental conspiracy, and in both films the male body and its perceptions are fragmented. The extent to which the Unisols are under the control of medical and military personnel is indicated largely through the technological manipulation and mediation of their vision: they wear headsets that enable the military to track and direct their vision. GR 44's fragmented subjectivity is marked explicitly by the presence of technology that enhances/invades the body, as well as by flashbacks that—like the POV of the military's control room monitors—interrupt the continuity of his vision. Shots depicting the Unisols' point of view are either overlaid by graphic reminders of military control—the ubiquitous on-screen programming of their actions—or they are relayed through control room monitors. As Cynthia Fuchs argues in her reading of *Robocop*, a hysterical POV is constructed "through an impossible POV camera . . . indicated by grid screens, blinking instructions, and targeting mechanisms," a "cyborg performance" that "replays the hysteric's fear of lost body boundaries as an anxiety over frames of vision which constitute 'subjectivity' and 'character.' " [48] In their mission to release the Hoover Dam from terrorist takeover, the Unisols perform under the watchful look of the Special Forces colonel, a SWAT team, the police, and journalists, whose looks are marked in turn by binoculars, gun sights, and camera sights—all reminders of their technological power and mediation.

Significantly, not only GR 44 but also Ronnie is depicted as the product of a patriarchal system that mediates vision and understanding. Both are "framed" by technology, just as they are later "framed" for a crime they did not commit, the murder of Ronnie's cameraman. When Ronnie arrives on the site of the terrorist crisis at Hoover Dam, she looks like a rebel, a hard-boiled journalist who works against the system. She arrives late to the shoot: she sheds her hat, cigarette, and sunglasses and dons a blazer for the camera. As she prepares herself for the broadcast, we are given the cameraman's POV. Framed by the viewfinder, Ronnie is the model of professional femininity, blond and capable. Yet a quick tilt of the camera down to her sneakers—with the crack "nice shoes!"—draws attention to the constructed nature of her professional image even as it reinforces the character of the tough, ambitious woman who "always gets her story." Yet Ronnie as a journalist is caught up by the same system that has transformed Pfc. Luc Devreaux to an MIA and subsequently to GR 44, and the vulnerability of her position is confirmed by her transformation in the course of the film from authoritative voice and face of the newscaster into an outlaw, a conspirator on the run, a POW.

Just as in *Jacob's Ladder* perceptual difficulties originate inside the body (the bayonet wound, the hallucinogenic drugs), the Unisols are not only controlled through their headsets and memory-clearance drugs but are also surveyed from *inside* their genetically altered bodies. On the run from Colonel Perry and the Unisols, GR 44 and Veronica stop at a roadside service station; in a rest room, he undresses, saying, "There must be a tracking device on me. . . . I want you to look for something unusual . . . something hard." Looking down at his own naked body, seeing it apparently for the first time, 44 is bemused. As Ronnie gingerly proceeds to move her hands down his torso, 44 nods in the direction of his (off-screen) penis and asks, "Is *that* supposed to be there?" She reassures him that his penis is *not* the state apparatus they are looking for, that it is "perfectly natural," and continues, until she finds an implant on the back of his leg. Although Ronnie makes 44 cut it out, she probes the bloody wound for him (shown in close-up) and pulls the wire out with disgust. The scene is suggestive both of the extent to which governmental control penetrates the male body, and Ronnie's importance as the one who makes 44's body make sense outside the military. Subsequent to this scene, Ronnie will become increasingly protective of the lost monster, who in turn becomes increasingly infantilized after having been cut off from the military. Putting aside her role as journalist who mediates information for the public, she takes on the role of mother who mediates 44's understanding of his body and makes it coherent.

Once Ronnie strips GR 44 of technology—first the headset that links him to the monitors, then the bug—she proceeds to make sense of who he is, what his body and past might mean. After Ronnie searches for and removes the transmitter embedded in GR 44's body, they find access to the past and the "nature" of what he has become. In so doing, she takes on the role of the mother in the mirror stage who draws attention to the child's embodiment and affirms the wholeness of the reflected image. What Ronnie recognizes as 44's bodily symptoms (his extraordinary strength, his muteness, his imperviousness to pain, his tendency to over-heat) subsequently become clues to his identity. Ultimately, Ronnie will help 44 answer the questions she fires at him after the first demonstration of his strength and strangeness: "Who *are* you? Do you have a family? Is there a Mrs. 44 someplace?" In the course of the chase that dominates the film, Ronnie asserts and defends the lost monster's humanity—and he, in turn, incorporates Ronnie into the only emerging frame of reference he has, his past before Vietnam. *Jacob's Ladder*, *Universal Soldier*, and *House* are similar, then, in their rejection and criticism of institutional technologies that constrain or influence understanding and in their representation of anxieties about knowledge and the body. Likewise, the central fantasy at work in *Universal Soldier* is the same as that of *Jacob's Ladder* and *House*—the fiction of an escape into the past, into the family, safe from the evil shadow of demonic supernatural forces, governmental administration, and military control.

LOST BOYS, ANGRY GHOULS

[I]n its representation of the infant and child, bourgeois mythology has constructed a sign of the future that is . . . open yet closed.
— Vivian Sobchak, "Bringing It All Back Home: Family Economy and Generic Exchange"[49]

While memory emerges as a violent, even destructive, force in *House*, *Jacob's Ladder*, and *Universal Soldier*, all three films are also profoundly nostalgic, and their conclusions depend especially on the bourgeois ideal of the child who embodies, as Vivian Sobchak points out, not an image of future potential, but "longing backward toward the promise once possessed by the past" (180). The conclusions of the three films posit in different ways the family as a refuge from the manipulations of an aggressive government that exercises futuristic control over the soldier-body and from a violent past in Vietnam.

In *House* and *Jacob's Ladder*, Roger Cobb's and Jacob Singer's ultimate reunions with their dead and missing sons signal that the two men have come to terms with the past. Lured away from his computer by his missing son's voice, Roger finally ventures into the building's haunted skin. On the other side of the bathroom mirror, he follows his son's voice and finds him in Vietnam, trapped in a tiger cage like those of Con Son Island. Similarly, Jake Singer's reunion with his little boy, Eli (Macaulay Culkin), signals his release from a life that has become torture. Throughout *Jacob's Ladder*, Eli, who had been killed by a car before Jake went to Vietnam, lends continuity to his two lives: the little boy's presence marks the difference between Jake's life before and after Vietnam, and between his good family (his wife, Sarah [Patricia Kalember], and his three boys) and his postwar nightmare relationship with Jezebel (Elizabeth Peña). Although *Jacob's Ladder* is highly disjunctive in terms of representations of time and space, the film is rigidly structured in terms of family relations, and offers, in fact, another version of the story told by the earlier Adrian Lyne film, *Fatal Attraction* (1987). *Jacob's Ladder*, like *Fatal Attraction*, depicts a family threatened by illicit desire and a monstrous woman. Jezebel appears demonic: as she dances provocatively at a party, a reptilian tail caresses her thighs. Vampire-like, she has no reflection in her dressing table mirror—or her mirror image is distorted, so that her reflection is acephalic and horrifying to Jacob. When she snaps irritably at Jacob, she appears feral as her eyes dilate and her teeth distend. Half-persuaded by books on witchcraft that he is possessed by demons, Jacob reads Jezebel's appearance as a sign of her complicity in their manipulation of him: she both figures and contributes to Jacob's loss and torment. Jacob's lives before and after Vietnam are defined in terms of the good woman versus the bad, marriage versus cohabitation, three sons versus a childless relationship, and middle versus working class. In his prewar life with his family in their respectable home, Jacob is in graduate school; after Vietnam, he shares a tiny squalid apartment with Jezebel and works at the post office, because he "just didn't feel like thinking anymore." Early in the film, Jezebel destroys pre-Vietnam photographs of Jacob's sons in a fit of jealousy; afterwards, he is cut off from his prewar past as well as from his "good" family. The subsequent fragmentation of his perceptions, the confusion between the past and present and his victimization by the medical establishment proceed along the fault lines of his domestic estrangements and displacements. Jacob turns to religious and supernatural texts to find a pattern and an explanation for disturbances of his perceptual life; but finally, it is only in the familial that he can understand his experiences. In the penultimate sequence of the film, Jacob takes a taxi "home," only to find himself in the home he *might* have had with his family after the war, if things had worked out differently for him domestically, socially, and economically. He is greeted by the doorman of his and Sarah's posh apartment building as Dr. Singer. In his empty but opulent home, he sees signs of life with his wife and sons—photographs, schoolbooks. Here he is finally reunited with his dead son Eli, an "angel," who leads Jacob into a dazzling light. Jacob walks with the little boy out of a future that might have been (the doorman, the house, and family) up to the hereafter—defined nostalgically, by Eli's presence, in terms of the past.

Similarly, in *Universal Soldier*, GR 44/Devreaux resolves his traumatic relation to the past—and to the government and the military—by literally, as Andy's girlfriend put it in *Deathdream*, "picking up where he left off." After GR 44/Devreaux is hijacked by Ronnie, he becomes progressively infantilized. His electronic ties to the military severed, he is left with little knowledge of who he is or the world around him; and he has a single desire—to go home. Ronnie takes him home, first to the doctor who gave him life as a Unisol, and then to Louisiana and his family. As the reporter and the childlike monster venture further into the "backward" culture of the South, they also travel back to a time before Vietnam. The future for GR 44/Devreaux is thus transformed into an idealized past, Vietnam all but erased. Most important to the transformation of their future, however, is the transformation of Ronnie herself. After she delivers GR 44/Devreaux from the military she abandons her professional desires as a journalist, which align her with those forces that would exploit the veteran/monster, in order to take on a maternal role: he is no longer a story, but a personal cause. Thus, images of the family-as-refuge rely not only on the image of the child, but also on the idealized image of domestic femininity, the good mother. In contrast to the uncertainty of bonds between husband and wife in these post-Vietnam films, and in contrast to the representation of mother and son in *Deathdream*, the bond between parent and child in these films of the 1980s and 1990s is idealized. The cultural regeneration of these fictions is based on a nostalgic desire for the continuity of generations. The sense of a secure future can be offered only by a past defined in terms of family—thus women enter into these scenarios only as mothers. Women whose professional or sexual desires take them out of the home and out of the traditional familial role are either demonized (Jezebel in *Jacob's Ladder*, Roger Cobb's wife in *House*) or transformed (Cobb's wife in *House*, Ronnie in *Universal Soldier*). Thus, while the focus of these three films, as well as the earlier film *Deathdream*, is damaged, monstrous, hysterical masculinity, it is negotiated through the most tritely stereotypical models of "good" and "bad" femininity. In this way fantasies constructed around Vietnam's missing negotiate both troubled femininity and masculinity in the context of a patriarchal family in crisis.

The caption for the image that advertises *Universal Soldier*—"The Future has a Bad Attitude"—is significant in this context. Given that the film begins in 1969 Vietnam, then cuts to "Nevada—Present Day" and recounts the violent effects of memory on its monstrous protagonists, it would seem more to the point that the *past* has a bad attitude. But, if the caption is somewhat inaccurate factually, it is appropriate in tone. Directed toward the adolescent or adolescent-at-heart consumer of action films, the film blends spectacular violence with adolescent gross-out humor. The results of GR 44's reconditioning by the government and his subsequent liberation from their control are such that the fifty-year-old resurrected soldier with the body of a twenty-five-year-old regresses to early adolescence regarding both his relation to his body and culture.[50] Unlike time-travel plots (like those of *Terminator* [1984] and *Terminator 2* [1991]) that show the potentially profound effects of actions in the present on an apocalyptic future, *Universal Soldier* erases a difficult history and suggests a future that will be nostalgically familiar, an adolescent romp into the past.

At the same time that the masterful agency of the male subject is undercut in terms of knowledge and vision in these films of the 1980s and 1990s, narrative closure and containment of the effects of loss devolve on the image and construction of flawed or recuperated feminine subjectivity, specifically in the context of the patriarchal family. And masculine self-generation that fails in the context of the military and government in these films succeeds—however tenuously in the case of *Jacob's Ladder* and *Universal Soldier*—in images of sons finally returned to their families. The fear with which Jake, Ronnie, and Luc view the government, military, and media dramatizes the unlikelihood in the 1990s of the sort of national consensus imagined by United We Stand's 1969 representation of the nation/family. Nevertheless, we see how, in these films, the family offers shelter and nostalgic comfort. In images of the family, patriarchal "generation" attempts to create an affectively, if not intellectually, coherent link between the past and future. In this way, images of victimized missing and recovered soldiers facilitate a nostalgic return to reactionary patriarchal masculinity: at the same time that the missing American soldier is a reminder of the losses of the Vietnam War, he is also, clearly, a figure that allows for the disavowal of war's injuries. So, despite the obsessive focus of these films on loss and absence, they also demonstrate the way hegemonic masculinity—like Jean-Claude Van Damme—can "land on its feet."[51]

But it should be remembered that, at the same time that fantasies about the missing body facilitate a complex negotiation of loss, they also point back to it insistently and repeatedly—and, significantly, it is in terms of such loss that the Vietnam War has persisted as material for popular representations of masculinity and male subjectivity. Stepping outside the Hollywood film—or outside its diegesis, at least—one finds in the credits of *Universal Soldier* another example of how America's past in Vietnam is used to address present fears and desires, one that suggests the complexity of Vietnam's role in contemporary American culture. Ice-T's song "Body Count," which plays on the sound track over the closing credits, brings us back to the present, refiguring the past violence of Vietnam as current urban violence in the way that sirens blend with the sound of helicopters in accompaniment to the chorus "Body Count, bodycount, . . . VC, VC, VC." The song serves as a reminder of the way the struggle for authoritative interpretations of past events continues in the present and the way the "threatening tendencies of technology and state control [were] exposed by the Vietnam War."[52] In this music the slap-thud of Huey blades, aural cliché of the Vietnam War film (especially when it functions as a sound bridge between past and present, the United States and Vietnam, war and home fronts) bridges the violence of Vietnam and Los Angeles. As a symbol of surveillance and social control associated with the police as well as the military, the helicopter consolidates the most sinister manifestations of governmental power and patriarchal dominance found in POW/MIA fantasy; thus Ice-T's song offers a more radical (though not unrelated) critique of the repressive governmental power and violence than does the film itself. The credits are the place of any feature film that mediates between the diegesis and world of the cinema, the place where we are reminded of the material circumstances of the film's production. In the case of Ice-T's song, we are reminded that the material circumstances that produce *Universal Soldier*, with its fantasies of white masculinity in distress, are the violent manipulation and control of disenfranchised nonwhite bodies. In the way Ice-T's song "Body Count" indicts both the racist policies of the war itself and present racist violence inflicted on African American bodies, it serves as a timely reminder of what is at stake in even the most fantastic films that recount the horrors of war, injury, and the body.

NOTES

Very special thanks go to Troy Boone, who contributed his critical intelligence to nearly every stage of this essay's completion. I also thank Jan-Christopher Horak, who carefully read and commented on an early draft of this argument, and Mark Betz, who, as always, generously shared videos and insights.

1. Elaine Scarry, *The Body in Pain: The Making and Unmaking of the World* (New York: Oxford University Press, 1985), 64.
2. Roland Barthes, *Mythologies* (1957; reprint, selected and translated by Annette Lavers, New York: Noonday Press, 1972), 151.
3. House Select Committee on Missing Persons in Southeast Asia, *Americans Missing in Southeast Asia: Hearings before the Select Committee*, 94th Cong., 2d sess., 1976, pt. 5 (Washington, DC: GPO), 20–21.
4. A Canadian production, directed by Bob Clark. Also known as *Dead of Night*, *Night Walk*, and *The Veteran*. While there *were* Canadian soldiers in Vietnam, the setting of the film appears to be the rural United States.
5. While belief in the missing certainly depends on and sustains a denial of the effects of war on the body—whether the issue is finding identifiable remains after twenty years in a tropical climate or finding actual living prisoners of war—it also facilitates a continuing imaginary engagement with scenes of bodily trauma. Those who believe that prisoners are still alive also believe that the missing are living in terrible torment, a state of continual pain and torture. Bruce Franklin, author of *MIA: Or, Mythmaking in America* (Brooklyn: Lawrence Hill, 1992) effectively demonstrates the government's role in fostering widespread belief in the missing through misinformation for political gain. The persistence of belief, however, which he compares to religious faith, is more mysterious, especially as belief in living POWs offers no solace, but only pain to the most loyal: "While the belief in live POWs may allow some flicker of hope, it hardly offers comfort, for the missing are imagined to be in a place . . . like hell" (19). While my analysis offers no simple answer to this puzzle, it does seek to place this fascination with loss and pain in a cultural context whereby belief in the missing becomes more than just a matter of misinformation, or even the denial of the loss of the Vietnam War, but is part of a broader cultural negotiation of patriarchal power and authority. The model of unconscious fantasy that informs my theoretical assumptions offers a way of reading connections between different kinds of representations of the missing as well as of reading the multiple and shifting effects of this fiction.
6. My use of the terms "fetishism" and "voyeurism" derives from film theory and is most clearly indebted to Laura Mulvey's important essay "Visual Pleasure and Narrative Cinema," *Screen* 16, no. 3 (Autumn 1975): 8–18. Mulvey uses Freudian concepts of fetishism and voyeurism to delineate psychical mechanisms underpinning classic cinematic spectatorship and narrative representation: she describes how the male spectator's imaginary power and coherence are maintained by projecting lack onto the female body, which becomes either the site of fetishis-

tic overvaluation or of voyeuristic control and sadistic investigation. While Mulvey polemically asserts the division between male scopic activity and passive female receptivity to the look or "gaze," she also clearly demonstrates the extent to which spectatorial pleasure is balanced—on a razor's edge, so to speak—between loss and plenitude, pleasure and unpleasure. A number of feminist film theorists have subsequently complicated Mulvey's schema of identification and pleasure through an elaborated concept of unconscious fantasy. Reconsidered in the terms suggested especially by feminist readings of Freud's "'A Child Is Being Beaten,' " one sees how fetishistic and voyeuristic pleasures Mulvey describes in her essay depend on simultaneous, multiple identifications across lines of sexual difference: Mulvey's male spectator, like Freud's boy-fetishist, must identify with the woman in order to misrecognize the absence of her penis as a loss that can be disavowed. Likewise the voyeuristic/sadistic pleasures of investigating the "source" of lack (illness, criminality) in the female body and punishing it would depend on identification with both punisher and punished, aggressor and victim. Thus, the positions of active male viewer and passive female body that classic cinematic narrative presents as a natural gendered division and that the scopic organization of the cinematic apparatus strives to fix would be unfixed at the level of unconscious pleasure and fantasy. Sigmund Freud, "'A Child Is Being Beaten': A Contribution to the Study of the Origin of Sexual Perversions," in *The Standard Edition of the Complete Psychological Works of Sigmund Freud*, vol. 17, trans. and ed. James Strachey (London: Hogarth Press, 1953), 175–204. For feminist discussions of unconscious fantasy and sexual difference, see, for example, Janet Bergstrom, "Enunciation and Sexual Difference," *Camera Obscura*, nos. 3–4 (Summer 1979); and Elizabeth Cowie, "Fantasia," *m/f*, no. 9 (1984). In addition to these discussions of fantasy, fetishism, and voyeurism in film theory, the wide-ranging collection of essays edited by Emily Apter and William Pietz, *Fetishism as Cultural Discourse* (Ithaca: Cornell University Press, 1993), confirms the usefulness of the concept of fetishism for understanding the connections between desire, material history, representation, and social power in a variety of cultural contexts.

7. James Donald, "The Fantastic, the Sublime, and the Popular: Or, What's at Stake in Vampire Films?" in *Fantasy and the Cinema*, ed. James Donald (London: BFI, 1989), 247. Further references to this work will be noted parenthetically in the text.

8. See note 6.

9. By combining this logic with a rhetoric of "accountability"—both the Vietnamese government's accountability to the United States and the U.S. government's accountability to the families of the missing—Nixon's administration was able for over three years to block peace talks by demanding the return of prisoners prior to an agreement to end the war. See Franklin, *MIA*, 16–35, 57–64; and Captain Douglas L. Clarke, *The Missing Man: Politics and the MIA* (Washington, DC: National Defense University Press, 1979), 13–37, 51–55. Further references to these works will be included parenthetically in the text.

10. Ross Perot's United We Stand and VIVA (originally the Victory in Vietnam Association), in addition to the National League of Families and other

groups that formed in the early years of the Nixon administration, launched a huge education campaign that featured advertisements, interviews, and a diorama at the Capitol that portrayed the conditions endured by American prisoners of war. These organizations were tax-exempt and, in the case of the league, received benefits ranging from free long-distance phone service to free air transport from the government and military. The most successful and lucrative of all the awareness campaigns was VIVA's production and marketing of POW/MIA bracelets in 1970. The first one was presented to Mrs. Ross Perot. See Franklin, *MIA*, 49–54; and Clarke, *The Missing Man*, 29–37.

11. Jonathan Schell, "The Time of Illusion IV: For the Re-election of the President," in *The Time of Illusion* (New York: Knopf, 1976), 231. First published in the *New Yorker*, 23 June 1975.

12. The league was, apparently, bought out in 1973 by VIVA, the same organization that had originated the POW/MIA bracelet in 1970. After accepting a donation of $20,000 from VIVA, the league allowed nonfamily members, including many of VIVA's members, to join the league's staff and board of directors. For more on the history of the league, see also Elliot Gruner, *Prisoners of Culture: Representing the Vietnam POW* (New Brunswick: Rutgers University Press, 1993), 16–19; and Iris R. Powers, "National League of Families and the Development of Family Services," in *Family Separation and Reunion: Families of Prisoners of War and Servicemen Missing in Action*, ed. Hamilton I. McCubbin et al. (San Diego: Center for Prisoner of War Studies, 1974), 1–10.

13. Even though, logically, the passage of time itself reduced the likelihood of recovering live POWs. As Clarke points out, unlike immediate family members, especially wives who needed a sense of closure in order to continue their lives, "'concerned citizens' . . . were more likely to stand on principle in demanding an accounting, and to press for an indefinite suspension of status changes" (*The Missing Man*, 38).

14. House Select Committee on Missing Persons in Southeast Asia, *Final Report*, 94th Cong., 2d sess., 1976 (Washington, DC: GPO), vii.

15. At the same time that the missing serve as a focus for discontent with the government, they also, as Bruce Franklin points out, distract popular anger from more tangible issues of governmental neglect and misconduct, such as the unemployment rate and mental and physical health problems among those soldiers of Vietnam who did return. By 1988 there were between fifty thousand and one hundred thousand homeless Vietnam veterans; as of 1979, only six years after the war, there were already two hundred thousand veterans in the penal system (Franklin, *MIA*, 189).

16. Hamilton I. McCubbin and Philip J. Metres, Jr., "Maintaining Hope: The Dilemma of Parents of Sons Missing in Action," *Family Separation and Reunion*, ed. McCubbin et al., 177, 176.

17. As Franklin points out, the demand that Hanoi release American prisoners ignored the fact that "the U.S., like most nations, has never been involved in a war in which either side released all its prisoners prior to an agreement to end the

war. But through the strange logic of the administration's negotiating position and its masterful public relations campaign, the American prisoners of war had indeed been successfully transformed—in the public mind—into . . . 'hostages' held for 'ransom' " (*MIA*, 59).

18. Thomas Di Piero uses the term "hegemonic masculinity" to articulate the way "a system of oppression and ideological obfuscation [masquerades] as a simple phylogenic gender variety" and thus causes "gender identity to subsume the invidious work of other forms of oppression." The male subject "can never, of course, accede to the position occupied by the stable and ideally coherent imaginary patriarch. . . . Masculine identity, consequently, is always in flux. . . . What results . . . is hysteria, since the male subject can never fully identify with either of the gendered positions culturally articulated." Thomas Di Piero, "The Patriarch Is Not (Just) a Man," *Camera Obscura*, nos. 25–26 (January-May 1991): 104, 119.

19. For an account of the circumstances of their publication by Daniel Ellsberg, see Howard Zinn, *A People's History of the United States* (New York: Harper Colophon Books, 1980), 478–79.

20. Note, for instance, "Operation Rolling Thunder," the 4,000–strong biker demonstration that roared through New Jersey in 1990 on behalf of POW/MIAs. *Jersey Journal*, 17 September 1990.

21. William Stevenson and Monika Jensen-Stevenson, *Kiss the Boys Goodbye: How the United States Betrayed Its Own POWs in Vietnam* (New York: Dutton, 1990).

22. "The World According to Ross," *U.S. News and World Report*, 1 June 1992, 24–28.

23. Pete Boss, "Vile Bodies and Bad Medicine," *Screen* 27, no. 1(1986): 15.

24. Stories of governmental conspiracy featuring POW/MIAs and reports of live sightings of POWs have continued through the 1980s and 1990s: the most infamous report of "live sightings" was of course the 1979 testimony of U.S. Marine Lt. Robert Garwood (I. Peterson, "Return of Marine Buoying Hopes on Missing in Southeast Asia," *New York Times*, 25 May 1979, A3, A10). Based on such reports, a private raid into Laos was planned and led in November 1982 by former Green Beret Lt. Col. James (Bo) Gritz—a venture funded by William Shatner and Reagan's close friend Clint Eastwood (Franklin, *MIA*, 129–65). See also "Private Raid on Laos Reported," *New York Times*, 1 February 1993, A2; and Peter Ehrenhaus, "On Americans Held Prisoner in Southeast Asia: The POW Issue as 'Lesson' of Vietnam," in *Cultural Legacies of Vietnam: Uses of the Past in the Present*, ed. Richard Morris and Peter Ehrenhaus (Norwood: Ablex, 1990), 9–24. Colonel James Gritz gives his account of governmental conspiracy and the missing in *A Nation Betrayed* (Boulder City, NV: Lazarus Publishing, 1988).

25. Philip Brophy, "Horrality—The Textuality of Contemporary Horror Films," *Screen* 27, no. 1 (1986): 9. The horror of these films featuring the undead is similar to that of what Pete Boss calls the "hospital horror film," where the body is "part of a highly organized network of operations which eventually invade or manipulate subjectivity." Boss, "Vile Bodies," 18.

26. Julia Kristeva, *Powers of Horror: An Essay on Abjection*, trans. Leon S. Roudiez (New York: Columbia University Press, 1982), 2. Further references to this work will appear parenthetically in the text.

27. I have never read this story but heard it a number of times when I was a kid in the early 1970s. As I remember, the story's effect on its listeners depended on the successful portrayal of the parents' innocence and grief and on the storyteller's prolonging of the dead son's progress from grave to doorstep. The listener is clearly identified with the grieving family; the storyteller would heighten this identification by shifting the son's trajectory so that he is ultimately standing not just outside his family's door, but outside "our" door as well. The film offers an interesting variation on both of these important elements, insofar as it questions/pathologizes the parents' innocent desire for the son's return and focuses more on the son's trip *back* to, rather than from, the grave. Identification shifts in the film between family and Andy, thanks to the frequent presentation of Andy's perceptual point of view by the camera. Likewise, the generally unappealing characterization of Andy's family and neighbors gives the viewer a strong sense of the killer-zombie's mental POV, so we are scared both of *and* for him.

28. Rick Berg, "Losing Vietnam: Covering the War in an Age of Technology," in *From Hanoi to Hollywood*, ed. Linda Dittmar and Gene Michaud (New Brunswick: Rutgers University Press, 1990), 57, 58.

29. Judith Williamson, *Consuming Passions: The Dynamics of Popular Culture* (1980; New York: Marion Boyars, 1986), 11. Further references to this work will be included parenthetically in the text.

30. Jean Bethke Elshtain, *Women and War* (New York: Basic Books, 1987), 223.

31. Michael J. Arlen, *Living-Room War* (New York: Viking, 1969).

32. Margaret Morse, "The Television News Personality and Credibility," in *Studies in Entertainment*, ed. Tania Modleski (Bloomington: Indiana University Press, 1986), 74.

33. Nick Browne, "The Political Economy of the Television (Super) Text," in *Television: The Critical View*, 4th ed., ed. Horace Newcomb (New York: Oxford University Press, 1987), 588.

34. This depiction of the home audience also recalls Arlen's critiques of Vietnam coverage. And *Night of the Living Dead* makes specific reference to Vietnam when the newscaster announces "search and destroy operations" against the zombies ordered by the Pentagon. See Sumiko Higashi, "Night of the Living Dead: A Horror Film about the Horrors of the Vietnam Era," in *From Hanoi to Hollywood*, ed. Dittmar and Michaud, 176–88.

35. Robin Wood, *Hollywood from Vietnam to Reagan* (New York: Columbia University Press, 1986), 134. Further references to this work will appear parenthetically in the text.

36. In the epilogue of *Homeward Bound: American Families in the Cold War Era* (New York: Basic Books, 1988), Elaine Tyler May also notes, "consensus no longer prevailed. . . . The family landed squarely in the center of hotly contested politics" including affirmative action, legalized abortion, arms control, and equal

rights (225). Thus while one can certainly see the effort toward recuperation and reaction in what Robin Wood like Andrew Britton calls "Reaganite entertainment" (*Hollywood*, 162), the stress of contestation is also in evidence in films of the period. See also Andrew Britton, "Blissing Out: The Politics of Reaganite Entertainment," *Movie* 31/32 (1986/87): 1–42.

37. Susan Jeffords, *The Remasculinization of America: Gender and the Vietnam War* (Bloomington: Indiana University Press, 1989) offers an extensive account of how the recuperation of the Vietnam War for the popular imagination—in wartime and postwar novels, short stories, memoirs, literary criticism, and film— is figured as and contributes to a recuperation of phallic masculinity in American culture of the Reagan 1980s. Jeffords sees masculinity in crisis as a result of the Vietnam War as well as other cultural changes in the period following World War II, and argues that the primary function of recent representations of Vietnam is to "remasculinize" American culture. While I would suggest that remasculinization is an ongoing project for Hollywood-style film and that locating a crisis in masculinity in one particular event or time period is itself something of an obfuscatory gesture, Jeffords's work offers a powerful indictment of reactionary patriarchal fictions constructed around the war and effectively delineates the imaginary aims of Reagan-era representations of combat. Perhaps of greatest interest for this essay, however, is the way that, in the course of Jeffords's analysis, it also becomes clear that the status of the Vietnam War as a problem simultaneously covers over and displays a problematic masculinity.

38. Donald, "The Fantastic, the Sublime," 247.

39. Joseph Breuer and Sigmund Freud, *Studies on Hysteria* (1893–95), vol. 2, *Standard Edition*, trans. and ed. James Strachey (London: Hogarth, 1955; reprint, New York: Basic Books, n.d.), 7.

40. This representation of heroic white masculinity in the wilderness has a long history in American culture. Using the idea of myth set forth by Richard Slotkin in *Regeneration through Violence: The Mythology of the American Frontier, 1600–1860* (Middletown, CT: Wesleyan University Press, 1973), Elliot Gruner and Tony Williams link contemporary POW/MIA rescue films to American frontier narratives. See Gruner, *Prisoners of Culture*; and Tony Williams, "Missing in Action—The Vietnam Construction of the Movie Star," in *From Hanoi to Hollywood*, ed. Dittmar and Michaud, 129–45.

41. Jeanine Basinger, *The World War II Combat Film: Anatomy of a Genre* (New York: Columbia University Press, 1986), 212.

42. Fredric Jameson, "Postmodernism, or the Cultural Logic of Late Capitalism," *New Left Review* 146 (1984): 79–80.

43. See Berg, "Losing Vietnam."

44. Heavy-handed, tongue-in-cheek use of wide-angle lens, dreamlike steadycam movement, and a horror-film sound track to establish the sinister character of the house recall *Burnt Offerings* (1976), *The Amityville Horror* (1979), and *The Shining* (1980).

45. This motif, of Vietnam and the United States as parallel worlds that mirror one another uncannily, shows up in other films and television shows as

well. It is a dominant trope, for instance, in the series *China Beach*, which I discussed in "A Madwoman in Southeast Asia: Looking Back on *China Beach*" (paper presented at the Society for Cinema Studies Annual Conference, New Orleans, 1993).

46. According to Carol Clover, "the language and imagery of the occult film is . . . a language and imagery of bodily orifices and insides (or a once-removed but transparently related language of doors, gates, portals, channels, inner rooms)." *Men, Women, and Chainsaws: Gender in the Modern Horror Film* (Princeton: Princeton University Press, 1992), 101.

47. The government's technology of vision and surveillance figures centrally in the POW/MIA issue, as Bruce Franklin points out. "The United States has an intricate intelligence network operating in Indochina, has interrogated many tens of thousands of refugees . . . has organized several cross-border raids to photograph suspected POW camps, and constantly monitors the area with satellites and high-altitude reconnaissance aircraft reputedly capable of photographing the letters on a license plate. So [believers and nonbelievers] . . . can agree: if there are any live POWs, the government would know about them" (Franklin, *MIA*, 35).

48. Cynthia Fuchs, "'Death Is Irrelevant': Cyborgs, Reproduction, and the Future of Male Hysteria," *Genders* 18 (Winter 1993): 116, 117. Fuchs argues convincingly that "cyborgs incarnate contradictions of masculine identity . . . they combine phallic masculinity and body permeability . . . multiple acts of penetration . . . reiterate the cyborg's own indeterminate self-identity" (114). Cyborgs, as models of masculinity in crisis, are "contestable, without desire or agency, and spectacularly incorporated" and are "emblematic of male hysteria over body limits, reproduction, and identities" (130).

49. Vivian Sobchak, "Bringing It All Back Home: Family Economy and Generic Exchange," in *American Horrors: Essays on the Modern American Horror Film*, ed. Gregory A. Waller (Chicago: University of Illinois Press, 1987), 180. Further references to this work will appear parenthetically in the text.

50. This is particularly interesting in the context of the marketing of the video of *Universal Soldier* to an audience technically too young to attend an R-rated movie in the theater. A 1–900 number for callers thirteen and older offers the chance to "*be* Jean-Claude Van Damme or Dolph Lungren . . . if you enter the *Universal Soldier* Sweepstakes" by taking a simple quiz: identify the weapons used by the two action stars.

51. As Constance Penley and Sharon Willis observe, "masculinity may be in trouble but it still knows how to land on its feet." Constance Penley and Sharon Willis, introduction to *Male Trouble*, ed. Constance Penley and Sharon Willis (Minneapolis: University of Minnesota Press, 1993), xviii.

52. Alasdair Spark, "Flight Controls: The Social History of the Helicopter as a Symbol of Vietnam," in *Vietnam Images: War and Representation*, ed. Jeffrey Walsh and James Aulich (New York: St. Martin's Press, 1989), 103.

Contributors

PURNIMA BOSE is Assistant Professor in the Department of English at Indiana University, Bloomington, where she teaches courses in feminist, post-colonial, and cultural studies. This chapter is part of a work-in-progress which treats women's organizing, writing, and nationalism in India and Ireland.

JULIA EMBERLEY is Assistant Professor of Women's Studies and teaches in the Women's Studies Program and Gender Studies Graduate Program at the University of Northern British Columbia. The author of *Thresholds of Difference: Feminist Critique, Native Women's Writings, Postcolonial Theory*, she is currently completing a manuscript on sexuality, cultural imperialism, and the politics of fur.

ELAINE FREEDGOOD is a Visiting Assistant Professor of English Literature at Swarthmore College. She is completing a book-length manuscript tentatively entitled *Locating Risk: Victorian Constructions of a Safe England in a Dangerous World*.

LAWRENCE HAMMAR is a Visiting Instructor of Anthropology at Lewis and Clark College. His chapter springs from *Crisis in the South Fly: The Problems of Sex and the Sex Industry on Daru Island, Western Province*, a nearly completed dissertation on the political economy of sex in the south coastal region of New Guinea. His research interests in cultural and medical anthropology include AIDS and venereology, gender technologies and relations, and sexuality and prostitution.

CHARLES HANNON, an instructor at the University of Alabama, is currently completing his book *Faulkner and the Discourses of Culture*. His

chapter is part of a work-in-progress on American women writers, tentatively entitled *Subversive Contexts*.

AMANDA HOWELL is a doctoral candidate in film at the University of Rochester. Her dissertation focuses on film and televisual representations of the family, history, and Vietnam.

CAROLINE J. HOWLETT is a graduate student at Jesus College, Cambridge, where she is currently completing a Ph.D. on feminism, gender, and identity in the literature of the British militant suffragette movement. She is co-editor with Hugh Stevens of a forthcoming collection of essays entitled *Modernism, Gender, and Sexuality*.

NADINE HUBBS has written on topics of nineteenth- and twentieth-century music and culture including Brahms, Schencker, Schoenberg, and the ideology of musical organicism. Her articles and reviews have appeared in *Theory and Practice, Perpectives on New Music*, and *Intégral*. She is Assistant Professor of Music (theory) at Wayne State University, and during 1995–96 a visiting member of the music faculty of the University of Oregon.

LELAND MONK teaches literature and film at Boston University, where he is Associate Professor of English. He is the author of *Standard Deviations: Chance and the Modern British Novel* (Stanford University Press, 1993) and is currently at work on a book about ideas of the homosexual at the turn of the century.

FRANCES L. RESTUCCIA is Associate Professor of English and women's studies at Boston College. The author of *James Joyce and the Law of the Father* (Yale University Press, 1989) and numerous articles in such journals as *Genre, American Imago, Contemporary Literature, Novel*, and *Raritan*, she is currently working on a book about pain in twentieth-century theory, contemporary women's fiction, and the experience of battered women.

JANELLE WILCOX is an African-Americanist interested in constructions of voice and subjectivity in African-American women's writing. She currently teaches in the English department at Washington State University. Her work-in-progress is a book on the textually constructed silences in the fiction of Gayl Jones, Alice Walker, and Toni Cade Bambara.

Guidelines for Prospective Contributors

Genders welcomes essays on art, literature, media, photography, film, and social theory. We are especially interested in essays that address theoretical issues relating sexuality and gender to social, political, racial, economic, or stylistic concerns.

All essays that are considered for publication are sent to board members for review. Your name is not included on the manuscript in this process. A decision on the essay is usually reached in about four months. Essays are grouped for publication only after the manuscript has been accepted.

We require that we have first right to any manuscript that we consider and that we have first publication of any manuscript that we accept. We will not consider any manuscript that is already under consideration with another publication or that has already been published.

The recommended length for essays is twenty-five pages of double-spaced text. Essays must be printed in letter-quality type. Quotatons in languages other than English must be accompanied by translations. Photocopies of illustrations are sufficient for initial review, but authors should be prepared to supply originals upon request.

Place the title of the essay and your name, address, and telephone number on a separate sheet at the front of the essay. You are welcome to include relevant information about yourself or the essay in a letter to the editor, but please be advised that institutional affiliation does not affect editorial policy. Since the majority of the manuscripts that we receive are photocopyies, we do not routinely return submissions. However, if you would like your copy returned, please enclose a self-addressed, stamped envelope.

To submit an essay for consideration, send *three* legible copies to:

Thomas Foster
Genders
Department of English
Ballantine Hall 442
Indiana University
Bloomington, IN 47405